New Religious Movements
in the Twenty-First Century

New Religious Movements
in the Twenty-First Century
Legal, Political, and Social Challenges
in Global Perspective

Edited by
Phillip Charles Lucas
and **Thomas Robbins**

ROUTLEDGE
NEW YORK AND LONDON

Published in 2004 by
Routledge
29 West 35th Street
New York, NY 10001
www.routledge-ny.com

Published in Great Britain by
Routledge
11 New Fetter Lane
London EC4P 4EE
www.routledge.co.uk

Routledge is an imprint of the Taylor & Francis Group.

10 9 8 7 6 5 4 3 2 1

Library of Congress Cataloging-in-Publication Data

New religious movements in the twenty-first century: legal, political, and social challenges in global perspective/edited by Phillip Charles Lucas and Thomas Robbins.
    p. cm.
Includes bibliographical references and index.
    ISBN 0-415-96576-4 (alk. paper)—ISBN 0-415-96577-2 (pbk. : alk. paper)
1. Cults.   2. Sects.   3. Religions.   4. Religion and law.   5. Religion and state.   6. Religion and sociology.   I. Lucas, Phillip Charles.   II. Robbins, Thomas, 1943–
    BP603.N495 2004
    200'.9'051—dc22

                                                        2003021305

We dedicate this book to a great advocate for religious tolerance and freedom, Dr. Earl W. Joiner, to his daughter, Ann Rouse Joiner, to Phillip's godson, Emerson Allen Rae, to Tom's Tonkinese cat, Bluberry, and to Phillip's late Silver Tabby cat, Smokey.

Contents

Part 4
North and South America

Part 5
Theoretical Considerations

Acknowledgments

This book is a collaborative effort and has benefited from the sage advice, research, and criticisms of a host of scholars. These include, among others, Eileen Barker, Massimo Introvigne, Jean-François Mayer, J. Gordon Melton, James T. Richardson, John R. Hall, James A. Beckford, Armin Geertz, Mikael Rothstein, Danièle Hervieu-Léger, Susan J. Palmer, Brigitte Schoen, Marat Shterin, Solveiga Krumina-Konkova, Brian Glyn Williams, Rosalind I. J. Hackett, Scott Lowe, Ian Reader, Robert T. Carpenter, Irving Hexham and Karla Poewe, Mark Sedgwick, Benjamin Zablocki, J. Anna Looney, Dick Anthony, Catherine Wessinger and Rebecca Moore (Co-General Editors of *Nova Religio*), Hubert Seiwert, Paul Froese, Gary D. Bouma, Willy Fautré, Lorne Dawson, Jeffrey Kaplan, Mimi Goldman, Michael Barkun, Rodney Stark, Jayne Docherty, and Jeff Kenney. We also wish to acknowledge the vital clerical and computer assistance of Kristen Asleson, Lisa Guenther, and June Sitler, and the editorial staff at Routledge, especially Gilad Foss, Bill Germano, Alan Kaplan, and Damian Treffs. Finally, we wish to acknowledge the many non-profit organizations, NGOs, and private individuals who work to expose and redress instances of religious intolerance, persecution, and bigotry in nations throughout the world.

Introduction
Alternative Religions, the State, and the Globe

THOMAS ROBBINS

Religious persecution, maintains Paul Marshall, is on the rise all over the world.

> Religious persecution, meaning violence in which the religion of the perse-
> cuted or the persecutor is a factor, affects all religious groups. Christians and
> animists in Sudan, Baha'is in Iran, Ahmadiyas in Pakistan. Buddhists in Tibet
> and Falun Gong in China are the most intensely persecuted, while Christians
> are the most widely persecuted group. But there is no group in the world that
> does not suffer because of its beliefs. All religions, whether large, such as Chris-
> tianity, Islam, Hinduism, or Buddhism, or small such as Baha'i, Jehovah's Wit-
> nesses, or Judaism suffer to some degree. In many cases these attacks come
> from their own religious groups (e.g., Sunni Muslims persecuting Shiite Mus-
> lims—*parenthetical added by T. Robbins*) . . . Religious freedom is also not con-
> fined to any one area or continent. There are relatively free countries in every
> continent and of every religious background. Perhaps surprisingly, South
> Korea, Taiwan, Japan, South Africa, Botswana, Mali, and Namibia are freer
> than France and Belgium. There are now absolutely no grounds for thinking
> that religious freedom is an exclusively Western desire or achievement.[1]

In short, "the dominant pattern is the increasing political influence of
religion coupled with increasing religious repression."[2] The enhanced
significance of religion and its heightened repression are clearly related:
religion is increasingly worth persecuting and state officials embrace
laissez-faire at their peril.

Religious persecution and religious conflict are presently ubiquitous.
Whether it is French officials' "war on sects," the Chinese government's

brutal suppression of Falun Gong, officials in Uzbekistan persecuting a number of groups to ward off a militant Islamic insurgency, or officials of the recently dismantled Taliban regime in Afghanistan prescribing death for attempts to convert Muslims to other faiths, the word is out that religion is a matter of vital importance and it cannot, therefore, be left alone by the state. A laissez-faire policy seems less and less tenable to political elites. Religion is now on the cutting edge of governmental social control.[3]

The present volume and its introductory essay focus primarily on the relations between new or alternative religions and the state in the contemporary world, and the factors that may now be rendering this relationship increasingly volatile.[4] Our volume is a significantly extended edition of a special symposium issue of the journal, *Nova Religio* (Vol. 4, No. 2, April 2001), which was devoted to "New Religions in their Political, Legal and Religious Contexts Around the World" and which was co-edited by Phillip Charles Lucas and this writer.

New, esoteric, and minority religious movements are emerging in many parts of the globe and often appear to be eliciting strong opposition and various degrees of governmental persecution. Scholars have been closely attending to this phenomenon, and a number of symposia and edited collections appeared prior to the Spring 2001 *Nova Religio* symposium that examined issues of church-state relations and religious freedom arising in connection with new and alternative religions.[5]

In preparing the original symposium in *Nova Religio,* Lucas and I sought to assemble a collection of original papers that probe these issues in various societies, states, and cultures around the globe. We suggested to the original contributors that they discuss the historical, social, and cultural contexts that are influencing the patterns of governmental response to new religious movements (NRMs) in particular nations or regions. We suggested that our authors might examine the role of a number of salient factors in the societies about which they are writing, including "anticult" mobilization, the structure of government and received pattern of church-state relations, the role of existing older churches, the linkage of controversies over new movements to other (e.g., ethnic, cultural, political) conflicts, the role of scholars, intelligentsia, and "cult experts," and the nature and (possibly disruptive) behavior of unconventional religious movements.

The present volume reprints revised and updated papers from the original journal issue and adds eight original papers. The new chapters in some cases fill gaps in the original symposium. The latter did not, for example, include a paper on Latin America, a deficiency that is now made up by Robert Carpenter's chapter dealing with Brazil's powerful surge of alternative spirituality. Given the popular "hunger for esotericism" to which it responds, this alternative spirituality appears too vast and diffuse a phenomenon to be seriously threatened by the apprehensive counterforces identified by Carpenter.

Religious Movements and Violence

A number of papers in the present volume deal with Al Qa'ida and more generally with apocalyptic violence and/or militant Islamic movements. Brian Williams' contribution describes governmental efforts to crush "Wahhabi Fundamentalist" movements in Central Asia, which Williams relates to the "worldwide struggle against al Qa'ida" and terrorism. A significant dimension of the paper looks at Sufism, which, as a diffuse folk religion, was able to withstand decades of Soviet repression. Such popular Sufism is held in contempt by Sunni reformers and is actually a target of Wahhabi revivalism. The latter aims to "purify" a tradition alleged to be polluted by magical Sufi practices and superstition. It is dynamic reformist Wahhabism, however, which is perceived as a threat to relatively secular post-Soviet political elites. Thus religion-state conflicts interface in various ways with interreligious tensions.

Al Qa'ida is also discussed in the theoretical essay by Mark Sedgwick.[6] Sedgwick explores the potentialities for applying the concept of "sect" and "sectarianism" from the sociology of religion to Islamic movements in a manner that will differentiate the groups to which it is applied from what might be viewed as Islamic "cults" and "denominations." A subtypology of Islamic sects is produced which distinguishes between *tariqa*, and *ta'ifa* and *firqa* movements. The latter are inherently unstable and more likely to become involved in violence. Al Qa'ida is said to have the characteristics of a *firqa*. Interestingly, Sedgwick rejects the applicability to Islamic groups of the voguish scholarly concept of "new religious movement." Scholars, Sedgwick maintains, have tended to use the "NRM" concept as a proxy for voluntary groups in tension with the environment. However, in Islam, old and institutionalized groups can be in tension with the surrounding environment, while some novel, voluntary movements may not be at all controversial. "What matters is not novelty in itself but voluntarism and tension," asserts Sedgwick.

"Research on NRMs in the post 9/11 World," a theoretical essay by Benjamin Zablocki and J. Anna Looney, presents a provocative overview of research on new movements. Zablocki compares older structural-essentialist models with newer interactive or process approaches. Zablocki maintains that questions of "why" need to make room for equally important "how" questions. We must shift our focus to the "social and cultural mechanisms used by NRMs for attaining cohesion and control and for mobilizing resources." How do such movements "continuously create and maintain themselves?" Zablocki and Looney usefully review pertinent research on new movements in a number of key areas including charismatic leadership and patterns of recruitment and defection. They also devote attention to stressful problems of "ideological disconnection" from the total society, particularly in the areas of apocalyptic violence and sex/gender roles.

Apocalyptic violence is the specific topic of John Hall's theoretical essay, "Apocalypse 9/11," which discusses Al Qa'ida and other groups and the significance of apocalyptic worldviews:

> The most radical apocalyptic narratives call on people to transcend their everyday lives, to undergo a rebirth of self and act in relation to special historical circumstances through collective social actions conducted in sectarian organizations of true believers. . . . The narrative of the generic "apocalyptic warning sect" . . . posits a struggle by the forces of good against those of evil as the necessary pathway to a post-apocalyptic tableau of salvation. The end of history can come only through a conflict in real historical time, and the warring sect makes inaugurating such a conflict its sacred enterprise.

However, "apocalyptic war [often] does not unfold as a one-sided series of terrorist actions. Rather it is an *interactive* process" (Hall's emphasis). As the state attempts to control apocalyptic violence it is strongly tempted *to become an apocalyptic actor itself* (my emphasis) with its own apocalyptic rationale for its social control policies. The classic example, as Hall notes, is President Bush's formulation of the "axis of evil" idea, which was applied to three historically disconnected or mutually estranged nations. "Bush thus invoked an encompassing historical struggle between good and evil, the forces of light, and the forces of darkness . . . the structure of the ideology is unmistakable: it is apocalyptic."

Hall's interactive analysis is convergent with the approach of Zablocki and Looney, who identify a process of "deviance amplification" at work in apocalyptic movements. Through this process, the continuous escalation of a conflict between a deviant group and agents of control is understood in terms of the deepening entrapment of both parties in interactive feedback loops of recrimination and estrangement such that the whole "amplification" process may spiral out of control.

Sources of Tension

Rosalind Hackett's paper on African states' response to "false prophets" also deals partly with explosively violent movements such as the notorious Movement for the Restoration of the Ten Commandments as well as religious movements with paramilitarist proclivities such as the Lord's Resistance Army (both groups, interestingly, emerged in Uganda). More generally, however, Hackett provides an excellent tripartite framework for looking at the basic challenges that NRMs pose to a society and its public authority, and for understanding the sources of tension between emergent movements and the state. Firstly, movements may pose a direct challenge to *political authority*, sometimes in tangible military terms, as instanced by the Lord's Resistance Army, "which plagued government troops in Uganda for a number of years in the late 1980s" (and recruited child soldiers). Secondly, new movements are often viewed as representing a threat to *public interests*, that is, the behavior of a group or its devotees or the beliefs being espoused are seen as inimical to basic cultural values. Hackett mentions Wilson Bushara, the leader of another controversial Ugandan group, who "offered space in Heaven after death in return for cash." The spectacular mass suicide/homicide of the Movement for the Restoration of the Ten Commandments is also placed in this category, as obviously may be the lethal behavior of groups such as the Peoples Temple, the Solar Temple, and Aum Shinrikyō, whose violence does not directly menace the state but is seen to embody a vile atrocity. Charges that sinister "cults" and their ruthless gurus "brainwash" and otherwise socially, financially and sexually exploit their members as well as "break up families" are also pertinent here, as are charges of "devil worship" and Satanism.

Thirdly, according to Hackett, new movements may mount challenges to the *religious power and authority* which older churches enjoy. A "new generation" of Evangelical/Pentecostal/charismatic modes of Christianity is making inroads at the expense of older churches; moreover, some Pentecostals actually engage in anti-Catholic preaching. Hackett's three foci of tension are obviously not mutually exclusive, e.g., competition between rival movements may lead to accusations of devil worship. Political and non-political (e.g., psychopathological) violence are not always easy to distinguish. Recruitment of child soldiers may be an offense to values (public interests) as well as part of a military threat.

In any case, the threats which new movements are perceived as posing to African states and societies are magnified by societal disorganization and the economic and political volatility of African states. "Faltering, debt-ridden African states must look to the management of religious pluralism as part of their plans of national integration lest it explode into conflict as in Nigeria and Sudan." Anticult literature is presently proliferating in Christian bookstores in Africa, where the government, the media, and churches increasingly treat new and deviant sects as a *single, generalized entity*.

Globalization

The currently fashionable concept of "globalization" (or "globalism") seems particularly useful for framing the whole issue of the interaction between the state and NRMs. Globalization provides a basis for contextualizing both the contemporary spread and growth of new movements and the tensions that surround them.

James Beckford has written a number of seminal papers looking at the interface of globalization and alternative religions.[7] Globalization, Beckford has previously noted, enhances the "frequency, volume, and interconnectedness of movements of ideas, materials, goods, information, pollution, money and people across national boundaries and between regions of the world."[8] Globalization thus facilitates the transnational and transcultural diffusion of symbolic movements and meanings. In so doing it encourages the emergence of new meanings and movements in part by facilitating syncretism and the "recombination of fragments of experiences" from various traditions. Thus, "all new religions incorporate, often indiscriminately, insights from other cultures and traditions."[9] Globalization thus tends to *increase religious diversity within societies and to implicitly deregulate religious markets*. In so doing, however, it may produce nativistic counterreactions against enhanced diversity, which may be experienced as unsettling. Particular hostility may be directed toward what Beckford has termed "religious multinationals" such as the Church of Scientology or the Unification Church.[10] Such groups are likely to appear *alien* from the standpoint of the nations and cultures into which they migrate.

In Beckford's paper in the present volume, certain paradoxes of the relationship of globalization and NRMs are laid bare. New movements emerging in the mid-twentieth century "have made strenuous efforts to crystallize forms of global consciousness" which "stress the interconnectiveness of human actions and social institutions at a global level." Movements such as Scientology, Unificationism, Soka Gakkai, and Transcendental Meditation "deliberately aspire to overcome national boundaries of ideology, religion, ethnicity, and citizenship in their drive toward a peaceful and harmonious world that is unified by what they consider to be universal values." On the other hand these putative universal values are being "conveyed by means of particularist ideologies." Particular meanings are embedded in concepts that are claimed to have universal meaning. Nonmembers thus do not generally view such movements as "disinterested purveyors of universalistic ideals." They are often seen as duplicitous and with hidden agendas. In Europe and elsewhere, they are frequently viewed as agents of American global hegemony and penetration of indigenous cultures. In fact, movements such as Hare Krishna, Unificationism, or Soka Gokkai are not of American origin, although they are often exported to various societies as American cultural products, and as such they elicit resentment. "Both France and Russia," Beckford notes, "are countries in which hostility to NRMs owes much to fear of American imperialism in the guise of globalization."

Beyond mere anti-Americanism, new movements are threatened by the ironic, culturally particularizing effect of globalism. Globalization threatens to relativize particularist cultural formations such that they may become more shrilly emphasized—partly at the expense of movements claiming to embody universal values—as they appear increasingly precarious. The overarching globalization process thus enhances the concerns of nations, regimes, and cultures (and national churches and dominant political groups) to preserve the integrity of their particularist cultures' identities, heritage, and values, which globalization threatens to relativize. "One of the marks of globalization is that it puts all ideologies and belief systems under pressure to clarify their place in relation to the new circumstance. They can no longer refuse to consider their position."[11]

The clearest example of this dynamic can be found in the Russian situation as delineated by Marat Shterin in this volume. Russian anticult media, notes Shterin, is increasingly "dominated by the motif of 'religious insecurity' supposedly inherent in the open religious marketplace." "Sectarianism" is alleged to undermine Russian statehood and lead to national disintegration. Partly imported from the United States, Russian anticultism nevertheless draws its strength from the strong support of the resurgent Russian Orthodox Church, which uses Western anticultism as the linchpin of what might be termed an implicit "re-establishmentarian" (our term) strategy entailing the denial of legitimacy to upstart alternatives to the historic National Church. Putatively alien sects are thus viewed as suspect, as are foreign religious missions such as the Salvation Army, which Moscow authorities recently attempted to destroy by denying it registration.

In a very different manner, France can be seen in Danièle Hervieu-Léger's chapter as defensively protecting its own very distinctive approach to religion from globalizing pressures and the threatened erosion of traditional "secular-Catholic" culture. What is vital here is not so much any overt Roman Catholic establishment but rather a distinctive secular-rationalist orientation, historically conditioned by the culturally formative episodes of the Enlightenment and the French Revolution, which sees religion as a dangerous irrational force with a destructive potential. The potential is hopefully contained by a "confessional system" of regulation that was originally developed to limit and compartmentalize the force of the traditionally dominant Roman Catholic Church. The system presupposes the organizational model of Catholicism as "the implicit reference for acceptable forms of religious expression—which the law intends to guarantee while simultaneously controlling for excesses." But, "French recognition of religious pluralism stops exactly at the borders of religions whose confessional organization assures adhesion to the values of the republic." Freedom of public worship is thus granted conditionally on the premise of the radical privatization of faith and the assimilation of each legitimated group to standard institutional forms. Cultural defense can be seen in the continuing strenuous efforts of the Interior Ministry to encourage a reorganization of French Islam on the model of the familiar Protestant Federation of France.

Hervieu-Léger observes a "presumption of risk" associated with religions that do not conform to approved confessional patterns and that may therefore degenerate into a "pathology of belief." What has evolved is thus an "implicit regime of recognized religions" that recognizes only a small number of religions as legitimate—their destructive potential tamed by their assimilation to the confessional system. Under the conditions of globalized postmodernity this implicit regulatory system is being undermined in France. "The mesh of the confessional net is strained by the multiplication of groups and movements claiming religious status and demanding the benefits of freedom taken for granted in democratic societies." The seemingly "anarchic proliferation of self-proclaimed and extradenominational religious groups" is evoking deep anxieties. A postmodern society of autonomous "believing subjects" free to "cobble together their own systems of meaning and create new forms of association for spiritual purposes" is a society in which institutional religious regulation will be precarious. The somewhat panic-stricken official response is to presume that the devotees of institutionally aberrant and unfamiliar movements are not autonomous and have succumbed to "mental manipulation." In an epilogue, Hervieu-Léger discusses the recent agitation against "sectarian danger" and "mind manipulation" that resulted in the law of May 2001. The careful, tortuous language of this statute introduces a notion of actionable, sectarian mental manipulation or implicitly coercive psychological domination without employing sensational terms such as "brainwashing" or even "mental manipulation." Since the law does not clearly define a "*secte*" (cult) it probably "has little chance of becoming an effective legal tool."

The present volume actually contains two papers dealing with the French milieu. Hervieu-Léger's paper deals with the cultural foundations of French discrimination. Susan Palmer's paper looks particularly at the impact of discrimination on the *sectes* and the divergent responses of various groups. Palmer comments:

> There were moments in my research when I felt I had walked into a veritable war zone. . . . the anticult war in France is mainly a war of words but there have been some attacks against individuals and property that have not been reported in the media. The Unification Church in Paris no longer exists, it was bombed in 1974 and again in 1995. . . .

According to Palmer, "hundreds of successful professional and responsible parents have been fired or lost custody of, or access to, their children, simply because of sect affiliation." The responses of most groups tend to be "culturally bilingual," that is, they disseminate apocalyptic expectations to their own adherents to confer meaning on their ordeals while using secular language and logic to argue with officials or appeal to the public.

Unlike the United States, where stigma and discrimination impinge most heavily on high-demand, "totalist" millenarian groups, French crusaders worry particularly about (putatively deceptive) low-key groups such as loosely organized meditation, faith-healing, and therapeutic circles. Their devotees are perceived as cultural infiltrators who will "mutate French culture from within" and undermine the primacy of reason.

The French situation is significant as a particularly stringent control system for deviant sects (particularly if the new law of 2001 is actually enforced) emerging in a basically democratic and pluralistic context. In contrast, the Chinese approach discussed by Scott Lowe represents a control pattern developing in an authoritarian (some might say still "totalitarian") setting.

For hundreds of years, China has constituted a relatively unified political community ruled under authoritarian auspices. Religion and governance have been closely interlocked such that the Western ideal of the "separation of church and state" has been totally alien to Chinese traditions. "Not surprisingly, unorthodox beliefs were seen more as treason than heresy." However, one effect of the interrelationship of religion and governance was that new religious visions tended to suggest new political arrangements and thus to imperil the state. Chinese history has thus been characterized by messianic religio-political insurgencies and aggressively theocratic movements. Fearful imperial ruling elites have fiercely persecuted clandestine brotherhoods and sectarian religious groups.

Lowe emphasizes the continuity between old imperial patterns and Maoist rule. Like past emperors, Chairman Mao "believed in the almost magical power of society-wide conformity and felt personally threatened by all ideological dissent." Post-Mao leaders have eased up a bit and allow tame, "patriotic" churches to be officially registered. The government still "deals harshly with unregistered groups, arresting leaders and raiding meeting places." The latter part of Lowe's chapter deals with the suppression of Falun Gong.[12] Lowe notes an interesting connection that may be developing between the Chinese government and American anticultists.[13]

According to Lowe, the present Chinese Constitution guarantees Chinese citizens' "freedom of religious belief" but "rather pointedly does not recognize the right to engage in religious practices or propagate religious teachings." This is a frequent pattern with authoritarian regimes that want to constrain independent sects. For a state to concede individual freedom of *belief* (which is essentially an intrapsychic modality) is really to concede very little. How would a government prevent a citizen from holding an inappropriate belief? If "freedom of religion" is conceived as the right to hold beliefs it is implicitly defined as something essentially individual and intrapsychic such that the implied constraint on the state is minimal. The constraint is more meaningful if the right of collective worship, the right to organize—to have a religious community—and the right to preach and proselytize are conceded. But simply guaranteeing the right to belief may not meaningfully circumscribe state authority, which is why regimes desiring to restrictively regulate religion nevertheless eagerly affirm citizens' freedom of belief. Oliver Cromwell prohibited the Catholic Mass, but in doing so denied that he was infringing freedom of conscience.

America, Globalism, and Religious Movements

As we have seen, James Beckford has noted how anti-Americanism is sometimes involved in the hostile reactions NRMs may elicit. Whatever their national origins, many "religious multinationals" appear to be exported to various societies as American cultural products.

Resentment of the world's remaining superpower is a salient element of contemporary globalization and its discontents: Globalization has allowed American corporations to penetrate the economies of various societies around the globe. It has permitted putatively vulgar American commercial products—colas, Big Macs, slick commercial entertainment—to invade other countries' home markets and crowd out the latter's more exquisite cultural and culinary creations. Indeed, it is tempting to conclude that American spiritual exports such as Scientology or Jehovah's Witnesses may be viewed in Europe as "fast religions" analogous to degraded American "fast food."

Sometimes anti-Americanism and a general xenophobic response to the pressures of globalization are difficult to distinguish. In Japan, notes Ian Reader, "the term cult has been applied less to *Japanese* new religious movements" than to imports from abroad. The Jehovah's Witnesses and the Unification Church, in particular, have been stigmatized and tend to be popularly equated with much more violent groups. There appears to be a resurgence of "Japanocentric modes of discourse that are clearly anti-Western and anti-foreign . . . with certain movements identified as much as anything because of their foreign provenance."

Reader's essay also highlights another key aspect of the interface of cult controversies and globalization: the emergence of a globalized "anticult" movement/network. In Japan this movement "has all but drowned out alternative voices and perspectives" and has grown rapidly in the aftermath of the sensational subway gassing perpetrated by Aum Shinrikyō. Japanese anticultism has benefited from the missionary activities of American crusaders against cults such as ex-Unificationist Steven Hassan. The latter warns against the menace of "brainwashing" in "cults," and his message provides "an easily grasped populist explanation of Aum."

As James Beckford notes, anticultists are now well established on the global Internet, as are alternative religions. However, in Beckford's view, the balance of Internet influence is presently shifting in favor of the anticultists. In any case, the worldwide net is an increasingly vital dimension of globalization and is also an active theater of cult/anticult confrontation conducted via proliferating missionary and activist websites.

Anti-Americanism is mentioned as a salient dimension of anticultism by a number of our contributors, but, interestingly has not been highlighted by Hervieu-Léger, notwithstanding known French resentments against certain exported American institutions such as McDonald's restaurants. Indeed, a French anticult activist is said to have referred to cults as "America's Trojan Horse" subverting the integrity of French culture.

In his report on Australia, James Richardson notes that successful attempts to prevent an amendment to the constitution (to add a Bill of Rights that would explicitly guarantee religious liberty) "have used the United States as a problematic example of what can happen with such formal guarantees of religious freedom." The deregulated religious market is a menacing specter to many persons, who view such guarantees as an encouragement to wild cults—candidates for tomorrow's Jonestowns and Wacos. Notwithstanding resistance to a formal guarantee of religious liberty, the situation in Australia is not that unfavorable to extensions of religious pluralism, according to Richardson.

This brings us to an interesting point. In relative terms, is the U.S. truly the "land of the free" in the sense of representing a citadel of religious liberty in which minimal regulation of the religious market provides a more favorable and less persecutory climate for new movements than democratic Western Europe? This is the forcefully stated view of two eminent sociologists of religion, Rodney Stark and Roger Finke:

> Europeans often claim that their nations, too, offer religious freedom, but to those accustomed to American standards of freedom, what is called freedom in Europe would only be called *toleration* in the United States—and often not that. In the abstract most nations of Western Europe assert freedom of worship, but permit almost unlimited discretion to bureaucrats and parliaments concerning specific policies and decisions to impose sanctions on minority religions, while not providing effective legal recourse as guaranteed in the United States.[14]

Germany, the authors imply, pursues particularly oppressive policies. German "free churches" that do not receive state support, are in fact "hindered, harassed and closely regulated" and are "stigmatized by the media and government" in a manner that "generates public disapproval."[15] However, in her essay for this volume, Brigitte Schoen maintains that in some respects Germany is less discriminatory in its policy toward new movements than are Western European nations such as France or Belgium. Schoen's essay rebuts what she views as exaggerated reports in the U.S. regarding the alleged persecution of Scientology in Germany.[16] Acknowledging that the German government considers Scientology a commercial rather than a religious organization (which may seriously disadvantage Scientology), Schoen claims that affirmative governmental action against Scientology has amounted to little more than surveillance (which a Berlin court has ordered discontinued) and the issuing of informational booklets containing some negative information.

In her essay (and more extensively in a personal dialogue with this writer), Schoen has noted certain factors which may challenge the widespread impression that the repression of esoteric religious minorities is substantially more severe in Western Europe and Germany than in the U.S. Compared to European countries, the U.S. has a relatively decentralized system of control such that discrimination "in the boondocks" against Neopagan or New Age groups may not be highly visible. While inflammatory statements against cults by European politicians and activists attract substantial publicity, court cases quietly won by controversial movements (for instance, a recent decision for the Jehovah's Witnesses in Germany's highest court) receive less attention. On the other hand, constitutional protection for "free speech" in the U.S. may make pejorative statements against NRMs as well as by NRMs in America less actionable.

Schoen notes that German law requires a balancing of the right to religious liberty with "the basic rights of other individuals, such as a child's right to freedom from injury in the case of Evangelicals calling for corporal punishment." As with other countries, the German legal system for organizing religions as corporate bodies "fosters a highly institutionalized, centralized organizational form for religions which one might call bureaucracies." Public funding for private anticult organizations (some of which had received state aid in the 1970s and '80s) has decreased while church support for anticultism has increased, as it has in several other countries.

Finally, the existence of an Al Qa'ida cell discovered in Hamburg and linked to the depredations of 9/11 has led to a change in the German law of associations. A religious exemption to the authority of the state to terminate associations linked to criminal or anti-constitutional activities is no longer operative. (One Muslim extremist organization has been banned to date.) German citizens are finding "the very notion of a terrorist variant of religion unsettling." Schoen notes the emotional effect of quiet, religious young men being revealed as mass murderers. Such a development "might kindle resentments against all kinds of minority religions. On the other hand, the new focus on Islamic extremism means that public attention no longer concentrates on the real or alleged dangers of [non-Islamic] new religions."

J. Gordon Melton's fairly sanguine report on the U.S. clearly supports the idea that the situation is more favorable to alternative religions in the U.S. than elsewhere. Melton reviews several key historical and legal events, including setbacks suffered by the American anticult movement. The movement, he maintains, is now little more than a "meddlesome nuisance." Melton makes a strong case, yet it may be somewhat overstated. He emphasizes the importance of the federal *Fishman* verdict in 1990, which excludes expert testimony about brainwashing from criminal trials on the grounds that the notion lacks scientific credibility. *Fishman,* however, transpired in a mere trial (lower) federal court, although it has been frequently cited. Yet *Fishman* could turn out to be a frail reed. The influence of horrendous tragedies such as the Uganda massacre or spectacular acts of "religious terrorism" such as produced the destruction of the World Trade Center may lead judges—whose legal reasoning may presuppose certain "scientific knowledge" about social behavior and the human psyche—to alter their "scientific" views. Melton does not highlight the earlier California Supreme Court verdict in the *Molko* case (1988), which affirmed that there is no *constitutional* or religious freedom barrier to tort actions relying on brainwashing claims in situations where a totalistic, encapsulating group employs recruitment practices that are substantially deceptive.[17]

As this writer recalls, the defeat of the anticult movement in the *Fishman* case was the result of a sort of successful fallback strategy employed by its opponents in the aftermath of *Molko*. The 1988 *Molko* verdict appeared to preclude the automatic dismissal, on First Amendment grounds, of litigation involving brainwashing claims against religious movements. However, the *Molko* court did not rule out a challenge to "expert" testimony about mind control on the grounds that it lacks "scientific" credibility. The *Fishman* verdict vindicated such a challenge in a criminal trial. The result has been to make the outcomes of civil and criminal litigation involving brainwashing claims frequently hinge on the resolution of pre-trial motions *in limine* to exclude testimony. In this connection the work of psychologist Dick Anthony, a key consultant in the *Fishman* case and in numerous subsequent cases, has been particularly valuable (from the standpoint of beleaguered movements) in frequently getting pseudoscientific mind control testimony excluded from evidentiary hearings.

The contribution of Robbins and Anthony in the present volume deals with legal strategies and rhetoric, and in particular with the convergence of three influential, quasi-legal discourses in which limitation of the scope of the First Amendment's protection of expressive speech acts is being advocated. In the areas of pornography, racist hate speech, and the indoctrination practices of "cults," it has been maintained that the speech acts are not "only words" but represent implicitly "coercive" abuses of speech which do not engage the critical intellect but rather operate viscerally to manipulate emotions. Robbins and Anthony are critical of this argument but are more concerned with its implications for the ambiguity of contemporary moral boundaries and the psychologizing of social control.

If, as Melton maintains, the situation is particularly favorable to alternative religions in the U.S., Great Britain, as reported by Eileen Barker, also seems to present a relatively favorable venue. Barker discusses the blemishes on the picture, including episodes of "Islamophobia" related to Al Qa'ida and the Ayatollah Khomeini, an ephemeral "satanic scare," and the dismissal of a Unificationist from a teaching position. The most important setback for pluralism may be the denial of official "charitable" status for Scientology (a lucrative status in terms of tax benefits). Barker notes the trend whereby the better known new religions increasingly "attempt to be accepted as 'normal' rather than insisting upon the ways in which they differ from the rest of society." This tendency has "defused somewhat at least some of the antagonisms that previously existed between the movements and the general British population."

In the remainder of this essay, I wish to touch upon some key factors that operate in various societies to influence the prospects for new religious movements. We have already looked at the role of *organized anticult agitation* in various countries: it is usually imported from the U.S., but its strength in a host country may be proportional to the support that is elicited from older churches, particularly formerly dominant churches seeking to maintain or regain a hegemonic status. Ironically, China, as Scott Lowe notes, is not very friendly to alternative religions, yet it does not have an independent anticult movement—Chinese anticultism is ultimately state controlled.

The Mandarin Factor

Perhaps because they are themselves scholars, a number of our contributors have been concerned with the role of scholars and intellectuals in influencing both the outcomes of cult controversies and the evolving milieus in various countries. Ian Reader's contribution is poignant concerning the "muted voices of academia" in post-Aum Japan. A very small number of Japanese and American scholars had been naïve about Aum Shinrikyō and had provided general legitimation for the movement and/or had refused to accept factually valid claims regarding criminal behavior of Aum and its messianic leader Asahara.[18] An exaggerated "prevailing image" of widespread academic complicity with sinister, lethal cults crystallized. "It is small wonder, then, that at present the ability of scholars to present an alternative to the views of the anticult movement has been severely diminished." This milieu is in contrast, notes Reader, to the intellectual milieux in the U.S. and the United Kingdom.

There is also a contrast with the Canadian situation reported here by Irving Hexham. Hexham's report combines a brief history of academic discourse about cults and sects in Canada with a sort of "rise and fall" narrative of Canadian anticultism. Hexham perceives the impact of Canadian scholars such as Nancy Nason-Clark, Saul Levine, Reginald Bibby, and Susan Palmer as representing a key factor in turning the tide against vociferous anticult agitation. It might be helpful to know more about why Canadian scholars should be particularly influential in their society. In any case, Hexham feels that it is necessary for scholars to reject not only the recent hostility and antipathy toward new movements but also the complacency and insensitivity toward possible abuses which may have replaced the earlier antagonism. What is needed is "a new skepticism that respects freedom of belief and association but looks closely at the implications of their actions and teachings for the society as a whole."

In Italy, a country having, according to Massimo Introvigne, a "surprisingly favorable" climate for religious minorities, scholars have "a history of being fairly pro-active in siding with underdogs, religious and otherwise." This is somewhat akin to the "adversarial" intellectual culture in the U.S. but is less the case with intellectuals in France and Germany. Influential intelligentsia in Italy tend to be libertarians—either of "new left" or "new right" persuasion—whereas French politics is dominated by paternalistic "old left" politicians with close ties to churches involved in anticult campaigns. However, Italian Protestants, remembering past persecution, are somewhat hesitant to recriminate against new minorities. It strikes this writer that omni-competent state *paternalism* may be one factor that renders European governments more prone to take action against stigmatized movements than their counterparts in the U.S., where "Big Government" has traditionally been distrusted.

Melton briefly discusses the dilemma of American scholars who are not necessarily enthusiastic supporters of controversial groups but who tend to oppose ideas such as brainwashing as explanations for recruitment and commitment to new movements. The fragility in the public mind of the distinction between opposing anticult claims on an objective basis and being a sympathizer with noxious groups is embodied in the derisive term "cult apologist." In some European nations, scholars who are not crusaders against controversial movements are excluded from influence and from participation in policy debates on these matters. Schoen notes that the Belgian (but not the German) Parliamentary Commission of Inquiry into possibly dangerous groups deliberately excluded social science and religious studies scholars as informants who might counter anticult perspectives. A French Commission, Introvigne has noted, did not include as witnesses scholars or faculty at any institution of higher learning. "When a number of scholars objected to the report, they were not only insulted as cult apologists by the tabloids but were harassed in many ways by authorities."[19] In France, an anticult leader was awarded the *Legion d'Honneur*, while a prominent social scientist, Eileen Barker, received a prestigious award in Britain.

Although anticult agitation has been discussed by many of our contributors, a more extended focus on particular scholars, clerical intelligentsia, and clinical/social science "experts" such as the French psychiatrist J.M. Abgrall, who spearhead crusades against alternative religions, would be a most interesting future direction for NRM scholarship.[20] Melton's essay gives some attention to Margaret Singer, who greatly assisted the American anticult movement in the last decades of the twentieth century. Armin Geertz and Michael Rothstein's report on Denmark includes a discussion of the countercult guru, Johannes Aagaard, and his arguably misnamed Dialog Centre at the University of Aarhus. My own recollection is that in the 1980s, Aagaard and his journal, *Update*, did foster genuine dialogue and was open to a plurality of views. But in the 1990s true dialogue appeared to be more or less replaced by a monotonic monologue featuring mainly attacks on new movements and treatises on the inferiority of Eastern spiritual ideas such as *karma* to Christian doctrines.

Finally, a number of contributors have highlighted the role of the *mass media* in fueling agitation against NRMs. Solveiga Krumina-Konkova concludes that the mass media as well as anticult groups have been largely responsible for the growing "moral panic" over new movements in Latvia and Lithuania in the last half decade. In Italy, according to Introvigne, there is an overrepresentation in the media of secularists, who tend toward anticultism. Nevertheless, overt anticult bias may be less significant than the sensationalist impulse to go after "lurid exposés of 'dangerous cults,'" which sell newspapers and draw in television audiences. Richardson reports that extremely negative, sensational coverage of the Unification Church in Australia fueled a controversy that caused a two-year delay in the granting of a permit to build a worship center. In Japan, as Reader notes, the media eagerly report the misdeeds of a wide variety of religious organizations.

Role of the Churches

The institutionalized churches play a key role in cult controversies. Although some churches may support religious liberty and the rights of small, nontraditional movements, it appears that anticult ideology is likely to become a significant societal force to the extent that it receives support from influential clergy. There are some exceptions—for example, the role of churches is not emphasized in Reader's report, and churches may be less important in Japan and in China. Although some clerics, such as the late Reverend Dean Kelley of the (American) National Council of Churches, may crusade for broad notions of religious liberty, clergy have often been active in social mobilization against cults.

As Shterin reports in Russia, the resurgent Orthodox Church is using imported Western anticultism to further its own implicitly re-establishmentarian purposes. The opposition of churches and clergy is one reason why a surge of religious diversity and alternative religions, which erupted after the fall of an authoritarian Communist regime, subsequently leveled off.[21]

In France, the Roman Catholic Church is in the somewhat ironic position of perhaps being a beneficiary of a system that was originally established to contain its influence. Although Hervieu-Léger says little about the attitude of French Catholic leaders, some observers believe that an "unholy alliance" against *sectes* exists between Catholic leaders and antireligious secularists. On the other hand, Hervieu-Léger notes that leaders of the respectable Protestant Federation in France are concerned with religious freedom and willing to offer admission to the Federation (which provides fairly effective protection from state persecution) to otherwise vulnerable Pentecostal and Adventist groups. In Italy, the Protestant churches have offered some support to the Jehovah's Witnesses. They recall, notes Introvigne, Mussolini's persecution of Protestant denominations, some of which were officially stigmatized as "sects" and "cults" under *Il Duce* and even well into the 1950s.

In several European states and elsewhere, certain sizeable and historic churches have a degree of "establishment" in the sense that the state plays a role in their funding. In a recent Hungarian statute, the state diverts a portion of citizens' tax payments to churches designated by taxpayers without requiring extra payments from them. However, smaller and less reputable churches are excluded from the system, and their members must pay their full taxes to the state plus extra dues to their church if they wish to support the latter. On the other hand, in some states such as Germany, the state collects church tithes through what amounts to a special, de facto "church tax" paid only by those taxpayers who acknowledge on their tax forms that they belong to a given (major) church. This system is believed by some to backfire in the sense that persons may leave established churches to avoid the church tax. It may also be significant that state funding puts clerics somewhat in the position of state bureaucrats. If the state sustains them they may have little incentive to develop a dynamic grassroots outreach.

They may resent actively evangelizing churches. According to one eminent German journalist, thousands of former German Catholics and Lutherans have left their churches and are gravitating toward new or more dynamic competitors. "Little wonder that the [major] churches have pressed the state to drive back the interlopers, and wherever the [Catholic] Church is particularly powerful, such as in predominantly Catholic Bavaria, the state has been particularly accommodating."[22] A threat to the Catholic Church is seen as a threat to the state and vice versa. This attitude has strong public support.

In Canada, according to Hexham, the churches have generally stayed clear of anticult crusaders. Notwithstanding their own vivid history of persecution and victimization, the Quakers may be something of an exception.

The Movements

It is worthwhile considering the groups being stigmatized or discriminated against. Are they simply innocent victims? What traits distinguish those groups that seem to elicit the greatest hostility? Why do certain groups, such as the Church of Scientology or Jehovah's Witnesses, so frequently get into hot water? (Parenthetically, the ubiquitous controversialism of the Witnesses outside of the U.S., where it is relatively reputable, may suggest that the "newness" criteria for identifying controversial and stigmatized movements may have been overemphasized.)

Of course, as discussed earlier, a handful of groups have become involved in spectacular mass mayhem (or lesser acts of violence). Only a small minority of "cults" are significantly violent.[23] Some groups, such as the Family of Love (formerly the Children of God), the Unification Church, and the Branch Davidians, manifest (presently or formerly) a "totalistic" organization in which devotees can be said to be more or less encapsulated and isolated from the broader culture and society. This may be problematic in two ways: 1) it appears to contravene norms of individuality and personal autonomy, which are strong in the U.S. and Britain; and 2) it potentially insulates participants from the norms and cultural standards of the general society and replaces these with strong, particularist group norms which may facilitate deviant and criminal behavior. Globalization, as we have noted, heightens cultural defensiveness in certain societies, and can thereby exacerbate the animus toward esoteric totalist sects that appear to withdraw members from the general culture.

In Africa, as Rosalind Hackett points out, movements such as the Lord's Resistance Army in Uganda may pose a military threat to state authority. A setting of political disorganization, in which ethnic-regional-political conflicts sometimes turn violent, may encourage a "revolutionary" or "terrorist" role for close-knit, messianic religious movements. But the instance of Aum Shinrikyō indicates that an anarchic general milieu is not necessary to instigate "religious terrorism."[24] The suspicious attitude of Chinese officials toward new movements, notes Scott Lowe, is influenced by a long history of the involvement of Chinese sects and secret societies in overt rebellions.

Some groups such as Scientology are highly diversified in their activities—particularly commercial operations. Arguably, this may be somewhat of a necessity for groups that lack the broad membership base for adequate internal, donative funding—they must somehow draw funds from nonmembers. Doubts naturally arise as to whether a particular diversified or "commercialized" movement is really a religion or is primarily a commercial, corporate organization.[25] Although the U.S., after much hesitation and acrimony, finally recognized Scientology as a "church" for tax purposes, in the U.K. Scientology has so far been denied the "charitable" status which would exempt it from taxation. It is worth noting that some new and alternative movements may be less involved, compared to more familiar churches, in activities that are "charitable" in the conventional sense. The result is the unwillingness of some (particularly European) governments to extend to alternative religions the tax privileges routinely granted to recognized "churches."

Some movements have apparently been involved in fraudulent commercial activities or deceptive proselytizing. The temptation to the latter is actually increased by the controversialism of certain groups, which become motivated to conceal their identity from prospective recruits in initial contact situations. Indeed, new movements may proselytize more vigorously and aggressively than institutionalized churches, which can produce irritation and perceived "invasion of privacy" even in the absence of misrepresentation. Some prophets and gurus have sexually or financially exploited their followers, a phenomenon which may become more likely when encapsulating totalism renders participants highly dependent on the group. The funding exigency created by a limited membership base may make it more likely that alternative religions will financially drain those members they do have and exploit devotees' unpaid labor.

To survive, a minority sect may need to become a disciplined "Gideon's Army" that excludes "free riders" or limited liability investors as well as troublesome dissidents. This is conducive to authoritarianism and to patterns of indoctrination and commitment building that are likely to be stigmatized as "mind control." Additionally, alternative movements are more likely than conventional groups to reject modern medicine and to use controversial methods of child rearing. Almost by definition, alternative religions cultivate *alternatives* to accepted norms, values, and procedures.

Finally, new movements are somewhat more likely to be possessed of both *charismatic leadership* and *apocalyptic perspectives*. Charismatic leadership is viewed by some scholars as inherently precarious and volatile. Apocalypticism and charismatic authority may be significant factors in facilitating the exodus of followers from conventional norms and received standards. This surely enhances the appeal of alternative groups to alienated and troubled persons. Falun Gong, according to Lowe, has apocalyptic teachings, which are being intensified under the impact of persecution.[26]

Marat Shterin notes that it is the perceived illegitimacy of new Russian groups per se and not their actual behavior that is the foundation of their stigma. Similarly, Hervieu-Léger observes that in France, the intense, exorbitant religious behavior of some groups is actually tolerated when the movements (Pentecostal groups, for example) belong to the Protestant Federation or to its familiar denominations. The lethal extremism of groups such as Aum Shinrikyō or the Solar Temple may have traumatized Europeans, but it may also serve as a convenient pretext for a more general repression of unconventional groups.

Two additional points need to be made. James Beckford has noted that, in different ways, movements such as the Unification Church, Scientology, Baha'i, Soka Gakkai, Transcendental Meditation, and Jehovah's Witnesses manifest their own *ideological visions of global order* or spiritual conceptions of the contemporary global crisis. Such visions tend to relativize or identify as superseded all other religions, cultures, and national identities.[27] Thus NRMs may be more likely to be at least implicitly exclusivist and "intolerant" than conventional Western churches, although many "New Age" and other groups are explicitly inclusive and affirm the legitimacy of pluralism. "Intolerant" faiths may appear disruptive and, moreover, may elicit hostility for reasons that evoke the Roman animus against early Christianity, which denied other gods and was thus stigmatized as perniciously atheist. As Reader notes, some new movements denounce competing movements as "false religions," thereby appearing to accept anti-cult mystiques about "destructive cults," themselves exempted.

Finally, our concluding essay by co-editor Phillip Charles Lucas presents a broad overview of five factors that are contributing to the emergence of an "increasingly repressive climate for new and alternative religions around the globe." The factors specified by Lucas are: 1. the end of the Cold War and the resultant shift from battles between capitalist democracies and their secular atheist (Communist) enemies to clashes between *religion*-based civilizations; 2. the destruction of the World Trade Center by Muslim extremists and the subsequent ratcheting up of the international "war on terrorism"; 3. sensational episodes of violence in NRMs such as the Branch Davidians, the Peoples Temple, and Aum Shinrikyō, and the subsequent growing perception that new and minority religions can constitute a mortal danger to social order; 4. the marginalization of academia in societal debates concerning cults and sects, and the concurrent internationalization and professionalization of the anticult and countercult movements; and 5. resurgent nationalism and religious traditionalism in countries trying to forge a "coherent national identity following radical regime changes." Lucas is persuaded that the forces of repression are growing around the world and that unless steps are taken to counteract increasing persecution in some countries, "Even citizens of nations such as the U.S. and Canada may soon find their religious rights threatened in ways that were inconceivable even a decade ago."

Conclusion: Freedom and Discrimination

In their important theoretical treatise on "religious economies," Rodney Stark and Roger Finke maintain that the growth of NRMs in Europe has sometimes been exaggerated. This may be particularly true of hyper-esoteric cults and guru groups. The real "potential wave of the future is to be found in energetic Christian and Islamic movements. . . . Indeed it is the fear of these movements that has motivated reactionary laws and policies in Eastern Europe and the nations of the former Soviet Union."[28] To some extent hostility to alternative religions in general may be partly a by-product of hostility to fervent Christian and Islamic sects, a point which is reinforced by Schoen's contention that a perceived Islamic threat may ramify into an apprehensiveness of esoteric, non-Christian groups in general. Krumina-Konkova's report on the Baltic States appears to highlight the hostility provoked by intolerant Christian movements such as the United Evangelical Congregation of God (which elicits antagonism in part because of its overt hostility to other Christian groups, particularly the Roman Catholic Church), Jehovah's Witnesses, and Christian Science.

Usually discrimination is tied to some kind of certification, registration, or licensing of what are considered to be the "bona fide" religious groups. In China, unregistered Protestant Evangelical groups may have their churches destroyed. Under Russia's 1996 legislation, unregistered groups such as the Salvation Army (at the time) may not be able to own property, employ persons, enter into contracts or hold public worship. In France, groups outside the confessional system may become objects of the state's "war on sects." In Denmark, however, as reported by Geertz and Rothstein, the consequences for groups whose application to become an "authorized" denomination under Danish law is denied do not appear to be very severe. Non-authorized or "outside" groups cannot conduct legal marriages but do not appear to be laboring under crippling disabilities.

Geertz and Rothstein report the interesting attempt by the Danish Advisory Council on Religious Denominations "to distinguish freedom of religion and conscience on the one hand and authorization of denominations on the other hand, with the privileges that the latter entails." Under Danish law, freedom of religion does not require that a group be empowered to exercise public executive authority, for instance, by performing marriages. The implicit distinction between effective denial of religious freedom and mere discrimination, though possibly at odds with American thinking, may appear valid in Denmark, where the burdens on non-authorized groups may be minimal. But at some point stronger discrimination would probably have to be seen as imperiling religious liberty. Where some sort of registration is essential for a religion to operate formally and publicly, discriminatory denial of certification is not compatible with religious liberty.[29]

It is worth noting that in modern, interdependent societies with a significant degree of state regulation, churches cannot easily operate without some support from public authorities. In the U.S.—the supposed fount of religious liberty—reputable churches are continually running afoul of zoning laws and other regulations when they try to expand their plant, build a new or larger parking lot, operate soup kitchens for the indigent, and so forth.

Finally, readers may want to consider that the criteria for authorization of denominations in Denmark as reported by Geertz and Rothstein (or other registration criteria in other nations) are prejudicial in the sense of mandating a particular organizational form of religion and excluding purported "religions" which do not meet what may be culturally particularistic criteria. Globalization is likely to enhance the salience of this issue.

Notes

1. Paul Marshall, "The First Freedom Under Siege," *First Things* 12 (April 2001): 18–20.
2. Ibid., 18.
3. Thomas Robbins, "Notes on the Contemporary Peril of Religious Freedom," in *Challenges to Religion*, eds. James Beckford and James Richardson (London: Routledge, forthcoming).
4. Ibid.
5. See James Richardson, ed., "Special Issues: Justice and New Religious Movements," *Social Justice Research* 12:4 (December 1999); Derek Davis, ed., *Religious Liberty in Northern Europe in the Twenty-First Century* (Waco, TX: Dawson Institute of Church-State Studies, 2000); Pauline Côté, ed., *Chercheurs de dieux l'espace publique [Frontier Religions in the Public Sphere]* (Ottawa: University of Ottawa Press, 2001); Robert Towler, ed. *New Religions in the New Europe* (Aarhus, Denmark: Aarhus University Press, 1995).
6. Mark Sedgwick, "Sects in the Islamic World," *Nova Religio* 3:2 (April 2000): 195–240.

7. James Beckford, "Religious Movements and Globalization," in *Global Social Movements*, eds. Robin Cohen and Shirin Rai (London: Athelone Press, 2000); see also, Irving Hexham and Karla Poewe, *New Religions as Global Cultures* (Boulder, CO: Westview, 1997).

8. Beckford, "Religious Movements and Globalization," 170.

9. Hexham and Poewe, *New Religions as Global Cultures*, 46.

10. James Beckford, "Cult Controversies in Three European Countries," *Journal of Oriental Studies* 8 (1998): 174–84.

11. Beckford, "Religious Movements and Globalization," 173.

12. On the Falun Gong sect and the fierce opposition it has encountered from the Chinese State, see the symposium on Falun Gong in *Nova Religio* 6:2 (Spring 2003) consisting of papers by Catherine Wessinger, Susan Palmer, David Ownby, Scott Lowe, Edward Irons, Bryan Edelman and James Richardson, Gareth Fisher, Craig Burdoff, and Mark Bell and Taylor Boas. See also the recent article by Patsy Rahn, "The Chemistry of a Conflict: The Chinese Government and Falun Gong," *Terrorism and Political Violence* 14:4 (Winter, 2002): 41–66.

13. In 2001, Herbert Rosedale, president of the anticult American Family Foundation, visited China and gave a presentation in Beijing to the China Anti-Cult Association, "Perspectives on Cults as Affected by the September 11 Tragedy" (see *Cultic Studies Review* 2:1 [2003]). Rosedale's paper strongly criticized the media's allegedly one-sided treatment of the Falun Gong controversy—its accounts of "persecution" combined with failure to expose the sinister cult—and neither praised nor criticized (indeed, barely mentioned) the extreme measures pursued by the Chinese state. An exchange between Rosedale and Thomas Robbins is forthcoming in *Cultic Studies Review*. On the mutual sympathy between the Chinese and French governments with regard to cults, see Joseph Bosco, "China's French Connection," *Washington Post*, 20 July 2001.

14. Rodney Stark and Roger Finke, *Acts of Faith: Examining the Human Side of Religion* (Berkeley: University of California Press, 2000), 232.

15. Ibid., 233.

16. Schoen cites two papers which she feels exaggerate the German persecution of Scientology and other groups: Irving Hexham and Karla Poewe, "Verfassungsfeindlich: Church, State and New Religions in Germany," *Nova Religio* 2 (1998): 208–27; Derek Davis, "Religious Persecution in Today's Germany: Old Habits Renewed," *Journal of Church and State* 40 (1998): 741–56.

17. See Dick Anthony and Thomas Robbins, "Law, Social Science and the 'Brainwashing' Exception to the First Amendment," *Behavioral Sciences and the Law* 10:1 (Winter 1992): 5–30.

18. See also Ian Reader, "Scholarship, Aum Shinrikyō and Integrity," *Nova Religio* 3:2 (Spring, 2000): 368–82.

19. Massimo Introvigne, "Blacklisting or Greenlisting: A European Perspective on the New Cult Wars," *Nova Religio* 18 (1998): 17.

20. Dick Anthony, "Pseudoscience and Minority Religions: Evaluation of the Brainwashing Theories of Jean-Marie Abgrall," *Social Justice Research* 12:4 (Dec. 1999): 421–56.

21. See, for example, P. Froese, "Hungary for Religion: A Supply-Side Interpretation of the Hungarian Religious Revival," *Journal for the Scientific Study of Religion* 40:2 (2001): 251–68.

22. Joseph Joffe, "Germany vs. the Scientologists," *New York Review of Books*, 24 April 1997, 16–21.

23. See the excellent overview by James Richardson, "Minority Religions and the Context of Violence: A Conflict/Interactionist Perspective," *Terrorism and Political Violence* 13:1 (Spring 2001): 103–33.

24. On the relationship between "cults" and "terrorists," see Christopher Centner, "Cults and Terrorism: Similarities and Differences," *Cultic Studies Review* 2:2 (2003).

25. See an interesting discussion of the conflicted religious status of the Church of Scientology, Nikos Passos and Manuel Castillo, "Scientology and its 'Clear' Business," *Behavioral Sciences and the Law* 10:1 (Winter 1992): 103–17.

26. See note 12.

27. Beckford, "Religious Movements and Globalization," 172–76. See also Hexham and Poewe, *New Religions as Global Cultures*, 46–47.

28. Stark and Finke, *Acts of Faith*, 257.

29. The situation in the republic of Belarus is instructive in this context. The Constitution of Belarus guarantees the right to faith but not the right to found religious organizations. The

influence of the larger Russian state and the Patriarchate of Moscow in Belarus is such that other purportedly "Orthodox" groups such as the "True Orthodox Church" are not allowed to register and are not recognized as authentic religious entities. As an official explained to reporters, the True Orthodox Church "does not exist in Belarus." Nevertheless the official denied that there is a ban on recognizing any Orthodox parishes outside of the Belarusian Exarchate of the Moscow Patriarchate. Unregistered religious activity in Belarus (and in one other post-Soviet republic) has been criminalized, and believers in unregistered communities can be punished if they conduct communal religious activity. They can meet and pray privately in their homes but not conduct a formal, public liturgy. Worldwide Religious News, 4 April 2003.

PART 1

Western Europe

CHAPTER 1

General Overview of the "Cult Scene" in Great Britain

EILEEN BARKER

Since 1559, the Church of England has been "by law established." There is also an established (Presbyterian) Church in Scotland; the Church of Ireland was disestablished in 1869; and the Church in Wales was disestablished in 1920. The sovereign of Britain is called "Defender of the Faith" and must promise on his or her accession to uphold the Church of England. Although Catholics and non-conformist Protestants have existed within a general tradition of dissent throughout the centuries, it was not until the second half of the nineteenth century that full civil and political rights were extended to all religions—in 1871 Parliament passed the Universities Test Act that opened Oxford and Cambridge to members of all religions, and in 1890 all government posts became open to members of the Jewish faith. Around the turn of the century, a number of alternative religions (widely defined), such as Theosophy, Spiritualism, Deism, Auguste Comte's Positivist Church of Humanity, and the Salvation Army, began to make their presence known. During the first half of the twentieth century, other new religions, most notably those of Eastern origin such as SUBUD, Vedanta, and the followers of Krishnamurti, gained popularity among a small but significant group of middle-class intellectuals.

In the late 1960s, protests against the Vietnam War and bourgeois imperialism in general broke out among the student population. This merged into the hippie period with "flower power" and the embracing of all manner of new kinds of religiosity and spirituality. Internationally operating movements came to Britain from the East and the West. The Church of Scientology had been one of the earliest of the current wave of new movements to appear on the scene, but it was soon followed by Krishna devotees chanting and dancing in the streets and the increased visibility of other new religions such as the Unification Church, the Rajneesh movement, the Children of God (later The Family), and the Divine Light Mission (later *Elan Vital*). Erhard Seminars Training *(est)* and other examples of the human potential movement joined indigenous new religions, such as the Emin, Exegesis, the Aetherius Society, the School of Economic Science, and the Findhorn community in the north of Scotland, and a number of small congregations within mainstream churches were labelled "cults" as they exhibited some of the more enthusiastic characteristics of new religions and their leaders. The Nine o'Clock Service, a Church of England congregation in Sheffield, was one of the more extreme examples.[1]

Another source of new (to Britain) religions was immigration, with several hundreds of black and Asian religions (such as Cherubim and Seraphim from Nigeria, and the followers of Swaminarayan from India) springing up around those areas (mainly large city conurbations) where the immigrant populations settled. On the whole, little attention is given to the black Afro-Caribbean churches, which have increased in number, largely due to immigration. However, widespread consternation accompanied the discovery of the torso of a young boy of African origin who was found in the Thames in September 2001. The investigation into what is widely assumed to have been a ritual killing still continues, with the enquiry extending to African villages where police are trying to discover the boy's origins through DNA sampling.

Despite the fact that the vast majority of the two million or so Muslims in Britain are well integrated into the country and perfectly law-abiding citizens, the apparently growing (but unknown) number of young, well educated Christians converting to Islam has been giving rise to apprehension in some quarters. An incipient Islamophobia was fanned by the *fatwa* placed by Ayatollah Khomeini on Salman Rushdie after the publication of his book, *The Satanic Verses*, and by the bombing of the World Trade Center and the Pentagon in the United States on September 11, 2001. This has been exacerbated by the existence of a few militant new movements, such as Hizb ut-Tahrir, Al Muhajiroun, and the Nation of Islam. Two additional incidents, both involving converts to Islam, raised the level of public fear. First, there was the so-called shoe-bomber, Richard Reid, who has been jailed for life in the United States for attempting to blow up a trans-Atlantic flight with 197 people on board. Second, an imam at a south London mosque, Sheikh Abdullah el-Faisal, who was reportedly a former supporter of Osama bin Laden, has been jailed for soliciting murder and inciting hatred against non-Muslims.

Like some other countries, Britain had its "Satanic scare," but it did not last very long, largely due to a thorough investigation being carried out with a grant from the government which revealed that almost all the incidents in which so-called ritual abuse had been conducted on children were, in fact, either "ordinary abuse" or complete fabrications.[2] In 1975, the first of the contemporary anticult organizations appeared on the scene.[3] Known as FAIR, the initials originally stood for Family Action Information and Rescue, but this was changed in 1994 to Family Action Information and Resource when it was decided that the erstwhile practice of forcible deprogramming carried out by some of its members was no longer acceptable. FAIR, which was founded by Paul Rose, MP, consisted mainly, but by no means only, of distressed parents who were later joined by some disillusioned ex-members. Two Christian countercult movements also appeared (the Deo Gloria Trust and the Reachout Trust). Later, other anticult groups, such as the Cult Information Centre (run by a man who had spent a few days with a group in Canada that had successfully cured him of smoking), Catalyst, and some groups specifically designed to warn the public of the dangers of particular movements, also joined the scene.[4]

Although there have been some excellent reports by journalists who have written books about British alternative religions (such as William Shaw's *Spying in Guru Land*[5] and Jon Ronson's *Them: Adventures with Extremists*[6]), as elsewhere around the world, the British media have tended to relate the more sensational stories about "the cults." Some of these have resulted in court cases, such as the libel case that the Unification Church lost against the *Daily Mail* when the tabloid accused it of brainwashing and breaking up families.[7] The jury, as a result of its deliberations, not only declared the *Daily Mail* to be vindicated in its accusations, but also requested that the Attorney General remove the church's charitable status. However, after a lengthy investigation, it was decided that there were no legal grounds for doing this. Another case was a successful libel suit against the *Daily Telegraph* for quoting an anticultist's remarks that a barrister and his wife constituted a cult. In the longest trial ever to take place in the Family Court, a grandmother lost her plea to have custody of her daughter's child while her daughter was a member of The Family. This was, however, only after the daughter and The Family had been required by Lord Justice Ward to renounce some of the teachings of their leader, David Berg.[8]

So far as the law is concerned, both Conservative and Labour governments have made it clear that, although they do not like many of the new religions, they have no intention of introducing any special laws to deal with them. So long as the NRMs act within the common and criminal law, they are as free as anyone else to believe and do what they wish.[9] This does not mean that there has been no discrimination against the movements, however. In 1968, restrictions were imposed on foreigners entering the

U.K. to study or work for Scientology. Following the Foster Report, these restrictions were lifted in 1980. In 1986, Louis Farrakhan was denied entry to visit his followers in the Nation of Islam, and successive Home Secretaries have upheld the ban in the courts. In 1995, Mr. Justice Sedley ruled that the then Home Secretary, Michael Howard, had used unlawful means to prevent Sun Myung Moon from entering the country "by reason of procedural unfairness," but in May 2003 a letter was sent to Moon stating that the current Home Secretary, David Blunkett, had personally directed that he "should be excluded from the United Kingdom on grounds that your [Moon's] presence here would not be conducive to the public good for reasons of public order." At the time of this writing, the church is in the process of appealing this decision.

There have also been a few cases where members of new or minority religions have been discriminated against in the courts.[10] In one instance, a teacher was dismissed because of her unconventional (Unification) beliefs (even though it was agreed that she had not attempted to pass these on to her pupils); in another instance, a case involving the use of Bhaktivedanta Manor was taken through the British Courts system before ISKCON devotees were finally allowed to use the manor for religious festivities.[11] Moving to the universities, a few new religions (such as the International Churches of Christ and Hizb ut-Tahrir) have been banned by Students' Unions from some campuses; but, generally speaking, religious groups are free to speak wherever they wish, so long as they do not cause a disturbance.

Towards the end of the 1980s, amid cries from anticultists and others that "something needed to be done," the Home Office and mainstream churches decided to support the founding of an independent charity which would supply enquirers with information about NRMs that was as objective and up to date as possible. INFORM (Information Network Focus on Religious Movements), which is based at the London School of Economics and employs staff trained in the methods of the social sciences, now deals with over one thousand inquiries each year, produces literature about the movements, and provides twice-yearly seminars and talks for various organizations. It is the only "cult-watching group" that has received official support from the British churches, the government, and the police.[12]

Although in the 1970s discrimination on the grounds of race or sex was outlawed, Northern Ireland has been the only part of the United Kingdom in which discrimination on grounds of religion was not permitted. On October 1, 2000, however, a new Human Rights Bill, incorporating the European Convention on Human Rights into U.K. law, was made legally binding. Although there has been a considerable amount of speculation as to what difference this will make, it is still too early to judge its effects.

While the government does not discriminate among religions—apart from the special status accorded the Established Church—the Charity

Commissioners do so, and whether or not they decide to grant charitable status to a group will have considerable financial consequences so far as tax exemption is concerned. Generally speaking, there are four grounds on which a group may claim charitable status: 1. the relief of the poor, handicapped and the aged; 2. the advancement of education; 3. the advancement of religion; 4. other charitable purposes which help and benefit the community.[13] Charity law is not clear on exactly what these criteria entail, and recent efforts to clarify the position have not been entirely satisfactory for any of the people concerned. The Church of Scientology has not succeeded in persuading the Commissioners that it is a religion. The Pagan Federation has objected to the fact that one of its caring facilities has not been accepted—although, unlike Rastafarians, Scientology, and the Nation of Islam, it is allowed to have a chaplain visiting its members who are in prison. In fact, there is considerable ambiguity about Paganism in Britain. On the one hand, Pagans are depicted as spiritually aware and ecologically concerned citizens with high standards of morality;[14] on the other hand, they are vilified as evil witches involved in black magic and Satanic rituals. The Pagan Federation's first national youth manager was suspended from his job as a drama teacher in a state secondary school when it was discovered that he was a "witch"—although he had never used his position to promote his beliefs and was subsequently reinstated.[15] There was, furthermore, a considerable furor when the then incoming Archbishop of Canterbury, Rowan Williams, "became a druid"—or, more accurately, was inducted into the Gorsedd of Bards, by donning white robes and partaking in an ancient ceremony honoring Welsh-speaking poets, musicians, and other artists.[16]

Although it is probable that most people, if asked, would "know" that "cults are a bad thing," it is also true that most people in Britain do not give the matter much thought. There may be a few demonstrators outside the Albert Hall when Mataji or Maharaj Ji are giving a talk to their respective actual and potential followers, but such events will, on the whole, pass unnoticed. There are, of course, individual members of Parliament and of the traditional churches who share the view of the anticult movement that NRMs should be subject to special restrictions and control. But although they clearly do not agree with the beliefs of other religions, the Established Church, the Free Church Council, and the Roman Catholic Church have exhibited a generally tolerant attitude towards them. Successive archbishops of Canterbury have strongly supported the approach taken by the government and INFORM, rather than that of the anticultists. That is, that it is necessary to provide accurate and balanced knowledge of the movements to public and official bodies, but that the movements and their members should not be treated in law any differently from the rest of the population.

It should be recognized that over the past quarter of a century several changes have taken place within the better known new religions themselves, making them more likely to wish to be accepted as "normal" rather than insisting upon the ways in which they differ from the rest of society.[17] This and other factors, such as more easily accessible knowledge of the movements' beliefs and practices, have defused somewhat at least some of the antagonisms that previously existed between the movements and the general British population. Indeed, several of the new religious movements have become accepted as significant contributors to some of the more influential sections of British culture. Thus, one might find members of the Brahma Kumaris at a reception at Lambeth Palace (the official residence of the Archbishop of Canterbury); a representative of the Baha'i at a Foreign and Commonwealth Office function; a member of the Friends of the Western Buddhist Order at a BBC gathering; and an ISKCON devotee representing the Hindu community in a religious broadcast on the BBC World Service.

It is impossible to estimate accurately the number of NRMs to be found in Britain today (one problem is the definition of a new religion—whether, for example, one includes self-development groups and/or all the small congregations within mainstream religions), but the number could be anywhere from 900 to 2000. This, however, does not mean that the number of core members of NRMs is anything but a very small proportion of the general population, largely because of the high turnover in most of the movements. Of those movements that were best known for active proselytizing in the 1970s and 1980s, most have assumed a lower profile and are likely to rely on second-generation membership as much as, if not more than, persuading new converts to join their ranks. Most of the movements have no more than a few hundred members—many have but a score or so. It is also the case that those movements which claim large numbers often include people who once took one of their courses, or were given a mantra, but have since had no connection with them.[18] Other movements, such as Swaminarayan, Sai Baba, or ISKCON, have large congregations of British Asians who may attend several temples and would not consider themselves to be involved in anything that differed from their traditional beliefs and practices.

Another problem with trying to estimate the statistical significance of NRMs is the widespread interest in Eastern and New Age concepts, which are used as an almost absent-minded resource by a growing number of the population without their belonging to any particular movement.[19] Such people are likely to draw on these and other, possibly contradictory, ideas as and when they seem appropriate, without having any well thought out or systematic theology. According to some polls, for example, nearly a quarter of the British population will say that they believe in reincarnation,[20] although a more recent survey, presenting a slightly different choice, gives only seven percent choosing reincarnation as opposed to other beliefs about life after death.[21]

Be that as it may, a general shift away from institutionalized religion to less institutionalized spirituality would seem to be a general trend in contemporary Britain. One aspect of this shift could be discerned in the 2001 U.K. census, which, for the first time since 1851, included a question on religion. The preliminary results revealed that 71.6 percent of the population considered themselves to be Christians of one sort or another; 2.7 percent were Muslims; 1 percent Hindu; with the next largest percentage being Jedi Knights (the galactic order of warriors from the Star Wars films), scoring 0.7 percent with over 390,000 respondents,[22] more than those belonging to the Sikh (0.6 percent), Jewish (0.5 percent), "Other" (0.3 percent) or Buddhist (0.3 percent) religions.[23]

To conclude, the situation with regard to new religions in Britain is not clear cut. Although it is apparent to some Britons that some groups and some sets of beliefs are clearly a danger to the individual and society, exactly what comprises a "cult" or new religion is by no means clear in all cases. While they may not be welcomed with open arms by many apart from their own members, compared with the situation in other parts of Europe the new religions are, on the whole, a more or less reluctantly accepted component of the complicated religious pluralism that typifies contemporary Britain.

Notes

1. Roland Howard, *The Rise and Fall of the Nine o'Clock Service: A Cult within the Church?* (London: Mowbray, 1996).
2. Jean S. La Fontaine, *The Extent and Nature of Organised and Ritual Abuse: Research Findings* (London: HMSO, Department of Health, 1994).
3. James Beckford, *Cult Controversies: The Societal Response to the New Religious Movements* (London: Tavistock, 1985), 225.
4. George D. Chryssides, "Britain's Anti-cult Movement," in *New Religious Movements: Challenge and Response*, eds. Bryan Wilson and Jamie Cresswell (London: Routledge, 1999), 257–73.
5. William Shaw, *Spying in Guru Land: Inside Britain's Cults* (London: Fourth Estate, 1994).
6. Jon Ronson, *Them: Adventures with Extremists* (London: Picador, 2001).
7. Eileen Barker, *The Making of a Moonie: Brainwashing or Choice?* (Aldershot: Ashgate, 1993), 121ff.
8. James R. Lewis and J. Gordon Melton, eds., *Sex, Slander, and Salvation: Investigating the Family/Children of God* (Stanford, CA: Center for Academic Publishing, 1994).
9. It might be noted, however, that witchcraft was illegal until 1951.
10. Eileen Barker, "The British Right to Discriminate," in *Church-State Relations: Tensions and Transitions*, eds. Thomas Robbins and Roland Robertson (New Brunswick, NJ: Transaction, 1987), 269–80; "Tolerant Discrimination: New Religious Movements in Relation to Church, State and Society," in *Religion, State and Society in Modern Britain*, ed. Paul Badham (Lewiston, NY: Edwin Mellen Press, 1989), 185–208.
11. Malory Nye, "ISKCON and Hindus in Britain," *ISKCON Communications Journal* 5:2 (December 1997): 5–14.
12. Despite persistent statements by certain anticultists that the Home Office has removed its financial support for INFORM, it actually increased it by 50 percent to £30,000 per annum in 2002.
13. See http://www.charity-commission.gov.uk, accessed 1 April 2003. The Scottish situation differs slightly from that in England and Wales.

14. Tania M. Luhrmann, *Persuasions of the Witch's Craft: Ritual Magic in Contemporary England* (Cambridge, MA: Harvard University Press, 1989).

15. Robert Mendick, "Pagan teacher to be disciplined by school," *Independent (Education)*, 9 April 2000; "Paganism finds growing interest among UK children," CNSNews, London, 23 March 2003, www.mcjonline.com/news/00b/20000828b.htm, accessed 29 March 2003; Melanie McGrath, "The witching hour," *The Guardian*, 28 October 2000.

16. Rebecca Allison, "Incoming Archbishop becomes a druid," *The Guardian*, 6 August 2002.

17. Eileen Barker and Jean-François Mayer, eds., *Twenty Years On: Changes in New Religious Movements* (London: Sage, 1995), especially 165–80.

18. Eileen Barker, *New Religious Movements: A Practical Introduction* (London: HMSO, 1989), 145–55.

19. Grace Davie, *Religion in Britain since 1945* (Oxford: Blackwell, 1994).

20. David Barker, Loek Halman, and Astrid Vloet, *The European Values Study 1981–1990: Summary Report* (Tilburg, Netherlands: European Values Group, 1993).

21. This is data I have collected as part of the Religious and Moral Pluralism project which has yet to be published.

22. This was as a result of a campaign on the Internet around the time of the census, inviting those who protested at being asked about their beliefs—or, the e-mail concluded, "Do it because you love Star Wars. If not, just do it to annoy people."

23. There were also 15.5 percent classified as "no religion" and 7.3 percent who gave "no answer."

CHAPTER 2

Religious Minorities and New Religious Movements in Denmark

ARMIN W. GEERTZ AND MIKAEL ROTHSTEIN[1]

The debate on new religious movements (NRMs) has been on the public agenda in Denmark for the past twenty-five years, and probably little can be said regarding this country which is not apparent in other places as well. However, one might point to one or two conditions that have been of special importance for the Danish situation compared to the situation in other European countries and in the United States. In short, Denmark has not seen the same kinds of conflicts that have emerged in some other countries, and it is worthwhile considering why.

The Danish debate on NRMs is not very different from what has transpired elsewhere. In Denmark, though, the general attitude towards new religions is not as unconditionally hostile as in Germany, France, Greece, Belgium, and Russia. Although the vast majority of people will express an unsympathetic attitude towards the new religions, most are basically uninterested in or ignorant of the subject. This lack of interest may point to a general indifference regarding religion among many Danes and to a tendency to perceive religious belief and religious affiliation as an entirely personal affair. One might also claim that negative sentiments are limited by the well established tradition for democracy and freedom of belief in this country. We would suggest that general cultural mores may have prevented the development of a radical hostility towards religious minorities and new religions.

It should also be noted that most of the new or emergent religions have a very modest, and generally insignificant, following in Denmark. A guess would identify slightly under 2000 individuals in Denmark firmly committed to and personally engaged in one of the new non-Christian religious movements that have emerged since World War II. This means that approximately 0.035 percent of the population is engaged in one of the new religions on a permanent basis.[2] In Denmark, religious pluralism is primarily understood with reference to the religions of immigrant and refugee groups, and the debate on Islam is permanently ongoing and much more problematic than that on new religions.[3]

In our opinion, religious minorities and new religions live a fairly secure life in Denmark, and actual violations of their rights are exceptional. In recent years two interrelated problems of principal concern have surfaced: political discussions concerning restrictions and privileges regarding minority religions and new religions, and in this connection a discussion about what kind of expertise the authorities should make use of when dealing with these cases.

The Legal Situation and Administrative Practice

Denmark is a constitutional monarchy[4] enjoying freedom of conscience and religion. Church historian Frands Ole Overgaard has summed up the situation:

> The freedom of not only religion, but also of expression, association, assembly and printing was an essential part of the first democratic constitution in 1849, even if the words "freedom of religion" were not used. The citizens were entitled to freedom of worship. They had the right to unite in a community to worship God according to their convictions, on the condition that nothing was taught or carried out that was inconsistent with morality and public order. The legislators were precluded from regulating the activities of a religious community if these related to or took aim at worship. Organization, financing and rites could not be banned. The freedom of thought, conscience, religion and belief included freedom to establish and maintain places for purpose of worship and association. No one was any longer obliged to contribute to a religion the person concerned did not affiliate with. Nobody could be deprived of civil and political rights because of his or her religious conscience.[5]

There is not, however, religious equality. This is because article 4 of the Constitution of the Kingdom of Denmark of 1849 (amended in 1866, 1915, 1920, and 1953) establishes the Evangelical Lutheran Church as the Church of Denmark (called *Folkekirken* in Danish, that is the "People's Church"), which "shall as such be supported by the State." This establishment introduced two sets of rights and privileges, namely, those of the Church of Denmark and those of the minority churches.[6] An important legal point in the status of the Church of Denmark is that it has no constitution even though Article 66 of the Danish Constitution states that the constitution of the church shall be laid down by statute. The relations of the church have instead been regulated by separate acts.

In a report published in 1999 by the Commissioner of the Council of the Baltic Sea States on Democratic Institutions and Human Rights, including the Rights of Persons belonging to Minorities, it is stated that:

> The aim of Article 66 was to establish a constitution and a regulation of the Folk Church, which separates it from the rest of the public administration. This was seen as an important part of the establishment of religious liberty. However, the proposed autonomy of the Folk Church has never been established, and it is in many ways still closely linked to the state. Because of its special status . . . it has never been under and is still outside the control of the Danish Parliament.[7]

In our opinion, however, even though the proposed autonomy of the Church of Denmark was never realized by constitutional law, the church is very much under the control of the Danish Parliament. The Ombudsman of the Danish Parliament, Hans Gammeltoft-Hansen, noted at a conference on the Constitution and the Church of Denmark that the Ruling Assembly of the Church of Denmark is in fact the Danish Parliament, the government, and the Minister of Ecclesiastical Affairs. He stated that this Assembly has authority over the internal and external affairs of the church. The many inquiries and investigations initiated by the Parliament and its subcommittees indicate that the Parliament takes an active interest in the affairs of the Church of Denmark. Furthermore, authoritative bodies within the Church of Denmark itself do not have the power to rescind, restrict, or affect laws and regulations enacted by the Parliament. Thus it can be stated that the favored status of the Church of Denmark, which includes among other things financial support from public funds, prevents the church from enjoying the autonomy that the freedom of religion should entail.

Furthermore, the rights and privileges of the minority churches are in certain crucial areas incumbent on de jure recognition from the Ministry of Ecclesiastical Affairs. Related to this recognition, the Danish Constitution states in Article 69 that "rules for religious bodies dissenting from the established Church shall be laid down by statute." This has not occurred, with the result that these matters are regulated by administrative authorities. Because of this, Hanne Fledelius and Birgitte Juul conclude in their report on the freedom of religion in Denmark that such regulation is without parliamentary control. However, it seems relevant here to remember the above mentioned comments by Hans Gammeltoft-Hansen.[8]

During the period between 1849 and 1969 certain religious communities were recognized by Royal Decree, which allowed them to perform christenings and marriages with civil validity, to keep a church registry of births and deaths in Denmark, and to avail themselves of certain tax and other benefits. Several were recognized in 1849, but the list only includes the Jewish community and ten Christian communities.[9] Communities that did not attain recognition were the Jehovah's Witnesses, the Mormons, the Adventists, and a group called Islam Denmark.

In 1969, the parliament passed a new Marriage Act allowing church weddings with civil validity to take place in the Church of Denmark, in the recognized denominations, as well as in other religious communities which have obtained authorization by the Minister of Ecclesiastical Affairs. Since then, sixty-six denominations have received authorization. Among these are groups that failed to receive recognition before 1969 as well as a number of ethnic and new religions such as various Buddhist groups, ISKCON, the Sai Baba movement, an Anthroposophical Christian Fellowship group, Brahma Kumaris, and the Baha'i religion. Among the groups that applied but were rejected are fringe Christian organizations (the majority) and NRMs such as The Family, Proudiest Universal, Siddha Yoga, "A Course in Miracles" group, the esoteric White Eagle Centre, and Scientology.

To a large degree this model seems to work, but there are, of course, problems. For one thing the groups may not live up to the legal idea of what a religious group is. To meet the requirements, a religious denomination, according to the Brief of the Marriage Act, must be

> a genuine religious community in the normal sense of this word—i.e. not just a religious "movement" or a religious or philosophical society, but an association or assembly (a religious community) whose primary aim is worship of God (cult) in accordance with an elaborated doctrine and ritual.[10]

Until recently, the Ministry of Ecclesiastical Affairs consulted the Bishop of Copenhagen concerning these applications in order to help it determine whether the applicants fulfill these requirements. This procedure has been criticized by religious groups, scholars of religion, and the public.[11] In 1992, jurists at the Danish Center for Human Rights (affiliated with the University of Copenhagen) opposed the fact that the Bishop of Copenhagen and his pastoral advisor were the only official consultants used by the state in questions regarding the legal status of minority religions. They argued that a secular state should not allow representatives of one religion to be consultants in questions regarding other religions. Rather, it was suggested that the state should draw on the expertise of "professors of religion."[12] The mounting criticism moved the then Minister of Ecclesiastical Affairs, Ole Vig Jensen, to establish an advisory committee in 1998 chaired by historian of religions Armin W. Geertz and further consisting of sociologist of religion Ole Riis, professor of law Eva Smith, and theologian Jørgen Stenbæk. In 2001 Margit Warburg replaced Ole Riis as the committee's sociologist of religion.

Attempting to bring coherency and transparency to the process of evaluation—both as a gesture to religious minorities and as a foundation for its work—the committee concentrated on interpreting the law and making it operational. Thus the committee published an eight-page analysis in Danish on the laws and procedures for the evaluation process which it uses in its deliberations.[13]

The complex situation of Danish practice raises interesting perspectives from a legal point of view, especially in the context of the Universal Declaration of Human Rights of 1948, the International Convention on the Elimination of All Forms of Racial Discrimination of 1965, the International Covenant on Civil and Political Rights of 1966, and the European Convention on Human Rights of 1950. The Advisory Committee on Religious Denominations has attempted to distinguish between freedom of religion and conscience on the one hand, and authorization of denominations on the other hand—considering the privileges that the latter entails. It seems that according to the law, freedom of religion does not imply that any organization claiming to be religious automatically receives authorization by the Ministry of Ecclesiastical Affairs. Since ministerial authorization in effect confers an extension of executive power to an authorized denomination—however minor that extension of power may be—the authorization process rests on the assumption that the Minister of Ecclesiastical Affairs can and should decide whether the authorization of a particular applicant is reasonable in terms of administrative law. From this perspective, it is evident that the government does not find Danish law and administrative practice to be in violation of the above mentioned conventions.

The situation involves, nevertheless, potential sources of conflict from human, institutional, and principle perspectives. Thus knowledge of the administrative practices of the Ministry of Ecclesiastical Affairs, the Ministry of the Interior, the Ministry of Justice, the Church of Denmark, the courts of law, law enforcers, and county and municipal authorities is essential to an understanding of the judicial situation of new and minority religions in Denmark. It will be interesting in the future to see if any court cases on these issues will arise in Denmark or in the international courts. So far, no cases concerning religious freedom have arisen in Danish courts of law. Cases have arisen on matters under the jurisdiction of other laws, such as illegal ritual slaughter, exemption from military conscription, and determining custody of children in divorce proceedings, but none dealing with the articles on religion. In the early 1980s, Scientology legally contested a decision by the Directorate of Immigration not to extend residence permits to two Scientology missionaries. The suit was brought to the European Commission for Human Rights in Strasbourg on the grounds, among other things, of Article 9 (on freedom of religion) in the Convention of 1950. The suit was turned down on the formal grounds that local redress had not been attempted according to Convention Article 26, but the commission also noted that the granting or refusal of residence permits cannot be regarded as a "civil right" as defined in Article 6.[14]

Areas of Concern

Danes basically hold liberal attitudes with regard to religion and see it as essentially an individual concern. Attention is paid, however, to minority groups of any kind that in the media appear to contravene public ideals or mores. The use of headscarves by Muslim women, for instance, is often considered to be in disregard of women's rights. The denial by Jehovah's Witnesses of blood transfusions to their sick children is deemed to be in negligent disregard of the right to proper medical care. Scientology's filings of the auditing records of individual members (the so-called "PC folders") is considered to be in contravention of the very strict laws on files and records ("Registerloven").[15] A final example is the practice of ritual slaughter performed by Muslims, which has led to legal prosecution.

Such matters reflect the commonly held view that the public should maintain legal insight into religious communities especially in relation to public laws and ordinances and to monitoring the use of public funds and tax exemptions. Other areas of concern include minority religions and public schooling, military service, and disinterment practices. All of these areas potentially involve judicial and social problems for minority members as well as for society at large. With few exceptions—most notably exemption from military service—most of the problems have been practical rather than judicial.

A further area of concern deals with a variety of needs from the perspective of individual citizens and aliens. The individual has the right of appeal in judicial and administrative decisions. In relation to the question of human rights, society has the duty to protect minority and individual rights. In questions concerning the rights of family members, children must be guaranteed the freedom of conscience and of religion as specified by the above mentioned conventions on human rights.[16] Another important problem that concerns many new and minority religions is the active role played by the newspaper and other mass media in criticizing minorities. Sometimes reports in the media are exaggerated and gratuitous. However, as indicated above, the Danish news media have been much less aggressive than their counterparts in other countries.

An offshoot of the attention that has been paid to Scientology through the years is the interesting case of a book published by a historian of religions. The case, though only indirectly involving Scientology, indicates a fundamental Danish steadiness and at the same time points to the potential for future turmoil. In November 1997, a debate surfaced in Danish newspapers concerning a historian of religions, Dorthe Refslund Christensen, who was a Ph.D. candidate at the University of Aarhus at the time and who had published a book about Scientology for the secondary schools.[17] The book deliberately avoided discussing the controversies surrounding Scientology, but focused instead on how and why this group could be understood and interpreted as a religion. The book focused among other things on the hagiography of L. Ron Hubbard, the development from Dianetics to Scientology, and Scientology's soteriological notions. One right-wing member of Parliament asked the Minister of Education (who also happened to be the Minister of Ecclesiastical Affairs) to dissociate himself from the book. The minister, however, stood firm. The book was posing no problem, he said.[18] The same conclusion was reached by those within the political and educational systems as well as by scholars who discussed the book. The new book about Scientology was composed in the same way as most educational books on religion in Denmark. Most people added, though, that it would be natural to include critical approaches of other kinds in the process of education in order to contextualize the issues. This was the first book ever to be put on the political agenda in this way, and the first schoolbook in modern times to be reviewed in a political forum.[19]

The Christian Response

The Church of Denmark has no official position on minority and new religions. There are, however, individual bishops and pastors who have quite clear positions. One very prominent person is Kjeld Holm, the Bishop of Aarhus. He has been politically active throughout his career and was Chair of the Board for Ethnic Equality (appointed by the Ministry of the Interior in 1997) until it was closed down in 2001. The board consisted of representatives from national, regional, and local authorities, major non-governmental organizations, the Danish Center for Human Rights, and the umbrella organizations and advisory boards of ethnic minority groups. Its primary purpose was to advise the parliament, the government, central and local authorities, private organizations, and other institutions on questions concerning discrimination and ethnic equality. It was also active in disclosing direct and indirect discrimination and in creating viable opportunities for ethnic minorities. The board has conducted investigations, held conferences, and produced books and publications to educate the Danish public on the concerns and needs of minority groups.[20] The reason the board was closed down was because of pressure from the Danish Folk Party. Originally, the party wanted to close down the Danish Centre for Human Rights. After realizing that this was impossible, they threatened to remove support for the 2002 fiscal budget. The resulting compromise was typically Danish: both the Danish Centre for Human Rights and the Board of Ethnic Equality were "incorporated into" a new Institute for Human Rights with a new board of directors. Some of the staff members from the former two bodies are now employed by the institute.

The Church of Denmark has set up a small network of pastors with special interests in new religions and alternative spirituality. The idea is to keep abreast of developments, not because the new religions themselves are of interest to the church, but because it is considered to be a matter of pastoral concern in guiding and educating people with regard to these religions. Although there is tolerance and respect for individual freedom of conscience and religion, their attitude is clearly critical and apologetic. It should also be noted, however, that a number of pastors in the church have expressed favorable attitudes towards some New Age ideas, claiming that Christians might well learn from other religious traditions.

Denmark has become world famous for the activities of a now retired professor of theology at the University of Aarhus, Johannes Aagaard. Certainly he is well known to scholars of new religions. He established a small Department of Missiology and Ecumenical Theology and the Center for New Religious Studies at the Faculty of Theology in Aarhus. The center is arguably one of the largest archives on new religions in northern Europe. Outside of the university context, Aagaard founded a Christian missionary organization called the Dialogue Center over twenty-five years ago. The Dialogue Center is a private organization, and Aagaard has kept his university activities and missionary practices separate. However, it should be noted that Aagaard's apologetic focus has been the same in both contexts, which means that his university work over the years has corresponded closely with his efforts in the Dialogue Center. This has led many people to believe that the two institutions are identical. The university, however, and especially the Faculty of Theology, have through the years insisted on a legal separation between the two.

Aagaard's response to the new religions was from the beginning programmatically critical. New religions were seen as a threat to individual and societal norms. Aagaard has consistently claimed that politicians and the Church of Denmark are far too reluctant to meet the threat of and challenges from the new religions. He promotes instead Protestant Christian virtues, identifying himself and his organization with the founding fathers of the Christian Church. Apart from the intense use of the media and an extensive lecturing schedule, many books, pamphlets, and other educational materials have been published by the Dialogue Center. These publications have quite often been used as resource materials by the press, schoolteachers, and Christian congregations.

The Dialogue Center has been associated with anticult activities in Russia and other Eastern European countries. Aagaard has personally promoted the prominent Russian anticultist, Alexander L. Dvorkin, who is considered to be one of the Dialogue Center's top associates in Moscow. Dvorkin is also Vice President of the Dialogue Center's international branch (the Dialogue Center International, the other Vice President being another prominent anticultist, German theologian Thomas Gandow).[21] While not wishing to draw guilt-by-association conclusions, it should be noted that Dvorkin and Gandow are currently among the most vigorous anticultists in Europe, and Aagaard's support of them most likely signifies something crucial about the Dialogue Center's ideology, if not its affiliations.

The Dialogue Center has been globalized. It has its own website, produces several magazines in different languages,[22] and has branches in approximately twenty countries throughout the world.[23]

In 1992 and 1993, a group of dissatisfied members of the group broke with Aagaard and formed their own organization, IKON, with the express purpose of engaging in "real dialogue" with other religious groups.[24] The new body has apparently succeeded. They made a breakthrough in 1993 with The Family, and soon other new religions showed a similar willingness to cooperate, including Danish New Age leader Jes Bertelsen, ISKCON, Jehovah's Witnesses, the Mormons, Sai Baba devotees, and various others. This was a new situation not only for the new religions but also for the general public. IKON's style is different than that of the Dialogue Center in that it provides its members with a platform for interreligious dialogue.

Small human rights organizations formed by members of the new religions (primarily Scientologists) in opposition to the Dialogue Center, on the contrary, have had little impact on the Danish scene.[25] On more than one occasion people have tried to establish human rights groups in opposition to the Dialogue Center, but apparently the need for such task forces, when all is said and done, does not exist. The interests of minority groups are generally attended to by the authorities, and thus human rights groups very quickly decline or vanish.

Independent Bodies

In 1992, the Parliamentary Assembly of the Council of Europe adopted "Recommendation 1178 (1992) on sects and new religious movements," which asks the member states to adopt educational, legislative, and other measures "in response to the problems raised by some of the activities of sects or new religious movements" (Article 6) with due consideration to the freedom of conscience and religion guaranteed by Article 9 of the European Convention on Human Rights. It is recommended that the basic educational curriculum should include "objective factual information concerning established religions and their major variants, concerning the principles of comparative religion and concerning the ethics and personal and social rights" (Article 7.i) and similar information on the nature and activities of sects and new religious movements. Furthermore, it is recommended that independent bodies should be established to collect and circulate such information (Article 7.ii). In Denmark, education concerning NRMs has been going on for many years.

With regard to research, mention should be made of the establishment of a research network by the Danish Council for the Humanities called Research Network on New Religions (RENNER). RENNER was established in order to coordinate scholarship on new religions in Denmark, analyze the material already collected (by, for instance, the Center for New Religious Studies), and establish cooperation with colleagues and similar organizations worldwide. Many colleagues have not understood the nature of RENNER because it is not an information center, and it does not have any official position on new religions except that of scholarship as commonly understood in the humanities and social sciences. Perhaps the most difficult thing to understand is that the executive board consists of sociologists, historians of religions, and theologians. Even though individual members of the board may object to one another's private activities, the essential Danish mentality of negotiation and compromise is as true in the politics of research as it is in parliamentary politics. RENNER has hosted a number of conferences, funded various research projects, published a newsletter, established two publication series, and encouraged young scholars to pursue research in new religions.[26]

Concluding Remarks

In education as well as in research, systematic attempts are being made to educate the public on the nature of and issues surrounding new and minority religions. With the establishment of the above mentioned Advisory Committee, the excellent relationship between governmental institutions and university researchers has borne fruit, and thus academic rather than confessional insight has some influence on administrative practice. This does not mean that we do not have problems and conflicts in Denmark. In the first version of this paper, we wrote that on the whole Denmark is more fortunate in its relations with minority and new religions than a number of other European countries. Since then, a new coalition government has come to power on the wave of popular dissatisfaction with immigration and refugee policies. The new, more restrictive, policies have effectively reduced the number of refugees by half. On the other hand, efforts are being made to develop more effective integration policies. Despite this more conservative tendency, the confrontation is not only between religions. Rather, the more restrictive policies can also be understood partly as measures to defend against perceived threats to the mores and ideals of Danish secular society.

Notes

1. This paper is based on two separate papers: Armin W. Geertz, "Religious Minorities in Denmark," paper read at a conference on Ethnic Minority Rights hosted by the North/South Priority Research Area at the University of Copenhagen in May 1999, and Mikael Rothstein, "New Religions, State Policy and Anti-Cult Activities: Aspects of the Danish Discussion," in *Gudars och gudinnors återkomst. Studier i nyreligiositet* (*The Return of Gods and Goddesses: Studies on New Religiosity*), eds. Carl-Gustav Carlsson and Liselotte Frisk (Umeå: Umeå University, 2000), 219–29.

2. No exact figures are available on every group. These findings are based on Mikael Rothstein's fieldwork and personal communication with people in charge of organizational matters in the various groups. According to the Danish Information Office, 84.3 percent of the population are members of the Evangelical Lutheran Church, which is the state's church. See *Statistisk Årbog 2002* (*Statistical Yearbook 2002*) (Copenhagen: Danmarks Statistik, 2002), 98. This means that the church has 4,527,000 members.

3. At least two right-wing political parties, Dansk Folkeparti (Danish Folk Party) and Fremskridtspartiet (Progressive Party), understand Muslim immigrants to be the greatest threat to Danish welfare and national identity, and because of the fairly broad appeal of this populist stance, every political party in Denmark addresses the question of Muslim immigration on a regular basis. As far as we know, no party has NRMs on its agenda. Only two of the Danish parliament's nine political parties explicitly mention Christianity as part of the ideological basis of their party program. The Social Democratic coalition government lost the 2001 elections mainly because of an unclear immigration and refugee policy. This resulted in a coalition government run by the Liberal Party and the Conservative Folk Party with parliamentary support from the Danish Folk Party.

4. The legislative power is held jointly by the hereditary monarch (who is without personal political power) and the unicameral Parliament. Executive power is exercised by the monarch through a cabinet led by the Prime Minister, who is responsible to the Parliament.

5. Frands Ole Overgaard, "New Religious Movements in 20th Century Denmark," in *New Religious Movements and the Law in the European Union: Proceedings of the Meeting* (Lisbon: Giuffrè Editore, 1999), 113–14.

6. In 1849, about 98 percent of the population were members of the Church of Denmark.

7. Ole Espersen, *The Right to Freedom of Religion and Religious Associations: A Survey of Recommendations* (Copenhagen: The Council of the Baltic Sea States, 1999), 19.

8. Hanne Fledelius and Birgitte Juul, *Freedom of Religion in Denmark* (Copenhagen: The Danish Centre for Human Rights, 1992), 31.

9. These were Roman Catholics, Reformed Community in Fredericia, the French Reform in Copenhagen, the German Reform in Copenhagen, the Methodists, Baptists, Orthodox Russians, the Norwegian Community in Copenhagen, the Swedish Gustav Association in Copenhagen, and St. Alban's English Church in Copenhagen.

10. *Folketingstidende* 1968–69, tillæg B, sp. 1927–30.

11. Margit Warburg, "Lige ret for Loke så vel som for Thor? Religionsbegreber og retspraksis i forbindelse med religioner udenfor Folkekirken (Equality for Loki as well as Thor? Con-

cepts of religion and judicial practice in relation to religions outside the Church of Denmark)," *Chaos* (1996): 9–32; and "Restrictions and Privileges: Legal and Administrative Practice and Minority Religions in USA and in Denmark," in *New Religions and New Religiosity* (RENNER Studies on New Religions, vol. 4), eds. Eileen Barker and Margit Warburg (Aarhus, Denmark: Aarhus University Press, 1998), 262–75.

12. Fledelius and Juul, *Freedom of Religion in Denmark*, 104–06.

13. Armin W. Geertz has argued recently that seen in this light, analytical and judicial definitions of religion have little to do with one another. See his "Religion eller trossamfund? Ordforklaring som strategi (Religion or Denomination? Definition as Strategy)," *IKON* 28 (1999): 9–11. The analysis is available on line at www.teo.au.dk/html/geertz/udvalg/vejledningrev02.pdf or at the website of the Ministry of Ecclesiastics at www.km.dk/publikationer/20020912_retningslinier.pdf.

14. Commission's Decisions 12097/86, 12436/86, 12468/86, discussed in Hagel-Sørensen and Holst-Christensen, *Ugeskrift for Retsvæsen* (*Legal Weekly*) (1989): B, 277; and in Peter Garde, "Legal Status of Minority Churches and Religious Communities in the Kingdom of Denmark: Liberty without Equality," in *The Legal Status of Religious Minorities in the Countries of the European Union: Proceedings of the Meeting, Thessaloniki 1993*, European Consortium for Church-State Research (Thessaloniki, Greece: Sakkoulas Publications and Milano: Giuffrè Editore, 1994), 81–114. See especially the discussion on page 91.

15. In 1987, a court ruled that Scientology's auditing records were illegal, and for many years the group had to manage in alternative ways because the PC folders are needed during auditing sessions. Nine years later, in 1996, a judge decided that Scientology could keep "logs" relating to specific individuals at the organization's headquarters during periods when people were actively participating in auditing.

16. See the interesting discussion on this difficult topic in Rex J. Ahdar, "Children's Religious Freedom, Devout Parents and the State," in *Law and Religion in Contemporary Society: Communities, Individualism and the State*, eds. Peter W. Edge and Graham Harvey (Aldershot, U.K.: Ashgate Publishing, 2000), 93–114.

17. The case was primarily debated in the newspaper *Dagbladet Information* during November 1997. The book is entitled *Scientology: En ny religion* (*Scientology: A New Religion*) (Copenhagen: Munksgaard, 1997).

18. This statement was quoted in the press but a more thorough argumentation was given during the Minister's answer to the Parliament's committee of education (Undervisningsministerens talepapir, Ministertale, samråd A, alm.del—bilag 168, 16 December 1997).

19. The Danish educational system is autonomous to a high degree. School books do not need approval by the state, but examination requirements are regularly reviewed through spot tests by the Ministry of Education. The responsibility for educational materials is placed on the schools and the teachers.

20. See their recent publication with English summaries, Lisbet Christoffersen and Jørgen Bæk Simonsen, eds., *Visioner for religionsfrihed, demokrati og etnisk ligestilling* (*Visions of Religious Freedom, Democracy and Ethnic Equality*) (Copenhagen: Nævnet for Etnisk Ligestilling, 1999).

21. Dvorkin occasionally writes for the Dialogue Center's magazine (for instance, *Den Nye Dialog* 5:3 [1993]: 21), and he is associated with the Dialog Center's branch in Moscow. On Alexander L. Dvorkin's status and contributions, see a report by Marat S. Shterin (*New Religions, Cults and Sects in Russia: A Critique and Brief Account of the Problems*) and his writings on the influence of Western anticult movements in Russia (available at CESNUR's website).

22. *Den Nye Dialog* (*The New Dialogue*), *Netop Nu* (*Current Events*), *Kirken Arbejder* (*The Church at Work*), in cooporation with the Danish Missionary Council, *Spirituality in East and West*, *UPDATE* (renamed *Aeropagus*), *Berliner Dialog* (*Berlin Dialogue*) and others. Magazines are in preparation for the Baltic countries, Russia, and several other countries. The Dialogue Center's website is found at http://www.dci.dk.

23. For instance, the Dialogue Center International (DCI) in Bombay, Delhi, and Bangkok. The group has spread into most European countries, including the former Communist countries where missionaries from the Dialogue Center are very active. In Moscow the group is associated with the Paulus Society, and in India another Dialogue Center branch is the Saint Thomas Society. The Dialogue Center has also established a youth branch known

as International Dialogue (ID). Finally ABCD (A Buddhist Christian Dialogue) has been founded. On the globalization of the Dialogue Center compared to developments in other religious groups, see Mikael Rothstein, "Patterns of Diffusion and Religious Globalization: An Empirical Survey of New Religious Movements," *Temenos* 32 (1996): 195–220.

24. The acronym stands for Informations- og Samtaleforum Om Kristendom og Nyreligiøsitet (Forum for Information and Dialogue on Christianity and New Religiosity).

25. An organization imitating the name of the Dialogue Center and the layout of its magazine was established around 1995. It is called Den Ægte Dialog (The Real Dialogue). After a court case, which was settled by compromise, this organization was forced to alter its name, but their target remains Johannes Aagaard and the Dialogue Center.

26. The two series are called *RENNER Studies on New Religions* (Aarhus: Aarhus University Press), and one in Danish, *Gyldendal Nye Religioner* (*Gyldendal New Religions*) (Copenhagen: Gyldendal Publishers).

CHAPTER **3**

France's Obsession
with the "Sectarian Threat"

DANIÈLE HERVIEU-LÉGER

The Sectarian Issue in France:
A Problem of a "Pathology of Belief"

On February 8, 2000, the entire French press commented on the report
submitted to Prime Minister Lionel Jospin the previous day by the *Mission
Interministérielle de Lutte contre les Sectes* (MILS—Interministerial Mission on Combating Sects). On the whole, the commentaries applauded the
idea that was being explored of soon banning two groups considered particularly dangerous (the Church of Scientology and the Order of the Solar
Temple). Whatever their political bent, left or right, the newspapers hailed
the determination of the mission, created in 1998 to help the government
effectively combat threats to individual liberties and public safety posed by
sects in France. In fact, this concern considerably predates the creation of
the mission and has garnered broad public support. Since the early 1980s,
a series of official reports have been published, and a parliamentary commission was created in 1995 to assess the scope of the "sectarian threat." In
1996, a report compiled by this commission defined a set of "danger criteria" that enabled them to identify a number of "groups at risk" displaying
at least one of these criteria. Thus was compiled a list of 173 groups requiring particular watchfulness on behalf of society and the public authorities.
The work of the MILS, charged with the constant surveillance of the

sectarian landscape, continues this previous activity in protecting citizens from the danger of "sect-like groupings."

A few months after the MILS report was published, the National Assembly voted unanimously in favor of a bill aiming to reinforce the legal means to conduct this battle. Socialist deputies introduced the bill on June 22, 2000, but the measure essentially restated a text already presented before the Senate by a senator from the Right that was designed to facilitate the banning of dangerous groups. At the center of the proposed legislation was the notion of "psychological manipulation." This "manipulation" was viewed as a crime that should be incorporated into the Penal Code. While acknowledging the potential value of this notion "so as to allow victims to be heard in court," Justice Minister Elisabeth Guigou immediately emphasized the looming difficulties of legally defining such a crime and the risks that such a notion might jeopardize "basic liberties such as the freedom of association or liberty of conscience." The deputies did not heed this appeal for caution. They sought to outdo each other during the debate by introducing amendments designed to elaborate even more rigorous protective devices. This arsenal of repressive measures has been examined by the Senate, and now has a definitive legislative status.[1]

But beyond the discussion of the text itself and its main lines, we must first point out the remarkable unanimity with which parliament members from the entire political spectrum hastened to establish anti-sect legislation, despite the fact that the MILS itself had discarded the idea, and the government had underscored the extreme difficulty of enforcing such a measure. Every voice was heard when the text was put to vote in the Assembly. The same was true in the Senate during debate on the About amendment, which suggested reactivating a 1936 sedition law in order to apply it to sects. In the context of French political discussion, the "sectarian question" is one of the very rare "social topics" (perhaps the only one!) that enables the various ideological families to set aside their differences. It is hard to tell if this unanimity arises from an exceptional agreement of the people's representatives on the issue or if, more prosaically, it results from identical pressures put on members of parliament by their constituents. But this does not alter the main fact: in France there is a broad consensus (vigorously sustained by the media) that the fight against sects should be a necessary aspect of the protection of individual liberties and that this fight should prevail, in the final analysis, over the defense of the right of each individual to freedom of religion.

Seen from abroad, the concern over sects that unites French public opinion and political authorities seems surprising, all the more so since it occurs in a nation where controversial NRMs have appeared in smaller numbers than in other countries.[2] To explain this particular situation, we must first point out that public opinion's aversion to religious manifestations considered excessive and dangerous to individuals does not apply in the same way to all groups displaying intense spiritual and religious preoccupations and offering their members what Max Weber called a "unitarian sense of life." Groups that are directly and officially affiliated with religious traditions whose long history roots them incontestably in the national cultural soil (the two variants of Christianity, Roman Catholicism and Lutheran-Reformed Protestantism, as well as Judaism) are spared this repugnance. More recently established religious groupings in France, whose qualifications as "major religions" do not appear debatable, receive intermediate treatment. Buddhism, especially the Tibetan version, is looked on favorably as a vehicle of tolerance and open-mindedness that is embodied in the revered figure of the Dalai Lama.[3] Islam—whatever the fears about the barely controllable proliferation of associations and the doubts expressed with regard to its intrinsic capacity to adapt to French institutions, customs, and political culture—now constitutes an incontrovertible reality in the French religious landscape. French society will have to adapt to this reality in one way or another over the long term. What is basically at stake in the collective anxiety manifested toward sects is the emergence and proliferation of poorly identified beliefs that at any time might dictate deviant behavior and engender social formations that threaten public order and conventional social ties. It is as if religious sentiment, when it escapes the major "organized religions," *by its very nature* can only degenerate into a "pathology of belief" that is basically contrary to freedom of thought and individual autonomy. In this perspective, all "sects" (if we apply this term out of convenience to all groups that display this "unframed" religious sentiment) are supposed to have an enormous potential for deviance from which society must protect itself. To combat this pathology—which is termed "sectarism" in the MILS report—the state has assigned itself the mission of placing all sects under strict surveillance, since it is unable to eradicate the untamed—and therefore threatening—religious sentiment that they embody.

Seeing sects in terms of a "pathology of belief" establishes a difference in the way groups considered authentically religious—because they are affiliated with "major organized religions"—and groups that lack such an affiliation and supposedly usurp the "religious" status they claim are treated. A "sect" in the most widely shared French perspective (including from the standpoint of government authorities) is a group that *abusively* asserts its quality as a religious entity. From this perspective, combating the supposedly evil influence of sects does not constitute a problem of religious freedom. The problem is actually one of public hygiene and suppression of fraud. The main question posed by this approach to battling sects is obviously one of definitions and the limits the state and public opinion assign by mutual agreement to the very notion of religious pluralism. Before discussing principles, this fact must be grasped as a historical given, the significance of which becomes clear only when examined in the light of the entire array of relations between the state and religion in the French context.

Managing Religion within the Limits of the Republic: The Confessional Model of Religious Pluralism

The situation is in fact incomprehensible unless it is examined within the context of the ambivalent relationship that French-style secularism *(la laïcité à la française)* has maintained and continues to maintain with religion. Throughout its entire history, the *laïque* perspective seems to have been torn between the democratic objective of guaranteeing religious freedom—as long as worship remains limited to the private sphere—and a desire to "tear minds from the influence of beliefs deemed to be in stark contradiction to reason and autonomy," a desire that harbors an ingrained wariness toward religious belief as such.[4] In establishing the hard-reached compromise that in 1905 led to legally instituting the separation of church and state, the elaboration of the confessional framework to manage "religion within the limits of the Republic" was subordinated to achieving a preliminary aim: to normalize religious belief as private belief, its "normal" collective manifestation being ensured by the worship assembly, placed under the guarantee and protection of the state. Outside this confessional framework confining religious belief to the privacy of the individual conscience and limiting its collective expression to approved forms of worship, religion does not have a socially identifiable place. Even more, when it emerges in a primitive and uncontrolled form, it is still thought to threaten individual consciences with political alienation, psychological dependence, and intellectual obscurantism.

This "presumption of risk" associated with outward manifestations of religions that do not benefit from a denominational *(confessionnelle)* authorization clearly shows that *laïcité* creates an "implicit regime of recognized religions," which can be viewed as a product of the long and indelible history of France's Christian and Roman Catholic past.[5] To base the state on this indifference to religion—which is the foundation of the French rationale of Separation—it had to create a legal and practical apparatus to clearly demarcate the space within which religious freedom—an integral part of civil liberties in any democratic country—can be legitimately exercised. Outside of this framework, however, the question of religion as a social and collective fact cannot be posed calmly. More precisely, it simply cannot be posed. The state, radically separated from accredited confessions in whose activities it does not get involved, absolutely denies itself the right to judge the contents of belief or even to define religion. It takes cognizance of the existence of belief as an irreducibly private reality, but it cannot formally recognize the social existence of these beliefs if they are not integrated into the confessional framework that indicates they accept the rules of the republican game which delimits this space for them.

It is essential here to remember that the confessional system, which has become the framework for the legitimate expression of religious pluralism in France, was set up both to prevent any interference of the Roman Catholic Church in the public sphere and to limit its hold on the public conscience, particularly its influence on young minds. The institutional apparatus set up by the law of Separation, created mainly to contain the Roman Catholic Church within the limits of a specialized religious sphere, at the same time made the organizational model of Roman Catholicism the implicit reference for acceptable forms of religious expression—which the law intends to guarantee while simultaneously controlling possible excesses. The Roman Catholic model—in which the cultural practice of the religion and the gathering of its specialized professionals and its community in buildings devoted to worship have a major importance—irresistibly dominates society's representation and the *laïque* definition of "normal religion." The massive presence of the dominant religion in the national history and culture has strongly reinforced this specifically French equivalence between "religion" and "Roman Catholicism." Third Republic members of parliament debated the role of religion in society, but it was the Roman Catholic Church they had in mind.[6]

In order to be accredited, minority religions—the recognition of which is an integral part of the battle against the symbolic monopoly and the political encroachment of the Roman Catholic Church—had to conform to this model and adjust their organization to the confessional apparatus that legally and administratively demarcates the territory of legitimate religion in France. The major Lutheran and Reformed Protestant churches obviously had no problem fitting into this mold. The Jewish Consistory instituted by Napoleon in 1808 transmuted the "Jewish nation" into an "Israelite confession" that publicly expressed in its places of worship a religious identity supposedly reduced to the private beliefs of its members—members whom the emancipation proclamation of 1791 had made full-fledged citizens. When the Interior ministers of today deploy all their efforts to bring about an organization of Islam ("on the model," suggested Jean-Pierre Chevènement, "of the Protestant Federation of France") and invite Muslims in France to create their own representative bodies, they are pursuing the same aims, all of them adamantly denying that they are "acting like Napoleon"! The issue is still one of stabilizing a French-style Islam that is acculturated to the rules of the republican game, the public expression of which could legitimately (and as much as possible exclusively) develop within the confines of the well-identified space of its places of worship. As for the state, it recommends that townships provide financial support to build mosques so that the Republic can insure the "free exercise of worship" for all in acceptable and dignified conditions.[7]

Thus French recognition of religious pluralism stops exactly at the borders of religions whose confessional organization assures adhesion to the values of the republic. This definition—which may appear surprisingly restrictive—did not pose a problem as long as the Roman Catholic monopoly on the religious sphere was challenged only by "historical" religious minorities (Protestants and Jews). These religious communities, in the eyes of the Republic, were hallowed with a particular "resistance legitimacy" because of the persecutions they had endured at the instigation of the dominant religion under the Ancient Regime. One of the first concerns of the 1789 revolutionaries was, moreover, to grant full citizenship to the faithful of these religious minorities, which was done in 1789 for the Protestants and in 1791 for the Jews. This recognition at the same time required preventing the Roman Catholic Church from being recognized as the official state religion. The political-religious conflict that ignited the nation for over a century and a half was partly rooted in the Constituent Assembly's refusal (three times over) to grant the Roman Catholic Church recognition of privileged status.

But this system topples when the mesh of the confessional net is strained by the multiplication of groups and movements claiming religious status and demanding the benefits of a freedom taken for granted in democratic societies. In reaction to the anarchic proliferation of self-proclaimed and extradenominational religious groups, *laïcité*'s deep-rooted suspicion that religious alienation poses a constant threat to freedom of conscience is tending to resurface. But it should be understood that the problem does not spring from the intensity experienced within little groups of spiritual virtuosos. As proof we have seen that groups with similar features but that are protected by the institutional wing of organized religions (such as charismatic Roman Catholic groups) remain theoretically exempt from state investigations.[8] Beyond the manifest desire to prevent excessive or misdirected religious sentiment, it is mainly the institutional deregulation of the religious sphere inherent in the weakening of the confessional model that is at the heart of the issue of combating sects in France.

To function properly, this model presumes that religious institutions themselves will indeed handle regulation of the religious sphere. For the state to maintain both the absolute neutrality it claims and its punctilious refusal to interfere in the religious sphere, religious institutions have to do their own policing. *Laïcité* precludes any encroachment outside of the specialized sphere in which the state is entitled to intervene. But it also requires that religious institutions be capable of organizing and controlling their own sphere of intervention. According to the French Separation law, in order for state regulation of the religious sphere to be exercised exclusively *ad extra*, the *ad intra* religious regulation must be clearly entrusted to uncontested institutional authorities. It is precisely this regulatory capacity of religious institutions that is currently in difficulty. In a society of individuals who have won their autonomy in all areas, religious devotees themselves tend more and more to think of themselves as autonomous "believing subjects," personally in charge of identifying the truths in which they believe and determining the obligations that they will associate with these beliefs. This movement of believers' individual emancipation destabilizes the means of validating and harmonizing the collective belief sustained by institutions. It frees floating believers to cobble together their own systems of meaning and to create new forms of association for spiritual purposes. These new forms almost completely elude the legal status of "worship association" *(association cultuelle)* that provides public accreditation for legitimate religions.

The Crisis of Secularism and the Collapse of Roman Catholic Culture: Two Inseparable Phenomena

The current proliferation of self-regulated spiritual associations is directly related to the increasing powerlessness of France's major religious institutions to steer religious belief as they had in the past. But the question of religious regulation arises not only because fewer and fewer members of major churches make up the bulk of those who declare themselves "believers." In a country like France, which for a long time was, to use J. P. Willaime's excellent phrase, "a secular country with a Catholic culture,"[9] the regulatory structure of Roman Catholicism functioned well beyond the restricted group of regular or periodic church-goers. Many French who never set foot in church have long kept the references, beliefs, and memories, that (often remotely) structure the elaboration of significations by which they give meaning to their lives (and especially their deaths). Those who rejected this Roman Catholic religious environment did so deliberately, referring to values, moral precepts, and beliefs (in science, progress, and so forth) that conflicted directly with the metaphysical and ethical conceptions of Roman Catholicism.

This implicit dual "secular-Catholic" regulation of belief long hindered the dissemination of religious beliefs. According to the amusing expression coined by British sociologist David Martin, the republican model in fact contributed to the spread in France of a sort of "Catholicism without Christianity." Today the dike built from this Christian and Roman Catholic cultural stock against limitless dimensions of belief has probably given way. In any case it no longer constitutes an obstacle to the flow of individual beliefs, which is accelerated by the collapse of ascribed religious and ideological traditions. The challenge of secularism is no longer to contain the influence of Roman Catholicism on the public conscience to ensure citizens their liberty of conscience. It is to manage the proliferation of voluntary groupings of believers that this individualistic turn in religious striving has fostered. The legal and administrative tools for managing denominational religions seem decidedly inadequate to deal with this uncontrolled dynamics of association.

One might wonder in the end if the specific anxiety of French public opinion with regard to sects is not, at least to a certain extent, a reaction to the cultural marginalization that the country's main religious institution is subjected to—a marginalization that opens (well beyond the problem of sects) an era of increased competition in the now deregulated market of symbolic goods. The dividing line drawn for two centuries between those who "had religion" (Roman Catholics for a large majority) and those who decided not to have any is now blurred. Believers are found in multiple, shifting, and often unstable forms of affiliation, borrowing their spiritual references from a broad cultural toolkit that includes Christian and Roman Catholic traditions among many others. This alarms the Roman Catholic Church and deprives the Republic of a simple regulatory device that, after much bitter conflict, has recently entered into a more serene *modus operandi*.[10] Public opinion senses that the erosion of devices for ideological identification—be they religious, political, or philosophical— which have so durably organized individual classifications and self-classifications in this country, may well leave them highly vulnerable to the multiplication of symbolic service enterprises now encouraged by the deregulation of the market. The "fight against sects" undertaken by government authorities can, from this standpoint, be perceived as revealing the end of an inseparably cultural, religious, and political singularity specific to France.

Epilogue: The Law of May 2001

In May 2001 the parliamentary discussion on the bill sponsored by the right-wing Senator Nicolas About—which concerned the provision of legal tools to stem "the criminal activities of sectarian groups that seriously threaten the integrity of the State and citizens"—came to an end. In its original 1998 version, the law aimed to treat sects as "militias," thereby placing them within the jurisdiction of a 1936 law giving the President the power to disband movements that seriously jeopardized state security. This measure was rapidly abandoned, but a revised version authored by socialist deputy Catherine Picard tried to target more precisely the "sectarian danger" by introducing the notion of "mind manipulation" as a new count of criminal indictment. This proposal, overwhelmingly accepted by the National Assembly in March 1999, has sparked a very intense public debate. First, the Minister of Justice warned the Assembly about the difficulty of defining objective criteria for "mind manipulation." Following this train of thought, the representatives of the churches (Roman Catholic and Protestant) expressed severe reservations concerning the notion. "Could you show me the distinction," asked Jean-Arnold de Clermont, President of the French Protestant Federation, "between 'mental manipulation' and an impassioned sermon?" Various associations of lawyers, the powerful League for the Defense of Human Rights, and the National Consultative Committee for Human Rights (whose advice was officially solicited by the Minister of Justice) were highly critical of the recommendation, stressing the risk of an excessive use of the new legal device. In the end, a parliamentary conference concluded that the introduction of a notion of "mind manipulation" into the criminal law was inappropriate. Following these discussions, a new version of the bill was tabled, including the rewriting of an existing article (313–4) of the criminal law concerning "the abuses of ignorance and weakness." This article does not attack sectarian practices as such, but rather attacks all attempts to take advantage of persons and their property by exploiting situations of personal frailty. Approved unanimously by the deputies (with one exception) in May 2001, the law prohibits the location of sects near "sensitive places" (such as schools, hospitals, and houses for the elderly) and makes provision for disbanding groups whose leaders have been convicted of illegal conduct in the courts. The very important difference between the first version and the final law is of course the change of direction in defining the possible illegality of "sectarian practices": in the first version, the notion of "mind manipulation" would have incriminated the practices as such; the law of May 2001 makes it necessary to document the "situation of weakness" that makes these practices dangerous and illegal. But a major problem remains: the law has abandoned the idea of defining a *secte*, except by identifying illegal practices that are covered by existing civil and penal laws.

In the end, it appears more and more clear that the law of May 2001, because it fails to define what a sect is from a legal point of view, has little chance of being an effective legal tool. To date the law has yet to be used to take a group to court. Does this mean that it is, in fact, a "law for nothing"?

The issue is more nuanced than this. A provisional analysis of the parliamentary process is that the law has primarily an emblematic function, attesting, before a very worried public, to the determination of the state to protect its citizens from dangerous *sectes*. But the measure is actually a compromise agreement, aiming to address the recurrent anxiety in France concerning the possible contradiction between freedom of thought and freedom of religion in the contemporary context of a massive deregulation of the "confessional system" regulating religious pluralism.

In May 2002, the right-wing parties won the general elections and formed a new government. This change does not mean any reorientation of public policy towards sects: on the contrary, one is struck by the remarkable *continuity* of discourse concerning this question. This continuity seems to confirm a policy of appeasement that commenced, paradoxically, with the vote on the law. Significantly, the Mission Interministérielle de Lutte contre les Sectes (Interministerial Mission on Combating Sects) has changed its name to Mission Interministérielle de Vigilance et de Lutte contre les Dérives Sectaires (Interministerial Mission on Watching and Combating Sectarian Disorders). The insistence placed on the fight against burgeoning sects and the responsibility for keeping a close eye on the "pathology of belief" is also a way to euphemize—to a certain extent at least— the missionary vocation of the committee to eradicate "false religions." The general orientation remains the same, but the less strident tone of public discourse reflects the growing indifference of public opinion with regard to groups that are seen, after September 11, as a very marginal threat in an ocean of perils.

Notes

1. In a memo to the Prime Minister in September 2000, the MILS suggested that the proposal to include the crime of "psychological manipulation" in the Civil Code was untimely and should probably be removed from the text that would be submitted to the deputies for a final vote. As a result of this and other criticisms of the original language in the legislation, certain changes were made in the bill's final draft. See the Epilogue of this article.
2. Alain Vivien, president of the MILS, estimates the number of people linked to groups considered sects at 500,000. Other reliable sources set this figure at 250,000. The truth probably lies somewhere in between.
3. The number of people having a fairly regular tie with Buddhist groups is estimated at 600,000. On the phenomenal expansion of Buddhism in France, see F. Lenoir, *Le bouddhisme en France* (Paris: Fayard, 1999).
4. On this issue, see P. Bouretz, "La democratie française eu risque du monde," in *La démocratie en France*, ed. M. Sadoun (Paris: Gallimard, 2000), 27–137.
5. Article 1 of the law of 1905 specifies that "the Republic does not acknowledge or subsidize any form of religion."
6. Today they debate the place of sects in society, but it is Scientology that they have in mind.
7. Interview given by Interior Minister J. P. Chevènement to *Le Monde* on February 19, 2000, on the shape of French-style Islam.
8. Independent Protestant churches at risk of appearing towards the top of the list of groups placed under high surveillance have well grasped the meaning of this differential treatment

and perceived that the only way to escape stigmatization is to join the ranks of "official" Protestantism as quickly as possible. In the eyes of the public authorities this official Protestantism is embodied in the Fédération Protestante de France. As soon as the first report of the parliamentary commission was published in 1996, Pentecostal and Adventist churches entered into negotiations to obtain "institutional protection." Neither Pastor J. Tartier nor Pastor J. A. de Clermont, successive presidents of the Federation, denied them this protection, out of a concern widely shared in the Protestant church for preserving minority rights.

9. J. P. Willaime, "Laïcité et religion en France," in *Identités religieuses en Europe*, eds. G. Davie and D. Hervieu-Léger (Paris: La Découverte, 1996), 153–71.

10. D. Hervieu-Léger, "The Past in the Present: Redefining *Laïcité* in a Multicultural France," in *The Limits of Social Cohesion: Conflict and Mediation in Pluralist Societies*, ed. Peter Berger (Boulder, CO: Westview Press, 1998), 38–83.

CHAPTER 4

The *Secte* Response to Religious Discrimination

Subversives, Martyrs, or Freedom Fighters in the French Sect Wars?

SUSAN J. PALMER

In 2001, France ranked sixth among countries that limited religious freedom through legal and social measures, according to *Le Monde.*[1] As a direct consequence of the Guyard Report and the Picard/About law, France joined a rogue's gallery that included countries such as China, Indonesia, Sudan, Nigeria, and Turkmenistan. The fierce intolerance of the government-sponsored watchdog bureaucracy—MILS (Interministry Mission for the Fight Against Sects)—was reflected in a statement made at the National Assembly debate over the About/Picard law, which was adopted on May 30, 2001: "It is unfortunate that we cannot have a *grand soir* of sects which would allow us to regulate everything all at once."[2] In France the term *grand soir* refers to terrible moments in history: the St Bartholomew's Day Massacre, or the mass immolations of the French Revolution.

In a previous study,[3] I outlined the six methods of social control adopted by French authorities in their effort to eradicate *les sectes* from their social midst. The purpose of this paper is to examine the effects of France's anticult policies on NRMs in general, to document the responses of these quite disparate spiritual/therapeutic groups to these policies of social control, and to focus specifically on two groups listed in the 1996 Guyard Report as *sectes*, Aumism (better known as Mandarom), and the

French Raelian Movement. I conclude with some general statements about France's "cult wars."

My findings are based on field research conducted during three trips to France in 2000–2001, when I interviewed leaders and members of 14 groups labelled as *sectes* and distributed a questionnaire. I have also written legal letters as a scholar for the Canadian Raelian Movement, a group that I have studied in some depth. As for Aumism, I visited their (now defunct) Quebec ashram, stayed at the Holy City of Mandarom, attended their court hearing in Digne as an observer, and participated in the Aumists' Evolution of Consciousness conference in Paris on March 9–10, 2002.

There were moments in the course of my research when I felt I had walked into a veritable war zone. France's persecution of religious dissidents is not nearly as ferocious as the Chinese government's draconian treatment of Falun Gong. The anticult war in France is mainly a war of words, but there have been some disturbing attacks against individuals and property that have not been reported in the media. The Unification Church in Paris no longer exists; it was bombed in 1974 and again in 1995. The New Acropolis in Paris, the Church of Scientology in Angers, and the Pélerins d'Arès have been recent targets of bombs or bomb threats. Horus, a New Age farming commune, became a target for vandals and arsonists after a negative TV documentary was aired on Envoyé Spécial. A car's gas tank blew up, a garage was torched, animals were stolen, sheep were strangled, and gunshots were fired into the farm at night. While only a few deaths can be considered a direct result of France's anti-sect campaign, many religious leaders have weathered death threats and assassination attempts. A "guru" means a spiritual master or teacher of truth in India, but *gourou* is a stigmatizing term of abuse in the French media. Hundreds of "acting leaders" (*responsables* in France, meaning administrators) of new religions and in many cases the computer-literate members who worked in their commune's office have been arrested for questioning, held without charges, and forced to spend several nights or weeks in prison.

The Word *Secte* in France

The conflicts of many NRMs with society began when they found their organization on the Guyard Commission's list of 172 *sectes* (published in 1996 as the Guyard Report). The word *secte* cannot be precisely translated as "cult." In fact, a *culte* is a respectable religion that offers a public forum for worship and is eligible for legal status as a voluntary association. Indeed, several *sectes* (notably Aumism) aspire for recognition as a *culte*. The stereotypical portrait of a *secte* found in government reports and in media stories has a Gallic flavor of its own, making it quite different from the North American "cult" stereotype.

In France, *secte* denotes a secretive group, usually apocalyptic in orientation. In North America we are accustomed to Bible prophecy and millennial currents in mainstream Protestant churches; the French are not so accustomed, and apocalyptic means potentially violent. The *gourou* of a *secte* is seen as a con artist and closet pedophile; members are seen as subversives, deceptively normal middle-class professionals who are victims of "mental manipulation"—hence incapable of rational thought.

An extraordinary situation exists in France: hundreds of successful professionals and responsible parents have been fired or denied promotion in their place of work, or have lost custody of or access to their children, simply because of sect affiliation.[4] NRMs are denied access to public space for their conferences and become the target of financial probes and stigmatizing media reports.

According to my informants, many members were aghast to find the name of their spiritual/therapeutic community on the infamous *liste*, alongside "Moonisme," the Hare Krishnas, the Children of God, and Scientology, and they tried to both correct and challenge this categorization. Many contacted the government-sponsored anticult agencies and asked for a definition or set of characteristics of a *secte* so that they could demonstrate the ways in which their group did not conform. They found that there was no definition and that France's leading anticultists actually make a point of evading a clear definition and keeping the term deliberately nebulous.

French anti-sect literature is careful to avoid a precise definition of *secte*, which makes it all the more stigmatizing. Fournier and Monroy write, "the word '*secte*' is ambiguous, because it described at times in history the minority religious groups."[5] These psychologists choose an even vaguer term, *sectarisme*, and argue that such groups in history were "religious," but that today's *sectarisme* is characterized by "the quest for power, through methods of manipulation of adepts, and not by their spiritual character."[6]

But while French bureaucrats involved in the *lutte* (battle) against sects won't define exactly what a *secte* is, they all agree they are bad news. Janine Tavernier of UNADFI (Union Nationale de l'Association pour la Défense des Familles et des Individus) notes, "the existence of these cults is an absolute menace to our society."[7] Jean-Marie Abgrall (France's leading "mental manipulation" theorist) said on television that "notwithstanding what they claim, sects are not religious movements but rather criminal movements organized by gurus who use brainwashing to manipulate their victims."[8]

It is illegal in France to query the government's criteria of a *secte* and its sources of information. This information is gathered by the Renseignement Générale (RG), an agency that, like the CIA, operates in secret, so there is no legal or practical way of verifying sources of information on *sectes* in government documents. The parliamentary committee of the Guyard Commission adopted the RG's list of 172 sects, so it became impossible to access the criteria used by RG, because of secrecy laws. Moreover, it is forbidden to query the parliamentary commission's sources of information because of immunity laws. Hence, NRMs are plunged into a nightmarish labyrinth of dead ends and harassment at the hands of *le fisc* (fiscal control office), the media, the mayor's office, and the *gendarmie*.

The chief battleground for the "war of words" is located in the media. The French media has thus far enjoyed open season on *sectes*, particularly since the Solar Temple events of 1994–97. Stories on *sectes* appear frequently in national daily newspapers such as *Le Figaro, Le Quotidien de Paris, L'Humanité*, and in popular magazines such as *VSD, L'Express, Lyon Mag, Marianne*, and *Echo Savanne. Sectes* are a hot topic for TV talk shows such as *Ciel Mon Mardi, Des Racines et des Ailes, Zone Interdite*, and *Sans Aucune Doute.*

French news reports on new religions are particularly badly researched and cliché-ridden, even more so than the breezy, tongue-in-cheek articles on "cults" that appear in North America. France's "cult" reportage tends to exhibit a hostile, even hysterical tone, and a disregard for factual accuracy (including spelling and dates). French journalists play an important role in fostering public intolerance towards obscure spiritual or philosophical movements. They debase intellectual standards of journalism such as objectivity, values-free research, and the fair presentation of dissenting opinions. In this regard, French news reports of *sectes* can be fairly described as propaganda or hate literature.

Journalists rely heavily on the anticult organization, ADFI, and on the reports of the Renseignement Générale. Anticult propaganda is issued by state-sponsored watchdog groups such as MILS (La Mission Interministrielle de lutte contre les sects) and CCMM (Le Centre contre manipulation mentale) and distributed in French schools.

Since the bureaucrats receiving government salaries for gathering information and writing about religious minorities actually pride themselves on boycotting first-hand research, on "having nothing to do with the groups we are fighting against," it is not surprising that their information is biased, selective, and out of date.[9]

An example of this methodology is found in Janine Tavernier's (the former president of UNADFI) statement in the magazine *Don Bosco Aujourd'hui* claiming, "We don't approach/go towards the groups, we do not have the time."[10] On another occasion, Tavernier was interviewed on a national television show, where a fellow guest was the widow of a Dr. Julien, who had just committed suicide after his professional reputation had been assaulted by media reports quoting UNADFI officials who claimed he was a *gourou* of a *secte*. The talk show hostess asked Tavernier if she herself, as president of UNADFI, had done a proper investigation of Dr. Julien's activities, and Tavernier responded (translation): "We do not do the investigation. Precisely, our role is extremely difficult, extremely perilous because our association is there to denounce the acts of cults, of the persons who trap the future victims, but our role is also to welcome the victims of cults."[11]

On the basis of my perusal of French magazine stories on *les sectes* since the Solar Temple events of 1994, I have noted a strong media consensus in fabricating an unrealistic, stereotypical portrait of a *secte*. In France a "typical" *secte* has a charismatic leader who became wealthy through fraudulent means and whose sexual tastes run unfailingly towards pedophilia. The members appear on the surface to be respectable pillars of society—successful professionals and responsible family members—but are "secret" adepts of *les sectes*. "Secret" means they are probably planning a mass suicide that will include their children. If the members are not secretive, but talk openly and casually about their spiritual affiliation in the workplace, they are then seen as a threat to any vulnerable, easily influenced person and therefore guilty of attempting *manipulation mentale* (a theoretically more vague version of brainwashing).

Another important difference is that there are very few scholars or academics foolhardy enough to study *les sectes* in France. Reputable scholars in the fields of sociology, history of religions, or theology are not invited to participate in government investigations or reports on *sectes*. It appears that no dissenting opinions are permitted, and those that are quoted for the obligatory "different view" in journalism are framed in such a way as to discredit the speaker. The public is cued that the protesting cultist is stupid, lying, or brainwashed, and the sociologist is a "cult apologist," a "so-called expert," or a "revisionist for the cults," paid to cover up the atrocities perpetrated in the cults' concentration camps. If this seems exaggerated, a study of French media will show that the ashrams or summer camps of religious minorities are routinely compared to concentration camps.

NRM Responses to "Mediabolization"

Under French law, the media are obliged to honor the *droit de reponse*—the legal right of parties receiving media coverage to respond to what they feel is inaccurate or unfair treatment, and to have their correctional letter published in the same newspaper or magazine. All NRMs I contacted in France complained of the devastating effects of demonization in the media. Some groups spend considerable energy correcting or suing the newspapers. Others, such as Mahikari, Mankind Enlightenment Love, and the Sri Chinmoy Association, ignore the media and do not even keep news reports in their files. Although the Pélerins d'Arès have sent out many *droit de reponse* letters to the media, none have been published.

The responses of the groups I visited can be placed within a continuum from active protest to head in the sand to outright flight. Several fleeing groups established new centers in Quebec, so as to make a gradual move, or have relocated their headquarters. The Raelians, for example, moved their headquarters to Quebec. MAEV (a New Age publishing company) moved to Quebec after finding themselves among the 172 *sectes*. The Aumists established an ashram in Quebec and a (now schismatic) ashram in Vancouver. At least twenty French Raelians have moved to Quebec to escape persecution and be near their prophet. One French Raelian has moved to Canada and is seeking refugee status, claiming that as a member of a minority religion he is persecuted in France. Many parents from groups whose home schooling, spiritual healing, or herbal medicine has led to social workers' investigations or custody battles, have fled France with their children to other countries of Europe.

The Dilemma of Solidarity

A network of groups protesting the discrimination against France's spiritual and therapeutic minorities has been forming since the 1990s. The first example was FIREPHIM (Fédération internationale des religions et philosophies minoritaires), founded by Rael in 1992 in response to the murder of a French ufologist. FIREPHIM soon had the support of other NRMs, including Scientology and the Unification Church.

Jean Migueres was a famous contactee, author, and founder of CEIRUS, a center for the scientific study of UFOs. While working as a paramedic, he had a near-death experience in which he claimed aliens had appeared and saved his life. His father-in-law, Roger Dorysse, became aware of Miguere's "suspect activities" (giving speeches and writing books on UFOs) through his contacts with ADFI and applied for custody of his granddaughter. Upon losing the legal battle and hearing that her parents were considering moving to Canada, Dorysse murdered Migueres on a crowded street, chasing him and shooting him repeatedly with a rifle. Several newspapers mention that Dorysse had a relationship with, or was a member of, ADFI. Yvette Genosy, a president of ADFI, was quoted making sense of the murder by stressing the victim's bizarre ideas.[12]

Whether ADFI was responsible for stirring up Dorysse's anticult phobia is not clear. However, it is clear on whose side the media stands. The murderer received sympathetic treatment in several stories, where he was portrayed as a devoted grandparent, driven mad with longing to see his granddaughter. The victim is consistently portrayed as a dangerous *secte* leader who deserved his fate.

After the Guyard Commission released its list of 172 *sectes*, additional efforts were made to unite stigmatized minority groups in a resistance movement. In 1996, Joël Labruyère, a journalist, artist, and former Rosicrucian, began visiting groups on the "list" to ask them to sign a petition protesting discrimination. He founded L'Omnium des Libertés, a religious freedom organization that currently numbers 1,000 members, and has organized fifteen press conferences (to date) where victims of religious persecution offer their testimonies and lawyers speak on civil rights. In 2000, a coalition of Scientologists and individuals (members who indirectly represent 40 different NRMs) formed CAP (Coordination des associations et particuliers pour la liberté de conscience). CAP has gathered 9,000 signatures for their petition defending freedom of conscience and are trying to register as an association. CAP also set up a network of lawyers who specialize in the defence of religious minorities and offer a referral service for people suffering from discrimination in the workplace or in custody disputes.

Many of the groups, appalled to find themselves on the *liste*, were invited to join these resistance groups but confronted a new dilemma. Many leaders I interviewed expressed their resentment at being lumped together with other groups whose views on the nature of God and on sexual and family mores conflict with their own. Some of my informants had uncritically imbibed media stereotypes concerning other *sectes*. There was the danger that any perceived solidarity between NRMs protesting religious discrimination would render one vulnerable to the media rumor that La Republique was threatened by a cartel of *sectes*. Thus, to participate in L'Omnium des Libertés or CAP would reinforce anticult stereotypes and invite the wrath that was already visited upon Scientology and Mandarom. Among the least activist associations were the Rudolph Steiner Schools (Anthroposophy), Soka Gakkai, and the Sri Chinmoy Association. CAP and L'Omnium sought to sidestep this dilemma by placing the emphasis on individuals whose rights as French citizens were threatened while underplaying their organizational affiliations.

Some groups have gained strength through solidarity. A well-organized battle for religious freedom spearheaded by the Church of Scientology filed a Human Rights Application against the French government before the European Court of Human Rights in August 2001 and gathered over 1,000 signatures protesting the May 2001 Picard/About law. Among the most active protesters were the Church of Scientology and the French Raelian Movement. Other groups, such as the Twelve Tribes and Aumism, chose to pursue independent courses of legal self-defense while continuing to struggle for social legitimacy. The Jehovah's Witnesses had a team of lawyers contesting their disestablishment and subsequent tax claims while their members handed out tracts.[13]

Most of the groups responded to discrimination in ways that were culturally bilingual. That is, they forged apocalyptic scenarios and theodicies to account for their suffering for the benefit of members inside the group, but they used secular language and arguments when they dealt with lawyers, mayors, and journalists in the larger society. Several groups interpreted their collective experience of persecution exclusively within the framework of their apocalyptic theory. The Apostles of Infinite Love were a striking example of this. When I asked permission from Quebec's mystical pope, Gregory XVII, to stay at their mother house in Clémery, France, his deputy replied, "We have reason to believe that France will no longer exist by next summer." The leaders in Scientology, Lectorium Rosicrucianum, and the Raelian Movement, in contrast, shared their secular, historically-based interpretations of France's sect wars with me. Their responses to discrimination were pragmatic. The Aumists' response was more complex; they were fervently apocalyptic, but they were also litigious, defending their rights in court and holding press conferences to ameliorate the relentlessly negative or satirical news coverage they had received since 1990.[14]

What follows are two case histories illustrating various responses of NRMs to France's strategies for eradicating *sectes* from its religious landscape. These two cases are Aumism and the Raelian Movement.

The Case of Aumism

The ashram of Mandarom was founded in the French Alps in the 1980s by Gilbert Bourdin (Hamsah Manarah), a yoga teacher and swami initiated by Swami Sivananda of the well-known Sivananda Yoga Society. In 1990 Bourdin performed the coronation of the "Cosmoplanetary Messiah," to which the press were invited. According to Aumists who were present, Janine Tavernier of ADFI attended the occasion, pretending to be a journalist. Since then, Mandarom has been the target of media harassment. Initially, *le fisc* demanded commercial taxes from Mandarom, a monastery. Next, the Aumists' right to build statues and temples was challenged. The permit for the eighth Pyramid Temple, which was a key element in Hamsah Manarah's millenarian prophecy, was denied. The 33-meter statue of the Cosmoplanetary Messiah, whose face bears a striking resemblance to the late Hamsah Manarah, was constructed with a legal permit that was later revoked. The order to destroy the statue was invalid because of another technicality (the organization had changed its name since) but the structure was nevertheless destroyed on September 6, 2001. Finally, Mandarom's resident spiritual master was prosecuted for alleged criminal behavior and spent weeks in prison.

The response of the Aumists has always been to pursue an independent, self-reliant course of legal self-defense and damage control through holding press conferences. While the Aumists do cooperate with Scientology and the other religious freedom networks on occasion, they tend to work alone and hold ecumenical conferences that emphasize the universality and global relevance of Hamsah Manarah's vision for the world's religions. The head administrator of the Vajra Triumphant Association, Christine Amory, expressed these differences as follows: "I am a Frenchwoman. We Aumists wish to educate the French government gently. We are optimistic that France will find a way to accommodate us. So we do not wish to ally with American groups that judge France by their own standards of religious liberty, and want to humiliate and destroy the French government!"[15]

In 1996, the Vajra Triumphant Association was preoccupied with hundreds of defamation cases. Amory showed me graphs she had drawn over a six-year period recording the number of *droit de reponse* letters published and the results of court actions. In a separate column she listed the number of negative news reports the following year. As a scientist, she was interested in testing the efficacy and longterm effects of her organization's self-defense strategies. Her graphs made it clear that the media was more cautious in their statements after being repeatedly sued.

The Aumists seek social legitimacy by organizing ecumenical conferences on universal spiritual themes and inviting academics and officials from orthodox religions. They are applying for recognition as an *Association Cultuelle*, or *culte*. In France this means recognition as a tax-exempt organization for "worship" or "culture." In order to prove they are an authentic *culte*, however, they must offer proof of their symbols, rituals, priests, and provide a public worship ceremony. To this end, the Aumists started holding a public *culte* in Paris, to which the public was invited.[16] Since wearing liturgical robes was necessary for their *culte* status, the Aumists went to Chirac's office to press their suit, wearing their colorful red and yellow cloaks and mirrored headdresses. They were stopped by the police and warned that if they continued to walk the streets of Paris in their sacred garb, they would be arrested for posing a threat to public order.

The French Raelian Movement

The Raelians were the first NRM in France to found a religious freedom organization as a means of protesting discrimination. In 1992, Rael founded FIREPHIM, an organization dedicated to protecting the rights of religious, racial, and sexual minorities. Rael was galvanized into action by the assassination of his friend and fellow contactee/ufologist, Jean Migueres.

The first controversy sparked by the Raelians was over their effort to found a political party, the "*géniocratie*," whose goal was to create a one-world government elected by citizens with high IQs and ruled by genuises. This model was based on the extraterrestrial system of government that

Rael observed during his journey to their planet in the 1970s. The Raelians succeeded in electing one of their members as mayor of a small town, but this unleashed a series of arrests, searches, and seizures of documents at the homes of Rael and his followers. The newspapers labeled the Raelians a dangerous "fascist" organization, referring to their swastika medallion. Rael prudently disbanded the geniocracy and defused the conflict.

Rael was invited to appear on a popular live talk show, *Ciel Mon Mardi*, in 1992. When he arrived, Rael found that the host, Christophe Dechavannes, had arranged for an ex-Raelian, Jean Parraga, to confront him. Parraga launched into a tirade, accusing Rael of breaking up his family, stealing his two daughters, brainwashing his wife, and presiding over negligent homicides of children at a summer camp. Elegantly dressed, Jean Parraga came across as a concerned father defending the sanctity of the family against the depraved cult leader. What was not mentioned was his criminal career and recent conviction for attempting to smuggle hashish across international borders. As a result of this defamatory broadcast, Rael received death threats, was forced to leave France, and applied (successfully) for Canadian citizenship. Incensed by Dechavannes' ambush journalism, Raelians flooded the TV station with letters demanding an apology and the right to be heard. Dechavannes countered by charging Rael with incitement to violence.

Besides resorting to legal suits and *droits de reponse* letters, the Raelians have responded to discrimination through public demonstrations and street theater. At a festival commemorating the fiftieth anniversary of the Universal Declaration of Human Rights, eighty Raelians met at the Place du Trocadero in Paris wearing large yellow star stickers on their clothes inscribed "member of a *secte*." They carried banners with slogans demanding respect for religious minorities, but were herded into a tiny parking space and circled by the Paris police. Raelian "Guides" who sat in cafes were refused service.[17]

The Raelians adopted the same strategy to protest their ostracization from public space. Guides I interviewed in Paris estimated that, over the past three years, 70 percent of their contracts for rented spaces had been annulled at the last minute. In 2000, they were turned away at the last minute by order of the Mayor of Castre, who feared "a risk of threats to public order due to potential violent confrontations with people opposing the conference." When Raelians showed up for their monthly meeting, a police barrier barred them from entering the rented premises. A TV crew was waiting, hoping to film the "violence," with a representative from ADFI. The Raelian Bishop in charge, Marcel Terrusse, pulled out a yellow star and pinned it to his chest for the benefit of the TV crew.[18]

Unlike the Church of Scientology and the Aumists, who seek legitimate religious status and cultivate cordial relations with the Fedérations of Muslims and Protestant churches in Paris, the Raelians have chosen to express their rage at their marginal social status by attacking the Catholic Church. The Raelians have a long history of anti-papal, anti-Catholic demonstrations. Angered at what they perceived as a double standard, they founded NOPEDO.

It is customary for the French media to refer to NRM leaders as pedophiles. The Raelians have been consistently characterized in this way in spite of a lack of evidence and several successful lawsuits. Rael is often said to preach pedophilia, although his advice on parents' sex education for their children is consistent with Dr. Spock's. Among the 55,000 baptized Raelians worldwide, ADFI discovered one member with a troubled history of pedophilia and relayed the information to the media, which in turn released a new flood of Raelians-as-pedophiles stories. "We're sick of being called pedophiles," said Raelian Guide Benoit Aymonier. "We're not pedophiles. Every time a newspaper calls us that, we send a *droit de reponse*, but they never print it. We could sue, but it's not worth it. So, we created NOPEDO, our organization to educate the public on the dangers of pedophilia."[19]

Following the passage of the About/Picard Law in May 2001 (which stipulated, among other things, that if a sect leader was found guilty of a felony, the whole association could be dissolved), NOPEDO adopted a pro-active stance towards the media stigmatization of their religion. They did this by pointing out the double standard that applies to new and old religions. In July 2001, Raelians distributed flyers on the streets of Italy and Switzerland warning parents not to send their children to Catholic confession, since 100 priests had been convicted of child molestation in France alone. They were subsequently sued for libel by the Diocese of Geneva.

Voluntary organizations are still free to distribute their literature on the streets in France, and the Raelians continue to do so in spite of the public's negative reactions (spitting, verbal abuse, beatings, and even death threats). It is interesting to note that the Raelians are the only NRM in my study whose French membership has increased (from 4,000 in 1990 to 5,000 in 2002) in spite of intense persecution and mediabolization in the wake of the 1996 Guyard Report.

General Observations

France is a country where conspiracy theories abound. The anticult campaign is fueled by a counter-subversion ideology reminiscent of the American Anti-Satanism movement. The public fears the contaminating influence of the seemingly respectable Frenchman/woman who is a secret member of a *secte*. The fear is that these infiltrators will mutate French culture from within, pervert or exploit France's future citizens, its children, and undermine (through their fanaticism and superstition) the hard-won "reason" of secular humanism.

For this reason, it is the middle-aged professional and parent (who belongs to a *secte*) who is perceived as a threat. They are the target of scapegoating processes in France's anticult campaign. Once their unconventional religious affiliation is rooted out by ADFI, these people often lose their livelihoods and the custody of their children.

The best documented examples of these discrimination cases is in a booklet compiled by CAP (Coordination des associations et particuliers pour la liberté de conscience) of 50 testimonials given at the press conferences organized by Joël Labruyère.[20] Martin Weightman of the Church of Scientology, who assisted in preparing the 2001 suit against the French government before the European Court of Human Rights, claimed he personally knew of around one thousand undocumented cases. In the course of my research, I spoke to many members who experienced setbacks in their careers as the result of discrimination in the workplace, and who knew of similar cases.

The American anticult movement has, since the 1970s, tended to focus on "world rejecting" NRMs that are "totalistic," communal, millenarian, and high demand—often requiring their middle-class youthful converts to drop out of college and the career market. The French anticult movement, on the other hand, worries about the type of groups that we, in North America, would consider "low key" and non-threatening. Oriental meditation groups, "third force" human potential therapies, or faith-healing circles demand little in terms of time, money, or loyalty from their members. When mature artists and wealthy professionals like Tina Turner, Tom Cruise, or Jerry Rubin turn to chanting, auditing, or meditating to enhance their spirituality, creativity, and careers, the general assumption of the American public is they are grownups and can handle it. These members tend to be more mature and well integrated into society, but in France, for this reason, they are seen as posing a threat to society. Perhaps this is a consequence of the Solar Temple's (OTS) tragic "carnage" of 1994–97, when the media made much of the horrifying enigma that the suicidal/homicidal Templars were wealthy, attractive, upper-class French or Swiss, with brilliant careers, beautiful homes, impeccable taste, and solid family connections. There is a widespread horror of mature, seemingly "normal" and successful professionals with seemingly happy families, who are covert "cultists" intent on spreading their ideological deviance through *manipulation mentale* so as to undermine French values and culture from within.

One interesting side effect of this situation is the graying of NRMs in France. I was struck by the prevalence of retired pensioners who acted as administrators and public representatives for their NRMs. They had nothing to lose in terms of profession, finance, or child custody. Many of these senior spiritual seekers spoke of their adult children as respectful of their parents' religion/philosophy.

Postscript

Since 2002, a new government has discarded the strong anticult stance of Vivien and Picard, and introduced a new model of the French laïcité that fosters education in the world's religions in the public schools and attempts to "normalize" the presence of Islam in the Republic.[21] France is deliberately cultivating an image of a tolerant, religiously diverse nation that values religious freedom. Whether this new official stance will filter down to journalists, local mayors, the gendarmes, and the men and women on the street remains to be seen and would be an interesting focus for future field research.

Notes

1. See "Libertés Religeuses: La Chine et la France épinglées," *Le Monde*, 30 June 2001, 5.
2. See *Bulletin de liaison pour l'étude des sectes*, No. 32, 4eme trimester, 1991.
3. "Field Notes: France's Anti-Sect Wars," *Nova Religio* 6:1 (Oct. 2002): 174–82.
4. Joël Labruyère, *L'Etat Inquisiteur: la spiritualité en danger* (Auxerre, France: Editions des Monts, 2000).
5. Anne Fournier and Michel Monroy, *La dérive sectaire*, 1. éd. (Paris: Presses universitaires de France, 1999).
6. Michel Monroy and Anne Fournier, *Les Sectes* (Milan: Centre Roger Ikor, 1995), 5.
7. *Cult Observer*, May/June 1996, 15.
8. Massimo Introvigne, "Réaction hysterique du sectretaire générale de la mission interministerielle de lutte contre les sectes," Press Release, CESNUR, 1 April 1998.
9. See "les propos troublants de JeanneTavernier," *CAP* No. 2, April 2001, regarding Tavernier's statement made in an interview on a TV talk show, *Vie Privée*, Vie Publique on France 2, 21 March 2001.
10. *Don Bosco Aujourd'hui*, November/December 1996. Tavernier's statement was, "Nous n'allons pas vers les groupes, nous n'avons pas le temps."
11. TV talk show, *Vie Privée*, Vie Publique on France 2, 21 March 2001.
12. "Au nom de l'enfant," *Le Figaro Lyon*, 30 July 1992.
13. *The Watchtower*, 1 September 2001, 19.
14. For example, they saw a cause and effect relationship between the September 11 tragedy and the detonation of their giant statue of the Cosmoplanetary Messiah on September 6.
15. Christine Amory, interview with author, Paris, 30 June 2001.
16. "*Culte publique de l'Aumisme*," (flyer, n.d.) invites the public to seven Sundays of worship between September 2001 and June 2002.
17. Martine Forestier, "France, Country of Human Rights, Where are you?" *Apocalypse* 113:53 (1998): 17–18.
18. "A small lesson of freedom for French authorities who are instituting intolerance," *Apocalypse* 115:55 (2000): 41.
19. Benoit Aymonier (Raelian Guide), interview with author, Paris, 20 July 2001.
20. See CAP, *Le Rapport sur la discrimination a l'encontrèdes minoritaires spirituelles et therapeutique en France*, October 2000.
21. Blandine Chelini-Pont, "Resume sur la gestion publique du pluralisme religieux en France entre 2002 et 2003," paper presented at the "Public Management of Religious Diversity" conference at Laval University, Quebec, Canada, 26 Sepember 2003.

CHAPTER 5

Italy's Surprisingly Favorable Environment for Religious Minorities

MASSIMO INTROVIGNE

International sources, including yearly reports on religious liberty issued by the U.S. Department of State,[1] the Helsinki Commission, and the United Nations, suggest that Italy, comparatively speaking, offers one of the best environments for religious minorities. Unlike France, Germany, and Belgium,[2] there is no official anticult activity, although there is some police watching of "cults." However, when a police report (although more moderate than its French or Belgian counterparts) was disclosed in 1998,[3] political criticism was directed primarily against the police for possible breaches of religious liberty rather than against the "cults" themselves. Anticult movements in Italy are small, underfinanced, and not particularly active. Even the most controversial religious movements operate in Italy in a climate of freedom and have consistently won their most important court cases.

On November 15, 1991, the Rome Court determined that "flirty-fishing," as practiced by The Family (formerly known as the Children of God), was not tantamount to prostitution and not illegal per se under Italian law.[4] The Supreme Court has also determined, on two separate occasions, that Scientology is a religion,[5] although it also maintained that Narconon, the drug rehabilitation program run by Scientology, is not in itself religious and, in consequence, not tax-exempt.[6] A leading judge in Rome investigating the Unification Church for possible mistreatment of its members closed the case with no indictments in 1980. Jehovah's Witnesses, denounced in France as the epitome of dangerous "sects," have entered into a concordat signed by the Italian Prime Minister on March 20, 2000, allowing them to receive public funding (the concordat is due for ratification by Parliament, and some opposition is expected). The Assemblies of God and the Seventh-day Adventists, investigated as possible "cults" in Belgium, already receive taxpayers' money under similar concordats in Italy. All this may seem rather strange, when one considers that religious liberty is a fairly recent phenomenon in Italy (it was only incorporated into the country's new Constitution after World War II), and Catholic influence is probably more dominant here than anywhere else in the world. This paper lists seven reasons that may explain why Italy's situation is apparently so favorable in terms of religious minorities. It also details some emerging trends that may cause this situation to change.

1. First, religious minorities are not seen as particularly threatening in Italy, simply because they are comparatively small. The *Encyclopedia of Religions in Italy* (co-edited by this writer)[7] lists more than six hundred religious bodies active on Italian soil. However, the combined membership of such bodies (excluding the Roman Catholic Church) amounts only to 1.92 percent of the total Italian population. The situation changes somewhat, however, when one considers not only the Italian population but also foreign workers and legal and illegal immigrants (who are not Italian citizens). In this case, members of religious minorities amount roughly to 3.50 percent of Italy's total population. Most immigrants, however, are not members of new religious movements (NRMs), but are Muslims (with, in consequence, a growing Islamophobia in certain quarters), or Eastern Orthodox Christians from Romania, Yugoslavia, and Russia (this latter religious minority is not regarded as particularly threatening). Religious minorities other than Islam, therefore, are often perceived as a mere footnote to the Italian religious scene as a whole, and voices are even heard among academics claiming that funds should not be wasted on social scientific studies of them.

2. A crucial role is played by the Italian legal system, which is based on the post-war Constitution and the 1984 revision of the Concordat with the Roman Catholic Church. Under the present system (unlike in Germany, for instance), all Italian citizens are obliged to pay a church tax amounting to 0.8 percent of their total income tax bill. While in Germany taxpayers claiming to be secular may abstain from paying the religious tax, in Italy the religious tax payment is statutory. The law does allow, however, for taxpayers to opt that their payment be given to a state charity managing historical buildings and museums, or to leave the corresponding section on the tax form blank. In that case, their money is divided among the religious

bodies that have elected to participate in the corresponding division. Although the Constitution provides that only the treaty with the Catholic Church is given the status of a "Concordat" (with a capital C), a number of other denominations and churches have smaller concordats called *intese*, which grant them very similar financial and other benefits. Participating religious bodies include Waldensians and Methodists (in 1975 these two churches merged their administrative bodies, although remaining separate religious institutions), Baptists, Lutherans, Jews, the Assemblies of God, and the Seventh-day Adventists. In 2000, the Prime Minister Massimo d'Alema signed concordats with the Italian Buddhist Union and the Jehovah's Witnesses, and these await parliamentary approval at the time of this writing. Negotiations with the Church of Jesus Christ of Latter-Day Saints (the Mormon Church), the Apostolic Church (another Pentecostal body), the Greek Orthodox Church, a Federation of Hindu Organizations, and Soka Gakkai (which is both the largest Buddhist body in Italy and not a member of the Italian Buddhist Union) are on their way. Polls show that a very large majority of Italians support the system. Secular humanist organizations are generally fairly vocal opponents, although one of them, the National Union of Atheists and Rationalist Agnostics, once claimed to be a religion and tried unsuccessfully to enter into a concordat itself. Although these secularist organizations have a limited number of members, they are somewhat overrepresented both among the media and the intellectual elite and are regarded by religionists as a real threat. This explains why mainline churches are often reluctant to oppose new entries into the concordats-religious tax system. They are afraid to rock the boat, and to open the whole system (extremely beneficial to them) to debate and controversy. Although Jehovah's Witnesses are not particularly popular among other religions, most Protestant bodies supported their application for a concordat, and the Roman Catholic Church remained officially silent (although criticism from individual priests and bishops was not uncommon).

3. Protestants have a history of discrimination in Italy, under the Fascist regime in particular, when Mussolini tried to appease and accommodate an initially suspicious Roman Catholic Church.[8] Some Protestant denominations were defined as "cults" and "sects" in official documents, including in the post-World War II period, and were subject to discrimination well into the 1950s. It was only during the 1960s, in a number of Supreme Court decisions, that what remained of the anti-Protestant measures were effectively dismantled (after Vatican II, with no opposition and the full approval of the Roman Catholic Church). The memory of this period of discrimination is still painful for Protestants and explains why Evangelical countercultism has such a limited presence in Italy. When foreign material written against groups such as the Jehovah's Witnesses or the Mormons is translated by Italian Evangelicals, a foreword usually

explains that strong theological criticism does not imply that these groups should be discriminated against by the state. The Fascist regime also introduced criminal legislation against *plagio*, a word whose contemporary translation into English should in fact be "brainwashing" (although Italian legislation was passed well before this word was coined in the U.S.). On June 8, 1981,[9] the Constitutional Court declared Section 603 of the Italian Criminal Code incompatible with a democratic constitution, thus eliminating *plagio* from Italian law and making it more difficult to reintroduce anti-brainwashing legislation.

4. "Cult" and "sect" were labels frequently used by the Roman Catholic Church and by left-wing political critics against Italian Freemasonry, an organization that for decades was often the most vocal exponent of secular humanism (for which it had to sever its ties with British and American Masonic bodies). Freemasonry was also a vocal critic of the large Italian Communist Party. The only anticult legislation proposed and occasionally passed in Italy was, in fact, anti-Masonic. In the 1980s and 1990s, after two Masonic scandals, left-wing governments passed laws and administrative regulations (still in force) preventing Freemasons from holding positions in the national judiciary or as presidents, for instance, of some of the country's Chambers of Commerce. While in France and other countries secular "continental" Masonic bodies (separated from non-anticlerical British and American Freemasonry) are very active in promoting anticult crusades, Italian Freemasonry has, understandably, developed a very different attitude over the years, simply because it has learned through experience that anticult campaigns in Italy often provoke new anti-Masonic legislation.

5. Scholars in Italy have (as in the United States, and unlike France and Germany) a history of being fairly pro-active and of siding with underdogs, religious and otherwise. Unlike the situation in France and Germany, however, there has also been a substantial body of empirical research on NRMs since, at least, the 1980s. Published social scientific and historical literature about NRMs is possibly twice as large as in France and Germany put together. A good seventy percent of this literature, in the form of some fifty books and hundreds of journal articles and chapters, has been produced by scholars associated with the Center for Studies on New Religions (CESNUR), established in Turin in 1988. From its very beginning, CESNUR has had an international board whose most active members are internationally well-known critics of the anticult movement. During its twelve years of existence, CESNUR has entered into several consultancy agreements with public institutions, law enforcement agencies, and mainline religious bodies; its courses, seminars, and reports (supplemented by many hundreds of media interviews) have helped spread a non-anticult perspective on religious minority issues in Italy.

6. The memory of the Fascist persecution of religious minorities makes Italian politicians extremely reluctant to act against "cults" or "sects." In nearby France, politics is still dominated by a secular humanist "old left" with a paternalistic view of government and state. In Germany, anticult crusades are often led by an "old right" that enjoys close connections with established churches and a general law-and-order attitude. In Italian politics, by contrast, there is a certain prevalence of a "new left" and a "new right," obviously different from each other, but both anti-paternalistic and libertarian. Both have opposed any attempt to widen state control of religion or anticult activity. A graphic illustration of this point is the joint representation by two senior lawyers on behalf of the Church of Scientology in recent court cases. One of the lawyers was a former cabinet minister from the libertarian wing of the conservative party "Forza Italia," and the other an equally libertarian MP from a small neo-Marxist left-wing party. Such legal representation on behalf of Scientology by prominent politicians who also happen to be lawyers would be unthinkable in France or Germany.

7. Italian anticultism has concentrated its efforts on establishing an on-line presence, but has found it difficult to achieve off-line results in a country where both media and politicians are quite reluctant to use unverified Internet gossip as sources. Some of the most extreme anticult websites are run by Italians, although they are occasionally hosted by foreign providers in order to bypass Italian law restrictions.[10] The Italian Roman Catholic countercult organization GRIS also had a significant international on-line and off-line presence both in Europe and in Latin America (although its Internet activities seem to be in a state of decline, and the once very active Rome section no longer has its own website). Several Italian anticultists operate almost exclusively on-line and have a very limited off-line presence. Their websites are better known abroad than in Italy. There is, for instance, an entire website (operated by a former Italian leader of New Acropolis) devoted to slandering scholars associated with CESNUR (although this website has not been updated since November 2001, and its sponsors seem to have focused on facets of anti-Americanism other than the struggle against "American" cults after the events of September 11). In this case, however, several hundreds of pages have been on-line for years without generating (as far as I know) a single line of comment in any of the mainline Italian media. On the other hand, the anti-CESNUR website (which includes many pages in languages other than Italian) has been quoted within the framework of local campaigns against "cults" (and "cult apologists") in France and Germany. An anti-Soka Gakkai page based in Italy, and a large anti-Scientology website run by a pseudonymous "Martini" also had a larger impact abroad than in Italy. GRIS, as mentioned earlier, is a somewhat different organization, with a real presence in several

Italian cities. It boasts of having the approval of the National Conference of Catholic Bishops (although several dozens of Catholic associations are similarly "approved," and "approval" does not give GRIS the right to speak for the Church). In recent years, it has been plagued by internecine struggles, has exhibited different attitudes within its own local chapters, and its presence at the national level appears to be declining. It still maintains contacts, however, with several Italian Catholic bishops and with countercult bishops and priests in Germany, Latin America, and elsewhere. Generally speaking, there is only a limited degree of (off-line) secular anticult and Catholic countercult activity in Italy. True, the Italian media are just as interested in publishing lurid exposés of "dangerous cults" as anywhere else. And while the overall domestic impact of Italian anticultism has been quite limited, Italian anticultists have been lionized by the international anticult movement. Because a number of Italian scholars of NRMs (both associated, and not associated, with CESNUR), as well as some Italian politicians and legal experts, are among the most vocal critics of European (particularly French) anticultism, European anticultists have a vested interest in claiming that these "cult apologists" are "controversial" at home. It is also worth noting that both Jehovah's Witnesses and Soka Gakkai have their largest European constituencies in Italy, and the same may well be true for Scientology, although in Scientology's case hard statistics are notoriously difficult to obtain. Anticultists in countries such as Germany and France, understandably, like to claim that these larger Italian bodies are as controversial in Italy as they are in their respective countries. Although it would be an exaggeration to claim that Italian Internet anticultism has no impact whatsoever in Italy, it would be true to say that the material is mostly produced for export and use in other countries.

In 2000, a self-styled "disgruntled former Italian anticultist" published an exposé and several documents on the controversial U.S. website tellitall.org (where anybody is allowed to post all sorts of outrageous claims, with anonymity guaranteed). The claim was made that extreme Italian anticult websites (particularly the anti-Scientology site run by "Martini") are operated by a group involved in a number of illegal activities with the secret help of Ministry of Internal Affairs officials. The Church of Scientology called the attention of several MPs to the exposé, and both a parliamentary discussion and an official investigation followed. The latter suggested that, contrary to the claims on tellitall.org, no governmental officer has been shown to cooperate with the extreme anticult websites, and the concerned MPs were told that any illegal activity carried out by these websites will, in the future, be monitored and prosecuted. It remains unclear who exactly was responsible for the exposé on tellitall.org (with critics obviously pointing their fingers at the Church of Scientology itself), but the whole story illustrates that in official quarters, extreme anticultists in Italy are regarded more as part of the problem than as part of the solution. There have also been suggestions that intelligence services of countries with a more aggressive anticult attitude may play a part in the whole Italian imbroglio surrounding the "anticult terrorism via the Internet." A certain pressure exerted by France against the concordat with the Jehovah's Witnesses has undoubtedly been felt during 2000–2001. Just as Italian anticultism is mostly a product intended for foreign export, anticultism from countries such as Germany and France may well be imported into Italy (although the new French government announced in 2002 that it is less interested in anticult activism in general, and in exporting anticultism abroad in particular, than its Socialist predecessor was).

Apart from international influences, there are also several domestic negative factors that may influence the situation of religious minorities in Italy in the near future:

1. The discussion about the possibility of a concordat with one of the Italian Islamic bodies became very heated in the aftermath of September 11. In fact, five such bodies applied for a concordat, with no negotiations taking place so far. A concordat with Islam would involve special problems, since three of the applicant bodies represent only a tiny proportion of Italy's estimated 600,000 Muslims and one has close ties with a foreign government (Saudi Arabia). The fifth, the Unione delle Comunità e Organizzazioni Islamiche in Italia (UCOII), although the most representative Islamic body in Italy, still cannot claim to represent the majority of Italian Muslims, and found itself under criticism from various quarters since most of its leadership belong to the fundamentalist Islamic Brotherhood. The Italian branch of the Islamic Brotherhood belongs to that part of the fundamentalist camp that does not advocate violence. Islamic fundamentalism, however, tends to dominate any political discussion about Islam, especially after both 9/11 and the arrest of several Al Qa'ida operatives who had formed cells in several Italian cities connected with some of the most radically fundamentalist mosques. In turn, doubts about the wisdom of a concordat with the Islamic bodies (shared by a sizeable proportion of scholars both of Constitutional law and of Islam) were used by both secular humanists and Catholic countercultists (including the national secretary of GRIS) to argue that there are now too many concordats around, and that the number of concordats should be limited to those already in force. Most of these discussions took place during the discussion about a new draft law on religious liberty, introduced by the current government with large bipartisan support. Although the new law mostly collects in a single text provisions already existing in a number of different laws or resulting from decisions of the Constitutional Court (immediately enforceable in Italy), the parliamentary debate about

this text (progressively amended to become more restrictive) was largely transformed into a controversy pro or con the new concordats and about the government's answer to the Islamic requests for concordat negotiations.

2. 9/11 displaced from the first page of Italian daily newspapers the most prominent media story in Italy during summer 2001. It concerned Monsignor Emmanuel Milingo, a Roman Catholic bishop—born in Zambia, but a longtime resident of Italy, where he was immensely popular—who, on May 27, 2001, shocked the Catholic world by being married to Korean acupuncturist Maria Sung by Reverend Sun Myung Moon. Milingo then shocked the Unification movement by leaving Maria and returning to the Catholic fold. Accusations of brainwashing were traded quite liberally between the Catholic media,[11] and the Unification Church and Maria Sung, who themselves used the word "brainwashing" to explain Milingo's return to the Catholic Church. Many facets of the affair remain unclear, including what the Unification Church really thought it could achieve through the whole Milingo incident. Prominent Unificationists told both the media and religious scholars that one aim was a dialogue with the Roman Catholic Church. This was, of course, incredibly naïve at best, and the result has been just the opposite. The Milingo case has re-energized an almost dying Catholic countercult movement, which has received new funding and resources and is now taken much more seriously by the hierarchy than it was before Milingo married Maria Sung. Countercultists were able to persuade several Catholic Bishops that leaving the "cults" alone would simply no longer do: "cults" are not leaving Catholics alone and are daring to enter the Vatican to "steal" and claim as their own one of the bishops working in the Roman curia (where Milingo was an officer). Although Italian countercultists did not overcome their internal problems, clearly the Milingo affair created new possibilities for them.

3. Stories about pedophile Catholic priests in the United States and elsewhere led the media to investigate possible connections between pedophilia and religion. Since incidents concerning Catholic priests were scarce in Italy, some media turned their attention to new religious movements. Old stories about The Family were revived on TV talk shows with the liberal participation of anticultists, who often confused The Family with its small Italian splinter group Orizzonti Nuovi. The latter publicizes old Children of God doctrines and practices about sexuality now repudiated by The Family. The leader of Orizzonti Nuovi is facing several trials for a variety of sex-related offenses. In the first case tried, he was found not guilty based on a legal technicality. Possible pedophilia by Satanists has also received new media attention, although the largest Italian Satanist body, the Children of Satan (Bambini di Satana), was repeatedly found not guilty of alleged instances of child abuse by the courts. In other cases, it is

unclear whether the pedophiles involved had any real connection with Satanism or simply used "Satanic" trappings in order to terrorize their victims. Be that as it may be, a small number of Catholic priests devoted to exposing publicly "the Satanist threat" have emerged. With the help of an anticult anthropologist, Dr. Cecilia Gatto Trocchi, who is also associated with GRIS (an organization which these priests regard as "soft on Satanism"), they have attracted considerable media attention, often associating the alleged "growing threat" of Satanism with "cults" in general.

4. The largest NRM in Italy (if one does not consider Jehovah's Witnesses a NRM) is Soka Gakkai. In 2001 and 2002, its Italian chapter experienced internal conflicts with two (or perhaps three) factions competing for leadership. Even sympathetic scholars such as sociologists Maria Immacolata Macioti[12] and Karel Dobbelaere called the attention of the international headquarters to the dysfunctional situation in Italy. The Italian media took an interest in the conflict because it seemed to involve political issues (some leaders were regarded as close to the present Italian government, and others were associated with the opposition). In fact, the situation was much more complicated. Although, as of November 2002, most issues appear to have been resolved through the intervention of the Japanese leadership, both former members and current members particularly unhappy with the Italian leadership have recently fed lurid stories about Soka Gakkai to the media. Reporters not particularly familiar with the intricacies of Nichiren Buddhism reinterpreted complaints about specific issues through an anticult frame of reference, and the discussion as usual extended to "cults" in general.

5. Italy does not have as many television preachers as the United States, but it does have a sizeable number of psychics both on national and local television. In 2001 and 2002 there were several scandals involving prominent television psychics and their sponsors; some were arrested for fraud for selling worthless preparations as "magical" remedies at exorbitant prices. Secular anticult organizations and professional skeptics immediately claimed these arrests as victories and insisted that "cults" operate "just like television psychics."

These factors, however, should not be blown out of proportion. Under the influence of countercultists and anticultists, proposals to set up official commissions to investigate Italian "cults," as has already occurred in France and Germany, have been introduced by some members of the Italian Parliament. To date these proposals have not been taken terribly seriously, and a large bipartisan consensus on religious liberty still prevails in the Parliament. However, the proposals may herald increasing anticult activity in the future and a general mistrust of minorities, religious and otherwise, typical of the post-September 11 era.

84 • Massimo Introvigne

Notes

1. U.S. Department of State, *International Religious Freedom Report for 2002* (Washington, D.C.: U.S. Department of State, 2002).
2. See James T. Richardson and Massimo Introvigne, " 'Brainwashing Theories' in European Parliamentary and Administrative Reports on 'Cults' and 'Sects,'" *Journal for the Scientific Study of Religion* 40:2 (June 2001): 143–68.
3. Ministero dell'Interno, Dipartimento della Pubblica Sicurezza—Direzione Centrale Polizia di Prevenzione, *Sette religiose e nuovi movimenti magici in Italia* (Rome: Ministero dell'Interno, 1998).
4. Tribunale Penale di Roma (Criminal Court of Rome), *Berg e altri*, unpublished decision of 15 Nov. 1991 in the collection of CESNUR (Center for Studies on New Religions, Torino, Italy) and in the archives of the Criminal Court of Rome (RG 3841/84).
5. Corte di Cassazione, *Segalla e altri*, decision no. 1329 of 8 Oct. 1997, text available at http://www.cesnur.org/testi/Milano.htm.
6. Corte di Cassazione, *Bellei e altri*, decision of 16 Dec. 1999–23 Feb. 2000, text available at http://www.cesnur.org/testi/scie_mar2000_txt.htm.
7. Massimo Introvigne, PierLuigi Zoccatelli, Nelly Ippolito Màcrina, and Verónica Roldán, *Enciclopedia delle religioni in Italia* (Leumann [Turin]: Elledici, 2001).
8. See Giorgio Rochat, *Regime fascista e Chiese Evangeliche. Direttive e articolazioni del controllo e della repressione* (Turin: Claudiana, 1990).
9. Corte Costituzionale, *Grasso*, decision no. 96 of 8 June 1981, *Giurisprudenza Costituzionale* 1 (1981): 806–34.
10. Massimo Introvigne, "So Many Evil Things: Anti-cult Terrorism via the Internet," in *Religion on the Internet: Research Prospects and Promises*, eds. Jeffrey K. Hadden and Douglas E. Cowan (New York: JAI Press, 2000), 277–306.
11. And later by Milingo himself (or by his editors) after his return to the Catholic Church: see Emmanuel Milingo, *Il pesce ripescato dal fango. Conversazioni con Michele Zanzucchi* (San Paolo: Cinisello Balsamo [Milan], 2002).
12. See Maria Immacolata Macioti, "L'Istituto Buddhista Italiano Soka Gakkai a un bivio," *La Critica Sociologica* 141 (Spring 2002): 89–96.

CHAPTER 6

New Religions in Germany
The Publicity of the Public Square

BRIGITTE SCHOEN

The Setting

The Reformation has left its traces on Germany's religious landscape, which still shows a distinctively regional distribution of Roman Catholics and Lutheran and Reformed Protestants. While in 1950, 94 percent of the population belonged to the two churches,[1] membership has dropped rapidly since then. In 2000, 27 million members or about 33 percent of the population belonged to each church.[2] Ex-members remain largely unchurched. Reunification also brought a significant increase in the number of non-believers. Within this framework dominated by the two established Christian churches, minority religions continue to seek a place for themselves. They are estimated to have five million members, or about six percent of the population, with the largest minority religion, Islam, numbering about three million members. Though not a new religion itself, Islam is a relatively new phenomenon in Germany, and as the most influential minority religion it has raised many issues which directly affect new religions. Figures for new religions vary considerably.[3] While there is disagreement concerning numbers as well as which communities count as new religions, they certainly are a fringe phenomenon. The typical size of new religions ranges from several hundred to a few thousand members.

Freedom of Religion and Modern Church-State Relations

The fundamentals of religious freedom and church-state relations are laid out in the basic law, the Constitution of 1949, which has become binding for East Germany as well since German reunification. A major intention of the Constitution has been to strengthen the basic human rights which are understood to govern the basic law.[4] These basic human rights are binding on legislative, executive, and judicial branches of government and are directly enforceable law (Article 1 III GG). Their essential content must not be infringed (Article 19 II GG). Freedom of religion is guaranteed through Article 4 GG, which rules that freedom of creed, of conscience, and freedom to profess a religious or non-religious faith are inviolable; that the undisturbed practice of religion is guaranteed; and that conscientious objection against military service is respected. Article 4 GG does not state an explicit limitation on religious freedom, which means that this right finds its limits only in the constitutional order as a whole as well as in the basic rights of other individuals. This means that a compelling state interest does not suffice to restrict religious freedom unless it is based on the above-named limits. On the other hand, the basic rights of others have to be guaranteed, such as a child's right to freedom from injury in the case of Evangelicals calling for corporal punishment.[5] To sum up, constitutional guarantees of religious freedom are extensive in present-day Germany.

Church-state relations are the result of a double compromise, the compromise of the Weimar Constitution of 1919 being incorporated into the basic law of 1949 because in both cases debates over how to reform the system could not be resolved politically. The constitutions merely prohibit a state church, they do not ask for a strict separation of church and state. Religions are organized either under public or under private law. A corporate body under public law is usually carrying out tasks of the state and therefore is granted a number of state powers, such as the right to levy a tax on its members; the purpose of this organizational form is to have an independent unit of public administration. Organizing religions in this fashion is of course a remnant of the former state-church system. The Weimar Constitution produced an interesting compromise by making public law status accessible to all religions and *Weltanschauungen* which by their constitution and by the number of their members guarantee longevity.[6] This meant in effect that the established churches did not lose privileges, but now had to contend with competition. The struggle of the Jehovah's Witnesses to gain public law status shows, however, how difficult it is to find a balance between religious self-determination and regulation of the special powers connected with this status. In an important decision the constitutional court has specified that a religion applying for this status must in principle display loyalty towards the law; it also must give the guarantee that its future behavior will not endanger the principles of the Constitution, the basic rights of third parties that are protected by the state, and the liberal principles of church-state relations as laid down in the Constitution. The constitutional court sent the case back to the lower courts in order to establish whether basic rights of third parties as guaranteed by the state might pose an obstacle to granting public law status to the Jehovah's Witnesses.[7] Several Muslim organizations have also tried to gain public law status. They have so far been unsuccessful since they are lacking a stable central institution representing all or a substantial part of the Muslims living in Germany. This clearly shows that the system of organizing religions as corporate bodies fosters a highly institutionalized, centralized organizational form for religions which one might call religious bureaucracies.

Religions that do not meet the requirements for public law status organize according to private law; there is no special legal form for them. On the whole the system increases the differences between large and influential religions and small minority religions. Quite often, however, different treatment does not derive from public or private law status but from the fact that those religions holding public law status also have far higher numbers of members. For instance, religious instruction in public schools does not depend on public law status but on whether sufficient numbers of students exist to form classes.[8] The right to public declaration of one's faith and to public recruitment—that is, the acknowledgement of a public mission of religion—is granted to all.[9]

The Concept of Religion in Jurisdiction

The constitutional court stressed early that the right to freedom of religion has to be interpreted broadly.[10] There is no concluding definition of religion; a working definition of the constitutional court merely requires that members of a religion or *Weltanschauung* share and testify to a consensus on the meaning of human life and how to cope with it. This means a minimum of organizational form, a consensus on the meaning of human existence, and bearing witness to that consensus.[11] As a result, the acknowledgment of new religions has been unproblematic. Neither political activities[12] nor predominant engagement in economic activities[13] hinder the religious character of an organization. Only when religious teachings are alleged to be simply a pretext for economic activities—that is, if the community in effect exclusively pursues economic interests—will it lose the guarantees of Article 4 GG.[14] So far only Scientology has been affected by this stipulation.[15] The constitutional court has not had a chance to discuss the nature of Scientology at this juncture, but in another decision it has made clear that a community's own insistence that it is religious may not suffice. Finally, it is the task of the courts to examine and decide these issues in terms of the meaning and aim of the constitutional provisions for the basic right of religious freedom.[16]

The flip side of this generally pro-religious jurisdiction can be seen in the public square, where Christian predominance is clearly felt. The state court of Hessia ruled in 1965 that school prayer would violate the negative religious freedom of the nonbeliever.[17] However, the constitutional court in 1979 still held school prayer to be permissible as long as students were free to decide whether to participate or not.[18] A significant alteration was effected in the so-called crucifix decision of the constitutional court in 1995, which stated that crosses in the classrooms of Bavarian public schools violated the plaintiffs' religious freedom, since the children were legally required to attend school and thus to be confronted with the cross, a situation which differs from casual encounters with religious symbols of different faiths in daily life.[19] This decision attempted to resolve tensions between different faiths by at least removing religious symbols in situations where confrontation is unavoidable. However, it will not generally affect the presence of religious symbols in public. This active support for minority faiths against the predominant culture has been a comparatively late development, but because of the increasing numbers of non-Christians in Germany, this trend is likely to continue, Bavarian protests against the crucifix decision notwithstanding.

Government Activities

The most conspicuous activity of German government agencies has been the production of information booklets on new religions. One of the first of these was a published report by the Federal Government in 1979 to the Board of Petitions, which had called on the government to present a concept of how it was going to deal with certain problematic endeavors of new religions.[20] The government's report gave a general perspective on problems arising from new religions and specifically mentioned the Unification Church, the Children of God (Family of Love), ISKCON, Divine Light Mission, Scientology, Transcendental Meditation, and the Bhagwan Rajneesh movement. The legal part of the paper ruled out any prohibition of new religions and emphasized the possibilities existing laws provide for eventual action.

This booklet, as well as others distributed by state governments, was challenged by lawsuits filed by the new religions affected. The courts then had to clarify the standard which the booklets needed to meet. They affirmed that authorities generally are bound by the precept of neutrality and tolerance, the principles of proportionality, legal necessity, and appropriateness, and the prohibition of excess.[21] While accurate factual statements are permissible, matters which are yet unclear are excluded, as are speculations and rumors. In the latter case, even speculations that appear as quotations from other sources must be excluded, since including them could lend them an air of authenticity.[22] An important controversy arose regarding the legal basis on which the booklets were issued, as they were taken to be an interference with the right to religious freedom of the religious groups cited.[23] While state governments can resort to police power that is situated at the state level, the federal government cannot. The constitutional court has finally ended a longstanding debate by affirming the right of the government and its organs to discuss publicly—even critically—religions and religious people, their aims and their activities. The court stressed that the principle of state religious neutrality has to be observed, which demands restraint. It explicitly prohibited defamatory, discriminating, or distorting representations of religious communities. As for the legal basis of the booklet, the court stated that the federal government can legitimately inform the public in matters in which it carries a national responsibility.[24]

The booklets themselves are of very mixed quality. Despite a large amount of legal information, the booklets aim to be accessible to the general public, and therefore often tend to oversimplify. Because of the above-mentioned court rulings, the booklets now mainly rely on quotations from publications of the religions in question. State warnings against new religions on the one hand seem drastic because of their publicity; on the other hand, everybody is free to ignore them, as was pointed out by the federal administrative court.[25] While it is important that new religions protest against booklets which they perceive to be unfair, the courts have held this public form of debate to be legitimate. Still, the booklets' actual influence on public opinion should not be overestimated.[26]

In 1996, the German Parliament appointed an Enquete Commission entitled "So-called Sects and Psychotherapy Groups." The purpose of an Enquete Commission is to provide parliament with background information on complex and important issues. The task of this commission was not to deal with particular organizations, but to analyze and to mitigate the potential for conflict in a range of new religious and ideological communities and psychotherapy groups.[27] As the commission was initiated at the request of critics of new religions, and as the majority of the commission's members can be counted among critics, the commission's results were all the more surprising. It concluded that at present new religious and ideological communities and psychotherapy groups presented no danger to state and society or to socially relevant areas.[28] Reasons for these moderate results can be seen in the presence of experts as permanent members of the commission, most notably among them Hubert Seiwert, who has analyzed the behind-the-scenes political conflicts and compromises within the commission.[29] The commission not only drew on social scientific research, but ordered a number of research projects the results of which could not be ignored.[30] This is a significant contrast to the French Enquete Commission of 1996, which largely relied on intelligence service reports, or the Belgian Enquete Commission of 1997, which viewed sociologists and historians of religion as mere theorists who would only study the doctrines and texts of these movements and would use very vague categories for qualifying groups as new religious movements. As a result, the Belgian commission found that the conclusions of scholars were insufficiently grounded and judged that their work was not really appropriate for the task of the commission, since the sociologists did not study the harmful aspects of the organizations in question.[31]

In 1997, the conference of the Ministers of the Interior decided to put Scientology under surveillance. As the decision came in the wake of Scientology's international campaign against Germany, it certainly was influenced by public pressure on the government to act. The basis of the decision was the legal expertise of a task force of the intelligence service.[32] While there is general agreement that the state of affairs warrants surveillance, it is debatable as to whether it warrants it compellingly. Helmut Albert has raised the interesting question whether surveillance would actually bring substantially new information, since the intelligence service has to rely mainly on open sources, due to legal restrictions on the tapping of telecommunications.[33] So far, the surveillance has resulted in the production of further information booklets on Scientology.[34] The Berlin administrative court ruled that the state of Berlin must not use secret agents to gather information on Scientology since the state did not bring forward substantiated arguments establishing the necessity of such means. Other intelligence means are not affected by this decision.[35] On the whole, public interest as well as the interest of politicians to pursue the issue have dropped drastically.

Taken together, governmental activities have mainly influenced the sphere of public opinion through the collection of information by the Enquete Commission and the intelligence service (on Scientology) as well as through the distribution of information to the general public. This of course means a high degree of publicity for the debate on new religions in Germany. On the other hand, governmental activity did not go beyond the collection and distribution of infomation, mainly because of the restrictions arising from the extensive constitutional guarantees for religious freedom and the fact that new religions have been recognized as proper religions by the courts. This recognition has been an important factor especially in dealing with local public administrations. It remains open to debate how far other tools of the state have been instrumentalized for political purposes. The Enquete Commission for its part has arrived at an independent position, and the intelligence service has refused to monitor new religions other than Scientology.[36]

Anticult Organizations

It does not seem appropriate to speak of a grassroots German anticult movement, as the degree of institutionalization of the organizations is high, as is cooperation between organizations. The prominent role of the churches makes it easy to overlook the fact that one is dealing with a number of quite distinct organizations ranging from concerned parents' initiatives to full-time church counsellors. Attitudes towards new religions also vary. Large differences occur especially within the Protestant Church, which accommodates both the generally moderate information center Evangelische Zentralstelle für Weltanschauungsfragen (EZW) as well as the aggressive anticultist Pastor Thomas Gandow.

During the late 1970s and the 1980s some anticult organizations received state funding, a practice which was stopped by the courts since such funding violates the principle of neutrality if the sponsored organization operates on a religious or ideological basis. In addition, private persons can rely on freedom of speech and do not face the same restrictions as public authorities; therefore authorities must not sponsor tendentious organizations in order to circumvent these restrictions.[37] Loss of state funding for private organizations on the other hand meant that the churches became more attractive partners for cooperation and funding. It also led to the foundation of information centers which operate on a neutral basis and therefore may receive state funding, such as the Informations- und Dokumentationszentrum Sogenannte Sekten/Psychokulte (IDZ) in Cologne. This is an interesting development which may help to balance the predominance of Christian countercult information.

The Impact of Islam on New Religions in Germany

Islam is Germany's largest and most influential minority religion, and as such decisions concerning it quite often have a spin-off effect for smaller religions, including new religions. Originally made up mainly of immigrants, many of its members are now second or third generation natives. Still, the process of societal integration is very slow. One of the most controversial issues is religion in the workplace. Here in many cases a balance between employers' and employees' interests has yet to be found. Muslims' efforts to have their religious rights affirmed can be seen as test cases which are setting precedents for other minority faiths.

Islam's more dominant influence in comparison to other minority religions does not necessarily lead to successful outcomes in the legal arena. In a decision denying the claim to public school employment for a Muslim teacher wearing a head scarf, the federal administrative court ruled that such a display of a religious symbol violates the religious neutrality of the state as represented by the teacher. Because a teacher is a role model for the pupils, he/she must not confront minors with a specific faith in such a continuous and conspicuous fashion. This decision is consistent with an earlier one concerning the followers of Bhagwan Sri Rajneesh, who in the 1980s were forbidden to wear the then mandatory shades of red colors when teaching in a public school.[38] These decisions notwithstanding, a quick glance at today's public schools confirms that Christian symbols usually are tolerated. In the interest of equal treatment of all religions it would be prudent for teachers to exercise restraint in wearing religious symbols of any kind, including Christian ones.

The terrorist attacks of September 11, 2001, were linked to Germany in a most shocking way, since Germany served as a safe haven for the headquarters of the Al Qa'ida cell that planned and carried out the attack. Legislators had already been aware that the laws against terrorism were inadequate, since they did not deal with the fact that terrorist organizations have developed global networks. While most legislative changes passed in the resulting two so-called security packages have no direct connection to religion, the change in the law of associations has. The privilege of religion had exempted religious associations from termination, which authorities can impose on associations in cases of criminal or anti-constitutional activities. The abrogation of this privilege has already led to the ban of a Muslim extremist organization called the Caliphate State.[39] While only fullgrown terrorist gangs fall under such a ban and therefore the banishment of new religions is out of the question, the very notion of a terrorist variant of religion has been unsettling. Efforts of state officials stressing that this was not "real" Islam show a noble intention to save law-abiding Muslims from the stigma of terrorism, but of course state officials must refrain from attempting to define what "really" constitutes a specific religion.

Much more difficult to grasp is the emotional effect of unobtrusive, well-behaving, religious young men turning out to be mass murderers. Though primarily an issue of public acceptance of the Muslim community, these developments might kindle resentments against all kinds of minority religions. On the other hand, the new focus on Islamist extremism means that public attention no longer concentrates on the real or alleged dangers of new religions.

Conclusion

Some observers of the German situation may be surprised not to have read anything more alarming. After all, the United States granted political asylum to a German Scientologist in 1997 on religious persecution grounds.[40] Some scholars have also claimed that German courts would rule according to the information they have been fed by church "cult" investigators;[41] or that Germans descend into a frenzy of persecution in periodic cycles[42] because the German psyche associates nontraditional religions with destabilizing political movements.[43] Numerous factual errors notwithstanding, such publications seem to enjoy a certain popularity.[44]

Part of the predominantly negative view derives from the fact that there has been a very contentious public debate about new religions in Germany. Even the German government has participated in this debate, and the style some politicians have employed has been much frowned upon. But these stylistic concerns have to be seen in the context of a quite favorable constitutional and jurisdictional background. The supportive stance of the courts did not make it into the news because it was not controversial. Still, public opinion on new religions has been quite negative, and Scientology's campaign against Germany led to an escalation of the situation in the mid-1990s. It was interesting to see that even in the case of Scientology the government's options for action turned out to be very limited. Instead, officials mainly concentrated on influencing public opinion on the issue. The attempt of the anticultist initiators of the Enquete Commission to jump on the train of current anticult sentiment eventually backfired, as the commission was not able to find evidence for the alleged dangers of new religions. If anything, these official results have had a moderating influence on public opinion.

A general evaluation of the situation of new religions in Germany must take into account the balance between the legal situation, jurisdiction, political action, as well as anticult activities and public opinion. It may be argued, therefore, that the bitter public dispute on new religions is best seen as a counterreaction to the comparatively favorable climate provided for by the legal situation and jurisdiction. Religion old or new is not restricted to the private sphere, nor is the discussion of religions. The price for a presence in the public square seems to be a public debate, which in the case of new religions in Germany has often taken a negative tone.

Notes

1. Lutheran and Reformed Protestants are organized in a joint institution, the Evangelische Kirche Deutschland (EKD).
2. For this and the following cf. *Nationalatlas der BRD: Gesellschaft und Staat*, ed. Institut für Landeskunde, Leipzig (Heidelberg, Berlin: Spektrum Akademischer Verlag, 2000), 102–05.
3. See also www.remid.de/remid_info_zahlen.htm.

4. Reinhard Mußgnug, "Entstehen der BRD," in *Handbuch des Staatsrechts der BRD,* eds. Josef Isensee and Paul Kirchhof, vol. I (Heidelberg: C.F. Müller, 1987), 239.

5. This is a major conflict between the Berlin Senate and the Gemeinde auf dem Weg, an evangelical community, which has prompted the Senate to issue a warning.

6. Art.137.5 WRV.

7. BVerfG, U.v. 19.12.2000–2 BvR 1500/97–, see www.bundesverfassungsgericht.de. Currently the case is pending at the OVG Berlin.

8. Cf. Josef Jurina, "Die Religionsgemeinschaften mit privatrechtlichem Rechtsstatus," in *Handbuch des Staatskirchenrechts der Bundesrepublik Deutschland,* eds. Joseph Listl and Dietrich Pirson, vol. I (Berlin: Duncker und Humblot, 2nd edition, 1994), 689–713, 701.

9. Ibid., 699.

10. Cf. Karl Herrmann Kästner, "Das Grundrecht auf Religions- und Weltanschauungsfreiheit in der neueren höchstrichterlichen Rechtsprechung," Rechtsprechungsübersicht, *AöR* (1998): 408–43. See also Winfried Hassemer and Dieter Hönig, "Die Rechtsprechung des Bundesverfassungsgerichts im Bereich der Bekenntnisfreiheit," *EuGRZ* (1999): 525–36. For the situation of new religions see also Ralf Bernd Abel, "Die Entwicklung der Rechtsprechung zu neueren Glaubensgemeinschaften," *NJW* (1996): 91–95, and "Die aktuelle Entwicklung der Rechtsprechung zu neueren Glaubensgemeinschaften," *NJW* (1997): 426–32.

11. Rainer Scholz in summing up the jurisdiction of the constitutional court, in " 'Neue Jugendreligionen' und Grundrechtsschutz nach Art. 4 GG," *NVwZ* (1992): 1152f. For a similar definition of the BVerwG see Kästner, 414.

12. BVerwG U.v. 23.03.1971 - BVerwG I C 54/66-, *DöV* (1971): S.777–81.

13. BVerwG, U.v. 27.03.1992 - 7 C 21/90–, *NJW* (1992): 2496–500.

14. Ibid.

15. BAG, ruling of 22 March 1995 - 5 AZB 21/94-, *NJW* (1996): 143–52.

16. BVerfG, B.v. 05.02.1991 - 2 BvR 263/86-*BVerfGE* 83, Nr. 18, 341–62; interestingly, this passage was an aside and did not concern the plaintiff in this case.

17. HessStGH, U.v. 27.10.1965 - P.St. 388-, *NJW* (1966): 31–36.

18. BVerfG, B.v. 16.10.1979 - 1 BvR 647/70-, *EuGRZ* (1980): 13–19.

19. BVerfG, B.v. 16.05.1995 - 1 BvR 1087/91-, *EuGRZ* (1995): 359ff. The plaintiffs are Anthroposophists.

20. "Jugendreligionen in der Bundesrepublik Deutschland," Bericht der Bundesregierung an den Petitionsausschuß des Deutschen Bundestages. Reihe Berichte und Dokumentationen 21, Bonn 1980.

21. Cf. Rainer Scholz, " 'Neue Jugendreligionen' und Äußerungsrecht," *NVwZ* (1994): 127–33.

22. Ibid.

23. Cf. Stefan Muckel, "Staatliche Warnungen vor sog. Jugendsekten," *JA* (1995): 343–49; Markus Heintzen, "Staatliche Warnungen als Grundrechtsproblem," *Verwaltungsarchiv* 81 (1991): 532–56; Christoph Gusy, "Anmerkung zum BVerwG Urteil vom 23.5.1989," *JZ* 21 (1989): 1003–5; Wolfgang Schatzschneider, "Informationshandeln im Bundesstaat," *NJW* (1991): 3202–203; Rainer Wahl and Johannes Masing, "Schutz durch Eingriff," *JZ* (1990): 553–63; and Hans Alberts, "Die schwierige Toleranz," *NVwZ* (1992): 1164–166.

24. BVerfG, B.v. 26.06.2002-1 BvR 670/91-, *NJW* (2002): 2626–632.

25. U.v. 23.05.1989—7 C 2/87-, *NJW* (1989): 2276.

26. Cf. Jürgen Eiben, "Erfolg um jeden Preis? Die Scientology-Organisation in der gesellschaftlichen und politischen Auseinandersetzung," *Die Scientology-Organisation. Methoden und Struktur, Rechtsprechung, gesellschaftliche Auseinandersetzung. 2. Bericht des Ministeriums für Arbeit, Gesundheit und Soziales des Landes Nordrhein-Westfalen* (Köln: 1997), 25–46.

27. *Endbericht der Enquete-Kommission "Sogenannte Sekten und Psychogruppen,"* ed. Deutscher Bundestag (Bonn: 1998), 19.

28. Ibid., 294.

29. Hubert Seiwert, "The German Enquete Commission on Sects: Political Conflicts and Compromises," *Social Justice Research* 12 (1999): 323–40.

30. *Neue religiöse und ideologische Gemeinschaften und Psychogruppen: Forschungsberichte und Gutachten der Enquete-Kommission "Sogenannte Sekten und Psychogruppen,"* ed. Deutscher Bundestag (Hamm: Hoheneck, 1998).

31. Enquete Parlementaire visant à élaborer une politique en vue de lutter contre les pratiques illégales des sectes et le danger qu'elles représentent pour la société et pour les personnes, particulièrement les mineurs d'âge: Rapport, 313/8-95/96, 28.04.1997, Partie II, 114, 117, 118.

32. *Abschlußbericht der Arbeitsgruppe SC der Verfassungsschutzbehörden: Zur Frage der Beobachtung der Scientology-Organisation durch die Verfassungsschutzbehörden,* ed. Innenministerium NRW (Düsseldorf, 1997).

33. Helmut Albert, "Beobachtung der Scientology-Organisation durch die Verfassungsschutzbehörden?" *Die Öffentliche Verwaltung* (1997): 810–16.

34. See www.verfassungsschutz.nrw.de and www.hamburg.de/Behoerden/LfV/publika.htm.

35. *Berliner Zeitung,* "Gericht schränkt Beobachtung von Scientology ein," 14 Dec. 2001.

36. *Abschlußbericht der Arbeitsgruppe SC der Verfassungsschutzbehörden zur Frage der Beobachtung der Scientology-Organisation durch die Verfassungsschutzbehörden,* ed. Innenministerium des Landes Nordrhein-Westfalen (Düsseldorf: 1997), 125.

37. BVerwG, U.v. 27.03.1992 - 7 C 21/90-, *NJW* (1992): 2496–500.

38. BVerwG, U.v. 04.07.2002 2 C 21.01 , see www.BVerwG.de; and BVerwG, B.v. 08.03.1988 2 B 92/87-, *NVwZ* (1988): 937–38.

39. For the political measures taken see *Der 11. September 2001 und seine Folgen. Dokumentation aus dem Bundesministerium des Innern,* ed. Bundesministerium des Innern, Berlin 2002, www.bmi.bund.de/downloadde/19336/Download.pdf. On the ban of the Caliphate State see BVerwG, U.v. 27.11.2002 - 6 A 1.02, 6 A 3.02, G A 4.02 and 6 A 9.02-, on-line at www.BVerwG.de.

40. For the background see *Stern,* "Der große Bluff," 29 June 2000; according to *Stern,* Scientologist Victore tried to escape a tax office bill. Victore had argued that she was not able to earn a living in Germany since employers would not hire Scientologists; however employers' letters refusing to hire her seem to have been written by fellow Scientologists at her request. For a general legal discussion see Arthur C. Helton and Jochen Münker, "Religion and Persecution: Should the United States Provide Refuge to German Scientologists?" *International Journal of Refugee Law* 11 (1999): 310–28.

41. Irving Hexham and Karla Poewe, "Verfassungsfeindlich: Church, State, and New Religions in Germany," *Nova Religio* 2 (1999): 208–27.

42. Derek Davis, "Religious Persecution in Today's Germany: Old Habits Renewed," *Journal of Church and State* 40 (1998): 741–56.

43. Ibid., 754f.

44. For a historical perspective see Randall Collins, "German-Bashing and the Theory of Democratic Modernization," *Zeitschrift für Soziologie* (1995): 3–21.

PART 2

Eastern Europe and Eurasia

CHAPTER 7

New Religions in the New Russia

MARAT SHTERIN

Post-communist Russia is in the process of remaking, with religion playing a considerable part in how individuals and their associations see and iden-tify themselves. The country is an exciting place for a social scientist to study how these new identities coexist, compete with, and try to delegit-imize each other. In addition, new religions and reactions to them may provide a revealing focus for understanding how the emerging mode of co-existence is affected by the country's historical legacy and new institutions, as well as by global transformations and political contingencies.

Religion and the Modernization of Russia

Despite its commonly held image as an Orthodox country, Russia has long been religiously diverse, with large ethnic religious minorities—such as Muslims, Jews, Roman Catholics, Protestants, Buddhists, and Shaman-ists—and ever present religious innovation and dissent, from the Old Believers to G. I. Gurdjieff and Pyotr D. Uspenski. Although suppressed, religious culture in various forms continued during the Soviet period; a "cultic milieu" became increasingly prominent beginning in the 1970s.

At the same time, the country has a long history of suppression in man-aging this diversity. Before the adoption of the Edict of Toleration in 1905, official policy was guided by the ideology of the inseparable unity of the Orthodox Faith, Russian State, and Russian Land, which was inimical to proselytizing by non-Orthodox groups.[1] Religious minorities were seen as enclaves in the Orthodox Land, which, according to the imperial legislation, were either "tolerated," e.g., ethnic faiths, or "persecuted," e.g., "sects."[2] A short period (1905–1917) of attempts to institutionalize religious toleration was followed by decades of another type of "organic unity"—that of the Communist Ideology, Soviet State, and Soviet Land, which relegated all faiths to a position of "tolerated" or persecuted minorities and justified the institutionalized destruction of religion.

It seems useful to place these policies in the wider context of the "challenge of modernity" that Russia has faced throughout its history and that has been described as attempts to "catch up with the West," and/or assert its own vision of modernity. This challenge characteristically compelled the imperial state to incomplete reforms, which were often associated with Westernization and caused anxieties over imminent erosion of the country's cultural identity.[3] One expression of this was the *Westernizers versus Slavophiles* discourse dating from the 1830s that made a major imprint on the Russian intellectual tradition. It has been argued that this discourse reflected Russia's generally ambiguous attitude to the West, which was looked upon with a mixture of frustration and infatuation.[4] Soviet modernization led to the country's political isolation, partly out of the fear of external ideological contamination.

Religion was deeply imbedded in the politics of Russian modernization. In the continuing absence of representative political institutions, and in the face of more technologically advanced Western competitors, the state and some sections of society continued to define the country as a unitary spiritual as opposed to political space. Thus, the multi-ethnic and multi-religious empire with its 200 different ethnic groups was seen as a Russian Orthodox country.[5] This situation reached a dramatic turn at the *fin de siècle*, when an ethno-religious reawakening and the spread of militant secularism within many ethnic groups were met with strenuous proselytizing by the imperial state and church.

The Soviet modernizing project declared religion a major obstacle to its success. The vision of a "new historic community of the Soviet people" was aggressively secularist. At the same time, the promised "flourishing of nationalities" in the Soviet Union was predicated on abandoning traditional ethno-religious links. However, the actual policy of Soviet nation building included a communist "political religion" designed to unite people around a set of prescribed ideas, symbols, and rituals and at the same time to distinguish these people from other nations.[6] Furthermore, Soviet nationalism increasingly referred back to the pre-Revolutionary symbolism of imperial might and to Russian high culture with its profound religious overtones.

The post-communist modernization involved the country's increasing exposure to global economic, political, and cultural forces. At the same time, the integration with the outside world coincided with internal disintegrative processes—the collapse of the USSR, the crisis of the federal system, ethnic conflicts, and economic decline. "Regionalization" of Russia was a particularly salient expression of the post-Soviet transition. It had partly to do with the attempt by regional political elites to decentralize the politico-administrative structure in order to protect local interests and gain maximum benefits from the post-Soviet exposure to "market forces." However, in the so-called ethnic "autonomous" regions it was also an effort to reclaim ethno-cultural identities after the damage of Russianization and Sovietization.

Again, the issue of Russian *national* integrity and identity came to the fore. After the decades of social and cultural homogenization, imposition of the Soviet identity, and hostility to difference, the question of what now united all citizens of this vast country proved difficult to answer. Even more difficult was the question of how to deal with the emerging diversity, in particular given the generally democratic post-communist ethos and the global human rights regime in which the country now operated. The response so far has been a mixed blessing, ranging from relative tolerance and will for compromise in some situations to the brutal use of force in Chechnya.

In the post-Soviet remaking of identities, religion re-emerged as a potent resource, both uniting and dividing. At one level, ethnic Russians, Tatars, and Kalmyks increasingly self-identified with reference to their traditional religion, as Russian Orthodox, Muslims, or Buddhists. This facilitated the involvement of religion in ethno-politics through activities of ethno-religious entrepreneurs and regional political elites. At the same time, the perceived disintegrating impact of both this new diversity and "globalization" encouraged ideological reinterpretations of the geopolitical space that used to be the USSR. For some, such as Eurasianists, Russia remains a separate civilization defined by its peculiar ethno-religious composition, or "balance," to use the current phrase. For others, its identity is defined by Christian Orthodoxy as the guardian against alien civilizations and globalism.

Post-communism also opened the country to other religions that are not affiliated with any of Russia's ethnic groups or whose reinterpretations of religious tradition deviates from the traditional mainstream. It seems that societal reactions to these religions provide a most interesting test of what is new and old in the new Russia. The controversies over religious legislation are a telling example of this test.

Religious Legislation and Related Controversies

The 1990 Law on Freedom of Religions and the provisions of the 1993 Constitution of the Russian Federation reflect the early liberalizing aspects of post-communism. For the first time in Russian history, the 1990 law treated religious freedom as among "the inalienable rights of Russian citizens" and extended these rights to any individual residing in Russia, irrespective of their citizenship. The law contained strong clauses that deprived various state agencies of the means to control religion. Compulsory registration of religious associations was abolished unless tax exemption was sought. Strong nonestablishment clauses were designed to guarantee the ideological neutrality of the state and the legal equality of all faiths.

Initially, the liberating effects of the 1990 law were almost unanimously welcomed—even by the Moscow Patriarchate. However, the consequent enormous increase in religious diversity was not readily translated into religious pluralism. In general terms, the primacy of *individual* rights and *equality* of faiths was in conflict with the vision of a *hierarchy of religions* based on their *historical* links with the country and its various ethnic groups. A corollary of this vision was the demand to limit proselytizing by "foreign faiths." This was initially justified by reference to the post-communist disadvantage of Russian historical faiths in their competition with "well-off" foreign missionaries. However, the opposition to the 1990 law also tapped into the basic challenges of post-communist politics—creation of a utilitarian democratic state and the search for cohesion and unity in nation building.

From the mid-1990s, opponents of the 1990 law increasingly referred to Russia as a *civilization* defined by its historically established "ethno-religious balance." New "sects," therefore, threatened to destroy Russia's cultural and political integrity. However, this argument alone would have been unlikely to strike a chord with Russia's politicians had it not been buttressed by reference to Western-like concepts about the general dangers from "cults."[7]

The new 1997 Law on Freedom of Conscience and Religious Associations had the obvious signs of a political compromise.[8] It retained the basic provisions for freedom of religion and nonestablishment, but introduced different statuses for different religious associations. Its preamble favored the role of Russian historical faiths, in particular Eastern Orthodoxy, which arguably received quasi-establishment status. According to the 1997 law, those religious associations that have existed in Russia for no less than 15 years could be registered as *organizations* and enjoy the full rights of a legal entity. Others, with less historical links with Russia, could operate as *groups* whose rights were seriously restricted. The new law also limited the rights of foreigners to proselytize. Finally, in apparent reference to NRMs, the law specifically prohibits the "use of hypnosis," "break-up of the family," and "actions against the Russian State."

The adoption of the 1997 law did not prevent further attempts at legal protection of the "Russian spiritual space." There have been numerous draft laws designed to give more explicit privileges to "traditional religions" and to place more restrictions on other faiths. Furthermore, in contemporary Russia, the operation of constitutional and other legal provisions is profoundly affected by a *legal culture* that tends to "give permission" for political considerations and cultural sentiments to take precedence over legal requirements.[9] The laws introduced during the transitional period have often been perceived as lacking full legitimacy on the grounds that they were against national or regional interests. Thus, many Russian regions have adopted their own laws and regulations that contradict both the 1990 and the 1997 laws.[10] Religious minorities are often dependent on the discretion of local officials who monitor their activities in close cooperation with other regional authorities, including the police and security agencies, and Orthodox diocesan authorities.

NRMs in the Russian "Religious Market"

Western NRMs were only part of the recent influx of "foreign religions" and occurred against the background of a resurgence of Russian historical religions and the emergence of indigenous religious innovation. Current data indicate that the groups that would normally be seen as NRMs make up only a small segment of the Russian religious scene, and it is unlikely that there have been more than 40,000 committed members—about 0.025 percent of the population—at any given time in the 1990s.[11] At the same time, "Charismatic Protestant" groups and "established sects" such as Jehovah's Witnesses and Mormons may have 300,000 members—about 0.2 percent of the population. However, conversion to "foreign" and new indigenous faiths took place against the background of rapid extension of the cultic milieu, particularly in urban areas, which contributed to the impression that the country was being overwhelmed by a tide of "alien religions." Indeed, some semi-official sources spoke of between 3,000,000 and 5,000,000 "sectarians" in Russia.[12] While the total membership in NRMs probably reached a plateau in the mid-1990s, the data clearly indicate increasing diversification of the new religious segment of the Russian scene over the last decade. However, this diversity—about 100 different NRMs and 1,000 local communities in the late 1990s—is still at a lower level than in Britain or the United States.

Opponents of NRMs have found little evidence of antisocial, let alone criminal activities among their members in Russia, and not for lack of trying.[13] If we assume that one of the defining characteristics of NRMs is that they represent the first generation of believers, then in Russia we can expect to find similar features in the behavior of many groups that would not normally be described as NRMs. After the decades of suppression of religious activism, the country has seen simultaneous conversion to a whole spectrum of religions, from the Russian Orthodox Church to Islam and Buddhism. Indeed, complaints resembling those of members of anticult groups have been made about the behavior of new converts to different religions, including traditional faiths. An example is the Moscow Patriarchate's grievances about certain practices of some of its younger priests and converts.[14] However, the allegedly negative effects of participation in newer religious groups are usually attributed to their coercive policies and mental manipulation, whereas explanations for other groups are usually quite different. This may be seen as further evidence that the plausibility of such allegations derives from the perceived lack of legitimacy of certain groups rather than their practices per se.

I would hazard the generalization that over the last decade, imported and indigenous NRMs have undergone a rapid evolution towards *depoliticization* and *deradicalization*. This is probably due, in part, to socio-demographic changes similar to those observed by Eileen Barker in Western societies.[15] However, there may be some additional factors in Russia that reflect the relationship between the emergence of NRMs and the overall systemic change in the country. Thus, the initial radical millenarian message of some indigenous NRMs was mainly concerned with the anticipation of the collapse of the "evil" Soviet regime (the Mother of God Center), or with the anxieties of early post-communism (the Great White Brotherhood, and the Vissarion Movement).[16] Subsequently, with the demise of the Soviet system and the shifts in public concerns in the 1990s, these radical theologies lost their appeal, and this contributed to their rapid evolution towards a more accommodating stance. At the same time, the initial appeal of some imported NRMs and their thrust to contribute to cultural and social transformation were attenuated as the search for *traditional* roots and suspicion of external influences came into prominence. We should also remember that many imported NRMs that had caused anxieties in the West had already undergone considerable accommodative changes before they arrived in Russia. However, some aspects of Russian societal responses to NRMs, and in particular imported ones, did not reflect these changes, but rather political expediency and fears of the unknown.

Unwelcome Guests of Mother Russia

In many ways, the sequence of societal reactions to NRMs in Russia was similar to that in many Western societies and moved from a mixture of welcome, curiosity, and some apprehension to outright hostility. However, even the initial positive response was politically colored, and the arrival of foreign missionaries in the early 1990s was generally welcomed as symbolic of the country's exit from isolation. Also, before that time Russia had relatively little exposure to the negative views embedded in the Western "cult controversies."

The first symptom of the Russian "cult syndrome" was the response to indigenous groups whose emergence was typically attributed to the legacy of the "totalitarian past." This was seen most clearly in the media responses to the Great White Brotherhood.[17] Ironically perhaps, with the flow of negative information from the West—in particular with regard to Aum Shinrikyō and the Solar Temple—and the buildup of the effects of the "negative summary event,"[18] the anticult media became increasingly dominated by the motif of "religious insecurity" supposedly inherent in the open religious marketplace. There was also a considerable polarization in the media along politico-ideological lines, with their anti-Western sections interweaving the antisectarian rhetoric with the general theme of *spiritual aggression against Russia*. In contrast, some liberal (or pro-Western) sections of the media tended to regard anticultism with considerable skepticism as they saw it as playing into the hands of traditionalists.

In some ways the Russian objectors to NRMs were similar to those in the West, and they formed a network connected with their Western counterparts.[19] However, the overarching ideology of Russian anticultism and its mode of operation have some distinctive features.

The current Russian anticult (or antisectarian) ideology sees the issue of "sects" as a matter of national survival in the face of the insecurities of the country's transitional state. One motif is that of *cultural subversion,* which rationalizes fears of foreign proselytizing by portraying it as destroying the "Russian civilization code," or "ethno-religious balance," or "Russian cultural identity."[20] At the same time, the motif of danger from "totalitarian sects" specifically points to NRMs as presenting particular social and political risks; they are portrayed as "mafiosi structures" and "criminal organizations" and even agents of espionage.[21] These two motifs tend to merge into the theme that *sectarianism* undermines Russian statehood and leads to disintegration of the Russian nation. This ideology stems from a combination of cultural assumptions grounded in an idealized vision of past history (Russia versus other "civilizations") and negative representations of NRMs ("totalitarian sects") mainly based on the Western anticult images, put in the framework of contemporary Russian anxieties ("crime," "mafia," and threat of disintegration). It is *political* in its ethos, appealing to the state to take over the antisectarian agenda as its most serious concern.

Two segments of the opposition to NRMs emerged almost simultaneously, reflecting different but rapidly converging parental and ecclesiastical concerns. Like their counterparts in the West, the first Russian parental groups were initially mainly concerned about the effects of conversion to NRMs on individual careers and family relations.[22] The Russian versions of the brainwashing metaphor, such as "coding," "zombification," or "programming," provided simple early explanations, and the overall aim was to "salvage" the converts. At their initial stage, the parental groups found themselves in considerable social isolation, as governmental agencies were reluctant to offer them support and their lack of material resources and relevant experience prevented them from developing their own organizational structures. However, they soon found their concerns heard by the St. Ireneus of Lyon Information Center (SILIC), whose status was determined by its affiliation with a department of the Moscow Patriarchate of the Russian Orthodox Church.

Alexander Dvorkin, an American citizen and a Russian ex-expatriate, was the founder of SILIC and initially provided what the Moscow Patriarchate was looking for—access to Western anticult circles, in particular the Danish Dialogue Centre and its branch in Berlin.[23] Through this cooperation and the affiliation with the Moscow Patriarchate, SILIC legitimized its approach and conveyed the Western anticult images and concepts to the public through the mass media. The Western material was used to construe the "cult issue" in mainly political and "criminal" terms. However, initially the emphasis was on the alleged threat to the fledgling Russian democracy, and the adoption of the anticult policies was presented by Dvorkin and his Western supporters as a necessary part of Russia's integration into the "civilized world."[24]

The Moscow Patriarchate has been generally opposed to proselytizing by other religious groups on the "absolutist" grounds that "Russia is a canonical territory of the Russian Orthodox Church." The church put increasing emphasis on its historical role in the formation of the Russian nation, which justified its present claim to integrate Russian society and to contribute to the restoration of Russian statehood.[25] The corollary of this is the anti-proselytizing stance of the church and its reference to "sectarianism" as a major threat to "the integrity of our consciousness and our national identity." However, the church has so far refrained from a direct appeal for reestablishment, probably for pragmatic reasons. Instead, the church has chosen what can be called the tactics of *reestablishment through denial*, which focuses on appeals to the state for protection on the grounds of the illegitimacy of foreign proselytizing. Undoubtedly, the political and criminal charges against NRMs, disseminated by SILIC on the basis of Western material, provided useful evidence. In this sense, Western anticultism serves as a substitute for theological arguments on the place of ecclesiastical antisectarianism, and as a political argument supporting the church's claim for restoration of its historical role. Indeed, the Missionary Department of the church supports its appeal for the "greater religious security" of Russia by reference to Western experts on "mind control" and the Russian historical tradition of using the secret police to "regulate spiritual affairs."[26]

Interestingly, in recent years some young church theologians have rejected Western anticultism and attempted to elaborate an "authentic" Orthodox countercult approach. For example, Roman Kon' of the Saint-Trinity Spiritual Academy has argued, in somewhat fundamentalist fashion, that the "Protestant" and secular notions of "brainwashing" and "mind control" are not acceptable for the Russian Church, which remains the only repository of Christian truth. For him, membership in "sects" is a heretical free choice and therefore should be regarded as sin.

Some mental health professionals adopted a similar politically colored combination of Russian indigenous and Western rhetoric. In the search for a socio-psychological norm that could replace what was laid down by the Soviet "political religion," they adopted the concept of the authentically Russian psychological makeup formed by the traditional religions. However, the apparent lack of definition of this "traditional norm" is handled by reference to foreign faiths representing deviation from it. In this context, Western anticult concepts of mental manipulation are used opportunistically for rationalizing the psychological mechanism of the asserted deviation from the "traditional norm." However, these concepts proved unnecessary for some Russian anticult psychiatrists who interpret and treat "sectarian deviations" in the light of Russian Orthodox teachings.[27] Others explain conversion to foreign faiths by reference to the concept of socially induced "delusion" which used to be routinely employed by Soviet punitive psychiatry.[28] All these perspectives tend to enter the political master narrative of Russian anticultism. Thus, the publications of the leading Russian institution for forensic psychiatry cite Western anticult sources to corroborate its general claim that NRMs are in fact "criminal formations" that destroy Russian "national spirituality" and the "spiritual symphony" between the "traditional religions and the State," and even "engage in espionage."[29]

It is worth considering the implications of the differences in the cross-cultural usage of the concepts of coercive mental manipulation by NRMs. In the West, and in particular in the United States, these concepts originally gained credibility during the Cold War; "mental manipulation" was used as a plausible explanation for the communist "mass indoctrination." The key question concerning conversion to NRMs was formulated in a similar fashion as that of how an individual could possibly give up the crucial human capacity for and right to free choice.[30] The mental manipulation discourse was central for opposition to NRMs. In contrast, in the

Russian settings, the references to the concepts of mental manipulation arise not so much from general cultural preoccupation with free choice, but from the political intention to use them as forensic evidence to delegitimize deviation from *the tradition*. The Western concepts that were originally developed to show the abnormality of conversion to specific NRMs proved their versatility in application to a wider range of minority faiths that were perceived as legitimate in the Western settings but are assumed to be subversive in the Russian situation.

The Russian anticult ideology was finally shaped and gathered momentum in the mid-1990s following the shifts in Russian politics towards integration and traditional understanding of nationhood. The increasing emphasis on the necessity for historically rooted Russian statehood gave rise to a confluence of interests between the Russian Orthodox Church and state agencies. At the same time, the rhetoric of "spiritual aggression" was attuned to the increasing preoccupation with issues of national security, which was further highlighted by the continuing Chechen war and its frequent association with the general threat of imported "Islamic radicalism" (see below).

Both professed allegiance to historical religions and a negative attitude towards "sects" became valuable resources for claiming political legitimacy. Antisectarian and pro-Orthodox statements were included in a series of agreements between certain governmental bodies and the Russian Orthodox Church, and similar statements were contained in political manifestos of the major political blocks during the 1995 parliamentary and 1996 presidential campaigns. The *Doctrine of National Security* (2000) makes a point about "spiritual security," which is spelled out as support for "traditional religions" and counteracting "spiritual aggression." Further, the recent Law on Extremism (2002) has been debated since 2000 and its eventual adoption was facilitated by the events of September 11. It defines political extremism so broadly that it can easily capture any controversial religion.

However, the stridency and even grossness of the official antisectarian rhetoric has not yet been translated into a consistent policy. There remains a degree of pragmatism in relation to sects as traditionalism is unlikely to be seen as the sole source of political legitimacy in the new Russia. The federal and regional authorities have been under continuous internal and external pressure to comply with their constitutional and international obligations. In the light of these pressures, the Constitutional Court decided in November 1999 that the "15-year rule" on the length of existence in Russia does not apply to the associations that were registered under the 1990 law. Nevertheless, the negative image of "sects" that lump together disparate religious minorities continues to tap into powerful trends in Russian politics. External political pressure for freedom of religion is counterbalanced by the antisectarian caveats embedded in the resolutions of the European Parliament and the Council of Europe and the anticult policies of some Western governments.[31] Indeed, this decision of the Constitutional Court refers to these resolutions in justification of the right of the state to

> prohibit legalization of sects which violate the rights of the individual and practice illegal and criminal activities, as well as to prohibit missionary activity (including the problem of proselytizing), if it is accompanied by psychological pressure or threat of violence.[32]

Finally, the negative assumptions about "sects" have encouraged several legal actions against certain NRMs, mostly brought by parental anticult committees. Parental grievances were usually supported by recycled evidence and concepts from Western anticult literature and the general antisectarian rhetoric. Considering the lack of autonomy within the Russian legal system, the judiciary in these cases characteristically found themselves torn between the apparent lack of what would normally be seen as evidence and considerable social and political pressure.[33] While their outcomes have varied, these cases characteristically lasted for a long period of time, with the judiciary delaying their decisions. Thus the case against the Moscow congregation of Jehovah's Witnesses has been pending since 1998, and so far has produced no evidence for the antisocial activities of which the group was accused.[34]

Controversies over "Islamic Radicalism" in Russia

Similar to its reactions to NRMs, Russia's policies towards "Islamic revival" reveal many of the dilemmas, insecurities, and uncertainties of the post-communist approach to religion, much of which Russia shares with the rest of the world. On the other hand, the similarities with reactions to NRMs become even more pronounced if we consider the ways in which generalizations are made in relation to manifestations of Islam.

According to different estimates, ethnic Muslims constitute between 12 and 17 million people, or between 8 and 12 percent of the population. They constitute the majority in seven of Russia's "autonomous republics" that are located in the parts of Russia that are crucial economically, such as Tatarstan and Bashkortostan in the Volga area, or geopolitically, in particular Chechnya and Dagestan in the Northern Caucasus. In addition, the recent migration of ethnic Muslims from the devastated or deprived areas of the Caucasus has considerably changed the ethnic composition of some of Russia's urban areas, with around one million estimated ethnic Muslims now living in Moscow alone.

These developments may appear to be a justification for geopolitical anxieties, if combined with manifestations of "Islamic revival" and "Islamist terrorism" in Chechnya and with its real and alleged connections with "international Islamist networks." This language alone may mislead us into overlooking what Russia's Muslims have in common with the rest of the country as well as the differences and rifts within Russia's Muslim population itself.

The post-communist "Islamic revival" has much in common with the restoration of ethno-religious links among Russia's non-Muslim ethnic groups. Despite the increased prominence of these links, most of Russia's Muslims remain secular in their orientation and lifestyle and aware of their Russian national as well as ethnic identity.[35]

On the other hand, while sharing the same world religion and common aspects of history, Muslim ethnic minorities differ in the kind of Islam that survived with them, the centrality of the religion to their ethnic identity, and its involvement in current ethnopolitics.[36] Post-communist ethno-religious entrepreneurs and ethno-political elites have used the Islamic faith in their endeavor to replace or re-legitimize the local ruling clans of the Soviet period. Depending on local issues, this ranged from attempts to promote a moderate, secular-friendly, "European Islam" in Tatarstan to the appeal to *sharia* and subsequently radical Islamism in war-ridden Chechnya. Elsewhere, Bashkir ethno-nationalists apparently have more grievances against their Tatar co-believers than against the Russians. This is likely because the Bashkirs are only the third largest ethnic group in their "titular" republic, and an appeal to Islam would not reinforce the boundaries between them and the Tatars. In Dagestan, Islam has been more vibrant than in any other part of Russia and at some points of history was closely linked to resistance to Russian expansion. Nevertheless, the shared religion has not overridden the differences between the republic's 30 or so ethnic groups.

We are likely to find out more about what Russia's Muslims have in common if we adopt a generational viewpoint. I would risk the generalization, in an ideo-typical fashion, that in the post-communist era the most active Muslims are those who belong to the last Soviet and the first post-Soviet generations, but there are considerable differences between them. The last Soviet generation embarked on restoration of the traditional ethno-religious links and institutional revival of Islam—rebuilding mosques, publishing books, and training teachers. Many of them, for example Islamic activists in Tatarstan and Moscow or the Sufi *Young Imams* (or *Tariqatists*) in Dagestan, also challenged and eventually destroyed the legacy of the overcentralized administrative structure of Soviet Islam. A bitter rivalry ensued among the new Islamic leaders, both within and across ethnic boundaries.[37] Failing to achieve unity within Russia, this generation wanted to restore their links with the *umma*—the worldwide Muslim community. Finally, they brought the issue of *Muslim identity* into the Russian political arena, in many ways living *for* and *from* their politics of identity.

For the first post-Soviet generation of active believers, the issue of their Muslim identity was mainly about how to live it out, how to make sense of it in the post-Soviet reality of social insecurity, injustice, ubiquitous corruption, and crime on the one hand, and of incipient Western consumerism on the other. In a variety of ways and circumstances, they came to seek an Islam that could serve as a basis for an "authentic" way of individual and social transformation, something the socially inept Islam of the "forgotten" Soviet Muslims was unable to provide. They often saw the new religious leaders as compromising with the post-communist realities and seeking to restore a narrow, ethnically-based traditional Islam. This post-Soviet generation's search for an "authentic" Islam took a variety of forms, from some Muslim women's return to what they saw as a traditional lifestyle, to an interpretation of *jihad* in politically extremist ways. In some cases, this search found an affinity with, and was even ideologically shaped by, what became known as *Salafi* Islam. In reality, however, this umbrella term referred to a variety of versions of the faith spread by Muslim missionaries from abroad, including Saudi Arabia, Syria, Egypt, and Turkey, and by young Russian Muslims returning from training in these countries.

Salafi groups differ in their interpretation of the religion, degree of zeal, and political orientations, but above all in the kind of world that they seek to change. In Tatarstan in the 1990s, there were a few *madrassas* that sought to teach *Salafi* interpretations of Islam. In Mordovia, a non-Muslim republic with large Tatar enclaves, some vigorous *imams* in the village of Belozerye attempted to introduce aspects of *sharia* as a way of solving many local social problems. In Dagestan, *Salafi* groups were strongly affected by their rivalry with the traditionalist Sufi *Tariqatists* and by the war in neighboring Chechnya. In some extreme cases, young converts from different parts of Russia who had embraced the radical political interpretations of *jihad* found a battleground for their beliefs in Chechnya and Afghanistan.

Similarly, the dynamics of these groups have differed both across and within the regions. In fact, much research on the ground is needed to understand why these groups have either moderated (as in Belozerye) or radicalized (like some groups in Dagestan) over time. What is clear, however, is that a single-factor approach would not get us closer to a reliable answer, whether we focus on ideology, external influence (such as "Islamist networks"), or historical contingencies. Instead we need to look at all these and many other factors. In particular, the dire economic conditions and abject poverty in many parts of the Northern Caucasus and elsewhere in Russia can be a powerful radicalizing factor. What is also obvious is that both official reactions and mass media responses play a considerable role.

The Russian mass media was obsessed with the "Islamic threat" long before September 11. This obsession first surfaced in 1995–96 as the Islamic theme began to unfold in the war in Chechnya. It acquired further negative overtones after a series of unsolved bombings in Moscow and Volgodonsk in 1999 and reached its peak in the wake of September 11. Almost any expression of Islamic identity or religion-related claims came to be grafted onto the theme of Islamic terrorism. To describe this kind of Islam, the Russian media used the code word "Wahhabism," revealing the perception that "Russian Islam" was being overtaken by alien, "fundamentalist," Middle Eastern Islam.

One example will suffice. Since 1998, a group of Muslim women in Tatarstan have demanded that they should be allowed to cover their hair for passport photographs. After successive federal governments had alternated between positive and negative decisions, the issue eventually reached the law courts.[38] Commenting on the case, one of the popular newspapers apparently voiced both official and unofficial apprehension by saying:

> From this innocuous . . . request to cover the head for a passport photograph . . . they will proceed to demand—also through the courts—that the school curriculum be changed according to the Koran. . . . In *madrassa* they will begin to train Chechen terrorists. . . . And afterwards we won't be far away from another September 11.[39]

The hot debates in the Russian media reflected the polarization of society over what was presented as the issue of Islam. One extreme view, coming from a lapsed ethnic Muslim, demanded that "the world community must declare Islam a religion *non grata*." This was contested on the grounds that fundamentalist currents in Islam might present a challenge to the secular state, but they were also subject to evolution in the spectrum between democracy and extremism.[40]

To some extent, federal and regional responses to "Islamic radicalism" were also driven by pragmatic considerations, including the complexities of Russia's ethnopolitics. The regional policies seem to have sought to retain the links with and support from moderate Muslim groups, while outlawing what they saw as radicals. The authorities in Tatarstan have closed down all of the small number of *Salafi* groups. The latest republican law on religion bans any group outside the jurisdiction of the official Administration of the Muslims of Tatarstan and introduces licensing of preachers from abroad. A similar law has been adopted in Dagestan in the wake of a raid by Chechen rebels, supported by some local "Islamist radicals" (August–September 1999). The law covered not only radical—or, better, radicalized—Dagestani *Salafi* groups, but also moderate ones. In both republics, the official Islamic bodies (in Dagestan dominated by Sufi *Tariqatists)* supported these secular policies on the grounds that the local "extremist" groups were implantations of "alien" Islam from outside these regions.

The federal authorities face even more difficult dilemmas, given the factors mentioned at the beginning of this section. Despite occasional pejorative remarks, the government, including the president, has refrained from official anti-Islamic campaigns. However, the persistent official reference to the Chechen war as resulting predominantly from involvement of "international Islamic terrorists" provides a powerful source of anti-Islamic sentiments. Following September 11, the Russian government has persistently pointed to the Chechen war as Russia's contribution to the "war on international terrorism" declared by the Bush administration. In a paradoxical sense, the post-communist politics of common Muslim identity pursued by some Islamic activists in Russia have been met with official fears about this identity, which seems implicit in the following comment by President Putin in 2001:

> If extremist forces manage to get a hold in the Caucasus, this infection may spread up the Volga River, spread to other republics, and we either face the full Islamization of Russia, or we will have to agree to Russia's division into several independent states.[41]

These comments were compounded by widespread hostility towards migrants and ethnic minorities whose racial features have provoked several attacks by racist youth gangs in Russian cities as well as harassment by the police. The chain of association—migrant-Islam-terrorism—has been used as an additional justification for such actions. On the official side, after the recent terrorist act in a Moscow theater, the governor of the Moscow region decided to deport all migrants from Central Asia, an action that was eventually revoked and up to now has not become a trend. In the Volga Federal District, a different way of dealing with "alien Islam" has been suggested by young liberal reformers, who have come up with an ambitious project to promote, mainly through the educational system, a "Russian Islam" that is moderate, secular, and loyal to the Russian authorities. One wonders what kind of unintended consequences this attempt at social engineering may give rise to.

In these circumstances, Russia's Muslims have mixed feelings related to religious aspects of their identity and may face difficult choices. Already on September 12, 2001, while condemning the terror in New York, Talgat Tadjuddin, the Chief Mufti of the Central Spiritual Administration of Russia, commented, "America has attempted to serve as a world policeman. They are like pharaohs—boastful and arrogant, and seeking to act as if they were masters of the world."[42]

Some of Russia's Islamic activists shared the view of some of their co-religionists elsewhere that September 11 was the result of a Zionist-American conspiracy.[43] At the same time, after September 11, the label "Wahhabi terrorist" has been widely used by some rival Islamic leaders to delegitimize each other. However, in the complex realities of a post-atheist society, with its ethnopolitics, and post-September 11 contingencies, the main difficulties may be experienced by those Muslims for whom their faith has become a way of expressing their identity, as they can be found guilty of simply attempting to be what they feel they are.

Conclusion

The unfinished story of the present spiral of Russian modernization prompts caution against too definitive conclusions. Antisectarianism seems to have a useful *political* function in a society that lacks shared elements of national identity but has a tradition of identifying itself negatively through contrast with the West and the enemy within.[44] It can also be argued that part of the challenge stems from the country's general lack of experience in negotiating different interests in a society which has a multitude of legitimate ways of social expression, be this in religion, politics, or the economy. The emergence of a diversity of new religious phenomena requires a language to describe, concepts to interpret, and means to handle it. In this sense, the increasing familiarity with the Western social scientific approach to NRMs has contributed to a greater understanding of NRMs in Russia in recent years.[45] However, some aspects of the present treatment of NRMs are the results of Russia's exposure to Western "cult controversies." It can be argued that the anticult concepts tend to encourage a restrictive approach to legitimate religious expression and to hinder pluralistic accommodation. Russia's treatment of religious minorities has also provided a test for the country's ability to cope with the new variety of religious identities, in particular when forging these identities has controversial outcomes, or becomes associated with politically sensitive issues.

Notes

1. For a useful discussion of the origins of this ideology, see G. Hosking, "The Russian National Myth Repudiated," in *Myth and Nationhood*, eds. G. Hosking and G. Schoplin (London: Hurst and Company, 1995).
2. This notion of toleration was quite different from the modern understanding of tolerance. It referred to the right to practice religion as part of ethnic identity, but by no means to proselytize among the Russians, which was a criminal offence.
3. See D. Christian, *Imperial and Soviet Russia: Power, Privilege and Challenge of Modernity* (London: Macmillan Press, 1997).

4. See L. Greenfeld, *Nationalism: Five Roads to Modernity* (Cambridge, MA: Harvard University Press, 1992), 86–7, 222–23.

5. Ethnic Russians constituted only 43 percent of the population, although many other major ethnic groups in the Empire were also Russian Orthodox, mainly a result of Russian Orthodox missionary efforts.

6. Christel Lane, *The Rites and Rulers: Ritual in Industrial Society—the Soviet Case* (Cambridge, U.K.: Cambridge University Press, 1981).

7. See Marat Shterin and James Richardson, "Effects of the Western Anti-cult Movement on Development of Laws Concerning Religion in Post-Communist Russia," *Journal of Religion and State* 42 (2000): 247–71.

8. For a detailed discussion of the 1997 law, see C. Durham, Jr. and L. Homer, "Russia's 1997 Law on Freedom of Conscience and Religious Associations: An Analytical Appraisal," *Emory Law Review* 12 (1998): 101–246.

9. For fuller discussion, see Marat Shterin, "Legislating on Religion in the Face of Uncertainty," in *Law and Informal Practices in Post-Communist Society*, eds. J. Gallighan and M.Kurkchiyan (Oxford: Oxford University Press, 2002), 113–33.

10. See L. Homer and L. Uzell, "Federal and Provincial Religious Freedom Laws in Russia: A Struggle for and against Federalism and the Rule of Law," *Emory Law Review* 12 (1998): 247–312; and Marat Shterin and James Richardson, "Local Laws on Religion in Russia: Precursors of Russia's National Law," *Journal of Church and State* 40 (1998): 319–42.

11. This percentage is very similar to that estimated by James Beckford in 1985 with respect to Britain; see James Beckford, *Cult Controversies: The Societal Response to New Religious Movements* (London: Tavistock, 1985), 244. I justified my estimate for Russia in M. Shterin, "New Religious Movements in Russia in the 1990s," in *Religious Transition in Russia*, ed. M. Kotiranta (Helsinki: Alexander Institute, 2000), 185–88.

12. For example, *Report of the Ministry of Internal Affairs of the Russian Federation*, 23 October 1996.

13. Since 1997 the Office of the General Prosecutor of the Russian Federation has produced several letters intended to show the criminal nature of sectarianism. However, these documents have consistently failed to produce any evidence for this. Thus, according to the letter of March 29, 1997, there had been seven criminal investigations of members of NRMs, in which only one resulted in a criminal conviction. This conviction was later appealed and overturned.

14. The Holy Synod of the Russian Orthodox Church (*Zhurnal (Journal)* N 114, 29 December 1998) expressed its concern over "increasing cases of abuse" by some priests and monks. In particular, the practice of *mladostarchestvo* was criticized (but not named), whereby lay or religious clergy exercise a form of "charismatic authority" over the lives of their followers, including their family relations, financial matters, medical treatment, employment, and education.

15. Eileen Barker, "Plus ça change. . . ," *Social Compass* 42 (1995): 165–80.

16. It is interesting to note that in the early theologies of the Russian indigenous NRMs the Russia-centric and messianic overtones were more pronounced than in the general cultural ambience of the early 1990s, but were in tune with what was quite common within the Russian Orthodox Church.

17. See E. Borenstein, "Articles of Faith: the Media Response to Maria Devi Christos," *Religion* 25 (1995): 249–66.

18. James Beckford defines this as a "practice of creating continuity between episodic . . . stories by adding a capsule summary of the negative features of the phenomenon which is in focus." See James Beckford, "The Mass Media and New Religious Movements," in *New Religious Movements: Challenge and Response*, eds. Bryan Wilson and J. Cresswell (London and New York: Routledge, 1999), 103–19.

19. See Shterin and Richardson, "Effects of the Western Anti-cult Movement."

20. See L. Levinson and V. Polosin, *Belaya Kniga (The White Book)* (Moscow: Allegro, 1998).

21. See, for example, A. Dvorkin, *10 Voprosov Naviazchivomu Neznakomtsu: posobie dlia tekh, kto ne khochet byt' zaverbovannym (Ten Questions to the Intrusive Stranger: A Manual for Those Who Do Not Wish to Be Recruited)* (Moscow: Otdel Religioznogo Obrazovania Moskovskogo Patriarkhata, 1995).

22. The first anticult parental groups were formed in 1992 in Moscow (The Committee for Salvation of Youth from Totalitarian Sects) and St. Petersburg (The Committee for the Defence of the Individual and Family).

23. See Shterin and Richardson, "Effects of the Western Anti-cult Movement."
24. See, for example, Pastor Gandow's statement in the Russian Duma in 1995, quoted in Shterin and Richardson, "Effects of the Western Anti-cult Movement."
25. See, for example, *Vsemirnyi Russkiy Sobor* (*The World Russian Council*) (Moscow, 1995).
26. *Novye Religioznye Organzatsii Rossii Destructivnogo and Okkultnogo Kharaktera* (*Russia's New Religious Organizations of Destructive and Occult Character*) (Belgorod: Missionerski Otdel Moskovskogo Patriarkhata, 1997).
27. One of the leading psychiatric centers in Moscow requires a reference letter from an Orthodox priest for treatment of disorders allegedly caused by "cult involvement."
28. Undoubtedly, there is a great deal of continuation between Soviet punitive psychiatry and the present involvement of some Russian psychiatrists in the antisectarian struggle. The fact that the two main anticult experts continue to work for the Institute of Forensic Psychiatry, which was notorious for its involvement in suppression of Soviet dissidents, including religious activists, is suggestive.
29. F. Kondratiev, et al., *Mediko-Sotsial'nye Posedstvija Deiatel'nosti Totalitarnykh Sect: Analytichiskiy Obzor* (*Medico-Social Consequences of the Activities of Totalitarian Sects: An Analytical Overview*) (Moscow: Gosudarstvennyi Nauchno-Issledovatel'skiy Institut im. V.P. Serbskogo, 1998).
30. D. Anthony, "Pseudoscience and Minority Religions: An Evaluation of the Brainwashing Theories of Jean-Marie Abgrall," *Social Justice Research* 12 (1999): 421–56.
31. See Shterin and Richardson, "Effects of the Western Anti-cult Movement."
32. The full decision of the Constitutional Court on 23 November 1999 can be found at www.stetson.edu/~psteeves/relnews/9911a.html#07 (accessed 14 March 2003).
33. On the treatment of NRMs within different legal systems, see James Richardson, "Religion, Law and Social Control," in *Frontier Religion in the Public Sphere*, ed. P. Côté (Ottawa: University of Ottawa Press, 2000); see also, James Richardson and Marat Shterin, "Minority Religions and Social Justice in Russian Courts: An Analysis of Recent Cases," *Social Justice Research* 12 (1999): 393–408.
34. Characteristically, the prosecutor in that case insisted that the Jehovah's Witnesses' teachings are socially damaging in themselves as they destroy the mentality of the Russians. See G. Krylova, "The Jehovah's Witnesses Case in Moscow," a paper presented at CESNUR-99, Bryn Athyn, Pennsylvania, June 1999.
35. See Leokadia Drobizheva, ed., *Sotsial'naya i Kulturnaya Distantsii* [*Social and Cultural Distance*] (Moscow: Institut Sotsiologii, 1998), 111–151, 229–49, 271–89.
36. See Galina Yemelianova, *Russia and Islam: A Historical Survey* (London: Palgrave, 2002), 137–65.
37. See Alexei Malashenko, *Islamskoe Vozrozhdenie v Sovremennoi Rossii* [*The Islamic Revival in Contemporary Russia*] (Moscow: Carnegie Center, 1998).
38. On March 5, 2002, the Supreme Court upheld the earlier decision of the Tatarstan Republican Court that the ban imposed by the Ministry of Internal Affairs was justifiable. However, on May 15, 2003, the same court overturned its own earlier decision and upheld the demand of the Muslim women. Among other things, this episode exposes much of the general uncertainty in Russia about treatment of religious minorities.
39. *Izvestia*, 3 August 2002.
40. See the debate in *Izvestia*, 5 November 2002 and 19 November 2002.
41. UPI, 5 September 2002.
42. Reported by www.newsru.com, 12 September 2001.
43. See, e.g., *Kommersant*, 19 September 2001.
44. An interesting attempt to present a uniting national idea was Nikita Mikhalkov's recent film *The Barber of Siberia* (1999), which offered a highly idealized version of the Russian past dominated by Orthodox symbolism. However, even this image was constructed through references to the subversive influence of Western culture and enemies within (godless Russian revolutionaries).
45. Some Western scholars, in particular Eileen Barker and James Richardson, have visited Russia personally, and an increasing number of Russian scholars have gained access to Western scholarly approaches to NRMs through literature and personal contacts. Cole Durham of Brigham Young University has made a particularly substantial contribution to understanding by Russian academics and officials of scientific and legal treatment of NRMs in the West.

CHAPTER 8

New Religious Minorities in the Baltic States

SOLVEIGA KRUMINA-KONKOVA

Although Estonia, Latvia, and Lithuania are united by their common past under the Soviet regime, the religious situation is quite different in these three Baltic States today. The first difference relates to the religious demography in each country.

In Estonia, there are over 177,230 members of the Estonian Evangelical Lutheran Church, over 100,000 members of the Russian Orthodox Church (subordinated to the Moscow Patriarchate [EOCMP]), 18,000 members of the Estonian Apostolic Orthodox Church (EAOC),[1] and over 5,000 members of the Union of Estonian Old Believer congregations. The majority of believers are Lutherans and Orthodox. Nonetheless, there are also communities of Baptist (about 6,100 members), Methodist (about 2,000 members), Roman Catholic (about 3,500 members), and other Christian denominations. Among new religious minorities in Estonia, the Union of Jehovah's Witnesses (about 3,900 members), the Union of Estonian Evangelistic Christian Pentecostal Congregations (about 2,500 members), the Union of Estonian Full Gospel Congregations (about 1,000 members), and the Union of Estonian Christian Free Congregations (about 1,000 members) are the most active.[2] There is a small Jewish community with 2,500 members. There are also communities of Muslims, Buddhists, and many other denominations and faiths; however, each of these minority faiths has fewer than 6,000 adherents.[3]

Religious life in contemporary Latvia could be characterized by the co-existence of five equally strong Christian confessions that claim to represent the priority of Christian tradition in the life of Latvian society and are regarded by public opinion as the traditional confessions in Latvia. As of the beginning of 2002, these churches have provided the following estimates of church membership to the Latvian Ministry of Justice: about 400,000 Latvian Evangelical Lutheran believers, about 500,000 Roman Catholic believers, about 300,000 Orthodox believers, about 70,000 Old Believers, and about 6,000 Baptists.[4] These Christian denominations have endured historical vicissitudes for several centuries. They have demonstrated that their teachings and activities do not contradict Latvian norms of morality. The Jewish community (about 6,000 members) has also been accepted as a traditional denomination similar to the above-mentioned Christian confessions in Latvia. Although Latvian legislation has not officially defined what religions are recognized as *traditional* religions, the Law on Religious Organizations prescribes that in public schools religion may be taught on a voluntary basis only by representatives of the Evangelical Lutheran, Roman Catholic, Orthodox, Old Believer, Baptist, and Jewish religious communities.[5] Nontraditional denominations may provide religious education in private schools only.

On November 8, 2000, Latvian Justice Minister Ingrida Labucka and Apostolic Nuncio to the Baltic states Erwin Josef Ender signed an agreement between Latvia and the Vatican. The pact replaced the pre-World War II Concordat that was not implemented after the restoration of independence in 1991. In the new agreement, Latvia also guaranteed the inviolability of places of worship and respect for the secrecy of confession. The most controversial part of the document is the guarantee of restitution of property formerly owned by the Catholic Church. To avoid criticism that the Catholic Church was given special privileges, the Law on Religious Organizations has been amended to permit churches to sign agreements similar to the one between the state and traditional religions in Latvia. Following long debate the agreement between Roman Catholics and the state was ratified by the Latvian Parliament in September 2002.[6]

Jehovah's Witnesses (over 2,000 members), charismatic Christian congregations (over 20,000 members, although precise figures are not available) such as "Jauna Paaudze" (The New Generation) and "Prieka Vests" (Message of Joy), Pentecostals (about 6,000, although precise figures are not available), the New Apostolic Church of North Rhine-Westphalia (about 1,000 members), the Church of Jesus Christ of Latter-Day Saints (about 500 active members), Muslims (about 300 members), and the International Society for Krishna Consciousness (about 500 active members) are among the more active new religious minorities in Latvia.[7]

In Lithuania, the current religious situation is marked by the dominance of the Roman Catholic Church. In 1999, around 70 percent (3,210,000 members) of the entire population belonged to this church. In 2001, about 79 percent of the inhabitants considered themselves to be Roman Catholics. The second largest denomination was the Russian Orthodox Church with 141,000 members, and the third largest was the Old Believers with 27,000 members. An estimated 19,500 Lutherans were concentrated in the southwest. The Evangelical Reformed community had about 7,000 members. The Jewish community numbered about 4,000 members. Five Sunni Muslim communities numbered about 2,700 members. The New Apostolic Church (about 5,600 members), the Word of Faith movement (about 2,800 members), Jehovah's Witnesses (about 2,200 members), Pentecostals (about 1,800 members), Mormons (about 450 members) and the International Society for Krishna Consciousness (about 300 members) are among the more active new religious minorities. According to the Ministry of Justice, a total of 967 traditional and 184 nontraditional religious associations and communities are registered.[8]

In common with religious demography, the legislation governing relations between religious organizations and the state in the Baltic countries has both similarities and differences. Legislative acts concerning religions have two common elements in all three countries, namely, by the constitution the church is separated from the state, and there is no state religion. Moreover, there is a division into traditional and nontraditional religions in all three states. Thus, in Lithuania, according to Article 5 of the Law on Religious Communities and Associations adopted by the Seimas (Parliament) in 1995, nine religious communities, namely, Latin Rite Catholics, Greek Rite Catholics, Evangelical Lutherans, Evangelical Reformers, Orthodox, Old Believers, Jews, Sunni Muslims, and Karaites have been declared "traditional" religions. These communities do not have to pay social and health insurance for clergy and other employees; they can register marriages; they have the right to teach religion in state schools and buy land to build churches (other communities may rent it). Only their clergy and theological students are exempt from military service, and only their top religious leaders are eligible for diplomatic passports. They also may have military chaplains. In addition, they have the right to establish subsidiary institutions.[9]

As a consequence, "since in the law only the nine traditional religious communities were *recognized* by the state, the 'traditional' even in the later legislation became synonymous with 'recognized,' and the 'other' with nonrecognized, nontraditional, even 'sectarian' or destructive."[10]

On April 18, 2002, the Interior Ministry of Estonia finally registered the Estonian branch of the Russian Orthodox Church (subordinated to the

Moscow Patriarchate), ending a legal wrangle that began in 1993. The Interior Ministry has registered the statute of the Estonian Orthodox Church, and church representatives have collected the registration certificates. Although the question of property remains unresolved, the church will now be able to carry out functions previously denied to it.

With regard to the situation of new religious minorities, the constitutions of all three Baltic States build on Articles 8 and 9 of the Convention for the Protection of Human Rights and Fundamental Freedoms and declare that every individual has the freedom of conscience, religion, and thought. Everyone is free to profess their religion if they do not break the law. In the other legislation on religious organizations, the international understanding is also generally followed. At the same time, every Baltic state offers its specific model for the registration of new religious communities. These models reflect the individuality of the religious situation in these countries. Thus, in Estonia the 1993 Law on Churches and Religious Organizations requires all religious organizations to have at least twelve members and to be registered with the Interior Ministry and the Board of Religion. Leaders of religious organizations must be citizens with at least five years of residence in Estonia.[11] In June 2001, the Estonian Parliament adopted a revised law that contained a provision barring the registry of any church or union of congregations whose permanent or temporary administrative or economic management is performed by a leader or institution situated outside Estonia. Former President of Estonia Lennert Meri refused to promulgate the law, declaring, in part, that it constituted an intrusion into the autonomous sphere of religious institutions. Nevertheless, the Estonian Parliament adopted unanimously a revised law with amendments, which removed the earlier disputed provision in February 2002. On February 27, 2002, President Arnold Ruutel promulgated the law. It was scheduled to take effect on July 1, 2002.[12] Soon after this adoption the Estonian Interior Ministry rejected a second application by the Satanists to register as a religious organization. The Religious Affairs Department of this ministry returned the registration documents as they did not comply with the legal requirements.

Although the Latvian Government does not require the registration of religious groups, according to the Law on Religious Organizations, any ten citizens or permanent residents over the age of eighteen may apply to register a church. Congregations functioning in the country for the first time that do not belong to a church association already registered must re-register each year for ten years so that their loyalty to the state of Latvia and conformity to legislative regulations can be observed.[13] 82 congregations are undergoing this temporary registration process now. (Nine congregations that have separated themselves from the Evangelical Lutheran

Church and represent the Confessional Lutheran Church, or so-called Augsburg Confession, are among them).[14]

In Latvia, ten or more congregations of the same denomination that have permanent registration status may form a religious association. A decision to register a church is made by the Minister of Justice. Problems may arise because the Law on Religious Organizations does not permit simultaneous registration of more than one religious union (church) in a single confession. Therefore, the government cannot register any splinter groups, such as the Latvian Free Orthodox Church or a separate Old Believers group. In addition, Clause 11, Paragraph 3 of the Law on Religious Organizations provides that religious organizations shall not be registered "if their activities endanger national security, public harmony and order, or health and morals of other people, if they propagate religious intolerance and hostility; or if other of their activities contradict the Republic of Latvia Satversme (Constitution) and legislation."[15] As a consequence of this clause and because of serious opposition from the Latvian Doctors Association, the Christian Science Church was refused registration five times (on May 20, 1997; March 26, 1999; April 11, 2001; March 4, 2002, and June 6, 2002). Finally, it obtained registration on October 16, 2002.

The Latvian Law on Religious Organizations covers only registration of confessions. Several movements (the Sathya Sai Baba movement, for example) do not consider themselves as religious but rather as spiritual movements, which are not mentioned in the law. Lack of legal status can cause difficulties for such movements when it comes to the rental of premises and other matters.

In Lithuania, according to Article 11 of the Law on Religious Communities and Associations, nontraditional religious communities have to present an application, a founding statement signed by no less than fifteen members, and a description of their teaching and its aims to the Ministry of Justice. The ministry has to review the documents within six months.[16] Since these regulations were enacted, the Ministry of Justice has turned down two applications, those of the Osho Ojas Meditation Center and the Lithuanian Pagans Community (Old Sorcerer). In 1995, the Old Sorcerer community brought a case against the Ministry of Justice over registration, which it lost in the spring of 2002. The authorities concluded that both groups were nonreligious. With regard to the first case, the official statement claims that "Osho Meditation Center statutes did not present recognizable marks of the religious nature of the organization. The demand for the members to present an AIDS certificate, which would be valid for three months, could indicate activities that violate the morals of society, and the description of practice of 'therapy' was considered to be a possible violation of the Law on Health Care, since Osho Center did not possess the license. Osho Meditation Center was granted an appeal of this decision by the court, but it has not undertaken this as yet."[17]

In a society in which when the majority of individuals and all traditional religions are more or less critical of the growth of new religious minorities, the circumspection of the state is justifiable. Representatives of the state are conscious of the fact that the state assumes certain responsibilities and gives known guarantees for every nontraditional or new religious minority that is officially recognized by the process of registration. Therefore, state officials try to avoid foreseeable conflicts by setting strict criteria for official registration.

I have already mentioned the problems of Christian Scientists in Latvia. The same situation existed with the Jehovah's Witnesses in Latvia several years ago. This religion has for some time attracted a great deal of public attention. They submitted their application to the Religious Affairs Department of the Ministry of Justice in 1993. After much correspondence, the Ministry of Justice announced that, according to the then existing legislation of the Republic of Latvia, the registration of Jehovah' s Witnesses would be postponed for three years. In 1995, correspondence with the Religious Affairs Department was resumed to find out whether the Jehovah's Witnesses could be regarded as a new or an old religion in Latvia. The issue was brought before the Court of Zemgale Borough of Riga, which ruled on May 26, 1995, that "Jehovah's Witnesses started their activities in Latvia in 1933 under the name "International Society of Bible Researchers."[18] However, the Supreme Court of the Republic of Latvia overruled the judgment of the Court of Zemgale Borough on June 28, 1995.[19] Three congregations of Jehovah's Witnesses were registered in 1998 for a year only. By February 2000, the Ministry of Justice had registered eleven congregations of Jehovah's Witnesses.[20] However, Jehovah's Witnesses as well as other new religious minorities must reregister every year for the next ten years.

In reality, the greatest problem for the Jehovah's Witnesses relates to enrollment for military service. On February 27, 1997, the Law on Compulsory Military Service came into force. It did not provide for any alternative service, and the Jehovah's Witnesses' youths that had reached the age of conscription faced difficulties. For example, Roman Nemiro and Vladimir Gamayunov were conscripted into the standing army. Both of them lodged complaints with the Court of the Vidzeme municipality of Riga concerning the state's unlawful action, namely its decision to recruit them into military service in spite of the Commission of the Military Conscription Office's knowledge that their religious conviction forbids them to perform military service. Moreover, Gamayunov based his claims to exemption on the fact that he was a clergyman. The court rejected both complaints.[21] On

August 10, 2000, the Minister of Defense issued an announcement concerning its position on the question of alternative service. It also invited the Parliament, the government, and non-governmental organizations to come forth with their suggestions and comments on this matter.[22] The third draft of the Law on Alternative Service was accepted by the Parliament on May 30, 2002, and came into force on July 1, 2002. This law guarantees a person's religious freedom, but attempts to harmonize this freedom with a person's civic obligations toward the state. Under the new law, alternative service lasts twenty-four months, except for persons with university degrees, in which case the service lasts only eighteen months. The service can be rendered in state and municipal institutions, companies with state or municipal capital, or in public organizations that are engaged in different rescue operations, social care, medical service, and so forth.[23]

Despite isolated cases of hostility, the public attitude to Jehovah's Witnesses has changed for the better recently in Latvia. Although Jehovah's Witnesses create their own subculture, they join in the broader life of society as well. For example, the Witnesses are very conscientious employees in the workplace. As a consequence, many managers regard them favorably. According to the Jehovah's Witnesses themselves, there is no unemployment in their community. It is likely that this religious minority will continue to integrate itself into Latvian society in the future.

Although the majority of citizens are more or less critical of the growth of new religious minorities, it is also true that the general population in all three Baltic States is rather tolerant of new religions. Perhaps such a situation has emerged because religious matters do not greatly concern the majority of the population. Besides, both in Latvia and Estonia the greater part of the population consists of religious believers who lack strong commitment to any religious organization. In Estonia, for example, anecdotal evidence from local Lutheran churches indicates a 76 percent decrease in registered confirmations between 1990 and 2000. In Latvia, over half of those who claim some form of allegiance to the traditional Christian churches—around 69 percent of the population—eschew active participation in particular congregations. Possibly they take their association for granted because of family tradition or because they hold the widespread notion that Latvians are Lutherans, Russians are Orthodox or Old Believers, and inhabitants of Latgale are Catholics. Some Latvians are likely to be so-called "Christmas worshippers" who believe that tradition and custom impose on them an obligation to go to church on Christmas. This conclusion is partly confirmed by statistics. According to an updated poll, only half of all participants replied that religion plays an important part in their lives. Four percent could not answer this question at all.[24] These non-belonging believers are broadminded with regard to the unconventional choices of other people. In such a context, the new religious minorities can adapt themselves little by little to the social and cultural situation. Only a few minorities seem to cause discomfort among the larger citizenry.

In Latvia, for example, in contrast to Germany, Russia, and other countries, there are no serious conflicts with the Unification Church and the Church of Scientology at the present time, although the prevailing public attitude to these religions is negative. At the same time, the conflict between part of the population and the Christian-oriented, fundamentalist United Evangelical Congregation of God grows day by day. The core of this congregation consists of about two hundred people, but nationwide there are around one thousand people who accept the congregation's teaching. Although the Ministry of Justice has officially registered this congregation, it is at present considering the revocation of this registration.

The main impetus for this reaction is the intolerant attitude the congregation holds toward other Christian denominations and toward Roman Catholics in particular. Moreover, this congregation has been reproached for harboring a "wrong attitude" towards its children. For example, children are forbidden to take part in out-of-school activities, to watch TV, and to listen to the radio. It is obvious that the congregation has increasingly isolated itself and that its reaction to outside criticism has become more aggressive. It therefore becomes increasingly possible that state institutions will have to interfere in this conflict.

With regard to Lithuania, it is worthwhile noting the June 2000 conflict between the Lithuanian Ministry of Justice and the Collegiate Association for the Research of the Principle (the CARP). The Lithuanian Ministry of Justice has taken steps to force this association to discontinue "its religious activities in Lithuania because they contradict its own bylaws and violate the country's law on public organizations."[25] According to CARP's bylaws, the chief goal of the organization is to promote friendship and cooperation among students of different countries to ensure world peace.[26] CARP has repeatedly stressed that this organization is not religious in any sense; it only shares the pro-family policy of Rev. Sun Myung Moon. Moreover, CARP has warned some of its members not to commingle the religious and the social activities of the Unificationist movement. Nevertheless, the Ministry of Justice contends that events organized by CARP in Lithuania were aimed at recruiting young people into the religious community of the Unification Church.[27]

The main difficulties that exist between the new religious minorities and their host societies are: 1. The negative attitude toward these religious minorities on the part of mainstream churches; 2. The lack of accurate information about new religions and the prevalence of one-sided materials published by the mass media; 3. The development of anticult and countercult activities; 4. Isolationist and separatist tendencies on the part of some religious minorities.

Mainstream churches, with some exceptions, deny any official dialogue with the new religious minorities. Sometimes they try to support their theological positions with the help of political parties and official institutions. It is possible to assert that, from the point of view of mainstream churches, all new religions are "destructive sects and cults." The mainstream churches also support anticult activities every now and then. Still, these churches do not engage in serious countercult activities because they are fully preoccupied with their own renewal. For example, in Latvia an initiative to establish the Center for Apologetics Research—which would undertake countercult activities and education—only got off the ground in Summer 2000.

Nevertheless, if we compare the current situation with the situation five years ago, we can certainly say that the "moral panic" regarding new "sects" and "cults" in the Baltic States, except possibly Estonia, grows rather rapidly. The mass media and anticult groups have been largely responsible for the escalation of these "moral panics." For example, in 1992 and 1993, the Word of Faith movement (in Lithuania) and in 1998 and 1999 the congregation "Jauna Paaudze" (in Latvia) experienced active hostility from several anticult activists and a rise of negative publicity in the mass media. Articles about religion, especially about religious minorities, reveal negative or neutral points of view at best. In Latvia, an exception occurred recently, when positively slanted articles about members of the Last Testament's Church or Vissarion's Congregation appeared.[28] Incidentally, occult sciences and parapsychology receive increasing attention in the Latvian press. "Parallel Latvia," a new weekly edition devoted to these issues, emerged in 2002. It is interesting to observe that, while vampires, Satanism, and occult phenomena have been described in neutral terms, Christian religious minorities have garnered most of the press's criticism.

Negative stereotypes about new religious minorities "travel" from country to country. As regards the situation in Latvia, it should be remembered that the public attitude toward new religious minorities is greatly influenced by the rising tide of hostility in neighboring Russia and Lithuania.

In Lithuania, the first anticult group was "Mothers against Sects." Because of this group's lobbying of the Lithuanian government, the registration of new communities of the Word of Faith movement was delayed, and investigations were carried out by the prosecutor's office. Later, however, the activities of this anticult group decreased. K. Andriuskevicius founded another anticult group in the middle of 1999, perhaps influenced by Dialog Centre International. This group has contributed greatly towards the rise of an antisect disposition in Lithuanian society. Because of this disposition, the government decided on April 14, 2000, to establish an intergovernmental commission to investigate whether the activities of religious, esoteric, or spiritual groups comply with the law. It includes representatives of the Ministries of Justice, Interior, Education, Health, Foreign Affairs, the General Prosecutor's Office, and State Security. The Minister of Justice appoints the chairperson of the commission. The commission was established as a response to parliamentarians' calls for increased control of "sects" following negative coverage of some religious groups in the media.[29] In December 2001, Stanislovas Buskevicius, a nationalist Member of Parliament, proposed a draft law, "On Barring the Activities of Sects." The draft was discussed by the Parliament. Several state institutions have expressed concern regarding the legal shortcomings of the draft and indicated its inconsistencies with European legal practices.[30]

Parallel to these events in Lithuania were attempts in Latvia to establish an anticult center in 1998. The establishment of the "Revival," a "Center for the rehabilitation and mental recovery of the victims of destructive religious and psychological sects and cults," was announced officially in May 1999. The main tasks of this center are: 1. the rehabilitation and psychological and psychotherapeutic deprogramming of the victims of sects, free of charge; 2. psychological consultations for the relatives of victims, free of charge; 3. the exchange of information with similar organizations, such as the Bureau for the Fight against Sects in France and the American Family Foundation (AFF) in the United States; and 4. public lectures on sects, current psycho-techniques and methods of defense against "brainwashing," hypnosis, and suggestion.[31] To date, the founders of this center have yet to receive sufficient financial support.

As this brief overview suggests, state officials and most of society do not generally assist anticult activities at present. Nevertheless, this situation can change quickly. Thus, it is particularly urgent for the Baltic States to learn how to preserve their rather fragile social fabric and how to diminish tensions that could erupt into overt conflicts. One of the ways in which the situation could be made better is to offer accurate information about new religions and current religious issues.

Notes

1. These figures are published in the *Annual Report on International Religious Freedom*. Released by the Bureau of Democracy, Human Rights and Labor, U.S. Department of State, 7 October 2002.

2. See Ringo Ringvee, "Religions in Estonia," in *Beyond the Mainstream: The Emergence of Religious Pluralism in Finland, Estonia and Russia*, ed. Jeffrey Kaplan (Helsinki: SKS, 2000), 110–12.

3. These figures are published in the *Annual Report on International Religious Freedom*. Released by the Bureau of Democracy, Human Rights and Labor, U.S. Department of State, 7 October 2002.
4. Ibid.
5. According to Paragraph 6 of the Law on Religious Organizations, this right came into force beginning 17 July 1996. *Likums par religiskajam organizacijam.* (*The Law on Religious Organizations)—Zinotajs* (*Government Monitor*) 21, 2 November 1995.
6. More in Ilze Grinuma, "Par katoliem valsts rupesies ipasi" ("State will attend to Roman Catholics particularly")—*Diena*, 30 September 2002, 3.
7. Much of this data is from personal sources.
8. Statistics based on Donatas Glodenis and Holger Lahayne, eds., *Religijos Lietuvoje: The Annual Report on International Religious Freedom* (Siauliai, Lithuania: Nova Vita, 1999), released by the Bureau of Democracy, Human Rights and Labor, U.S. Department of State, 7 October 2002, and on data from personal sources.
9. In the *Annual Report on International Religious Freedom*, 7 October 2002.
10. In Donatas Glodenis, "New and Non-Traditional Religious Movements in Lithuania," paper read by Donatas Glodenis at CESNUR's fourteenth International Conference, "New Religiosity in the 21st Century," in Riga, Latvia, on 29 August 2000.
11. See "Zakon o Cerkvjah i obschinah" ("Law on Churches and Religious Organizations"), *Pravovije Akti Estonii* (*Legal Acts of Estonia*) 33, 3 September 1993.
12. See the *Annual Report on International Religious Freedom*, 7 October 2002.
13. The 8th paragraph, item 4 of the new "Law on Religious Organizations," see "Likums par religiskajam organizacijam" ("The Law on Religious Organizations"), *Zinotajs* (*Government Monitor*) 21, 2 November 1995.
14. In "New Religions in Latvia: The Way Towards the Recognition," paper read by Nikandrs Gills at CESNUR's fifteenth International Conference, Salt Lake City, 21 June 2002.
15. See "Likums par religiskajam organizacijam" ("The Law on Religious Organizations"), *Zinotajs* (*Government Monitor*) 21, 2 November 1995.
16. See the *Annual Report on International Religious Freedom*, 5 September 2000.
17. In "Law and Religion in Lithuania," paper read by Routa Ziliukaité and Donatas Glodenis at the conference, "Law, Religion and Democratic Society," Tartu, Estonia, 19–20 October 1999.
18. Judgment of the City of Riga Zemgale Borough Court, Case No. 2–2452, 26 May 1995.
19. Decision of the Republic of Latvia Supreme Court's Board, Case No. CK-1429, 28 June 1995.
20. This figure was published in the *Annual Report on International Religious Freedom*, 5 September 2000.
21. "Jehovah's Witnesses in the Social and Cultural Context of Contemporary Latvia," paper read by Nikandrs Gills at CESNUR's fourteenth International Conference, "New Religiosity in the 21st Century," in Riga, Latvia, 31 August 2000.
22. Ibid.
23. See "Alternativa dienesta likums" ("The Law on Alternative Service"), *Vestnesis* (*Gazette*) 91, 18 June 2002. Published also at http://www.mod.gov.lv/08akti/01_09alter.php.
24. "Pie kuras ticibas sevi pieskaitat?" ("Which confession do you set down as yours?"), *Diena*, 5 July 2000, 3.
25. "Lithuania orders Moon followers to stop religious activities in Lithuania," BBC Monitoring, Baltic news agency BNS, 28 June 2000.
26. Ibid.
27. Ibid.
28. More in "New Religions in Latvia: The Way Towards the Recognition," paper read by Nikandrs Gills at CESNUR's fifteenth International Conference, 21 June 2002.
29. See the *Annual Report on International Religious Freedom*, 5 September 2000.
30. See the *Annual Report on International Religious Freedom*, 7 October 2002.
31. From the announcement of this center, officially distributed in May 1999.

CHAPTER 9

Crushing Wahhabi Fundamentalists in Central Asia and the Caucasus

Subplot to the Global Struggle against Al Qa'ida or Suppression of Legitimate Religious Opposition?

BRIAN GLYN WILLIAMS

During the winter of 1996 I had the rare privilege of flying on a *Transaero* flight from Moscow to Almaty, the capital of the sprawling former Soviet republic of Kazakhstan, with a group of American missionaries from Texas. The evangelists from Houston were on their way to this landlocked Central Asian Muslim republic to spread the gospel of Christ and had a sense of enthusiasm that was nothing if not contagious. As their Texas twangs mingled in the airplane's cabin with the Turkic language of the Kazakhs, a people who in many ways still resemble their nomadic ancestors who conquered the world under Genghis Khan, I was intrigued by the notion of American missionaries converting these hard drinking, ex-Soviet Muslims of Inner Asia to Christianity.

I asked one of the missionaries if he felt that the post-Soviet Kazakhs, who were known for their watered-down, shamanistic version of mystic-Sufi Islam, represented fertile ground for the spreading of evangelical Christianity. I received a resounding affirmative. "Under the atheist government of the USSR," my missionary source replied, "believers of all faiths were repressed and now, since the fall of the Soviet Union, disillusioned people of all religious backgrounds are hungry for moral grounding, for something to replace the soulless system of Marxist materialism that previously provided them with their shallow sense of civic morality. Most importantly, they now crave something that has been missing in these lands for generations. . . . They crave God."

While I, as a Central Asianist, was inwardly bemused at the notion of Texans converting the mystic Muslim Kazakhs of Central Asia to their distinctly southern-American version of Christianity, I had to admit that the enthusiasm of the missionary was inspiring. And he did have a point. Many secularized Muslims of the former USSR were indeed searching for a deeper moral grounding on both a personal and communal level to replace the bankrupt Communist system that had dominated their lives for most of the twentieth century. Seventy-odd years of Soviet-imposed atheism had certainly taken its toll on the millions of non-Slavic Muslims who found themselves cut off from the outer Muslim world by the walls of the Communist Iron Curtain.

Throughout the Muslim borderlands of the USSR, thousands of mosques had been closed by the Kremlin. In addition, official Islamic clerics known as *mullahs* had been shot or exiled as "social parasites" by the KGB, and a rather sterile Soviet-Russian culture had replaced much of the colorful local Islamic traditions of the ethnic groups of this multi-national Communist imperium. As a result of this experience, the average Muslim I came in contact with in the republics of the former Soviet Union more closely resembled *Homo Sovieticus* than *Homo Islamicus*.

Official Orthodox Islam in the USSR was shattered by the anti-religious drives of the 1930s, and the only manifestations of Islam to survive this onslaught were the ancient, Sufi-based folk beliefs of the common people that operated below the surface throughout the Soviet period.

Sufi Islam, for example, enabled: 1. oppressed Soviet Muslims to visit ancient shrines and tombs in the mountains to obtain cures for illnesses; 2. *sheikhs*, or underground holy men, to marry Muslim couples who avoided the Orwellian People's Houses of Marriage designated by the Soviet government for marriage ceremonies; and 3. adherents of secret Islamic brotherhoods to gather away from the watchful eye of the KGB and chant Allah's name in mystic dances in order to achieve unity with the Creator.

From the sunny coasts of the Crimean Peninsula (home to secularized Muslim Crimean Tatars) to the religiously conservative oases of southern Uzbekistan and cliff top villages of the Caucasus, however, I found the Muslims of this region to be more familiar with the sayings of Marx than Muhammad. With the closing of their mosques, destruction of their Islamic literature, and execution of their trained official clerics, most manifestations of formal, Orthodox Islam in the USSR disappeared. Islamic morality and identity were sustained in this period only by the durable folk Islam of the Sufis that could not be destroyed despite the efforts by the Kremlin or its officials in the "backward" Muslim provinces.

In addition, during the Communist period, *the Soviet Muslims' own autonomous national-republic leaders* worked hard to stamp out any outward manifestation of grassroots Islam amongst their Muslim co-ethnics in the name of their Communist masters in the Kremlin (a tradition these entrenched native leaders were to continue after the fall of the USSR).

It should come as no surprise, then, that the Soviets' pervasive policies of secularization created a cultural and religious chasm between Muslims of the isolated USSR and the bulk of Sunni Muslims in conservative Middle Eastern countries. On many levels the Soviet Muslim peoples, such as the Chechen highlanders of the Caucasus Mountains, Kazakh shepherds of the Eurasian plains, and Tajik and Uzbek farmers of the oases of Central Asia, were psychologically and symbolically cut off from the *Dar al-Islam* (Islamic Heartland) by the Soviet experiment.

This isolating experience was to make this vast region a fertile proselytizing ground for foreign missionaries when the Communist USSR fell for, in many ways, the newly independent ex-Soviet Muslims of the 1990s were a people in need of a faith renewal. It was, however, not to be Texan Christians who were to find this area a fertile proselytizing ground, but Wahhabi missionaries from the religiously conservative states of the Arab world. In the process of offering the ex-Soviet Muslims a new sense of spirituality and a vehicle for opposition to post-Soviet dictatorships, however, the entrepreneurs of Arabic fundamentalist Islam were to threaten the traditional order in this lost Islamic realm. Most alarmingly, the extremists among them were to link this once-isolated Muslim land to the terrorist struggle of the world's most wanted terrorist, Osama bin Laden.

Allah's Foot Soldiers: The Export and Radicalization of Islamic Fundamentalism in the Arab World

Not surprisingly, the Communists' vast projects of societal reconfiguration created socio-cultural gaps between secularized Soviet Muslims and the Sunni (mainstream) Muslims in the heartland of the Islamic world. In Saudi Arabia, for example, a state-sponsored, austere form of fundamentalist Islam, known as *Wahhabism,* was actively enforced by the Committee for the Prevention of Vice and Promotion of Virtue (a force that was imitated by the Taliban), while Soviet Muslims were undergoing KGB-organized, anti-Islamic drives at the direction of Soviet General Secretaries Leonid Brezhnev and Yuri Andropov. While Soviet Muslims worked to construct a "workers' paradise" based on a utopian, Marxist-proletarian *future*, the Wahhabi fundamentalists in Saudi Arabia sought to turn back the hands of time and emulate an idyllic *past* as it had supposedly existed during the epoch of the Prophet Muhammad.

Seen in this light, it is no surprise that the fundamentalist movements in Saudi Arabia were diametrically opposed to the moderate, secular form of state-controlled Islam that existed below the surface in the atheist Soviet Union. This was in part because Islam in the Soviet Union was perceived by the Arab fundamentalists as being tainted with Western secular materialism in a Soviet form. Interestingly, this opposition to a freewheeling Soviet Islam also stemmed from the fact that the Central Asian and Caucasian Muslims of the USSR followed a mystical current of Islam (Sufism) that was full of pre-Islamic local traditions that the Saudi literalists considered to be "heretical superstitions." Although the strict fundamentalist movements in Saudi Arabia and the Gulf States were militantly intent on defending "pure" Islam from the contamination of Soviet atheism and Western secularism, *their most remarkable feature was their desire to cleanse Islam itself of its perceived impurities or false folk practices of the sort found in the traditional Sufism of the Central Asian and Caucasian Muslims.*

While the Arab fundamentalists took their *external* struggle against Soviet atheist imperialism to the battlefield by volunteering to fight alongside the Afghan *mujahedin* (holy warriors) in the 1980s *jihad* against the "godless Soviet invaders" of Afghanistan, the Arab puritans simultaneously waged an *internal* theological campaign. This campaign sought to purify Islam of its heretical impurities and return it to its ideal roots as they were imagined to have existed in Medieval Arabia at the time of the *Salafi* (the original Muslim community of Mecca and Medina). While this purification campaign was once limited to the Arabian peninsula, the 1980s saw the beginnings of an effort to export this puritanical interpretation of Islam throughout the Muslim world.

By the 1980s the Saudis were using their petrodollars to export their Wahhabi fundamentalist interpretation of Islam across the globe. This process began with the selective dissemination of funds only to radical fundamentalist mujahedin groups fighting against the Soviets in Afghanistan, a process that in many ways empowered a new militant version of global Islamic fundamentalism at the expense of moderate Islam. At this time Saudi charities also took advantage of the Qu'ran's injunction on pious Muslims to pay a *zakat* (tithe) to channel millions of dollars into exporting their rigid form of Islam to a wide array of local settings. These settings varied from Indonesia (where the local, moderate form of Islam was radicalized by such Saudi-sponsored groups as the *Jemaah Islamiya*, which has been held responsible for the October 2002 terrorist bombing in Bali) to the *madrassas* (seminaries) of Pakistan's Northwest Frontier that subsequently trained thousands of Pashtuns who would later form the backbone of the Taliban regime in Afghanistan. In these diverse ethnic and geographic contexts the Saudi version of Islam was to prove extremely disruptive to traditional indigenous Islamic orders *and* political systems.

The arrival of this new fundamentalist interpretation of Islam militarized local Muslims and contributed to the rise of *jihadi* (holy war) movements in areas such as Algeria, Kashmir, Basilan Island in the Philippines, the Molucca Islands in Indonesia, the Pashtun border regions of Pakistan, and post-Soviet Afghanistan. In the Afghan context, Saudi-sponsored *Talibs* (religious seminary students), who sought to emulate the fundamentalist regime of Saudi Arabia, succeeded in seizing power in 1996 and enforcing the strict Taliban-theocracy in a land traditionally known for its moderate form of Sufi Islam.

This trend was to be duplicated in the post-Soviet Central Asian and Caucasian contexts when Arab Wahhabi missionaries and Arab mujahedin veterans from Afghanistan began to disseminate both Qu'rans and AK-47 machine guns in the 1990s. In Central Asia and the Caucasus following the Soviet collapse, Arab-sponsored fundamentalist missions were to merge with newly formed, indigenous Islamic revivalist movements to forge political and military threats to the repressive ex-Communist regimes that maintained control of these newly independent republics (or small ethnoprovinces still found *within* Russia).

The export of this alien Wahhabi form of Islam throughout Eurasia in the late 1980s and 1990s was the natural outgrowth of a historic process of forced proselytizing that actually began in the late eighteenth century with the founding of Saudi Arabia. The kingdom of Saudi Arabia was founded when an Arabian Bedouin chief named Muhammad ibn Saud forged an alliance with an iconoclastic Muslim purifier named Muhammad ibn Abd al-Wahhab and seized control of central Arabia.

The Saudi regime has, since this time, become the political expression of an intolerant purifying sect that has sought to cleanse global Islam of its local "un-Islamic" traditions, *including the underground Sufi form of Islam that ironically enough sustained the Soviet Muslims' religious identity during the period of Communist-enforced atheism.* This purifying Saudi sect is unofficially known as Wahhabism after its spiritual founder, al-Wahhab, but its adherents in Saudi Arabia and fundamentalists in the post-Soviet Caucasus and Central Asia reject this term. Many modern Wahhabis who claim to emulate the *Salafi*, the original Muslims of Arabia during the time of the Prophet Muhammad, instead call themselves *Salafites* (Traditionalists or Unitarians).

Regardless of their collective name, al-Wahhab's followers took great satisfaction in destroying the ancient tombs of local saints in the Nejd region of central Arabia where their iconoclastic movement began. This destruction was then carried to Mecca and Medina where the Wahhabi zealots destroyed ancient domed edifices, tombs, and shrines. Al-Wahhab called for his followers in the Arabian peninsula to destroy all aspects of Arabian Islam that had strayed from the strictly-interpreted fundamentals of Orthodox Islam, and this included localized religious "deviations." The Wahhabis subsequently slaughtered many local Muslims for such "impure" practices as smoking or participating in pilgrimages to the shrines of venerated local saints.

It was not until Saudis began to send thousands of fighters and missionaries to Afghanistan in the 1980s, however, that the export and promulgation of this austere form of Islam was wedded to a new form of trans-national militancy that was to later prove so costly in human terms in the Muslim lands of post-Soviet Eurasia. The global export of Saudi Wahhabi fundamentalism and radical, Afghan-style jihadism in the 1980s thus served as a backdrop for the events surrounding the collapse of the USSR in 1991 and the emergence of five new Muslim nations in Central Asia (Kazakhstan, Kyrgyzstan, Tajikistan, Uzbekistan, and Turkmenistan).

With the demise of the USSR in 1991 and fall of the Communist-dominated Najibullah regime in Afghanistan in 1992, many newly unemployed Arab-Afghan mujahedin veterans, Arab religious charities, and Wahhabi missionaries refocused their sights on the millions of ex-Soviet Muslims in Central Asia.[1] The battle for the souls of Central Asia's 50 million secularized Sufi Muslims had begun. This broad-ranging battle was to lead to open warfare between secularists and Islamists in a land inhabited by Muslims who often knew the works of Vladimir Lenin better than the text of the Qu'ran.

Suppressing Wahhabi "Enemies of the People" in Post-Soviet Central Asia

Since the collapse of the USSR, the term *Vakhibity* (Russian for Wahhabis) has been widely used in post-Soviet Eurasia as a catchall phrase to refer to *all* Muslims who operate beyond the confines of official, state-sponsored moderate Islam. Ironically, many so-called Wahhabis in the region had never heard of Wahhabi puritanism in Saudi Arabia until they were saddled with the negative term by conservative ex-Communist governments in the early 1990s.

In the post-Soviet context, the term Wahhabi, or the more widely internalized alternative Salifite, refers to fundamentalist Islamists who seek to politicize the local Islamic culture. The post-Soviet version of Wahhabis also seek to introduce elements of *sharia* (Islamic law) into societies that they claim are dominated by lax secular laws stemming from the Soviet era or permeated with heretical Sufi traditions (such as membership in religious brotherhoods known as *tariqats*, making pilgrimages to local shrines or mausoleums, visiting Sufi sheikhs who engage in "magical rites," and chanting Allah's name in order to achieve unity with God). Many post-Soviet Wahhabi leaders were young men who trained in the mosques of the Middle East in the years following the collapse of the USSR. After returning to their homes in Central Asia or the Caucasus they confronted the traditional Sufi clergy, who often did not know Arabic or conform to the rigid interpretation of Islam the young trainees had encountered in the *madrassas* of the Arab world.

While the Islamists' secular opponents thus claim that the "Wahhabi" fundamentalist movements of post-Soviet Central Asia are led and funded by Arab sponsors, there is little doubt that these Islamic populist movements actually have home-grown roots that were seized upon by the ex-Soviet Muslims returning from the seminaries of the Arab world. During the late 1980s period of liberalization in the USSR known as *glasnost* (openness), Soviet leader Mikhail Gorbachev allowed for the emergence of an all-Soviet Islamic party known as the Islamic Renaissance Party (IRP). While this party was founded by Tatars (the most secular of the Muslim peoples of the USSR), its most resonant chord was struck with the Muslims of the backward mountain republic of Tajikistan.[2] As the USSR collapsed in 1991, Islamic fundamentalism and the IRP became something of a vogue for even the young people in Tajikistan who had, like young Muslims throughout the USSR, traditionally disdained attending mosques where only the elderly went to pray.

By 1992, opposition groups from throughout the newly independent republic of Tajikistan began to unite under the banner of the IRP in an effort to wrest power from the hands of an entrenched group of former Communists who retained power in the Tajik capital, Dushanbe. While the ex-Communist leadership accused their Islamic IRP opponents (who united with other regional and political opponents to form a political military coalition known as the United Tajik Opposition (UTO)) of being "Wahhabis" bent on seizing power and taking the country back to the Islamic Middle Ages, the IRP's goals were actually quite modest. The Islamists' agenda included the banning of such practices as the sale of alcohol, singing at weddings, ritualized mourning at funerals (local Sufi traditions), and the consumption of meat that was not cut in an Islamic fashion (that is, *hilal* Islamic culinary taboos similar to kosher practices).

As local politics and regional clan rivalries overlapped with the struggle between the Islamic opposition and the former Communist government in Dushanbe, full-scale civil war erupted in Tajikistan in 1992. This war between Islamists and the central government was to be the bloodiest conflict in the former Soviet space and came to involve all the neighboring states, including Russia, which became the defender of the former Communist government of Tajikistan. The ensuing conflict between the Islamists and the former Communists was to ebb and flow for five years until a UN-brokered peace agreement was signed in 1997.

As the conflict between the Islamic UTO opposition and the government took the lives of over 50,000 Tajiks, the stunned ex-Communist leaders of the neighboring Central Asian republics united to form a common front against the Wahhabi threat to secular stability in the region. For the most part, however, the fundamentalist threat never materialized in Kazakhstan, Kyrgyzstan, or Turkmenistan. This was largely because these peoples were former nomads who had a very watered-down, shamanistic version of ethnic Islam that was less strict than the Islam of the conservative, oasis-dwelling Tajiks and Uzbeks of southern Central Asia. When I spoke to Kazakhs of my interest in traveling to the traditional Islamic core of Central Asia, the Uzbek and Tajik areas to the south, these Russified former nomads felt it necessary to warn me of the conservative, patriarchal Islam that existed among their sedentary neighbors in Uzbekistan and Tajikistan.

Seen in the light of history and tradition, the activities of the Wahhabis in Central Asia were therefore limited to Uzbekistan, Tajikistan, and, to a much lesser extent, portions of Kyrgyzstan (namely the Osh region, a section of Kyrgyzstan that extends into the Uzbek-dominated Fergana Valley). There was nonetheless a real fear among the Kazakhs and Kyrgyz in the mid-1990s that the Islamic movements of the southern Tajiks and Uzbeks would threaten the stability of all Central Asia and even Russia.

While the bloodshed and destruction in Tajikistan proved that the Islamic fundamentalist threat to Central Asian stability was real, the subsequent 1997 peace treaty between the Islamist UTO rebels and the secularist Tajik government brought a gradual end to this conflict. In the process, this treaty also allowed for (relatively) free elections in which representatives of the Islamist opposition were included in the government in small numbers. This peace treaty may thus serve as an alternative path whereby secular regimes from Algeria to Uzbekistan can co-opt and disarm their Islamic opponents by including them in the government. While the Islamists in Tajikistan have made claims of fraud against the government since the elections, the Islamic resistance appears to have nonetheless accepted its role as a legal political opposition group operating *within* the existing political system, and this has moderated their demands to a considerable extent.

Since the end of the conflict, many so-called Wahhabis of Tajikistan have shaved off their once-vogue, Wahhabi-style beards, and calls for the forceful implementation of *sharia* Islamic law have subsided. In addition, the drinking of alcohol has returned to teetotaler villages that were once controlled by the austere Islamic opposition, and local Sufi traditions that were banned by the Islamic fundamentalists, such as singing at weddings and having picnics in family graveyards, are once again widespread.

In Uzbekistan, by contrast, the struggle to suppress Wahhabism continues unabated to this day. Wahhabis first appeared in Uzbekistan, the most populous country in post-Soviet Central Asia, in the early 1990s and began to spread their beliefs throughout this country with funding from Saudi Arabian NGO charities. I found tangible evidence of this dissemination of fundamentalist Islam in the form of unofficial mosques that sprang up throughout the Uzbek republic under the sponsorship of Saudi Wahhabis.

While the Russified urbanites in the Uzbek capital of Tashkent were less inclined to respond to the call of missionaries from Saudi Arabia, the overpopulated Fergana Valley in eastern Uzbekistan proved to be a fertile ground for entrepreneurs of radical fundamentalism. The Fergana Valley is home to ten million of Central Asia's fifty million inhabitants and provides a home to many desperate Uzbeks whose economic situation drastically deteriorated in the 1990s when the fall of the USSR brought hyperinflation. Many Uzbeks of the region blame their impoverished condition on the nepotism and rampant corruption of the "mafiocracy" that has firmly ruled Uzbekistan since the final days of the USSR. This popular resentment, combined with widespread unemployment, has served as a breeding ground for the radicalization of Islam in such diverse settings as the Gaza Strip and the streets of Karachi, Pakistan.

In the early 1990s, many Uzbek men in the Fergana Valley began to wear Wahhabi-style beards, and women began to discard their brightly colored folk dresses and to wear modest, *chador*-style dark dresses and headscarves. The most visible signs of this trend occurred in the Fergana Valley town of Namangan where unlicensed *imams* (preachers) who had recently been trained in Saudi Arabia began to preach a new form of Wahhabi fundamentalism. These *imams* called for the creation of an Islamic caliphate (theocracy) in the valley that would eventually expand to include all of Central Asia (including the Chinese province of Xingkiang). This was a bold challenge to the secular government of Islam Karimov, the president of the newly independent Uzbekistan, who had been appointed to be head of the republic just prior to the demise of the USSR.

As the emboldened Islamic militants began to call for the implementation of *sharia* law in Namangan, Karimov traveled to the Fergana Valley to meet with them in 1991. At this meeting the head of the Islamic extremists, Tohir Yoldeshev, a firebrand who wanted to turn Central Asia into a strict *sharia*-based state, insulted the president and forced him to swear on the Qu'ran that he would implement Islamic law. A furious President Karimov returned to the Uzbek capital of Tashkent and promptly launched a statewide campaign to destroy the Wahhabis, who were described in Soviet terms as "enemies of the people."

Since this time, unofficial mosques have been closed, their *imams* have been rounded up in police sweeps, thousands of suspected Wahhabis have been summarily arrested on trumped-up charges, and Islamists have been tortured or killed. To have a Wahhabi-style beard in Uzbekistan today is to ask to be arrested and shipped off to the dreaded Jaslyk prison camp, which was created to hold thousands of suspected Wahhabis. Few who enter this notorious prison, located in the barren lands south of the Aral Sea, are ever seen or heard from again.

After the Wahhabis of Uzbekistan were accused of fighting back against the authorities (most famously by killing and beheading a policeman in Fergana and attempting to kill President Karimov in a deadly bombing outside the president's palace in February 1999), Karimov announced, "Such people (Wahhabis) must be shot in the forehead! If necessary, I'll shoot them myself."[3]

Human rights groups have strongly criticized Karimov's government for its brutal policies, which have seen many innocent Muslims caught up in police sweeps and sentenced to jail for such minor infractions as carrying "Wahhabi agitation literature." The greatest crime in Uzbekistan today, however, consists of belonging to one of the country's two main Islamic "Wahhabi" parties, the Hizb ut-Tahrir al Islami (Party of Islamic Liberation), which calls for the peaceful overthrow of the secular authorities, or the Islamic Movement of Uzbekistan (IMU), which has aimed for the violent destruction of the "Godless" regime of Karimov. As a result of this oppression, however, one specialist on Wahhabism in Central Asia has written, "The radical measures of the authorities in the struggle with the religious opposition led to an increase in their ranks, to their radicalization, and to the inclusion in their ranks of foreign fighters who had experience in leading diversionary wars. One can say that the Uzbek authorities grew themselves enemies."[4]

The most feared of these enemies was an ex-Soviet paratrooper-turned-Islamic guerilla who went by the *nom de guerre* Juma Namangani. Namangani became the military head of the IMU in the late 1990s, and his fame quickly spread throughout Central Asia and beyond. Namangani's IMU, for example, made world headlines in 1999, 2000, and 2001 when his guerilla units, made up of Tajik, Uzbek, and Arab guerillas from Afghanistan, launched a series of military forays into the Batken region of Kyrgyzstan and into Uzbekistan's Fergana Valley. Many average Uzbeks saw Namangani as a contemporary Robin Hood fighting the corrupt Uzbek authorities in much the same way their ancestors had fought the Soviets during a series of "Basmachi" revolts in the 1920s.

Military analysts were, however, subsequently surprised to discover that the IMU guerillas were expertly trained in Afghan terrorist camps and equipped with rifles with laser sniper scopes, advanced communication equipment, rocket propelled grenades, and other powerful weaponry. It soon became apparent that Namangani's fighters had evolved from local boys fighting for their religious rights to something far more sinister.[5] It subsequently emerged that the IMU had forged an alliance with Osama bin Laden, who was at that time extending his influence in Taliban-controlled Afghanistan, and that Namangani's struggle had been submerged into bin Laden's wider-ranging global *jihad.*

In what was ultimately a strategic miscalculation, Namangani (like the Taliban regime itself) increasingly allowed his popular resistance to be hijacked by the transnational, anti-Western struggle of Al Qa'ida. As Namangani's fighters became further linked to the radical movement of jihadism at the expense of their previous interest in a popular religious revolution in Central Asia, they lost popularity among the vast majority of easygoing Uzbek moderates. In the final stage of this radicalization, Namangani was given command of Al Qa'ida's main fighting unit in Afghanistan, the hardened International 055 Brigade, on the eve of the September 11, 2001, attack on the United States by Al Qa'ida. Osama bin Laden and his followers were very interested in carrying the struggle they had commenced against the Soviets in Afghanistan into post-Soviet Central Asia, and Namangani's IMU was the perfect weapon for translating their grandiose plans into reality.

In the subsequent U.S.-led destruction of the Taliban regime and the 055 Brigade at Kunduz in northern Afghanistan in November 2001, however, Namangani and many of his Uzbek fighters were killed by U.S. bombers and the rest captured or dispersed. With U.S. support, President Karimov has followed up this unexpected eradication of his enemy by enacting further clampdowns on Wahhabi opposition in Uzbekistan. This brutal domestic policy has been carried out in the name of crushing "international terrorism." Today, Uzbekistan's jails are filled beyond capacity with thousands of suspected Hizb ut-Tahrir members, and there are no viable outlets for religious opposition in the republic of Uzbekistan. The extreme religious fringe has, in effect, given the Karimov dictatorship a pretext for eradicating even the moderate Islamic opposition in Uzbekistan, a process the U.S. supports in the context of its struggle to suppress Al Qa'ida terrorism. While many fear that the example of the U.S. support for the doomed Shah of Iran in the late 1970s may serve as a template for Uzbekistan, the example of Tajikistan beckons as an alternative.

Jihad in the Caucasus: Militant Wahhabism in Dagestan and Chechnya

The small *autonomous* Muslim ethnic enclaves of the Russian Federation's north Caucasus mountains constitute a second arena for the struggle between Wahhabi fundamentalists, and secularist governments and indigenous Sufi Muslims. This conflict in many ways stems from the independence struggle of the tiny secessionist Muslim republic of Chechnya, which led to a brutal war between Chechen guerillas and Russian Federation forces from 1994 to 1996.

While this first Russo-Chechen War was initially based on a Chechen national liberation struggle similar to the previous independence movements of the USSR's Baltic republics (Estonia, Latvia, and Lithuania), it later took on undertones of a *jihad*. As the hard pressed Chechen resistance fighters gradually realized that the West did not support them in their lopsided struggle for national independence from the powerful Russian Federation, they were only too willing to receive help from any source proffering military and financial assistance. The only aid for the beleaguered Chechen fighters at this time came from Arab mujahedin trained in Afghanistan and from Arab Wahhabi charities.

The David versus Goliath struggle of the Chechen highland guerillas against the might of the Russian Federation became a *cause celebre* for young Arab idealists and extremists who glamorized the notion of *jihad*. Many Arabs romanticized this bloody struggle in much the same way that American volunteers in the Spanish Civil War of the 1930s had earlier idealized that conflict. As the Russian Federation forces callously obliterated the Chechen capital of Grozny in an effort to subdue the rebels hiding in the city (turning a city of 400,000 into a devastated wasteland with hardly a murmur of protest from Western governments), Osama bin Laden and his militants began to see this uneven struggle for political independence as a conflict between Islam and Christianity.

Chechnya soon became, along with several similar zones of conflict between Muslims and non-Muslims (such as Bosnia), a prime destination for Arab *jihadi* volunteers who gradually radicalized the local Islam in Chechnya just as they had in Kashmir in the late 1980s.[6] Most of the transnational Islamic fighters who joined the Chechen guerillas espoused a strict form of Wahhabism. These volunteers saw themselves as holy warriors charged with the task of not only defending the Chechen Muslims from Russian infidel aggression but of purifying the wayward local Sufi Islam of its heretical practices.

The most important of the Arab volunteers to assist the Chechens was Emir Khattab, a Saudi Arabian jihadist who had previously fought in the ranks of the anti-Soviet mujahedin in Afghanistan. Khattab arrived in Chechnya in 1995 under the protection of a legendary Chechen field commander named Shamil Basayev and soon used his previous experience in ambushing Soviet military columns in the earlier Afghan *jihad* to annihilate a Russian Federation division on a winding mountain road in southern Chechnya. This spectacular, videotaped military success ensured Khattab's popularity among the outgunned Chechen fighters, and the ranks of his Islamic Battalion soon filled with idealistic young Chechen fighters and Arab volunteers who took great risks sneaking into the Russian-occupied republic to join the outgunned rebels. Chechens in the Islamic battalions began to wear Wahhabi-style beards, to outlaw alcohol, and to consider the Russian opponents they had once shared a Communist homeland with to be *kafirs* (infidels).

As the war progressed, many previously secular Chechen fighters began to wear headbands inscribed with the Arabic words, *Allahu Akbar* (God is Great), and Khattab's Arab holy fighters began to successfully graft the concept of *jihad* onto the Chechens' independence struggle.[7] When the war ended successfully for the Chechens in 1996 (resulting in de facto Chechen independence and the withdrawal of Russian forces), the Arab Wahhabis capitalized on this hard-earned foothold among certain Chechen radical fighters to extend their political and religious influence in the newly independent republic.

In a nutshell, the Russian invasion of Chechnya resulted in the intervention of Arab volunteers and the propagation of their fundamentalist beliefs in this military theater in much the same way that the Soviets' earlier invasion of Afghanistan had led to the spread of Saudi-sponsored Islamic fundamentalism and jihadism in that moderate Muslim country. As in post-Soviet Afghanistan, the horrific destruction wreaked on Chechen society by the Russian invasion of 1994–96 (over 45,000 Chechens were estimated to have been killed, many villages were destroyed, and most Chechens were jobless) planted seeds of resentment and despair that would eventually sprout and lead to the rise of Islamic militancy in a region previously known for its accommodating Sufi version of Islam.

As they had in other moderate Islamic regions from Indonesia to Bosnia, the Arab Wahhabis actively sponsored this radicalization of Islam in the northern Caucasus every step of the way. After the 1994–96 Russo-Chechen war, for example, a wealthy Jordanian Arab known only as Fathi used funding that may have come from Osama bin Laden to establish Islamic boarding schools for orphans in the Chechen town of Urus Martan and to support militant Wahhabi groups. Also at this time, Wahhabi-funded fundamentalist mosques were built in Urus Martan and Chechnya's second largest town, Gudermes.

This effort at fundamentalist proselytizing was paralleled by increased Wahhabi military activity and the simultaneous establishment of camps in the mountains of southeastern Chechnya to train young Muslim men from throughout this multi-ethnic region in the principles of Wahhabi Islam and *jihad*. In addition, a coalition of Arab mujahedin, Chechen fundamentalist opposition politicians with Arab-Wahhabi connections, and militant Chechen warlords subsequently pressured the weak, secular Chechen authorities to implement *sharia* law in the newly independent Chechen republic. This led to the horrific televised execution of two criminals by local Islamic courts, the closing down of stalls selling alcohol throughout the republic, and a series of congresses held by Wahhabis from Chechnya and the neighboring republic of Dagestan (a Muslim province still in Russia) calling for the overthrow of secular authorities in *both* republics.

As Wahhabi influence spread in Chechnya and in Dagestan, the armed fundamentalist radicals began to outlaw traditional Sufi practices and to pressure the traditionally free women of the North Caucasus (some of whom were former rebel fighters) to wear veils or *hijabs*. This increasing Wahhabi-led radicalization soon caused a major rift between the vast majority of moderate Chechens and Dagestanis—most of whom belonged to two ancient Sufi brotherhoods (the Naqshbandi and Qadiria orders), and the Wahhabi militants, whose goal was to unite with Muslim fundamentalist radicals in Dagestan and recreate a legendary nineteenth-century, *sharia*-based imamate (theocracy).

This conflict between the Wahhabis and the moderate secularists in Chechnya broke out into open warfare on two separate occasions in the late 1990s, with the Islamic extremists increasingly calling for the overthrow of Chechnya's moderate president, Aslan Maskhadov. Maskhadov (who was popularly elected by the Chechen people in 1997) and his secularist supporters, including the *Mufti* (chief cleric) of Chechnya, Akhmad Kadyrov, considered the attempts by Wahhabi "foreigners" to create an alien Arab-style fundamentalist theocracy in the Caucasus to be a threat to their moderate Sufi traditions. President Maskhadov even called on Russia to help him crush the Wahhabi extremists in his chaos-ridden statelet. But the calls of Chechnya's moderate authorities for help in expelling the militants struck a deaf ear among those in the Kremlin who were only too happy to see the destabilization of Chechnya at the hand of extremist gangs.

Historically, the Chechens and Dagestanis have gathered to perform *zikirs* (circles in which devotees seek ecstatic union with Allah through rhythmic singing and dancing), worshipped at the shrines of *evlias* (local saints), and have been very tolerant of their Russian neighbors. All of these traditions, but most importantly the notion of peaceful coexistence with the Russian infidels of the *Dar al-Harb* ("Realm of War"), were considered anathema to the Wahhabi-Arab volunteers and their local extremist allies in Chechnya and Dagestan. The extremists hoped for a further chance to humiliate the Russian "infidels" who had withdrawn so ignominiously from Chechnya in 1996. Many Western military analysts believed that a second Russo-Chechen war was inevitable.

In August 2002, I interviewed Abu Hamza al Misri, the notorious *imam* of the Finsbury Park Mosque in London who has called for celebrations of the attack of September 11 and who is suspected of recruiting followers for Al Qa'ida as well as the Chechen mujahedin "battalion." He informed me that several volunteer fighters in Chechnya from his mosque wanted to continue the *jihad* against Russia regardless of whether or not Moscow was occupying Chechnya. Many ordinary, war-weary Chechens who dreamed of establishing a national state feared that the Wahhabi extremists supported by Abu Hamza and his like would give Russia a pretext to once again invade and deprive them of their hard won independence. President Maskhadov, for example, complained that Arab fighters in his republic (including Khattab, whom he tried to have expelled from Chechnya) were intent on "raising the green flag of Islam above the Kremlin itself."

Most analysts feel that civil war between the Chechen moderates, headed by President Maskhadov and several Sufi sheikhs on the one hand, and the well-funded Wahhabis, led by militant field commanders Emir Khattab, Shamil Basayev, and Arbi Barayev (a fundamentalist militant whose nephew later took over 800 hostages in Moscow in October 2002) on the other hand, was headed off only by a massive Russian invasion of Chechnya in the fall of 1999. This attack was to dwarf the previous Russian invasion of 1994–96 in its scale and intensity and to see the destruction of all Chechnya's rebuilding progress since 1996. As many average Chechens had feared, the bloody second Russo-Chechen War of 1999-present came as a result of efforts by the Wahhabi fundamentalists in Chechnya to forge links with Wahhabis in the neighboring Muslim republic of Dagestan.

The rise of fundamentalism in Dagestan began in the late 1980s and early 1990s as Islamists began to open mosques in this mountainous region with funding from Wahhabi groups in the Arab world. A group of these Wahhabis in central Dagestan went on to clash with local Sufi Muslims who resented the increasing intrusion of this alien form of Islam in the late 1990s. As the local Dagestani authorities began to suppress this "foreign religious sect," the Wahhabis responded by declaring their towns in central Dagestan an independent "*sharia*-zone." When the Dagestani authorities, who were legendary for their corruption, called on Russian Federation forces to suppress the Wahhabis in August 1999, the Russian army responded by dropping deadly vacuum bombs (fuel air explosives similar to napalm) on the Wahhabi villages, killing scores of innocent Wahhabi civilians.

It surprised no one that the heavily armed Wahhabis in Chechnya under the command of Emir Khattab responded to this assault on their "brothers and sisters" by launching a full-scale invasion of Dagestan with as many as 1,200 fighters. Khattab's aim was to break through the lines of Russian Federation forces encircling the besieged Wahhabi villages of central Dagestan and save his beseiged fellow fundamentalists. But his actions instead gave the new Russian leader, Vladimir Putin, an excuse to launch a brutal invasion of the "terrorist republic" of Chechnya.

The second Russian invasion of Chechnya, which has cost thousands of lives, was thus launched in response to the reactionary invasion of Dagestan by Khattab and Basayev's Islamic Peacekeeping Battalion in August and September of 1999.[8] *In essence, Moscow's second Russian quagmire was begun as a response to the joint military activities of a small number of Wahhabi radicals in the Russian republic of Dagestan and the breakaway statelet of Chechnya who hardly represented the will of the vast majority of moderate Sufi Chechens or Dagestanis.* After Khattab, who was considered a hero by many Arabs for his bold defense of Chechnya during the second Russian invasion, was killed by a mysterious poison in April 2002, his role as head of the foreign fighters in Chechnya was taken over by a Saudi Arab named Abu al-Walid. Saudi money for approximately 150–300 well-armed foreign fighters and their allies in Chechnya continues to flow from Wahhabi charities such as Al Haramein, and this certainly contributes to the bloody conflict in Chechnya.

As the following interview with an average Chechen makes clear, the Wahhabi-sponsored Islamic brigades have the funds to recruit young Chechens who are embittered by Russia's bloody assaults on their villages: "Wahhabis offered young people something the official Maskhadov administration was powerless to provide. They gave them a steady income. It was blood money, of course, but who cared? If one person joined, he was issued a weapon and became a rank-and-file *mujahideen*. . . . If you brought a group of people with you, you were issued a wireless kit, an off-road vehicle, and weapons for everyone. . . . We were making an average of 100–300 dollars a month."[9]

The common people of Chechnya, who dislike the Wahhabi extremists, have suffered tremendously from such extremism and the Russian occupation of their homeland. Many Chechens blame the despised Wahhabis and fundamentalist field commanders for the slaughter of their people and the virtual destruction of their republic by Russian Federation forces. A large portion of the Chechens led by the former *Mufti* of Chechnya, Akhmed Kadyrov, have in fact gone over to the Russians in order to combat the influence of Wahhabi fundamentalism in their republic. On the other hand, independence-minded Chechen moderates, such as President Maskhadov, who have continued the struggle for freedom from the southern mountains, have been forced to ally themselves with the powerful Arab and Chechen Wahhabis whose well-funded Islamic *jamaats* (platoons) are useful in battling the Russian Federation forces. These radicals are not under Maskhadov's control, however, and often carry out bombings, assassinations, or ambushes of Russian forces without the consent of the secular Chechen government in hiding.

Sadly, a radical Wahhabi-jihadist fringe has thus hijacked the independence struggle of the Chechens. This has played directly into the hands of the Russian government, which cynically seeks to depict *all* Chechen resistance fighters (including those of Maskhadov and his moderates) as Osama bin Laden-funded terrorists. In a 2000 interview, Ilyas Akmadov, the moderate Chechen Foreign Minister, expressed his visceral dislike of the Wahhabi fundamentalists and their Arab supporters while nonetheless acknowledging that they increasingly played an important role in the struggle against Russia. It would appear that the extremists are taking advantage of the Russians' clumsy search-and-destroy operations (known as *zachistkas,* which target villages, maim civilians, and terrorize the bulk of moderate Chechens) to increase their influence among desperate young Chechen men. As more Chechens become victims (and *shaheeds* [martyrs]) of Russia's brutal campaign to destroy "international terrorism" in Chechnya, Islam in Chechnya becomes further radicalized and the influence of the Wahhabis at the expense of the Sufi moderates grows. The most recent manifestation of this radicalization has been the destruction of the Russian government's provisional headquarters in the heart of Grozny by Wahhabi-sponsored suicide bombers (killing approximately 80) in December 2002.

Conclusion

In the final analysis, the initial popularity of the Wahhabi Islamic movements of post-Soviet Central Asia and the Caucasus can be seen as an outgrowth of the new-found interest in Islam that swept these regions in the late 1980s and early 1990s. The efforts on the part of radical Wahhabi fundamentalists to translate their *religious* influence into *political* power (through military means) and to purify indigenous Sufi-style Islam have, however, been met with brutal suppression on the part of secular authorities and local religious leaders throughout the region. The propagation of an austere, alien form of politicized Islam from Saudi Arabia among the moderate Muslim populations of Central Asia and the Caucasus has destabilized these secularized Islamic societies and led to bitter conflicts costing the lives of tens of thousands. In effect, the militarization of the Wahhabi movements of the former Soviet Union (a process that is in itself partially a response to government-sponsored oppression of unofficial fundamentalist Islam) has led to full-scale warfare between proponents of the new creed and those representing the traditional religious-political order.

In perhaps no other modern global context has the introduction of a new religion led to such brutal warfare, widespread devastation, disruption of traditional societies, and misery as is the case with Wahhabism in the secularized, Sufi-Muslim lands of the former Soviet Union. The horrific violence resulting from the introduction of this radical religious movement is due, in part, to militant Islamists in the Arab world, such as Osama bin Laden, who see the overthrow of the entrenched secularist regimes of Central Asia and the struggle against the continued Russian presence in the Islamic north Caucasus flank as one of the primary objectives of their global *jihad*.

The Wahhabi extremists in the Middle East have thus funneled funds and fighters into strengthening the radical Islamists in this region in much the same way they focused their resources on fundamentalist mujahedin organizations (such as Gulbuddein Hekmatyar's fundamentalist Hezb-i Islami) during the Soviet-Afghan *jihad*. As a result, the spread of militant Wahhabism in this vast strategic region is seen as a serious threat to stability in post-Soviet Eurasia and is now increasingly viewed in the context of the post-September 11 war on transnational *jihadi* terrorism. This represents a radical transformation of a religious movement that once sought only to re-Islamize a region that had undergone 70-odd years of Soviet-sponsored atheist oppression.

While Wahhabis in the former USSR have been demonized as a result of their militarization and the links some undoubtedly have had to global Sunni Islamic terrorism, this uniquely post-Soviet version of Wahhabism must also be seen as social and moral protest by Muslim believers who are frustrated with the rampant corruption, materialism, and nepotism that is endemic to former Communist governments in the Caucasus and Central Asia.

Fortunately for the oppressive leaderships of these republics, the Wahhabis' gradual radicalization and crude efforts to seize political power in Uzbekistan, Dagestan, and Chechnya, as well as their hostility to local Sufi traditions, have alienated the moderate Muslim majorities in all these regions. This has given the local political authorities a popular mandate and pretext for cracking down on all manifestations of "Wahhabism," a term that has been broadly interpreted to refer to *any* form of religious opposition or grassroots Islam that is not officially sanctioned by the government.

The responses on the part of the entrenched political elites in this strategic region to the Wahhabi threat have invariably taken the form of mass arrests and a resounding display of military force designed to physically eradicate any Wahhabi opposition. In the process, Wahhabi fundamentalists throughout the region have been largely defeated in their efforts to seize power and establish *sharia*-based societies, and secular Central Asia has been preserved from the "Islamic threat."

Tajikistan is the only country in the region that has created a *modus vivendi* with the Islamic fundamentalists, and this came about only after a brutal civil war (1992–97) that proved that the Islamists could not be subdued through purely military means. The subsequent power-sharing agreement in that country, which effectively solved the conflict between the Wahhabis and secularist ex-Communists by co-opting the fundamentalists, may serve as an alternative solution to the emergence of Wahhabism in the Islamic states of the former USSR.

Notes

1. These fighters belonged to the Azzam Brigades, international fighters from Egypt, Algeria, Yemen, etc., who had been organized by Osama bin Laden's mentor, Abdullah Azzam.

2. For an analysis of the Tatars, the most secular Muslim nation in Eurasia, and the complete absence of extremist Islam among the Crimean Tatars, see Brian Glyn Williams, *The Crimean Tatars. The Diaspora Experience and the Forging of a Nation* (Leiden/Boston: Brill [Inner Asian Library], 2001).

3. "Republic of Uzbekistan Crackdown in the Farghona Valley," *Human Rights Watch* 10:4 (May 1998).

4. Sanobar Shermatova, "Tak Nazyvaemye Vakkabity (The So-Called Wahhabis)," *Chechnya i Rossiia: Obshchestva i Gosudarstva* (*Chechnya and Russia: Culture and State*), vol. 3 (2000): 408.

5. An Islamist website entitled, "Jihad Land: Uzbekistan," run by Azzam publications (which has links to Al Qa'ida supporters) proclaimed, "We are not fighting against Muslims and are not fighting against civilians. The president of Uzbekistan is a Zionist Jew and his army are communists who know what they are doing. . . . The battle is clearly one of Islam versus *kufr* (disbelief), and justice versus tyranny. Actually it is a battle of Islamic forces in Uzbekistan against a coalition of disbelieving nations backing Karimov. See http://66.96.205.195/azzam/html/landsmideastuzbekistan.htm, although this site has been shut down on occasion by the U.S. government since the commencement of the post-September 11 war on terrorism.

6. At this time radical militants from Pakistan began to invade the Indian province of Jammu and Kashmir, a Muslim-dominated land in predominantly Hindu India, in order to wage *jihad* against the Indian government. Local Kashmiri Muslims did not have a tradition of militant radicalism prior to this, and many were dismayed by the introduction of the new *jihadi* extremism by such groups as Haraket al Mijahideenr in their traditionally moderate land.

7. Arab volunteer militants tried to similarly graft the concept of *jihad* to the Albanian Kosovo Liberation Army's (KLA) struggle against the Serbs in 1999. Interestingly, the Muslim fighters of the KLA adamantly rejected links to Arab militants and expelled or betrayed Arab militants who came to Kosovo or Macedonia with the aim of Islamicizing conflicts in the former Yugoslavia. KLA fighters I interviewed in the spring of 2001 in Kosovo were secular nationalists who were conscious of the fact that their remarkable success was because NATO came to their aid in 1999, not Wahhabi volunteers. One can surmise that the same situation might have prevailed in Chechnya had the West offered the Chechen government aid packages after 1996 or made a stronger effort to halt Russian war crimes in Chechnya. The West's lack of support for the beleaguered Bosnian government led to the formation of an Arab Wahhabi Islamic Brigade in the Bosnian city of Zenica during the 1992–95 Bosnian War. These Arabs were moderately successful in radicalizing the local Bosnian Muslims, who were known for their tolerant version of secularized Islam.

8. For an in-depth analysis of this conflict and the role of Wahhabis in Dagestan and Chechnya, see Brian Glyn Williams, "The Russo-Chechen War: A Threat to Stability in the Middle East and Central Asia?" *Middle East Policy* 3:1 (March 2001).

9. D. Umalt, "Chechens Fear Wahhabi Threat," *Institute for War and Peace Reporting*, 21 December 2002.

PART **3**

Africa, Asia, and Australia

CHAPTER **10**

Prophets, "False Prophets," and the African State
Emergent Issues of Religious Freedom and Conflict

ROSALIND I. J. HACKETT

Introduction[1]

Africa's great ethnic and cultural diversity (approximately two thousand ethnic groups in more than fifty nation-states) is matched by an equally complex religious scene. One of the most interesting features of this religious landscape is not just the many Islams, Christianities, and numerous other movements (from Jehovah's Witnesses to Heaven's Gate) that have been brought to the continent and have taken root there amidst the great variety of local forms of indigenous practice, but also the creative and innovative responses of Africans themselves in forming their own religious movements.[2] Compared to parts of Europe and Asia, there would not appear to be the same degree of repression in Africa of non-mainstream or alternative, minority religions. Religious tolerance has historically been a more defining feature of African societies. In one form or another, all African constitutions enshrine the values of religious diversity and non-establishment as articulated in international human rights documents.[3]

However, in this chapter I intend to provide evidence of emerging patterns of conflict in several African states over newer religious formations. These conflicts can be conceptualized in political, social, and/or religious terms that I will discuss more systematically in the next section. I attribute the rise in tensions to the following factors:

1. new challenges from increasing religious pluralization and state management of this plurality;
2. a marked increase in religious revivalism and militancy, notably among Christians and Muslims;
3. the growing tendency to frame socio-political insecurities and economic failures in terms of encroaching satanic and occult forces;
4. the emergence of an increasingly mass-mediated public sphere and new religious publics;
5. an increase in discourses concerning human rights and religious freedom.

Let me elaborate briefly on some of these points by way of background, before offering a short historical overview of new religious movements (NRMs) in Africa.

In the slipstream of political liberalization and globalizing cultural and market forces in post-colonial Africa we are witnessing an attendant pluralization of religious options. This is altering the stakes of religious co-existence—creating conditions that are clearly more conducive to religious tension and conflict. The national scene becomes more competitive as religious institutions that were formerly privileged by colonial regimes now find themselves as just one of the players in the new pluralistic dispensation. The global discourse of human rights is increasingly localized and naturalized via state and civil society structures.[4] In the last few years, Africans are becoming more vocal about claiming their constitutional and international rights to freedom of expression and freedom of religion.[5] Some, notably Pentecostal and evangelical Christians, are aware of American interest in religious persecution issues in the form of the United States International Religious Freedom Act of 1998.[6] They may even have come across the "bestsellers" in the field, Paul Marshall's *Their Blood Cries Out* and Nina Shea's *In the Lion's Den*, with their emotive tropes of martyrdom and persecution.[7]

In short, religious issues impinge more than ever on ethnic, national, and transnational politics in many parts of Africa. For example, Nigerian political analyst and social commentator, Father Matthew Hassan Kukah, states that "the religious question . . . is now the single greatest threat to the existence of the Nigerian state."[8] African newspapers regularly report on the differing views of political and religious leaders as to the appropriate place of religion in the national setting. Faltering, debt-ridden African states must now look to the management of religious pluralism as part of their plans of national integration lest it explode into conflict as in Nigeria and Sudan, and more recently and unexpectedly, Ivory Coast and Niger. They must pay special attention to the mass media that have developed with intensity over the last decade throughout Africa. States and religious authorities are losing control over this rapidly privatizing and more participatory media sector, particularly at the level of newer, small-scale media production.[9] The new technologies of communication blur private and public spheres, opening up new possibilities for identity politics. It is particularly the younger generation of Muslims and Christians who are key players here. They are drawn to local and international prophets of religious revivalism who have proliferated in the last two decades, along with their "spiritual adjustment programs." The latter popularly refer to the efforts of the aforementioned prophets to counter the negative effects of structural adjustment programs, political misrule, and moral confusion. Many African states remain very autocratic and consistently fail to respect or protect the basic civil and economic rights of their citizens.[10]

New Religious Movements in Africa: An Overview

The study of Africa's NRMs has generated a vast, multidisciplinary literature from both African and Africanist scholars. However, much of the scholarship has focused on particular historical periods and/or particular movements, or types of movements.[11] It has also been more historical or theological in nature. A more comparative and contextual analysis is needed within the prevailing discourses on democratization, civil society, and religious freedom, and the role of these religious formations therein.[12] It hardly needs stating that such a goal cannot be accomplished within the confines of the present essay. Rather, I hope to show, by means of selected examples, some of the emergent patterns of conflict between the newer religions and the state. The death, predominantly murder, of nearly a thousand members of a Ugandan (post-) Catholic apocalyptic movement, the Movement for the Restoration of the Ten Commandments of God, in March 2000, may prove somewhat paradigmatic in this regard. But first, some historical background is needed.

One of Africa's earliest known religious movements, the Antonian movement, was founded in the late seventeenth century in a spirit of political resistance and religious independency in the former Kongo empire of Central Africa. The founder, Dona Béatrice or Kimpa Vita, was burned at the stake in 1706 for her efforts in trying to turn the Portuguese Catholic mission into a Kongo Catholic Church.[13] She laid the foundations for a long history of political resistance in the region.[14] It was not until the end of the nineteenth century that more religious forms of protest emerged in West and South Africa in the form of the Ethiopian churches. They broke away from mission control mainly for reasons of racial disparity.[15]

Yet, for many Africans questions of cultural and spiritual relevance were more pressing. By foregrounding dreams, visions, healing, and spirit possession they were not only validating their own cultural roots but actively negotiating new indigenous forms of Christianity. Good examples of this type of movement would be the Aladura churches in Nigeria and the Zionist churches in South Africa.[16] This type of revitalization movement occurred to a lesser extent in Islam,[17] and traditional religion.[18] The main thrust of this religious independency began in the later colonial period (end of nineteenth to beginning of twentieth century). It was most marked in those areas that had been missionized by Protestantism, although some regions, such as East Africa, do have more movements that grew out of the Roman Catholic Church.[19]

The social and cultural impact of these thousands of religious movements (perhaps over 12,000 according to some estimates)[20] and their more transnational successors—churches and movements of the evangelical/ Pentecostal/charismatic variety, has been considerable.[21] Because of the self-determining claims of the earlier movements that came to be known as African independent churches (African-initiated, African-instituted or "new generation" churches are now also popular labels), they have been subjected to discrimination and persecution at the hands of state and non-state actors.[22] They were frequently viewed as subversive by colonial governments and deviant by the older mission-related churches.[23] Colonial proscriptions on these movements were removed by several of the new African governments in the post-independence phase.[24] However, by then, as Claasen notes in the case of the independent churches in South Africa, "[I]t is rather ironic that these churches which took pride in their spiritual independence, were being coerced into dependence by government regulations."[25] The purported political acquiescence of the Zionist churches in both the apartheid and post-apartheid eras has been the subject of much debate.[26] It has variously been attributed to fear of state reprisals or failure to gain official recognition, poverty, lack of education, political naïveté, protest against political violence, and pietistic character. Bengt Sundkler, the pioneer of the study of South African independent churches, describes their political strategies as more counter-cultural and as a withdrawal from the then "dominating world of the whites."[27] He underscores the lack of government recognition of these African churches by pointing to the minimal number of official registrations their precursors, the Ethiopian churches, were granted over the course of several decades (eleven churches from 1925–65).[28]

The eclipsing of these older independent churches and the growing domination of the "new generation" evangelical/Pentecostal/charismatic forms of Christianity in many parts of the African continent has been well documented.[29] Their predilection for a more apolitical[30] or indirectly political,[31] "spiritual" orientation and conservative social stance—notwithstanding their modern lifestyles—has appealed to a number of Africa's political leaders.[32] Significantly, this development has arguably engendered less antagonism in terms of the religion-state relationship than in earlier periods.[33] Yet, this newer type of movement has also caused an escalation in inter-religious conflict. But we shall return to this below.

Areas of Conflict

Rather than try to treat current tensions between NRMs and African governments from a regional or state-centric perspective, I propose the following framework to identify the principal areas of conflict. In the first instance, religious movements may be seen as constituting a threat to *political authority*. Here is where the state (whether in the form of police, politicians, or presidents) takes action to protect itself from the efforts of religious movements to subvert or critique its authority. In the second category, NRMs are viewed as constituting a threat to *public interests*. Their activities may be considered as inimical to particular types of individuals (such as women and children) or to social order more generally. In the third instance, *religious power and authority* are threatened directly or indirectly by the religious claims of these newer groups. Needless to say, where there are close links between religious and political formations, as in Uganda, then ostensibly religious altercations have political ramifications.

In order to counteract these real or perceived threats, national and local governments, as well as the media and religious organizations, resort to various courses of action—ranging from extreme to mild—which may be legal, semi-official, or informal methods.[34] I shall now discuss, with the aid of selected, relevant examples, these types of conflict and the various responses.[35] These examples will serve to demonstrate the complex, multi-perspectival nature of these issues, and their overlap in several cases.[36] For, as the Igbo of Nigeria say, you don't stand in one place to watch a masquerade. I give one particular case study, the neo-traditionalist Mungiki movement of Kenya, more extensive analysis not just for its topicality but because its conflicted and ambiguous relationship with the authorities illustrates well the complex and volatile nature of these issues in Africa today.

Threats to Political Authority

By far the most serious clashes between states and NRMs occur when the latter challenge the ruling authorities. This is not surprising given the insecurity of many African regimes, whether democratically elected or not. Fighting "cults" may be good for re-election. Let us take the case of Kenya. Many religious groups there, with the exception of the Pentecostals, criticized the autocratic regime of former President Daniel Arap Moi.[37] The mainline churches have consistently spoken out in the name of freedom and democracy. The government has historically been unsympathetic to revivalist, traditionalist movements because of their appeal to the poor through anti-government rhetoric. Over the last decade they have harassed and banned the Tent of the Living God and arrested its pro-Gikuyu leader and members.[38] But it is the more politically oriented Mungiki which has given the government a run for its money. This group, which is an offshoot of the former, advocates in somewhat revolutionary terms the need for fair governance and the destruction of sites of "devil worship." Much to the ire of public officials, they have publicly declared war on the Freemasons. They also express anti-Christian sentiments. Claiming links to the earlier 1950s nationalist movement, Mau-Mau, they practice female circumcision, sing traditional songs, and wear dreadlocks. Mungiki members also sniff raw tobacco and dried and ground roots. They have been involved in frequent confrontations with police. In September 2000 they "merged with" or converted to Islam, claiming that it would "hasten the realisation of our goal."[39] This has transposed the conflict to another level.

In defense of the group, the Council of Imams asked the government to stop harassing Mungiki followers and depriving them of their right to assemble at any place in Kenya (several had been arrested for illegal association) or of freedom of worship. "The government is courting bloodshed by continuously subjecting Mungiki followers to harassment and it should learn a lesson from what is happening in Israel now," one of the Muslim leaders stated provocatively after Mungiki was subjected to a police ban in October 2000 on unlicensed meetings.[40] Ibrahim Ndura Waruinge, the Mungiki national coordinator, accused church leaders of inciting the police against the group's members, who were not affiliated to any political party. Cabinet Minister Joseph Kamotho had indeed publicly urged the churches to help counter it: "[the t]ime has come for the Church to condemn the practices of this sect which is promoting outdated cultural beliefs."[41]

In terms of religious movements that have actively sought to destabilize government authorities, the Mungiki group is perhaps less well known abroad than the Lord's Resistance Army, which plagued government troops in Uganda for a number of years in the late 1980s.[42] This group has been implicated by several human rights groups in the recruitment of child soldiers.[43] Operating mainly in the north, it has some connection with Alice Lakwena's Holy Spirit Movement, an earlier Acholi resistance movement.[44] Renowned for her mystical powers, Alice Lakwena sought to counter the economic and political marginalization of her people through increasing militancy and millennialist messages of social and moral reform.[45] She creatively linked the healing of an abused natural environment with Christian ideas.[46] In addition to describing its traditionalist roots,

Prunier also highlights the group's semi-modern discourses, with its combination of minority status human rights talk and possession by James Bond-type spirits or *jok*.[47]

Sometimes governments have moved to ban NRMs because they deem their mission to be antipathetic to nationalist goals. This occurred in Ghana in June 1989 when the PNDC (People's National Defense Council) Law 221 was promulgated requiring all religious bodies to register. According to Kwesi Dickson it was "ostensibly a way of controlling the activities of Christian sects that were multiplying very rapidly." However, Justice D. F. Annan, a member of the government, assured the sects that the purpose of the law was to regulate rather than control religious activities.[48] The law also provided an instrument for the PNDC to ban any church "whose activities it deemed incompatible with normal Ghanaian life." The Jehovah's Witnesses and Mormons fell into this category.[49] The mainline churches contested the ban. The matter remained unresolved until the law was repealed at the inauguration of the Fourth Republic in 1994. The Ghanaian Mormon community reestablished itself and will soon have its own temple in the capital, Accra—one of the few granted to Africans to date.

Registration/deregistration is a powerful tool used by governments not only to exert control but also to manipulate public opinion about nonmainstream movements. This was the subject of the important "Seminar on Freedom of Religion and Belief in the OSCE Region: Challenges to Law and Practice," convened by the Dutch Foreign Ministry in The Hague in June 2001.[50] It was noted that "the law and practice with respect to recognition and registration of religious organizations has emerged as a crucial test for evaluating a country's performance with respect to freedom of religion or belief."[51] In the African context, the authorities may claim that groups which refuse to register are suspect and lack transparency. In return, minority religious groups may challenge the moral or legal authority of the government to regulate their activities. For example, the Kenyan neo-traditionalist movement, Mungiki, has openly rejected government and public calls for its registration: "We will never do that. We do not need to be registered by [this] Government which only abets poverty, insecurity, killings and social instability."[52]

Registration mechanisms are often created or strengthened following a particularly critical incident. Sundkler notes that the violent clash between Enoch Mgijima's Israelites and government forces in 1921 in South Africa led to a set of conditions for church registration in 1925.[53] After the discovery of the "cult" killings in Uganda in 2000, William Ruto, Assistant Minister in the Office of the President, warned that the government would crack down on religious groups that endangered the safety of their adherents.[54] New steps are being taken to counter growing threats to national security.

One of these new measures will involve the monitoring of the "working programmes" of "churches and religious sects" by district security chiefs.[55] This recommendation was adopted as the result of a report by Makerere University Professor Byaruhanga Akiiki on the threat of religious extremism to the country's security. The head of the Lord's Resistance Army, Joseph Kony, was singled out in particular. The concern by the government to "assess current and potential threats," and its plans to counter these threats in the next 15 years, is clearly being conducted with the Movement for the Restoration of the Ten Commandments of God in mind, as well as growing fears about global security.[56]

The Uganda massacre provoked a "prise de conscience" in several African countries, and moves were announced to reinforce the surveillance of "sects." For example, the government of Burkina Faso expressed particular concern over the Raelians because of their rapid growth in the country's second city, Bobo Dioulasso, and their aggressive proselytizing techniques in homes, the workplace and hospitals, and exploitation of the poorer classes.[57] The Minister for Administration, Yéro Boly, declared that he would forbid the activity of the "*sectes*" each time they threatened public order and security. In 2000, the government of Togo set up an inter-ministerial commission to investigate the activities of all non-mainstream religious groups in the country "whose unorthodox mode of worship threatens to imperil the orderly well-being of the Togolese society."[58]

Sometimes historical patterns of manipulation of religious groups can be reflected in subsequent restrictions. In former Zaïre (now the Democratic Republic of Congo) the colonial government set in motion national and provincial mechanisms in 1938 for disbanding "*sectes*" and "*associations indigènes*" that were considered to be a threat to public order.[59] In his extensive efforts to construct an ideologically integrated Zairean state from 1965 onwards, the head of state, Mobutu Sese Seko, launched various laws to restrict the activities of religious groups. The law of December 31, 1971, regulated public worship and the conditions for recognition as a legal religious institution in Zaire.[60] It granted legal status to three established churches and ignored the Islamic community. Both the Jehovah's Witnesses and Seventh-day Adventists suffered years of harassment from the regime. Mobutu coerced the Muslims in 1972 into forming a unified group in order to gain recognition as a national religion.

In 1989, following a countrywide tour, the Zairean Minister of Justice introduced stricter measures against religious communities and sects which had not obtained official status. He ordered the immediate closing of temples and places of public worship (the ban included meetings in forests and private homes) but guaranteed the right of individuals to practice their religion alone in the privacy of their own residences.[61] He invited all religious organizations to register under the laws governing non-profit organizations.[62] The conditions to be met in order to qualify as a founder of such an organization were very demanding (theological education, financial deposit, no previous role in another religious organization, and so forth), with the additional burden of annual reports. In his analysis of these legal developments, Ludiongo observes that, despite the touting by the government of the benefits of official recognition, very few groups that were not Catholic or Protestant (Eglise du Christ au Zaïre) had been registered. He attributes this in part to ignorance or to bureaucratic delays. He also notes that the only group banned between 1965 and 1991 were the Jehovah's Witnesses, which he finds remarkable given the informal complaints that circulate about minority religious groups. He suggests that the fact that 234 religious groups could continue to function (as of 1991) despite their unregistered status (26.44 percent of the total surveyed) might indicate a degree of tolerance on the part of the government, particularly in view of the law which states that no one can publicly preach if he is member of a church or religious sect which does not have civil status.[63]

Using registration as a way of determining acceptable and unacceptable religious organizations is recently evidenced in the case of Eritrea. In 2002, the Government of Eritrea instituted new constraints on religious groups known collectively as "Pentes."[64] These include all groups that do not belong to the four principal religions—Orthodox Christian, Muslim, Roman Catholic, and Evangelical Christian—including Pentecostals, evangelicals or "born-again Christians," Seventh-day Adventists, Jehovah's Witnesses, Baha'is, Buddhists, and other Protestants. In 2001, the government began closing "Pente" facilities. Following a May 2002 government decree that all religious groups must register or cease all religious activities, religious facilities not belonging to the four recognized religions were closed by the end of July.[65]

A more subtle but quite effective method of limiting the activities of less favored religious groups (and this may be for ethnic or political rather than or as well as directly religious reasons) is to create bureaucratic obstacles for their legal recognition. Losing files, inventing problems, and demanding extra payments are common practices. However, we should not assume that registration is necessarily problematic for newer religious movements in Africa. In the late 1980s when the Ghanaian government decreed that all religious groups should obtain official registration, it was the mainline churches who furiously protested the order and refused to comply, protesting freedom of religion. In contrast, it was the smaller, independent churches who rushed to get registered and enjoy the new legitimation and status!

Closely connected to questions of registration is land allocation. This constitutes a strategic form of government control of minority religious groups. In Kenya, President Moi was renowned for maintaining strict control over this sector. In the north of Nigeria, where many states have recently imposed *sharia* (Islamic) law, Christian groups complain of the discriminatory treatment they receive in trying to obtain land for church or school expansion. In some cases, local authorities try to destroy or displace pre-existing buildings if they are deemed to be in Muslim-dominated areas. Under such restrictive conditions it is not uncommon for religious groups to utilize creatively school and university buildings, private homes, hotels, and cinemas. It also leads to new alliances among beleaguered groups. For instance, the Centre for Religious and Cultural Rights was founded in 2002 to protect both mainstream and independent Christian churches from demolition and illegal transactions.[66] Sometimes the police may seek to appropriate land from a religious movement in order to curtail its operations. Approximately five years ago, in Nigeria, the governor of the state tried to acquire the property of Guru Maharaj Ji's Divine Light Mission, an Eastern-oriented communtarian group with a prominently situated ashram along the Lagos-Ibadan expressway. The movement went to court and was able to prove legal ownership of the land.[67]

As a less stringent measure, the common tactic is to control the freedom of association of unpopular or targeted religious groups. In this way the authorities can not only operate a process of selective control but also surveillance. If done with obvious bias, there can be violent public backlash. This occurred in the northern Nigerian city of Kano in 1991 when authorities banned a visit from the controversial South African Muslim preacher, Ahmed Deedat, but allowed Reinhard Bonnke, the equally controversial German Pentecostal evangelist, to come and lead one of the mass crusades for which he is famous.[68] He never actually made it on to the stage as Muslim youths launched a violent attack on Christians and in the ensuing riot several hundreds were killed. When Bonnke visited southern Nigeria in November 2000 to lead the Great Millennium Crusade—purportedly attended by six million people—he was told publicly, and in no uncertain terms, by the Council of Ulamas to stay away from the predominantly Muslim north of the country.[69]

Charges of illegal activities, such as drug smuggling, can create the leeway for the authorities to harass particular groups. This was the case with the highly publicized Synagogue Church of All Nations, run by Prophet T. B. Joshua in Lagos, Nigeria, who was arrested but not prosecuted in 1996 on orders from the National Drug Enforcement Agency. While the charges have not been cleared, the prophet appears to have been exonerated by a recent confession of one of the agency members.[70] Moreover, his reputation as a healer is now so celebrated that he draws supplicants from all over the world whether pro football players or heads of state.[71]

In some cases, it is the real or imagined overseas connections of a movement that may provoke government fears or suspicions, and resultant clampdowns. The fact that the Brazilian leaders of the controversial Universal Church of the Kingdom of God have not mastered English or the local African languages counts against them in public opinion in several African countries. The Nasser regime in Egypt around 1960 dissolved the Baha'i and Watchtower communities, and placed restrictions on Ahmadiya missionaries from India, because they were suspected of having ties to Zionism.[72] Frequently it is the smaller independent Pentecostal movements who may be targeted for having foreign, rather than nationalist, loyalties. In 1977, Uganda's head of state, Idi Amin, proscribed these churches.[73] Their conservative ideology and American connections have made them appear inimical to the liberation struggles of southern Africa.[74] But that was then, and the Pentecostal/charismatic churches and para-church movements, such as the Full Gospel Businessmen's Fellowship International, have effectively penetrated the leadership of several African countries. Their upwardly mobile image, promises of blessings and miracles, and popular gospel music production are nothing short of seductive.[75] At least four African heads of state, Kérékou of the Republic of Benin, Chiluba of Zambia, Obasanjo of Nigeria, and Moi of Kenya, have openly declared their "born-again" status. Others have sympathies with this type of religious orientation through their spouses, family members, and aides (Museveni of Uganda being a case in point).

Public Interests

When Africans express their misgivings concerning the "proliferation of sects" in their countries, they are generally alluding to the risks of financial and social exploitation by the founders and leaders of such groups. The unchecked "mushrooming" of religious groups is linked in many people's minds with loss of tradition, lack of authority, and selfish opportunism.[76] It is not uncommon to read in the popular media of women impregnated by independent church leaders, children kidnapped, sick people deprived of expert medical attention, and men duped by fake prophets.[77] A classic example of this would be Wilson Bushara, leader of the World Message Last Warning Church in Uganda, who had offered space in heaven after death in return for cash; men were supposed to surrender their wives, and the wives then declared themselves unmarried.[78] Journalists are also fond of pointing to disparities between the comfortable, if not flamboyant, lifestyles of the leaders and their desperate and impoverished followers.[79]

More recently, the issue of noise pollution by exuberant Pentecostal and charismatic churches and the "right to sleep" for neighboring residents has become highly contentious. Local authorities or campus officials usually point to the loss of productivity and security risks of all-night services.[80] In Makalle, (Tigray) Ethiopia, near the end of 2002, followers of the Good Gospel Church staged a religious meeting at the town's stadium.[81] Following purportedly peaceful complaints from neighboring residents (mainly Ethiopian Orthodox Christians according to the newspaper report) about the "deafening noise," the police moved in, and between two to five deaths were reported. In January 2002, district officials in Gilgil, Kenya, stopped a religious meeting of the Emmanuel Church of God during a two-week crusade after local residents complained of continual wailing and screaming coming from the church.[82] Residents charged that the group was a cult and that its members had sold their property to prepare for the return of Jesus Christ. The allegations were denied by the church. In the 1990s, bans were initially placed by the Togolese authorities, then lifted, on "sects" because of the nuisance and noise they create.[83]

The problem, of course, is the imposition of a blanket ban on all new groups, or groups in a particular category, rather than singling out those who are the worst offenders. In defense of this, officials generally state that, since the majority of these churches are given to expressive forms of worship with the use of drums, electric musical instruments, and modern public address systems, this type of general restriction is justified. Furthermore, they would argue that they do not possess the means to address the complaints leveled at individual religious organizations for breach of public peace and order—unless this involves serious criminal action. It is not uncommon for African governments to ignore unregistered groups as they do not have the means to pursue them. Likewise, many of the religious groups themselves, notably the smaller, independent ones, manage to function without gaining official recognition.[84] But there is a significant difference between the minimal ability to function without registration on the one hand, and the ability to engage in activities such as managing religious property as a group rather than as individuals.[85]

Another justification for curtailing the activities of religious groups may be linked to healthcare. For instance, in Angola, a local government has closed down seventeen out of a list of 57 illegal groups and arrested six religious leaders. One of the reasons given by the provincial council of Cabinda is that "many of these sects indulge in unauthorised modern and traditional medicine which often puts people's lives at risk."[86]

Burundi journalist Agnes Nindorera links the efflorescence of (mainly Protestant-related) religious groups in her country to the breakdown of political and religious (Catholic) authority over the last decade, and the sheer quest for survival.[87] However, she claims that the enthusiasm for these newer movements was somewhat tempered by troubling information which came to public light in February 2000 about the antisocial activities of several movements. This was quickly followed in March by the news of the unfolding tragedy concerning one of Uganda's new religious movements.

On March 17, 2000, over three hundred followers of a Catholic-oriented, apocalyptic movement known as the Movement for the Restoration of the Ten Commandments of God died in Kanungu (Rukungiri district, Uganda), 217 miles southwest of the capital, Kampala.[88] The majority perished in an explosion and fire in the church; mass graves were later discovered of people who had died violent deaths. Some suicides have also been reported. The final count was close to 800. Needless to say, various theories and rumors have been advanced as to the reasons for the tragedy. Information on the leaders is available but it is unclear whether they escaped or died in the conflagration. The movement came into being in 1989 following apparitions of Jesus Christ and the Virgin Mary. Such experiences were common in this part of Uganda and neighboring Rwanda. Not all were endorsed by the Roman Catholic Church. The key figures of the movement were Paul Kashaku, who died before the events of March, his daughter, Credonia Mwerinde, a barmaid with a reputation for sexual promiscuity, Joseph Kibwetere, a former politician and locally prominent Catholic layman, and Dominic Kataribabo, a former Catholic priest and college-educated theologian. They had access to Marian literature from other parts of the world and produced some literature of their own, including a book, *A Timely Message from Heaven*. It remains unclear whether the final events were precipitated by apocalyptic fears or demands from members for the return of their funds. The group was in contact with the local authorities over registration and other issues. In fact they had even paid their taxes not long before March 2000. There are reports, nonetheless, of police ignoring appeals to investigate charges of child abuse and kidnapping in the group.[89]

It took no time at all before the Ugandan movement was being compared to Jonestown and Waco by the local and world press. The repercussions were manifold. The Ugandan government started clamping down on many minority religions, notably the "doomsday" groups, including several Pentecostal churches. The latter tried to turn the tables by casting aspersions on the normally unassailable Roman Catholic Church. The arrest in July 2000 of Wilson Bushara, leader of the World Message Last Warning Church, who had been on the run in Uganda for ten months, accused of embezzlement, unlawful assemblies, and sexual and child abuse, was much heralded by the media.[90] In July 2000, Kenyan human rights groups expressed fears about the Movement for the Restoration of the Ten Commandments of God being reincarnated in Kenya in the guise of another movement known as Choma. They appealed to the authorities to "move in and save the people of western Kenya from mass suicide that may be occasioned by the cult."[91] Several African governments, such as those of Botswana, Namibia, Kenya, and Rwanda, made it known to their populations that they were stepping up vigilance and/or control of "sects and cults." The media seemed readier than ever to cover and comment on the questionable activities of such groups, as when Heaven's Gate members purportedly entered Kenya recently to make contacts and distribute literature.[92] American self-styled anticult experts offered their services to the Ugandan government but reportedly did not get further than Nairobi as the government was not prepared to pay the asking price.[93]

The neo-traditionalist Mungiki movement in Kenya has continued to aggravate its opponents by allegedly leading a mob that attacked and stripped six women for wearing trousers in late 2000.[94] In response the police raided the estate in Kayole where the attack took place and seized arms, electronic goods, and thousands of liters of traditional brew. They went ahead as public clamor grew for the arrest of the alleged culprits. Film of the assault was screened on Nation TV, and the attackers were clearly shown. In one sequence they waved the women's trousers in triumph. Yet officials of the group distanced themselves from the attack. The coordinator, Ibrahim Ndura Waruinge, said the incident was "unfortunate and inhumane" and added that the movement did not support violence against women. He said allegations of harassment of the women by members of the sect were propaganda by the government and the press and could be attributed to an extremist Kikuyu group. He emphasized that women members of Mungiki wear trousers just like the women who were stripped and said they respected the rights of other people to wear what they wanted. In response to condemnations from women's groups, such as the Federation of Women Lawyers (Fida), Waruinge asked them to "leave us alone," complaining that they supported prostitution and male and female homosexuality.

The public complaints against Mungiki persisted several weeks after the stripping incident. A local Muslim leader condemned their actions and stated that Mungiki should not be associated with Islam. He urged the government to take stern action against Mungiki before they caused tremendous damage to the country and its citizens. Cabinet Minister Joseph Kamotho renewed calls for the Anglican Church to help counter Mungiki and to discourage young people from joining the sect because of its promotion of "outdated cultural beliefs." Sporting long or short trousers and chanting anti-Mungiki slogans, members of the Coalition on Violence Against Women demonstrated in the center of Nairobi in early November. They brandished placards reading, "I will wear whatever I want."[95] It was not long before there was a presidential directive to crack down on Mungiki and several arrests were made.[96]

In Nigeria, it was "Jesus of Oyingbo" who was the bane of the authorities for many years. The founder of the Universal College of Regeneration (UCR), Olufunmilayo Odumosu, ran a commune at his Lagos residence where women members became "wives" or "sisters." Procreation was alleged to be a goal of the group, and incest was reported.[97] The group disbanded following the death of its founder some years ago. More widely known is the case of the Divine Light Mission, a communitarian group predicated on Eastern spirituality run by Guru Maharaj Ji. There have been a number of attacks on their ashrams, mainly spearheaded by former members. For example, in 1989, Maharaj Ji was arrested when a former devotee claimed that the leader had killed and buried 200 people in the Ibadan ashram. No evidence was found of such claims after extensive digging by the police. In late July 2000, the leader was acquitted of murder charges after a Ghanaian devotee was beaten to death at the Lagos/Iju ashram. The judge reprimanded the police for their high-handedness and poor investigations.[98]

The Brazilian Pentecostal church, the Universal Church of the Kingdom of God, has generated controversy in at least three African countries to date. In Kenya, they were criticized for attracting people to the church via the media on the basis of unrealizable promises. In South Africa, the Human Rights Commission receives more complaints concerning this religious organization than any other in the country.[99] In Zambia, the movement was proscribed in 1998 on the grounds that it had not operated "within the laws of the land."[100] Former church members also publicly alleged that ritual murderers operated from within the church as members were purportedly required to donate blood for satanic rituals.

Religious Power and Authority

In the competitive public spheres of Africa's cities, clashes between mainstream and minority religious groups occur quite frequently. The accusations can be theological ("satanic") or social (dangerous, antisocial, corrupt) in nature, but the interests center on boundary maintenance. Loss of members to another organization entails loss of revenue and loss of prestige. Increasingly, these confrontations are played out in the media, which may only serve to heighten the disagreements.[101] They may not involve the government unless the latter is invoked in matters of registration, illegal operations, and so forth. Not infrequently it is the newer Christian movements who take the high moral ground in condemning the nefarious or unbiblical practices of others. For instance, a Zambian bishop of the Church of God suggested that the Evangelical Fellowship of Zambia be allowed to scrutinize applications of new churches for registration since government regulations were "very weak."[102]

To combat the "sheep-stealing" activities of the Mungiki group in Kenya, a seminar was organized in September 2000 by the National Council of Churches of Kenya to investigate the activities of the "sect" and to offer guidance on how to confront it.[103] Earlier strategies involved emphasizing through the media the group's unregistered status. The confrontation between Mungiki and church leaders escalated in October 2000, when Mungiki leaders issued a seven-day ultimatum to the Anglican Church of Kenya to apologize over its retired Archbishop Mannasses Kuria's assertion that it was satanic. The angered Mungiki members called on the Anglican Church to disassociate itself from the prelate's remarks or "we (Mungiki) in liaison with our Muslim brothers issue a fatwa (decree) on them." In a show of defiance, the head of the Anglican Church in Kenya, Bishop David Gitari, dismissed the Mungiki threat, saying his church would not want to engage in petty politics with a violent and unregistered group. "The church could only respond to the threats of fatwa by the Mungiki sect upon receipt of a written decree duly signed by sect leaders and their Muslim brothers," the *East African Standard* (Nairobi) quoted Gitari as saying some days later.[104]

It should be noted that these attacks and counterattacks have been occurring within a general context of socio-political insecurity and economic downturn in Kenya. Fears of "devil worship" involving the rich and powerful abound.[105] This more modernized, global type of witchcraft, with its conspiratorial interpretations, is believed to account for the child kidnappings and killings that have rocked Nairobi and Mombasa in recent times. It is also linked to serious corruption and illegal land transactions.[106] Any organization that is remotely secretive can fall prey to these accusations. The Freemasons constitute one such example, despite (or in some minds because of) their support from the Roman Catholic Church. The Kenyan government even went so far as to establish a Presidential Commission of Inquiry into Devil Worship in 1994 in response to public concern, mainly voiced by Christian clergy. Its report was presented to parliament in August 1999.[107]

According to the U.S. State Department's 2000 Annual Report for International Religious Freedom, "Satanists" in Kenya had allegedly infiltrated non-indigenous religious groups such as Jehovah's Witnesses, Mormons, and Christian Scientists, as well as the Freemasons and the Theosophical Society. The State Department report notes that most members of the commission making the report were "senior members of mainline Christian churches."[108] A local journalist wryly commented that "[t]he commissioners overlooked the fact that Kenya is a secular state and went on to prescribe standards that only Moses the Lawmaker could think of recommending to the Jews."[109] In a trenchant and humorous piece, *The Nation*

(Nairobi) journalist G. K. Waruhiu wrote, "[the report] is also highly defamatory, scandalous, and poorly presented, full of cliches and empty statements which were not properly researched, and which in the final analysis amount to a new-fangled Kenyan Spanish Inquisition, or simple witch-hunting."[110] He calls on the government to apologize for wasting taxpayers' time and money and putting minority religions at risk. For many Christians the non-release of the government report has spurred them to take their own action. The Christian Churches Education Association (CCEA) of Kenya, for example, set up its own commission in January 2001 to probe "devil worship" in learning institutions countrywide.[111]

Not much is said or known publicly about New Age, Rosicrucian, and Asian-derived movements in Africa. But there is a growing pattern of critical opposition to, if not outright harassment of, these movements by evangelical and conservative Christian groups in particular. Summit Lighthouse members reported to me in Calabar in August 1997 that they had been physically harassed and publicly abused by militant Christians, and eventually forced to cancel their planned public rally at the central sports stadium. As indicated earlier, media channels may be employed to identify the enemy or answer critics. Eckankar's local president in Liberia sought to dispel rumors in October 2000 about its "dubious and secret activities" in the country by publicly explaining its key tenets.[112] Likewise, Nigeria's Minister of Justice and Attorney General, Chief Bola Ige, took advantage of a major AMORC convention to chide critics of the Rosicrucian Order for their writing off the organization as a "secret cult" when, according to him, that is how Christianity began its life.[113] The New Age, Rosicrucian, and Asian-derived movements seem to enjoy greater tolerance in Ghana and South Africa because of their associations with the ruling classes. For example, Summit Lighthouse was closely associated with the Acheampong regime in Ghana in the 1970s. In South Africa, the New Age movement is growing—mainly among the white middle class—primarily as a quest for alternative healing strategies. On the whole these New Age, Rosicrucian, and Asian-derived movements have a limited appeal for most Africans. Ironically, while the secrecy cultivated by some of these groups is a source of stigma, it may eventually be what protects them. Some are dismissed as being "Eastern" or "Oriental" religions. Their public lectures are frequently held on university campuses. Economic demands on members, whether for initiation purposes or the purchase of inspirational/instructional materials, such as in the case of the Holy Grail Movement or AMORC, may also preclude or reduce access.

Sometimes the government can decide to intervene on matters of religious conflict. For instance, the Nigerian government banned religious broadcasting in the late 1980s in an effort to stem the tide of inter-religious conflict. In Uganda, at least a decade ago, Paul Gifford reports how the government became alarmed by the intolerance between churches, in particular the anti-Catholic preachings of the Pentecostals.[114] One of the measures they took was to place a ban in 1990 on television and radio programs by the Pentecostal churches. The infighting between the newer "born-again" churches has been exacerbated by the growing influence of demonic and satanic beliefs (this is also strong in Ghana, and South Africa)[115] and the tendencies of these churches to authoritarianism and totalitarianism.[116]

In Nigeria, it is precisely these newer groups that are tipping the balance of religious power relations despite the fact that they still number less than mainline church adherents. This development has been a major factor in the recent and ongoing religious conflicts that Nigeria has experienced over the last twenty years. Since late 1999, the violence between Muslims and Christians involving loss of life and property damage has been aggravated by the decision of several northern states to implement *sharia* as the predominant legal system. It is more often than not the newer generation churches who are the most vocal in contesting these developments because of their greater militant and millennialist tendencies.[117] As I have argued elsewhere, they have readily appropriated the large and small media in their efforts to proselytize.[118] Their congregations are younger and hence less bound to tradition and centralized authorities, whether local or international. Yet their influence reaches a wide cross-section of the population through their inspirational literature, gospel music, popular videos, and televangelism. While the larger movements carve out an image of apolitical, upright, and successful lifestyles replete with blessings and miracles, there is a dangerous undercurrent of conspiratorial and adversarial images of the Islamic other.

Moreover, it is often the evangelical, Pentecostal, and charismatic movements that are the most vocal in claiming their constitutional and international rights to religious freedom. This is due to the fact that their leaders may be more educated (many of these movements are born on university and college campuses) and their membership more middle class than in the independent or "spiritual" churches. It stems also from their links with similar United States-based organizations and the fact that a defining characteristic of their enterprise is proselytization. We should not underestimate the role played by the drive to disseminate one's religion in antagonizing relationships between religion and the state, and between different religious groups in Africa.[119] More often than not this has served to polarize religious groups and generate conflict as each group seeks to claim its own space and protect its own practices, rather than recognizing the need to negotiate contested issues and terrain. A good example of this would be the recent controversy over drumming in Ghana, which was much covered—some would say exacerbated—by the press. In 1998 and 1999, some Pentecostalists refused to accept an annual ban on drumming imposed by the Gan people in the capital, Accra, during an important traditional festival period. Some serious clashes resulted. A series of ecumenical moves prevented further outbreaks of violence in 2000.

Conclusion

As stated at the beginning of this essay, Africa has not seen the systematic suppressions of NRMs and minority religious groups found in, for example, China and Russia. One reason may be that the growth of the new religions in Africa has occurred over several decades and as a result of various configurations of local and international agency, rather than as a result of a sudden influx of exogenous proselytization as in Eastern Europe, for example. It is also linked to the fertile growth of Africa's own movements. Movements that some decades ago were sidelined politically and culturally may now be larger and more influential than their mainline counterparts. The Zion Christian Church in South Africa would be a case in point. As the largest of the independent churches in southern Africa, with between three and six million members, it has exceeded the membership of the Anglican and Dutch Reformed Churches. These facts notwithstanding, there is clear evidence of a new phase of inter-religious and religion-state tensions taking shape across Africa. As adumbrated above, these local conflicts are fueled by the globalizing discourses of human rights and religious freedom, and the rapid expansion of the mass media.

Moreover, African states and their citizens debate openly these days whether unbridled religious freedom is healthy. Yet the growing number of calls for more state regulation of religious groups can sometimes be countered with negative political and popular backlash. As is the pattern in Africa and elsewhere, it is the non-mainstream groups who come off worst, with the constitutional protection of religious freedom in many African states providing "cold comfort to religious groups disapproved of by the political authorities."[120] In the opinion of Kenyan legal scholar Makau Mutua, it is traditional African religions that have suffered the most at the hands of the state.[121]

So alongside the many voices condemning the proliferation of religious movements in their respective countries, there are those who would defend the constitutional right to freedom of religion, even if that means allowing undesirable competitors to co-exist in the public sphere. As a Kenyan journalist observed sagaciously not long after the Uganda crisis,

> Our government lacks the means through which to regulate these bodies without compromising the constitutional guarantee to freedom of worship. Society

also deems it improper to probe the groups. The only workable preventive strategy then is for the followers to be alert and not let anyone sway them into wayward, unorthodox practices.[122]

As evidence of a more proactive strategy, a non-governmental organization known as VOA (*"la voix des abusés et des opprimés"*) was established in October 2000 in the Democratic Republic of Congo to educate members of religious groups to view their patrimony as collective rather than being owned by the leader alone.[123] This seems like a practical step in the face of empty government rhetoric at festival time about the need for religious tolerance. The role of academics and missionary organizations in fostering dialogue and promoting education is also noteworthy in this respect.[124] But we should not overlook the ways in which they are more than capable of shaping public discourses on minority religions in a negative fashion.[125]

Much more research remains to be done on these emergent issues of religious freedom and conflict in Africa—not least to comprehend better the prevailing interconnections and tensions between religion, ethnicity, nationhood, globalization, and now international security concerns. The experiences and trajectories of individual movements, and types of movements, in their interactions with the state need to be documented and analyzed. As suggested earlier in this essay, hard and fast categories and generalizations can run afoul of the evidence—the burgeoning Pentecostal groups being the primary case in point. In addition, the varying influences of colonialist and political leaders on current interpretations of freedom of religion and belief in the respective African contexts merit further investigation. We need to look to the way different models of religious freedom (whether European, American, Muslim, Christian, traditional African) are informing public debates and policy-making—particularly given the current or proposed legal restrictions on "sects" and "cults" in several European countries that were former colonial powers. The role of the local and international media in shaping popular fears or understanding of the activities of NRMs is sorely in need of critical examination. United States-produced anticult and countercult literature has been on the bookshelves of Africa's Christian bookstores for some years now, but the activities of anticult organizations in Africa (whether local or foreign) would appear to be an under-researched and challenging new area for scholars of religion to engage.[126]

Africa's NRMs and minority religious groups may not trump the centrality of Christian-Muslim relations in shaping religion-state relationships. But with the trend by government, media, and churches to treat them as a generalized category they will likely grow in influence. Treatment of and attitudes toward these groups serve as important pointers to the differential power relations within each nation-state and reflect popular cultural attitudes of religious tolerance and intolerance. The cases of the Movement for the Restoration of the Ten Commandments of God in Uganda and Mungiki in Kenya, as well as many others, clearly illustrate how the mishandling or misreading of a minority religious group may have dire national and international repercussions.

Notes

1. I would like to acknowledge the help of Natalie Schwehr, Zachary Lomo, Sheila Braka, Robert Papini, Sunday Dare, and Samuel Amadi in preparing this essay. I also benefited from the probing comments and questions of colleagues when a version of this paper was presented at the Harvard Africa Seminar, 30 November 2000, and at the Boston University African Studies Center (Walter Rodney Seminar) on 5 February 2001. Portions of this paper were delivered at and benefited from an American Academy of Religion panel (cosponsored by the Millennialism Studies and New Religious Movements Groups) on the Movement for the Restoration of the Ten Commandments of God, Nashville, 20 November 2000.

2. See Terence O. Ranger, "Religious Movements and Politics in Sub-Saharan Africa," *African Studies Review* 29:2 (1986): 1–69; and Rosalind I. J. Hackett, ed., *New Religious Movements in Nigeria* (Lewiston, NY: Edwin Mellen Press, 1987). As suggested here, I am operating with a fairly broad understanding of what constitutes a "new religious movement" in the African context. This is essential given the fluidity and flux of African forms of religious expression, and a greater leaning toward this-worldly pragmatism. I am including both exogenous and indigenous movements which distinguish themselves from mainstream religious traditions (whether local, Christian, or Islamic) in terms of practice, belief, and values. In many cases the reformulation of religious identity has involved institutional rupture and structural innovation through the agency of prophetic figures. Such movements for the most part are perceived as minority religious groups for reasons of size, ideology, and social practice. However, by dint of popularity and growth, they may become major players politically, socially, and religiously. This would be the case of the newer independent churches of Pentecostal and charismatic orientation. The terms "sect" and "cult" do get used quite widely and generally pejoratively (that notwithstanding the anthropological uses of "cult" in the traditional context). In Nigeria, the use of the term "cult" has come to refer almost solely to the "secret cults" which have been the scourge of university campuses for more than two decades. These are fraternity-type organizations that engage in terrorist and extortionist activities to bolster their group solidarity and perceived nefarious powers. They are not explicitly religious but may employ religious symbols as part of their repertoire and discourse of secrecy. These organizations have been banned on many campuses and in some states. See, e.g., Mike Osunde and Ifedayo Sayo, "Edo Passes Law against Cultism in School, Service," *Guardian Online*, 7 February 2000.

3. See J. D. Van der Vyver, "Religious Freedom in African Constitutions," in *Proselytization and Communal Self-Determination in Africa*, ed. Abdullahi Ahmed An-Na'im (Maryknoll, NY: Orbis, 1999), 109–43.

4. See Abdullahi Ahmed An-Na'im and Francis M. Deng, eds., *Human Rights in Africa: Cross-Cultural Perspectives* (Washington, D.C.: Brookings Institution, 1990); and Louise Pirouet, "The Churches and Human Rights in Kenya and Uganda since Independence," in *Religion and Politics in East Africa: The Period Since Independence*, eds. Holger Bernt Hansen and Michael Twaddle (Athens, OH: Ohio University Press, 1995), 158.

5. See J. Kilian, ed., *Religious Freedom in South Africa*, vol. 44 (Pretoria: University of South Africa, 1993); J. M. Waliggo, "The Role of Christian Churches in the Democratisation Process in Uganda 1980–1993," in *The Christian Churches and the Democratisation of Africa*, ed. Paul Gifford (Leiden, Netherlands: E. J. Brill, 1995), 217–18; and Malory Nye, *Multiculturalism and Minority Religions in Britain: Krishna Consciousness, Religious Freedom, and the Politics of Location* (London: Curzon, 2001).

6. See Rosalind I. J. Hackett, Mark Silk, and Dennis Hoover, eds., *Religious Persecution as a U.S. Policy Issue* (Hartford, CT: Center for the Study of Religion in Public Life, 2000).

7. Paul Marshall, *Their Blood Cries Out* (Dallas: Word Publishing, 1997); and Nina Shea, *In the Lion's Den* (Nashville: Broadman and Holman Publishers, 1997). I have seen copies of these books circulating in Kenya, Nigeria, Ghana, and South Africa. See also his more recent report, Paul Marshall, ed., *Religious Freedom in the World: A Global Report on Persecution and Freedom* (New York: Broadman and Holman, 2000). As I was writing this article, the new book, *Today's Martyrs*, by religious statistician and editor of the *World Christian Encyclopedia*, David B. Barrett, was being announced.

8. Taken from a lecture, "Religion, Ethnicity and the Politics of Constitutionalism in Africa," delivered at Ohio University, Athens, Ohio, 13 November 2000, and reported in *Post Express* (Lagos), 13 November 2000.

9. Dale F. Eickelman and Jon W. Anderson, eds., *New Media in the Muslim World: The Emerging Public Sphere* (Bloomington, IN: Indiana University Press, 1999).

10. Cf. Richard Joseph, ed., *State, Conflict, and Democracy in Africa* (Boulder, CO: Lynn Rienner, 1999); Abdullahi Ahmed An-Na'im, "Competing Claims to Religious Freedom and Communal Self-Determination in Africa," in *Proselytization and Communal Self-Determination in Africa*, ed. An-Na'im, 9.

11. Harold W. Turner sought to collate these works through his Centre for the Study of New Religious Movements, first at the University of Aberdeen, then at Selly Oak Colleges in Birmingham, United Kingdom. See, for example, his now dated bibliography on African movements, *Bibliography of New Religious Movements in Primal Societies*, vol. 1, *Black Africa* (Boston: G. K. Hall, 1977). Adrian Hastings bemoans the lack of a satisfactory overall study of NRMs in Africa. His own bibliography is very helpful, despite the fact that he does not go beyond 1950, and his general antipathy toward (and hence non-inclusion of) social science accounts. See Adrian Hastings, *The Church in Africa 1450–1950* (Oxford: Clarendon, 1994), 669–76.

12. Such is intended by the new German journal, *Religion-Staat-Gesellschaft*. See also the very valuable special issue of *Social Justice Research* on "Justice and New Religious Movements" 12:4 (1999) edited by James T. Richardson on Europe, Canada, and Australia. However, it should be noted that there is as yet very little case law in the African context in this area. But media, archival, and ethnographic sources can offset this lack. There is a need to complement or even contest the predominant outside interest (of the media, Christian missionary organizations, and foreign governments, notably the United States) in Christian-Muslim relations. Véronique Faure makes the same observation about the southern African religious scene. See Véronique Faure, *Dynamiques Religieuses en Afrique Australe* (Paris: Karthala, 2000), 12. See Paul Gifford, *African Christianity: Its Public Role* (Bloomington, IN: Indiana University Press, 1998) for an excellent example of the type of scholarship needed on religion in Africa. Max Assimeng's *Saints and Social Structures* (Legon, Ghana: Ghana Publishing Company, 1986) is an earlier sociological analysis of NRMs in West and Central Africa that is both comparative and well-researched.

13. Adrian Hastings, *The Church in Africa 1450–1950*, 104–108; J. K. Thornton, *The Kongolese Saint Anthony: Dona Beatrix Kimpa Vita and the Antonian Movement, 1684–1706* (New York: Cambridge University Press, 1998).

14. Wyatt MacGaffey, *Modern Kongo Prophets: Religion in a Plural Society* (Bloomington, IN: Indiana University Press, 1983).

15. Jim Kiernan, "The African Independent Churches," in *Living Faiths in South Africa*, eds. Martin Prozesky and John de Gruchy (New York: St. Martin's Press, 1995), 118f. See also the extensive literature on the Watchtower and Kitawala movements, G. Shepperson and T. Price, *Independent African: John Chilembwe and the Origins, Setting and Significance of the Nyasaland Native Rising of 1915* (Edinburgh: Edinburgh University Press, 1958), and Karen E. Fields, *Revival and Rebellion in Colonial Central Africa* (Princeton, NJ: Princeton University Press, 1985).

16. See, for example, J. D. Y. Peel, *Aladura: A Religious Movement among the Yoruba* (London: International African Institute, 1968); Adrian Hastings, *The Church in Africa*, 493–539; G. C. Oosthuizen and Irving Hexham, eds., *Afro-Christian Religion at the Grassroots in South Africa* (Lewiston, NY: Edwin Mellen Press, 1991); Jim Kiernan, "The African Independent Churches," in *Living Faiths in South Africa*, eds. Martin Prozesky and John De Gruchy (New York: St. Martin's Press, 1995), 116–28.

17. Lamin Sanneh, *The Crown and the Turban: Muslims and West African Pluralism* (Boulder, CO: Westview Press, 1997); Sulayman S. Nyang, "Islamic Revivalism in West Africa: Histor-

ical Perspectives and Recent Developments," in *Religious Plurality in Africa: Essays in Honour of John S. Mbiti*, eds. Jacob K. Olupona and Sulayman S. Nyang (Berlin: Mouton de Gruyter, 1993), 231–72; David Westerlund and Eva Evers Rosander, eds., *African Islam and Islam in Africa: Encounters Between Sufis and Islamists* (London: Hurst, 1997).

18. Rosalind I. J. Hackett, "Revitalization in African Traditional Religion," in *African Traditional Religions in Contemporary Society*, ed. J. K. Olupona (New York: Paragon House, 1991), 135–48.

19. See Cynthia Hoehler-Fatton, *Women of Fire and Spirit: History, Faith, and Gender in Rojo Religion in Western Kenya* (New York: Oxford University Press, 1996).

20. In South Africa alone, 4,500 names of African independent churches were discovered in the 1996 census. See Marjorie Froise, *South African Christian Handbook* (Welkom, South African Christian Info, 2000), 61–65.

21. Cf. Harvey Cox, *Fire from Heaven: The Rise of Pentecostal Spirituality and the Reshaping of Religion in the Twenty-first Century* (London: Cassell, 1996), 243–62.

22. Cf. Hannah W. Kinoti, "Religious Fragmentation in Kenya," in *Proselytization and Communal Self-Determination in Africa*, ed. An-Na'im, 268–90; D. R. Boschman, "Religious Freedom in Botswana: The Cases of the Zion Christian Church and the Nazareth Church of Botswana," in *African Independent Churches Today: Kaleidoscope of Afro-Christianity*, ed. M. C. Kitshoff (Lewiston, NY: Edwin Mellen Press, 1996), 37–50.

23. Some even owed their very being to such a political goal. Witness the case of the neo-traditional movement, Godianism, founded by Chief K. O. K. Onyioha in Nigeria, as the religious wing of the National Council of Nigeria and the Cameroons.

24. J. N. K. Mugambi, "African Churches in Social Transformation," *Journal of International Affairs* 50:1 (1996): 194–220, 205.

25. Johan W. Claasen, "Independents Made Dependents: African Independent Churches and Government Recognition," *Journal of Theology for Southern Africa* 91 (June 1995): 15–34.

26. Matthew Schoffeleers, "Healing and Political Acquiescence in African Independent Churches," in *Religion and Politics in Southern Africa*, eds. Carl F. Hallencreutz and Mai Palmberg (Uppsala, Sweden: Scandanavian Institute of African Studies, 1991), 89–108; cf. Jean Comaroff, *Body of Power, Spirit of Resistance* (Chicago: University of Chicago, 1985).

27. Bengt Sundkler, "African Independent Churches and their Political Roles," in *Religion and Politics in Southern Africa*, eds. Hallencreutz and Palmberg, 87.

28. Ibid., 86.

29. In the new edition of the *World Christian Encyclopedia* edited by David B. Barrett, George T. Kurian, and Todd M. Johnson, *World Christian Encyclopedia: A Comparative Survey of Churches and Religions, A.D. 3–A.D. 2200* (New York: Oxford University Press, 2001), Barrett claims that those believing in and practicing such spiritual gifts as healing and speaking in tongues continue to be the fastest-growing segment of Christianity. Africa numbers 126 million who consider themselves to be Pentecostal or charismatic. See religiontoday.com (viewed 14 August 2000). Daneel contests the conflation and inflation of these figures in Pentecostalism in South Africa. See Marthinus L. Daneel, *African Initiated Churches in Southern Africa: Protest Movements or Mission Churches?* Vol. 33 (Boston: African Humanities Program, African Studies Center, 2000), 7. Gifford rightly indicates that perhaps South Africa, because of its later political liberation, is the only place in Africa where the older-style independent churches still flourish. See Gifford, *African Christianity*, 325. That notwithstanding, they are still marginalized. For example, at the conference of Christian World Communions held in Johannesburg in October 2000 they were not invited but met with separately. See "Christian World Communions Begin Conference," Panafrican News Agency, 23 October 2000. However, the South African Council of Churches is reconsidering its membership procedures because of new trends in application for membership, notably from the African Independent Churches. Also it is not uncommon now for the South African president to go on official visits to the larger independent churches. Information from Robert Papini, 17 November 2000.

30. Paul Gifford, *African Christianity*, 334.

31. Ruth Marshall, "Power in the Name of Jesus," *Review of African Political Economy* 52 (1991): 21–37.

32. In fact, Gifford, *African Christianity*, 245, 334, argues that the label of "sect" is inappropriate for these groups as they are not breaking away from power but seeking to become part of the establishment in many cases.

33. As stated unambiguously by the founder of the Abundant Life Church in Uganda, "[A]ny President with any sense would welcome born-again churches. We pray for them," Gifford, *African Christianity*, 174. There are naturally exceptions. Dr. Mensa Otabil, founder and senior pastor of the International Central Gospel Church in Accra, Ghana, has established himself as a thoughtful critic of Ghana's post-independence phase. See ibid., 80–84, 237–42, and the church's new website, centralgospel.com. See also Joseph Eastwood Anaba, *God's Endtime Militia: Winning the War Within and Without* (Oxford: n.p., 1993). A top example from Nigeria would be Tunde Bakare, founder of the Latter Rain Assembly in Lagos, who has drawn criticism for his outspoken prophecies. See Temitope Ogunjinmi, "Profile: A Fiery Priest," *The News* (Lagos), 14 June 1999.

34. Cf. Marat Shterin, "Legislating on Religion in the Face of Uncertainty," in *Law and Informal Practices in Russia*, eds. J. Callaghan and M. Kurkchian (Oxford: Clarendon Press, 2001).

35. North Africa is not covered in the present essay.

36. A relevant example here would be the radical Islamic movement in northern Nigeria, known as Maitatsine, which clashed with political and religious authorities in the late 1970s. Property was damaged and hundreds of lives were lost. There is also the recent case of the alleged killing of the popular Prophet Eddy Nawgu (Edwin Okeke) in Onitsha, Nigeria, in late 2000. See Geoffrey Ekenna, "Death of a Miracle Man," *Newswatch* (Lagos), 11 December 2000, 23, 32. Although popular with many for his divinatory skills and community-building activities, Prophet Eddy was reportedly involved in clashes with the Roman Catholic Church, the police, and local vigilantes over his criminal exploits. He was even the subject of a 1993 book, *Truth and the Oracle at Nawgu* (Nigeria: Hanoby Books, 1993), by a university lecturer, Anene Obianyido, who claimed that Okeke was guilty of numerous human rights abuses.

37. David Throup, " 'Render Unto Caesar the Things That are Caesar's': The Politics of Church-State Conflict in Kenya 1978–1990," in *Religion and Politics in East Africa*, eds. Hansen and Twaddle, 143–76; Louise Pirouet, "The Churches and Human Rights in Kenya and Uganda since Independence," ibid., 247–59.

38. Formed in 1965 by Ngonya wa Gakonya, the Tent of the Living God changed its name in 1988 from the Church of the Living God. It was deregistered by the Kenyan government in February 1990, which deemed it a source of disunity and anti-government sentiments (*The Weekly Review* [Nairobi], 16 February 1990). For details of continued harassment, see Edward Miller, "Kenya Wary as Traditional Religions Are Revived," *Washington Times*, 24 August 2000. See also Grace Nyatugah Wamue, "Mungiki Movement: Religion or Cult?" paper presented at the African Association for the Study of Religions regional conference, Nairobi, July 1999.

39. Murthui Mwai, "What makes Mungiki tick?" *Daily Nation* (Nairobi), 23 October 2000.

40. "Abong'o outlaws Mungiki meetings," *Daily Nation* (Nairobi), 26 October 2000.

41. "Exposed, Terror Gang of Kayole," *Daily Nation* (Nairobi), 25 October 2000.

42. Although it is interesting to note that Mungiki now features on several cult-watch websites in North America and Europe, such as the Apologetic Index and the Ross Institute for the Study of Destructive Cults, Controversial Groups and Movements (www.gospelcom.net and www.rickross.com). In contrast, the most recent U.S. State Department Annual Report on International Religious Freedom (2002) refers to Mungiki as follows: "a small, controversial, cultural and political movement based in part on Kikuyu ethnic traditions, which espouses political views and cultural practices that are controversial in mainstream Kenyan society. While religion may have played a role in the formation of the group, observers believe that it is not a key characteristic of the group. The Mungiki do not adhere to any single religion and members are free to choose their own religion; the group includes Muslims and Christians." http://www.state.gov/g/drl/rls/irf/2002/13839.htm (accessed 3 March 2003).

43. See Human Rights Watch, *The Scars of Death: Children Abducted by the Lord's Resistance Army in Uganda* (New York: Human Rights Watch, 1997). These accusations continue up to the present time. See Allan Thompson, "Hope for Child Soldiers: Canada Brokers Deal with Sudan," *Toronto Star*, 18 September 2000.

44. Gérard Prunier, "Le Mouvement d'Alice Lakwena, un Prophétisme Politique en Ouganda," in *L'Invention Religieuse en Afrique: Histoire et Religion en Afrique Noire*, ed. Jean-Pierre Chrétien (Paris: ACCT–Karthala, 1993), 409–30; Heike Behrend, "The Holy Spirit Movement and the Forces of Nature in the North of Uganda 1985–1987," in *Religion*

and Politics in East Africa, eds. Hansen and Twaddle, 59–71; idem, "War in Northern Uganda: The Holy Spirit Movements of Alice Lakwena, Severino Lukoya and Joseph Kony (1986–97)," in *African Guerillas*, ed. Christopher Clapham (Bloomington, IN: Indiana University Press, 1998), 107–18. Alice fled to Kenya where it is believed that she has remained since 1987.

45. Zachary Lomo, a student in Kampala at the time, argues that Lakwena's movement was a direct response to the political polarization introduced by Museveni when he came to power in 1986. Personal communication, 8 November 2000.

46. Heike Behrend, "The Holy Spirit Movement and the Forces of Nature in the North of Uganda 1985–1987," in *Religion and Politics in East Africa*, eds. Hansen and Twaddle, 69.

47. Gérard Prunier, "Le Mouvement d'Alice Lakwena, un Prophétisme Politique en Ouganda," in *L'Invention Religieuse en Afrique*, ed. Chrétien, 420.

48. Kwesi A. Dickson, "The Church and the Quest for Democracy in Ghana," in *The Christian Churches and the Democratisation of Africa*, ed. Paul Gifford (Leiden, Netherlands: E. J. Brill, 1995), 265–66.

49. "Jehovah's Witnesses: Are They Really Banned?" *Uhuru* 2 (1990).

50. *Seminar on Freedom of Religion or Belief in the OSCE Region: Challenges to Law and Practice* (The Hague: Netherlands Ministry of Foreign Affairs, 2001).

51. Ibid., 45.

52. Murthui Mwai, "What Makes Mungiki Tick?" *Daily Nation* (Nairobi), 23 October 2000.

53. Bengt Sundkler, "African Independent Churches and their Political Roles," in *Religion and Politics in Southern Africa*, eds. Hallencreutz and Palmberg, 86.

54. U.S. Department of State, *Report on International Religious Freedom* (September 2000), "Kenya," http://www.state.gov/www/global/human_rights/irf/irf (accessed 29 November 2000).

55. Geoffrey Kamali, "Security to Monitor Churches," *New Vision*, 7 November 2002, available at http://allafrica.com/stories/printable/200211080543.html (accessed 8 November 2002).

56. Ibid.

57. CIP 28.05.2000, www.shsf.net www.hrwf.net (accessed 1 June 2000).

58. *Ghanaian Chronicle*, 19 April 2000. Circulated by Human Rights Without Frontiers, Religious Intolerance and Discrimination news service, 26 April 2000.

59. See Ndombasi Ludiongo, "Rapport Sectes et Pouvoirs Politiques: Aspects Juridiques des Sectes," in *Sectes, Cultures et Sociétés: Les Enjeux Spirituels du Temps Présent* (Quatrième Colloque Internationale du Centre d'Etudes des Religions Africaines, Kinshasa, 14–21 November 1992) (Kinshasa: Facultés Catholiques de Kinshasa, 1994), 355–74. Also published as *Cahiers des Religions Africaines* 27–28, nos. 53–56 (1993–1994).

60. T. K. Biaya, "Postcolonial State Strategies, Sacralization of Power and Popular Proselytization in Congo-Zaire, 1960–1995," in *Proselytization and Communal Self-Determination in Africa*, ed. Abdullahi A. An-Na'im (Maryknoll, NY: Orbis, 1999).

61. Ibid., 367.

62. Decree of 18 September 1965; Law no. 71-02, 31 December 1971.

63. Article 1 of Law no. 71-0012, 31 December 1971. See Ludiongo, "Rapport Sectes et Pouvoirs Politiques," 373–74.

64. www.state.gov/g/drl/rls/irf/2002/13820.htm (accessed 6 March 2003).

65. WEA Religious Liberty Commission, "Eritrean government orders shutdown of almost all evangelical churches," HRWF, International Secretariat, 6 March 2002, http://www.hrwf.net/newhrwf/html/eritrea2002.htm. Interestingly, the U.S. State Department report, while criticizing the deterioration of respect for religious freedom in Eritrea during 2001–02, notes that social tolerance still exists.

66. "Group Cautions on Church Demolition," *ThisDay* (Lagos), 20 August 2002, http://allafrica.com/stories/printable/200208200119.html (accessed 26 August 2002).

67. Information from Dr. Matthews A. Ojo, 6 November 2000.

68. See Klaus Hock, *Der Islam-Komplex* (Hamburg: Lit Verlag, 1996).

69. "Great Millennium Crusade Kicks Off Today," *Post Express* (Lagos), 8 November 2000.

70. Joseph Aimienmwon, "Faithfuls Seek Clean Bill Over Joshua's Detention," *Post Express* (Lagos), 11 September 2000.

71. Anthony Okoro, "Nothing Can Disintegrate Nigeria-Prophet Joshua," *P.M. News* (Lagos), 19 June 2000. Nicholas Ibewuike, "Zambian President to Become Prophet Chiluba," Panafrican News Agency, 13 November 2000.

72. Johanna Pink, "New Religious Communities in Egypt: Islam, Public Order and Freedom of Belief," presented at the CESNUR International Conference on "Minority Religions, Social Change, and Freedom of Conscience," 20 June 2002, www.cesnur.org/2002/slc/pink.htm.

73. Kevin Ward, "The Church of Uganda Amidst Conflict: The Interplay between Church and Politics in Uganda since 1962," in *Religion and Politics in East Africa*, eds. Hansen and Twaddle, 82.

74. See, for example, Paul Gifford, *The New Crusaders: Christianity and the New Right in Southern Africa* (London: Pluto, 1991).

75. That notwithstanding, a Kenyan government minister ordered the Nigerian-based Winners' Chapel out of his district for its purported involvement in child abductions and anti-government activities. See "Nigerian Church Ordered Out of Kenyan District," Panafrican News Agency, 28 October 2000.

76. Figures illustrating this type of growth come from Kinshasa, Democratic Republic of Congo. See "2,177 églises et sectes recencées à Kinshasa," Panafrican News Agency, 27 October 2000. The report elicited much public criticism and concern.

77. For a classic story of a man being duped by a fake prophet, see Anthony Okoro, "Prey to Fake Prayers," *P.M. News* (Lagos), 13 November 2000.

78. "Uganda Doomsday Cult Arrested," Associated Press, 19 July 2000.

79. See Stefan Lovgren, "Cults, Some Deadly, Flourish in Africa. Some Governments Fear Groups Will Challenge Their Authority," www.msnbc.com/news/ (accessed 30 March 2000).

80. See Allan Turyaguma, "Ntungamo Bans Night Prayers," *New Vision*, 21 August 2002, http://allafrica.com/stories/printable/200208210289.html (accessed 20 January 2003).

81. Editorial, "Religious Tolerance Imperative," *Addis Tribune* (Addis Ababa), 3 January 2003, http://allafrica.com/stories/printable/200301030327.html (accessed 20 January 2003).

82. U.S. State Department report, "Kenya," www.state.gov/g/drl/rls/irf/2002/13839.htm.

83. Interview with Mawulé Kuamvi Kuakuvi, 20 September 2002. The U.S. State Department report notes that no action was subsequently taken, www.state.gov/g/drl/rls/irf/2002/13860.htm.

84. This is noted for Cameroon by the U.S. State Department report (2002), http://www.state.gov/g/drl/rls/irf/2002 (accessed 6 March 2003).

85. T. Jeremy Gunn, personal communication, 9 February 2003.

86. "Illegal Sects Banned," *Angola Press Agency* (Luanda), 24 October 2002, http://allafrica.com/stories/printable/200210240600.html (accessed 24 November 2002).

87. Personal communication, 11 November 2000.

88. See Massimo Introvigne, "Tragedy in Uganda: The Restoration of the Ten Commandments of God, a Post-Catholic Movement," www.cesnur.org (accessed on 14 November 2000), and Jean-François Mayer, "The Movement for the Restoration of the Ten Commandments of God: Between Facts and Fiction," report on a research trip to Uganda (unpublished and privately circulated), 13–23 August 2000. The Ugandan Human Rights Commission produced a periodical report in 2002, *The Kanungu Massacre: the Movement for the Restoration of the Ten Commandments of God Indicted*, www.uhrc.org/publications[1022501764]Kanungu%20report-website.htm (accessed 9 October 2002). In addition to the numerous press reports, local and international, on the movement, of varying reliability, see also, Irving Hexham, "What Really Happened in Uganda?" *Religion in the News* 3:2 (2000): 7–9.

89. See the journalistic analysis (" 'Mary's Flames': The Long Road to Horror in Kanungu," *The East African* (Nairobi), 8 February 2001) of the report produced by Makerere University's Department of Religious Studies authored by Gerard Banura, Chris Tuhirirwe, and Joseph Begumanya (published by Marianum Press of Kisibi, 2001). The authors of the report provide more information on the "chaotic situation" that developed in the camp when the earlier predictions regarding the end of the world on 31 December 1999 did not come to pass and the date was extended to 17 March 2000. The leaders started selling the followers' property and possessions, and persistent complainants were made to disappear. The report also states that Mwerinde and Kibwetere met (in 1988?) at an apparition site developed in the 1980s by Gauda Kamusha at Nyabugoto caves. They launched their own movement in 1990 and then moved in 1993 to Kanungu, registering in the same year as a religious NGO. They named the site "Ishayuuriro rya Maria," meaning "where Mary comes to the rescue of the spiritually stranded." The report claims that the movement attracted people (predomi-

nantly women and children) from various religions, classes, and professions, and was not limited to the illiterate as had been generally thought.

90. Jossy Muhangia, "Fugitive Cult Boss Arrested," *The New Vision* (Kampala), 19 July 2000.

91. "Ugandan Doomsday Cult Surfaces in Kenya," Panafrican News Agency, 31 July 2000.

92. "American Suicide Cult Invades Kenya," Panafrican News Agency, 27 October 2000. The report goes on to list all known recent "cults" around the world that have led to loss of life. It also mentions that the Kenyan government warned people in March 2000 that a British group, the Children of God, "known for sexually molesting children," had established a base in the country.

93. It was most likely the group known as Cult Solutions. Information from Massimo Introvigne, 18 November 2000. See Massimo Introvigne, "The Secular Anti-Cult and the Religious Counter-Cult Movement: Strange Bedfellows or Future Enemies?" in *New Religions and the New Europe*, ed. Robert Towler (Aarhus, Denmark: Aarhus University Press, 1995), 32–54, for the distinctions between the secular anticult and religious countercult movements.

94. "Exposed, Terror Gang of Kayole," *The Nation* (Nairobi), 25 October 2000. An additional incident occurred on 12 November 2000. See "Kenya's Outlawed Sect Members Arrested After Battling Police," Panafrican News Agency, 13 November 2000.

95. Hannah Gakuo, "Women in Demo over Dress Code," *Daily Nation* (Nairobi), 5 November 2000.

96. "Kenya's Outlawed Sect Members Arrested After Battling Police," Panafrican News Agency, 13 November 2000.

97. *Newswatch* (Lagos), 22 February 1988.

98. Information from Matthews A. Ojo, 6 November 2000.

99. Barney Pityana, Chair, South African Human Rights Commission, personal communication, 6 August 2000.

100. Namasiku Ilukena, "Zambia Church Banned for 'Satanism,' " *Mail and Guardian* (Johannesburg), 9 September 1998. They were banned under section 17 of the Societies Act. The church was founded in 1975 and came to Zambia in 1995.

101. Rosalind I. J. Hackett, "Managing or Manipulating Religious Conflict in the Nigerian Media," in *Mediating Religion: Conversations in Media, Religion and Culture*, eds. Jolyon Mitchell and Sophia Marriage (Edinburgh: T & T Clark, 2003).

102. Namasiku Ilukena, "Zambia Church Banned for 'Satanism,' " *Mail and Guardian* (Johannesburg), 9 September 1998.

103. "Kenyan Churches Alarmed By Spread of 'Mungiki' Sect," Panafrican News Agency, 3 September 2000.

104. Tervil Okoko, "Religious Bodies Trade Accusations Over Devil-Worship," Panafrican News Agency, 3 October 2000, Nairobi, Kenya, http://allafrica.com/stories/200010030005.html (accessed 24 October 2000).

105. For more general discussion of this phenomenon, see Rosalind I. J. Hackett, "Discours de diabolisation en Afrique et ailleurs," *Diogène* (UNESCO) 199 (juillet-septembre): 71–91.

106. For a litany of social and economic problems in Nyanza province attributed to "devil worship" (by the Provincial Commissioner himself), see Churchill Otieno, "PC in Devil Worship Claim," *The Nation* (Nairobi), 11 October 1999.

107. It was originally scheduled to remain under government wraps for four years but the report was leaked by the *Daily Nation* (Nairobi) newspaper.

108. www.state.gov/www/global/human_rights/irf/irf_rpt/irf_index.html (accessed 29 November 2000).

109. Otsieno Namwaya, "Dark Forces, Bloody Rituals under Probe," *The East African* (Nairobi), 17 August 1999.

110. "Devil Worship Report the Height of Naivete," *The Nation* (Nairobi), 13 August 1999.

111. "Religious Association Launches Cult Probe," Panafrican News Agency, 10 December 2000.

112. " 'We're Not in Dubious Activities': Eckankar Followers Dispel Rumours," *The News* (Monrovia), 23 October 2000.

113. Yakubu Musa, "Christianity Started As a Cult, Says Ige," *ThisDay* (Lagos), 19 November 2000.

114. Gifford, *African Christianity*, 175–76.

115. See, in particular, Birgit Meyer, " 'Delivered from the Powers of Darkness': Confessions about Satanic Riches in Christian Ghana," *Africa* 65:2 (1995): 236–55; and idem, *Translating the Devil: Religion and Modernity among the Ewe in Ghana* (Edinburgh: Edinburgh University Press, 1999). Véronique Faure, "L'occulte et le politique en Afrique du Sud," in

Dynamiques religieuses en Afrique australe, idem, 175–205. See also the attribution of recent ethnic clashes in Nigeria to "Satan" by a London-based Nigerian evangelist and writer, Matthew Ashimolowo, *P.M. News* (Lagos), 30 October 2000. He was speaking at a one-week Christian conference that he organized in Nigeria to address "the satanic forces bent on stifling the country's development." He urged Nigerians to turn to Christ to combat the government's demonstration of "demon-cracy."

116. See the call by Gospel Outreach Fellowship junior pastor, Alex Phiri, to the Zambian government to "come up with criteria to screen and scrutinise churches and their doctrines" and "to help churches acquire land to build more churches." Chisenga Kabuswe, "Church Leaders' Conduct Worries Rev. Chintala," *Post of Zambia* (Lusaka), 27 October 2000.

117. Rosalind I. J. Hackett, "Radical Christian Revivalism in Nigeria and Ghana: Recent Patterns of Conflict and Intolerance," in *Proselytization and Communal Self-Determination in Africa,* ed. An-Na'im, 246–67.

118. Rosalind I. J. Hackett, "Charismatic/Pentecostal Appropriation of Media Technologies in Nigeria and Ghana," *Journal of Religion in Africa* 26:4 (1998): 1–19.

119. The Kenyan government has made it clear that campaigns of competitive conversion are considered to be divisive and contrary to President Moi's *Nyayo* philosophy of "peace, love and unity." Donal B. Cruise O'Brien, "Coping with the Christians: The Muslim Predicament in Kenya," in *Religion and Politics in East Africa,* eds. Hansen and Twaddle, 209.

120. J. D. Van der Vyver, "Religious Freedom in African Constitutions," in *Proselytization and Communal Self-Determination in Africa,* ed. An-Na'im, 140.

121. Makau Mutua, "Returning to My Roots: African 'Religions' and the State," in *Proselytization and Communal Self-Determination in Africa,* ed. An-Na'im, 169–90. See also Hannah W. Kinoti, "Religious Fragmentation in Kenya," in ibid., 269.

122. Benson Kimathi, "Cults and their Followers," *The Nation* (Nairobi), 22 April 2000.

123. See "2,177 églises et sectes recencées à Kinshasa," Panafrican News Agency, 27 October 2000.

124. The Mennonites, for example, have long been active in providing theological education for the leaders of independent churches. The South African professor of religion, G.C. Oosthuizen, has for several decades, through his research unit at the University of Zululand and now from his home in Durban, championed research and publication on South Africa's independent churches, and organized annual conferences in which many independent church leaders participated.

125. In former Zaïre, now the Democratic Republic of Congo, numerous conferences have been held and research projects conducted on the country's proliferation of NRMs. The scholarship tends to reflect, however, the fact that the universities have official ecclesiastical connections (predominantly Roman Catholic). In the midst of very useful research data it is not uncommon to read statements about the cancerous growth, social problems, and threats to public order and the status quo constituted by such religious groups. See, for example, Centre d'Etudes des Religions Africaines, *Sectes, Cultures et Sociétés: Les Enjeux Spirituels du Temps Présent* (Kinshasa: Facultés Catholiques de Kinshasa, 1994).

126. Cf. Marat Shterin and James T. Richardson, "Effects of the Western Anti-Cult Movement on Development of Laws Concerning Religion in Post-Communist Russia," *Journal of Church and State* 42:2 (2000): 247–71. See also Anson Shupe and David Bromley, *Anti-Cult Movements in Cross-Cultural Perspective* (New York: Garland, 1994). James Beckford, *Cult Controversies: The Societal Response to the New Religious Movements* (New York: Tavistock, 1985). Interestingly, Bamesa Tshungu notes in his study of Satanic groups ("sectes lucifériennes") in Zaïre that several members reported that they were *attracted* to these movements through the anticult literature of popular authors such as Rebecca Brown.

CHAPTER **11**

Religion on a Leash
NRMs and the Limits of Chinese Freedom

SCOTT LOWE

Introduction

The government of the People's Republic of China (PRC) has managed to stay in the international spotlight for several years with its ongoing suppression of the *qigong*-based spiritual group Falun Gong (also called Falun Dafa). In its attempts to justify its behavior to an outraged West, China has relied primarily on finger pointing, claiming that many other nations, including the United States, regularly engage in similar practices of repression and control. In both official and quasi-official PRC websites, sources associated with the American anticult movement are cited with approval and used to demonstrate that Falun Gong is a "cult." These sites further imply that "cults" are evil and regularly prosecuted in the U.S.[1]

When facing censure over trade practices or international copyright violations, the Chinese have not been shy to claim exemption from the values and practices of Western societies on the basis of their long-standing distinctive cultural traditions. Yet, curiously, when it comes to the control and suppression of religious groups, the Chinese have made very little propaganda use of their venerable two-thousand-year-old tradition of monitoring and regulating major religions and harshly repressing *xie jiao* (literally "wicked teachings") and *hui* ("sworn brotherhoods" and "secret societies"), a broad group of "heterodox" teachings and clandestine orga-

nizations that resemble in a generic way what Western scholars call new religious movements (NRMs).[2]

Historical Overview

As C. K. Yang has convincingly demonstrated, from the time of the earliest
written records till the modern day, the dominant "Confucian" strand of
Chinese thought has placed a premium on society-wide ideological conformity.[3] The emperors of successive dynasties engaged in a demanding
schedule of time-hallowed rituals that were viewed by traditionalists as
a kind of religio-political governance process through which the ruler was
brought into harmony with Heaven, local deities, and the ancestors,
thereby securing the peace, prosperity, and order of the realm. A less elaborate ritual calendar dictated the corresponding performances of officers on
the provincial and district levels. Government officials at all levels, from
the imperial court down to the county magistrates, regularly functioned in
multiple capacities, serving in turn as investigators, public works managers, arbitrators, judges, and religious specialists. Traditional rituals, and
to a lesser extent the beliefs that accompanied them, were an essential part
of the governance process and believed to be a fundamental source of social harmony and cohesion.

Deviant beliefs were not simply eccentric, a matter of personal concern or choice, for if propagated widely they would inevitably threaten
the stability of the entire society. Not surprisingly, unorthodox beliefs
and practices were seen more as treason than heresy. The modern Western ideal of the separation of church and state not only would have
made no sense in traditional China, it would have been perceived as
threatening by most members of society, a seditious idea that any humane ruler ought to suppress. The Chinese *knew* beyond questioning
that in a balanced, harmonious empire there is no difference between
the religious and the political. In the last few decades, we have seen similar positions endorsed by Christian, Muslim, Hindu, and even Buddhist
neo-traditionalists around the globe.

With the arrival of Buddhist missionaries in the first century C.E., the
Chinese had their first known encounter with a spiritual tradition that was
separate from—and sometimes in conflict with—the shared beliefs and
practices of the surrounding community. Buddhism not only expanded
the spiritual horizons of the Chinese, it also brought the startlingly novel
concept of conversion. While all Chinese were familiar with the seasonal
celebrations of their communities and the ancient patterns of domestic
ritual—traditions that they had inherited without choice, like their local
languages and cultures—Buddhism offered something new: a comprehen-

sive way of life that could be studied, evaluated, formally accepted, and adopted. The conservatives were outraged.[4]

Once the idea of voluntary religious affiliation had entered China, it spread rapidly. In 184 C.E., the "Yellow Turbans," a NRM based on Taoist teachings, rose in revolt against the declining Han dynasty.[5] Five years later, a second group, the "Five Pecks of Rice" religion, a similar Taoist offshoot, rebelled, establishing a theocratic state in the southwest of China. Both these politically ambitious NRMs shared the prevailing orthodox view that religion and governance are inseparable; a new ideology both necessitates and legitimates the creation of a new political order. The potential for rebellion by the followers of millenarian or messianic leaders—often unrealized but always lurking in the background—is a recurring theme in subsequent Chinese history and explains much of the alarm with which the ruling elite has consistently viewed religious movements operating outside the government's tight system of control.

Governmental regulation of organized religion has been the norm in China for nearly two thousand years. The foreign "Great Traditions" practiced in China (Buddhism, Islam, and more recently Catholic and Protestant Christianity) and indigenous Taoist organizations have always been regulated and overseen by the bureaucracies of successive dynasties, both native and "barbarian," though the effectiveness of this oversight has not been consistent. Governments have reserved the right to limit ordination and determine the qualifications of Buddhist and Taoist clergy, periodically "cleaning house" and expelling monks and nuns who fail to measure up to the moral and academic standards set by the state.

Alarmed by the concentration of land and capital under the control of the great Buddhist monasteries, the rulers of the Tang dynasty (618–906 C.E.) attacked Buddhism on several occasions, confiscating enormous wealth and forcibly returning hundreds of thousands of monks and nuns to lay life. So severe was this assault that many scholars believe Chinese Buddhist monasticism never fully recovered from the "Great Persecution" of 845. From that time until the early twentieth century, academic Buddhist study and rigorous monastic practice were largely confined to a handful of major monasteries that were supported and regulated by the state.

During the centuries that Buddhism has been a force in China, Buddhist leaders have often enjoyed close, mutually advantageous (but unequal) relationships with civil authorities. Though the Buddhist establishment was sometimes wealthy and powerful, the state consistently held the upper hand. The suffocating regulation of monastic Buddhism since the founding of the PRC in 1949 might plausibly be viewed as a simple continuation of earlier patterns of state control, though it must be acknowledged that the

Chinese Communist Party (CCP) has proven far more efficient and severe than any of its predecessors.

Imperial support and patronage of minority religious traditions was also employed as a conscious mechanism of political control, especially in the cases of Islam in western China and Vajrayana Buddhism in Mongolia and the neighboring country of Tibet. Manipulation and interference in the internecine disputes of Tibetan high lamas and their monasteries, most notably by the Mongol Yuan (1271–1368) and the Manchu Qing (1644–1911) dynasties, forms a main basis of the Chinese claim to sovereignty over the vast Tibetan plateau.[6]

Of course, China has long been home to a wide range of local gods and distinctive ritual traditions. As long as these were the expressions of traditional regional cultures and posed no overt threat to the political order, they were generally tolerated. In fact, the imperial authorities consciously attempted to co-opt local deities by incorporating them into the official pantheon.[7] This was a clever, pragmatic response to the regional diversity found in an almost ungovernably large realm, and since local traditions tended to be politically conservative and strongly supportive of the status quo, there was usually little danger in the practice. Nonetheless, the elite classes were always on the lookout for nascent subversive tendencies.

By far the greatest regulation and persecution was reserved for the thousands of indigenous sectarian religious groups and secret societies that first flourished during the Yuan dynasty and have continued to the present day throughout the Chinese cultural sphere. The danger these NRMs posed for the established political order became painfully obvious during the Qing dynasty, when scarcely a decade passed without significant armed insurrections.

Study of the Qing legal code suggests that the ruling elite had a powerful fear of clandestine brotherhoods and sectarian religious groups, lumping them together into broad categories for prosecution and sentencing, and punishing their members with a ferocity that seems astonishing to modern observers.[8] Founders and leaders of any sort of proscribed group[9] were usually executed if the group was considered potentially troublesome and banished (after heavy caning) if innocuous.[10] Ordinary members received sentences ranging from execution through banishment to simple caning, depending on their degree of involvement. Strangely enough, these draconian punishments do not seem to have prevented the widespread proliferation of NRMs throughout the Qing and Republican (1911–1949) periods, suggesting that millions of Chinese must have felt a strong need for the spiritual and economic support these groups offered.

In the coached, formulaic "confessions" of NRM leaders preserved in official documents we can discern the motives that government inquisitors projected upon these groups. Under torture, leaders usually "confessed" to being frauds who had tricked their followers into seditious behavior in order to gain power and wealth. Many also confessed to outrageous acts of sexual license and flagrantly immoral behavior. It is significant that the charges brought against the leaders of Chinese NRMs hundreds of years ago are virtually indistinguishable from the accusations made today against modern "cult" leaders in the mass media, East and West. And, of course, these same formulaic charges of financial and sexual exploitation are currently being brought by the government of the PRC against the leaders of a wide range of NRMs.

The most popular NRMs of the Qing and Republican periods derive from rather disparate sources. While it falls outside the scope of this essay to treat them in detail, a brief overview of two important strands, the "White Lotus" and "Triad" traditions, may prove illustrative, especially since both these traditions continue to be influential in modern China. It should be kept in mind that as these groups proliferated their theologies, oral histories, and rituals evolved with great speed and creativity, so any general account will only approximately suggest the beliefs and practices of specific groups.

The so-called "White Lotus" groups usually share a creation myth centered on the "Unborn Ancient Progenitress" (*Wusheng Laomu*) and seek salvation through initiation into secret teachings and practices. According to the "Gnostic" myth shared by White Lotus groups, humans are the children of an ancient mother goddess who sent her offspring down to earth to play. Over time, the children became entangled in the world of matter and desire, forgetting their origins in pure spirit. Trapped in the realm of sensory pleasures, reincarnating again and again on earth, the children have grown increasingly coarse and vulgar, weighed down by progressively heavier burdens of evil karma. The Ancient Progenitress, still grieving for her lost offspring, has sent down a series of saviors to awaken her slumbering children, to little avail. Soon a great period of purifying disasters will come. (Inspired leaders usually insert their chosen date here.) The *kalpa* is about to turn, bringing with it a "black wind" that will annihilate all unbelievers.[11] The faithful few will then live happily ever after in a radically transformed, depopulated, and purified new world. Since time is running out, it is urgent that all spiritually salvageable individuals heed the message of a new savior (often a child identified by the NRM's leaders as Maitreya Buddha, though sometimes a sect leader will claim this role). With this powerful message, a charismatic leader, and suitable conditions, White Lotus groups were, and perhaps still are, capable of explosive growth.

Leaders of White Lotus groups usually emphasize the importance of vegetarianism and celibacy and often teach mantra recitation as an essential practice. Martial arts practices are featured prominently in some groups. Determining the exact moment of the *kalpa*'s turn is a crucial concern, and in the past rebellions often began when a sect leader exhorted his followers to revolt in order to hasten the onset of destruction.[12]

Triad-related "secret society" groups, on the other hand, tend to emphasize mutual support and invest most of their energy in overtly economic activities. However, most also engage in elaborate initiation ceremonies and express clear messianic expectations in their founding myths. Many of these groups trace their origins to a legendary clandestine band of Shaolin martial artist/monks who were dedicated to the nativist agenda of expelling the Manchu Qing dynasty and restoring the indigenous Ming.

The Triads and similar groups have often recruited most heavily from the ranks of unemployed and underemployed single men, providing them with economic opportunities and surrogate family ties. The loyalty and trust secret society members owe one another are rarely extended to the outer community, so it has been relatively easy for groups to move into predatory criminal activities without consciously repudiating their self-professed noble ideals.

When Sun Yat Sen and his fellow conspirators plotted against the tottering Qing dynasty, the Triads were quickly brought in as foot soldiers for the revolution. Though their actual effectiveness has been questioned, in the popular imagination of China the Triads and other secret societies were crucial to the ultimate success of the Republican Revolution of 1911. During the later struggle between the Kuomintang and the CCP, secret societies were courted by both sides. After the final Communist victory, Mao lost little time eliminating every organization potentially capable of resisting his rule, especially targeting those with experience in clandestine operations, since they posed a very real threat to his desired totalitarian control. The secret societies appeared to have been decimated; at the very least their activities were driven deeply underground, and their members, when caught, were treated as common criminals.[13]

The PRC

Though ostensibly a "communist" opposed to reactionary "Confucian" thought, Chairman Mao (1893–1976) was very much a product of his culture and in many ways perpetuated the views of earlier Chinese rulers. Like his imperial predecessors, he believed in the almost magical power of society-wide conformity and felt personally threatened by all ideological dissent. Since religions were sources of competing ideologies, providing alternate centers of power and allegiance, they ultimately had to be eliminated. As an exponent of a totalistic political system, Mao was incapable of allowing religion to exist in a separate (non-secular) realm independent of politics.

Although for the first few years after the communist victory Mao appeared willing to allow religion to die out gradually, in accord with Marxist theory, by the early 1950s Mao had become impatient, concluding that the apparently vigorous survival of a wide range of religious practices was a clear sign of obstinate reactionary subversion. From this point on, all public believers in any religion were subjected to re-education; those who continued to profess their faith faced imprisonment, torture, and even death. As the recent histories of Falun Gong, Zhong Gong, the Protestant Christian "Shouters," and other less well known groups have shown, twenty-first century NRM members still face re-education, imprisonment, torture, and death.

There is some irony in the fact that an atheist who criticized religion's stranglehold on the minds of the masses was responsible for creating (in the name of liberation!) one of the tightest systems of ideological control ever witnessed on earth. Mao's ambitious experiments in "group think" during the "Great Leap Forward" and the following "Cultural Revolution" brought a degree of ideological conformity to China that previous despots would certainly have envied. While the goals of Mao's wild utopian experiments were thoroughly materialistic, the fervor, devotion, and fanaticism expressed by hundreds of millions of Chinese during the peak of the Cultural Revolution were more reminiscent of a massive religious revival than a secular political movement.[14]

The legal system of the PRC plays an essential role in the government's efforts to restrict religious expression. Article 36 of the Constitution of the PRC states that "Citizens of the People's Republic of China have the freedom of religious belief." However, the Constitution rather pointedly does not recognize the right to engage in religious practices or propagate religious teachings. Since the founding of the People's Republic in 1949, several laws have been employed to restrict severely the outward expression of a wide range of religious practices found in Buddhist, Taoist, Muslim, Christian, sectarian, and popular traditions. Meanwhile the government has steadfastly maintained that the constitutional right to freedom of religious *belief* has always been observed in the PRC.

Starting in the early 1980s, the PRC began lifting its suppression of religious activities, in part because of the growing recognition that the Maoist ideals of self-sacrifice and public service had lost credibility in the increasingly cutthroat atmosphere arising from the new policies of economic liberalization. Simultaneously atheists and moral conservatives, the current leaders of China must feel ambivalent about the resurgence of religion. On the one hand, many leaders would presumably rather have citizens adhere to "superstitious" religious ethics than operate in a complete moral vacuum, yet on the other, it must be hard for even lukewarm communist ideologues to view the increase in religious activity as anything other than a step backwards. Moreover, as former bureaucrats scramble to get rich, it is simply too much work to keep track of everyone else's private business. However, one can easily overestimate the degree to which the police state is in decline; the forces of control are still strong and have recently demonstrated their power and the length of their reach.

In general, registered groups that are sanctioned by the Religious Affairs Bureau are allowed to operate freely, so long as they follow strict government regulations and engage in approved activities. The government still deals harshly with unregistered groups, arresting leaders and raiding meeting places. As in past centuries, enforcement of regulations varies widely by region. Unregistered groups, especially those that are involved in charitable work, are sometimes appreciated in one jurisdiction while harassed elsewhere.

There appears to be little friction between the members of the five officially recognized religions—Buddhism, Taoism, Catholic Christianity, Protestant Christianity, and Islam—but, as noted in International Religious Freedom Report 2002, relations between registered and unregistered Christian churches are often acrimonious.[15] In this context, it is surely significant that the number of practicing Christians, both Catholic and Protestant, affiliated with unregistered churches is thought to be much greater than the number in the official churches. While the beliefs and practices of many of the unregistered churches meet general standards of Roman Catholic or Evangelical Protestant orthodoxy, some deviate significantly. These less mainstream groups are not only unregistered but are also classified as xie jiao, or "cults," leading to intense governmental scrutiny.

As the disparities in income and opportunity continue to multiply across the PRC, economic uncertainty is certain to increase. It has been estimated that at any one time more than one hundred million workers are migrating across China seeking work. The elderly, most of whom spent their entire working lives "building socialism" at very low wages, are now often in desperate economic straits, since the social support system they were helping to construct has largely collapsed. These circumstances are ideal for the resurgence of "secret societies" and, of course, must be terrifying to those responsible for monitoring and controlling the behavior of 1.3 billion Chinese.

Complicating the matter is the fact that for several decades the PRC has attempted to rehabilitate traditional preventative medical and hygienic practices by severing them from their roots in Chinese religion. From 1982 till 1999, traditional qigong practices were widely promoted for their health benefits, and reputable scientists attempted to document the practical value of these exercises, thereby proving that they were not "religious" (that is, "superstitious").[16] These studies encouraged millions of Chinese, especially the elderly, who often have limited access to quality medical care, to take up *qigong*. Though many people started their practice without explicit spiritual intentions or interest, over time the exercises themselves seem to have awakened latent religious impulses, contributing to a growing spiritual revival in China.

In September 1999 the government's prohibition of Falun Gong was ambiguously extended to all organized *qigong* groups, regardless of their beliefs or leadership. This presumably means that the members of clubs and informal groups that once met every morning in parks across China can now be prosecuted at the whims of local officials or as part of a governmental crackdown. In practice, this has not happened, at least not in the big cities, where *qigong* groups have continued their public practice. Since both the government and the members of these groups have long insisted that *qigong* is not religious, practitioners are in a peculiar position to ask for international support as victims of religious persecution, and Western supporters face equal difficulties in attempting to shame the PRC into better behavior, since the government maintains that it is not attacking legitimate "religion" but merely protecting the public from evil "cults."

The events of 9/11 and the subsequent "war on terrorism" have further complicated the picture. In 2002, as part of an apparent, if murky, bid to gain Chinese support for military intervention in Iraq and the more general fight against terrorism, the U.S. declared an obscure Muslim group active on China's western frontier to be a terrorist organization. This public declaration was thought by many to indicate tacit U.S. support for the PRC's ongoing suppression of suspect Muslim groups in the western provinces. What impact this will have on non-Muslim NRMs in China is unknown, but it seems likely that the PRC may interpret this U.S. gesture as a subtle signal that China will face less pressure to conform to Western standards of religious freedom in other parts of the nation.

The brutal suppression of Falun Gong continued through 2002, crippling the group's prospects for further growth at present. Yet despite thousands of arrests, quick trials followed by harsh prison sentences, and the involuntary commitment of large numbers of defiant practitioners to mental hospitals, the movement managed to stage numerous spectacular protests, the most amazing of which included repeated hijackings of government cable TV signals and even the disruption of nationwide satellite television broadcasts. It seems unlikely that these dramatic and technologically impressive protests will produce long-term strategic benefits for the group, but they certainly serve to focus worldwide attention on Falun Gong's plight.

Perhaps the most intriguing news from China is that in 2002, five members of the Chinese Anti-Cult Association, a Beijing-based group of anti-cult professionals, were sent to Ohio to study treatment methods at the Wellspring Retreat and Resource Center. The Wellspring Center promotes itself as the only residential-treatment facility for former cult members in the U.S., and its director claims to focus on "destructive" and "very, very pathological" groups.[17] This suggests that at least some governmental figures in the PRC are looking beyond various forms of incarceration for members of proscribed religious groups and seeking more "humane" solutions to the vexing "problem" of religious adherence.

Conclusions

Due to its history and current form of government, the PRC presents a very different public face than most nations of the West. Since the government still attempts to control all aspects of civic life, there is no independent "anticult" movement, nor is there a media view of "cults" or NRMs at variance with official policy. As an officially atheist nation, there is no established church, unless one considers the CCP party line to be the national orthodoxy.

In the next few years, we should expect to see the PRC continue to struggle with the conflict between the people's growing expectations for personal liberties—including, of course, the free practice of religion—and the ruling elite's desire for control. As many sociologists of religion have noted, material possessions and physical comfort may initially satisfy people long deprived of them, but eventually a significant percentage of the population is likely to desire deeper spiritual meaning than mere comfort and security can provide. Anecdotal evidence strongly suggests that many of the beneficiaries of China's sustained economic growth are already seeking the higher values promised by religion. Meanwhile, the hundreds of millions of Chinese abandoned by the new economy and dependent on a failing social "safety net" for bare survival may be motivated to seek support and security in resurgent "secret societies" and mutual aid societies.

Though most Westerners naturally assume that the practitioners of "religion" in China are the "good guys" and the forces of repression are inherently evil, it is essential to reflect on the leading role taken by NRMs in violent rebellions during the last two thousand years of Chinese history if we wish to comprehend the fears motivating the leaders of the PRC. In China's self-understanding, NRM leaders have usually been villains.[18] This differs greatly from the post-Reformation Protestant sympathy for religious rebels that, in some instances, makes them out to be culture heroes (Wyclif, Huss, Luther, Calvin, Knox, and so on).[19] Most Chinese do not view religious innovators so favorably. Rather than seeing the charismatic founders of NRMs as role models, many Chinese tend to see them as malicious purveyors of destruction and mass suffering.[20] Given their history, it is not unreasonable for China's ruling elite to be alarmed by the explosive growth of movements they cannot understand or readily control. Further conflict seems inevitable.

Notes

1. As of September 2000, the English language translations of these sites were blocked, though the Chinese versions are still up. The reasons for denying access to the English language sites are unknown to me. The best of the old sites was www.ppflg.china.com.cn/baodao/ indexE.html.

2. Falun Gong is classified by the PRC as a *xie jiao*, since the authorities see it as primarily "religious" in focus. The Triads (Heaven and Earth Society) are an example of a *hui*. Both *xie jiao* and *hui* tend to be intensely focused upon ultimate concerns and meet many scholars' definitions of religious groups, though *hui* tend to have a more this-worldly political, or even criminal, orientation. Chinese NRMs possess several distinctive features that are not found in their Western counterparts, making all cross-cultural comparisons suspect and inaccurate. However, if (for purposes of illustration only!) these imprecise categories were applied to groups in the U.S., NRMs as diverse as Heaven's Gate, the TM Movement, and the Church Universal and Triumphant would probably be classified as *xie jiao*, while the Masons and the Montana Freemen would likely be lumped together as *hui*.

3. C. K. Yang, *Religion in Chinese Society* (Berkeley: University of California Press, 1961), 104–218.

4. Even during the twentieth century some Chinese traditionalists still attacked Buddhism as an evil "foreign superstition."

5. There are problems, of course, in calling groups that arose nearly two thousand years ago "New Religious Movements"; however, these groups share many features with their modern descendants and were certainly new at the time of their inception.

6. While these claims seem spurious to many Western observers and could easily be reversed to show that China has long been a part of the Tibetan motherland, it is undeniable that "Chinese" rulers (neither the Mongols nor the Manchus were ethnically Chinese) have long attempted to meddle in Tibetan religious affairs, and of course these "religious" affairs are also political.

7. For example, Mazu, a local deity worshipped primarily by fisher folk in Fujian, was given national rank and titles by the Yuan, Ming, and Qing dynasties. The title *Tian hou* ("Queen of Heaven"), given by the Ming, is still in common use.

8. In the 1500s, Europe experienced its own series of millennial rebellions, like the Anabaptist takeover of Münster. Little mercy was shown to the defenders of Münster when the forces of church and state finally made their move. If such rebellions had continued into the twentieth century in the West, our societies would certainly have less tolerance for religious dissent today. (The Taiping rebellion, led by an inspired millennial visionary, raged across China in the 1850s and 1860s, leading to at least 20 million deaths. If, say, the U.S. Civil War had been instigated by a NRM, would we even pay lip service today to the hallowed American right to free choice in matters of religion?) Of course, students of NRMs know that religious freedom and tolerance in the U.S. has always been more an ideal than a reality.

9. This category included mutual aid societies, scripture recitation societies, vegetarian groups, sworn brotherhoods of all sorts, etc. As mentioned previously, many of these groups seemed quite harmless and, in practice, were often ignored by local authorities. However, in times of unrest even the most innocuous groups could come under governmental attack.

10. See the following for examples: Robert J. Antony, "Brotherhoods, Secret Societies, and the Law in Qing-Dynasty China," in *"Secret Societies" Reconsidered: Perspectives on the Social History of Early Modern South China and Southeast Asia*, ed. David Ownby and Mary Somers Heidhues (Armonk, NY: M. E. Sharpe, 1993), 190–211; Daniel Overmyer, *Folk Buddhist Religion: Dissenting Sects in Late Traditional China* (Cambridge, MA: Harvard University Press, 1976); Susan Naquin, *Millenarian Rebellion in China: The Eight Trigrams Uprising of 1813* (New Haven, CT: Yale University Press,1976); *Shantung Rebellion: The Wang Lun Uprising of 1774* (New Haven: Yale University Press, 1981).

11. *Kalpa* is a Sanskrit word meaning eon. In Buddhist teachings, *kalpas* are enormously long expanses of time. Chinese NRMs dramatically shortened the duration of these periods.

12. One is reminded of the obsession with determining the exact date of the Second Coming that is found in so many Western millennial groups.

13. In fairness, it must be noted that the members of secret societies were widely feared as criminals by most Chinese and would have been regarded as such by law enforcement agencies in nearly every nation of the world. The arguably religious foundations of the groups would in no way exonerate their activities.

14. This has led some scholars to label Maoism a "quasi-religion." Clearly this is a matter of definition. If religion is defined as "ultimate concern," Maoism at its peak was clearly a full-blown "religion." Using this definition, groups like the Montana Freemen and the Chinese Triads are also religions, at least for their most sincere adherents. For a marvelous description of the religious ecstasy experienced during Mao's rare public appearances see Liang Heng and Judith Shapiro, *Son of the Revolution* (New York: Random House, 1983), 121–25.

15. See "China," International Religious Freedom Report 2002, U.S. Department of State, October 2002. Available at: www.state.gov/g/drl/rls/irf/2002/13870.htm.

16. The government's identification of religion with superstition has been so effective that even Chinese spiritual leaders assume that this highly questionable association is valid and universally recognized. The China-wide acceptance of this implicit definition of religion as superstitious nonsense leads people like Li Hongzhi, the founder of Falun Gong, to declare emphatically that his teachings are not "religious," even though their goal of enlightenment/salvation would make them appear so to most Western observers.

17. "Chinese Team Dealing With Falun Gong Visits Cult Rehab Center," Associated Press, 25 October 2002. This article is archived on the CESNUR website and can be accessed at: www.cesnur.org/2002/falun_007bis.htm.

18. Except in certain strands of Marxist scholarship where they are seen as proto-revolutionaries.

19. And even here, one person's inspired leader is another's charlatan.

20. A fascinating e-mail survey asking highly educated overseas Chinese their views of Falun Gong is summarized on the web at www.voicesofchinese.org/falun/surveyrpt.html. Since the respondents are individuals who are living outside the PRC, one may safely assume that they are not under pressure to adhere to the current party line. Many of the respondents also appear critical of *both* Chinese and Western media coverage of Falun Gong. Nonetheless, the respondents view Falun Gong and its leader, Li Hongzhi, with considerable skepticism. For example, 47 percent of respondents agree that Falun Gong is "harmful to Chinese society." 64 percent agree that it is "anti-scientific," while 59 percent believe that "Li Hongzhi is an imposter." Most important, 39 percent agree that Falun Gong "should be banned in China."

CHAPTER 12

Consensus Shattered

Japanese Paradigm Shift and Moral Panic in the Post-Aum Era

IAN READER

Introduction

Any discussion of the factors shaping attitudes to, and patterns of conflict over, new religious movements (NRMs) in Japan today, has to be conducted in the light of the activities of Aum Shinrikyō. For Japanese society, the "Aum affair" raised the specter of a legally registered religious organization enjoying freedom of worship, legal protection, and religious tax exemptions and yet abusing these privileges to finance the manufacture of chemical weapons and commit heinous crimes.

Inevitably, the question of Aum's position and continued existence under Japanese law became a matter of public and political debate. On the wider level, too, the Aum affair raised basic questions about the relationship between religion, society, and state in a modern, liberal society and about the extent to which such societies should offer protection to, and tolerate the existence of, religious movements that are inimical to normative social values. The affair also raised questions about the tax benefits given to religious movements and about the ways in which religious movements acquire their wealth. Such issues gave a powerful boost to the development of an anticult movement in Japan and gave added impetus to an aggressive mass media keen to expose "deviant" religious groups. The Aum affair also damaged the ability of academics in the field to offer balanced judgments on NRMs and virtually silenced academic researchers in the debates that arose during the post-Aum moral panic that gripped Japan.

Paradigm Shifts and Changing Eras:
The Post-War Consensus and its Origins

The Aum affair is a watershed moment in modern Japanese religious history, with scholars now referring to this as the post-Aum era (*posuto Oumu jidai*). This new era has seen a paradigm shift in public perceptions about the relationship between religion, state, and society, with the consensus that existed from the end of World War II until 1995 being replaced by one that is far less favorably disposed to the religious sphere. To understand this change, one needs to look briefly first at the factors that shaped the pre-Aum consensus.

The prevailing liberal democratic ethos upon which post-war Japanese society and the Japanese constitution of 1946 were based viewed religious movements as needing guaranteed protection from the possibilities of state intrusion and oppression. This view—and the resulting constitutional and legal safeguards—was a direct response to the repressive policies of pre-1945 Japan. These policies had transformed Shintō into a state religion centered on the Emperor as a unifying symbol of the nation and used this state religion to justify Japan's colonial and war-mongering policies. As Japan descended in the 1930s into its "black valley" (*kurodani*) of fascism and militarism, those who raised dissenting voices were invariably suppressed.

One movement so suppressed was the highly successful millenarian new religion Ōmotokyō, whose leader Deguchi Ōnisaburō[1] portrayed himself as a world savior while symbolically challenging the sacred status of the Emperor. Twice, in 1921 and most severely in 1935, Ōmotokyō was subjected to police raids, the incarceration of its leaders, and the razing of its religious centers. By responding to Deguchi's challenges and crushing Ōmotokyō, the state displayed its readiness to use force against any religion that opposed its ideology or threatened its power. Hereafter most religious movements in Japan—either cowed by fear of repression or motivated by a culturally and religiously ordained ideology of nationalism—fell into line with government dictates and with Japan's ideologically driven military expansion.[2] The few that did not were suppressed and their leaders imprisoned.

After Japan's defeat in 1945, the American-dominated occupation government promulgated a new, liberal constitution. Recognizing that religious repression had been crucial to the rise of fascism, the government implemented laws and constitutional articles formally separating religion and state, affording the right of freedom of religion to all, and granting religious organizations protection from state interference. These notions of individual religious freedom and the rights of religious groups became basic foundations for the modern, secular, liberal democratic state that emerged after the war.

Such constitutionally guaranteed religious freedoms did not necessarily transform Japan into a haven of religious tolerance. While free from the fear of state repression, religious movements found themselves subject to scrutiny (and frequent hostile attack) from the free press that emerged after the war. Indeed, it could be argued that the mass media in general took upon itself the role of public policeman of religious movements, publishing numerous exposés of religious organizations for financial irregularities and other scandals. While the media delighted in reporting misdeeds across the religious spectrum, from the financial misdeeds of Buddhist temples to the closet right-wing nationalist political associations of certain Shintō shrines, it was the new religions that bore the brunt of such criticism. They were frequently portrayed as dubious organizations intent on manipulating and fleecing the gullible masses.

Nevertheless, until 1995, religious movements were largely free from external intrusion. The civil authorities, fearful that any such action would be seen as an attempt to turn the clock back, rarely looked into the affairs of groups that were registered under the Japanese Religious Corporations Law, even when evidence of malpractice existed. This attitude helped Aum; although widely suspected of numerous crimes prior to the subway attack, it was not properly investigated, largely because the police feared being accused of breaching constitutional safeguards against religious persecution.

Consensus Shattered

This consensus was effectively shattered in March 1995 when public opinion and political necessity demanded a decisive police response to Aum's atrocities. That response—including mass raids on Aum centers and prominent displays of weapons, shields, and other military equipment—aroused for some observers disturbing parallels to the pre-war militaristic assaults on Ōmotokyō. The general public, however, fully supported the raids, turning a blind eye to any possible breaches of the civil liberties of Aum members and widely agreeing with the arrests, trials, and sentences (including several death sentences) passed on Aum leaders.

It was not just the immediate trauma of the Aum affair that affected public opinion and convinced the political authorities that they had to react. It was also the revelation that Aum had gathered a large amount of materials and weapons for the purpose of committing further violence against the populace.[3] This trend in public opinion has been a major factor in shaping attitudes to new religions in the post-Aum era. It has also encouraged the media to give saturation coverage to the Aum affair, endlessly reporting rumors, allegations, and facts, bringing in numerous "experts" (mostly critics who denounce Aum as a nefarious "cult") to discuss the affair and its possible meanings for Japan, and engaging in new exposés of Aum and other movements that might—in the media perspective—turn out to be "dangerous."

Aum provided Japan with an example of what *might* happen if religious movements were left unchecked. In the popular view the affair appeared to indicate that certain types of movements, especially ones that, like Aum, preached a message of rejection of normative social mores and values and that aspired to the formation of a new spiritual order, might prove dangerous to society. The new consensus that has emerged as a result is one which places less weight on the idea of protecting religious movements from the state, and which is more concerned with protecting state, society, and the general public *from* the potential dangers of religious groups.

Political and Public Responses to Aum

It was hardly surprising that the government felt impelled to amend the laws relating to religious movements. Some rather anodyne changes were made to the Religious Corporations Laws, while the question of whether to ban Aum—an action that raised major questions about individual religious freedoms—was given serious consideration. A commission was established to determine whether Aum could be proscribed under the Anti-Subversives Law (a repressive law implemented in 1952 as an anti-Communist measure, but never before applied to any movement), but it decided that Aum no longer posed a threat to public safety and hence should not be banned—a decision greeted with relief by liberals who feared that using this act against Aum would set a dangerous precedent for future religious repression, but resented by many who saw it as an act of excessive tolerance toward an undeserving movement. This latter view was the position taken by the Japanese Public Security Intelligence Agency, which would have overseen the use of the Anti-Subversives Law against Aum, and which has since sought to persuade the authorities to reconsider this decision.[4] Its concerns, and those of the wider public, were recognized by the government in 1999 when it passed a new law (described by some as "draconian") aimed specifically at Aum which required the movement to keep authorities closely informed of all its affairs and membership records.

Aum has tried hard to change its image and to convince the public that it is no longer a threat. It has issued public apologies for its actions and taken steps to pay reparations and fines levied on it for injuries inflicted on others. Now under new leadership, and distancing itself from its imprisoned guru Asahara Shōkō, it has renounced earlier doctrines that legitimated the killing of unbelievers and proclaimed itself a peaceful movement concerned to work for the public good. A name change, to Aleph, in 2000, was a further attempt to distance itself from the past. However, for most Japanese, such changes have been seen largely as window dressing. The movement is still usually referred to by the media and critics as "Aum," many people regard the changes as concealing a continuing antisocial agenda, and it continues to inspire a mixture of hostility and fear in others.

This has been manifest notably wherever Aum members have tried to establish homes or centers in Japan. Such attempts have frequently led to opposition from local citizens' groups and authorities, which have stated that they feared the presence of Aum followers in their neighborhoods would cause problems or danger to residents. Landlords who have rented out properties to Aum followers have been pressured to evict them, protest groups have picketed the homes and centers of followers, and local authorities have frequently refused to accept the residence registration of Aum members or to allow their children to attend local schools.

Such actions (notably refusing residence registration and school access) are illegal in Japan and have been declared so by frequent court rulings in favour of Aum. However, public opinion and media sympathies continue to side very much with the protesters and give support to continued attempts to hamper any activity the movement tries to carry out. The issue of civil rights, in this context, appears to be secondary for many people, as was illustrated by the comment of a Japanese friend in Tokyo who told me that, whatever the cost to civil rights, he wanted Aum to be disbanded and its followers made to renounce their beliefs. He and his family regularly used the subway and, although he was not personally injured in the attack, it had left a strong enough impression for him to fear that Aum still posed a threat to the well-being of his family. The freedom to follow one's own religion was secondary to the rights of others to go about their business safely, a point that is readily understandable given the circumstances of the Aum affair.

Such perceptions have conditioned attitudes not just toward Aum but to NRMs in general. Aum's continuing existence provides a constant reminder to the Japanese public concerning the dangers that *might* come from certain sorts of religious movements. This viewpoint has been widely articulated in the mass media which, never a shrinking violet where new religions and hints of scandal are concerned, have been emboldened to mount further high profile investigations of potentially "deviant" movements. Equally, the police, whose earlier reluctance to get involved with

Aum was quite conspicuous, have been keen not to repeat the error and have exhibited a greater readiness to investigate scandals surrounding registered religious groups. When, for example, allegations were made by disaffected former members against Hōnohana Sanpōgyō (a new religion which promoted costly divination practices), and the movement became subject to an intensive media exposé, the police began investigations which led to the movement being disbanded because of extensive fraud and financial abuse, and its leader, Fukunaga Hōgen, being arrested on fraud charges.[5] One suspects that, prior to the Aum affair, the former members would have been less vocal in airing their grievances—or in demanding recompense from the movement—and the police far less likely to have intervened.

"Dangerous Cults" and the Rise of the Anticult Movement

This climate of public hostility towards NRMs has been exacerbated by the emergence of an "anticult" movement that has all but drowned out alternative voices and perspectives. This movement, which barely existed prior to the Aum affair, grew rapidly in its aftermath, spurred by the activities of "anticult" activists from the United States such as Steve Hassan. Hassan visited Japan shortly after the subway attack to speak about the practice of "brainwashing" in "cults" such as Aum.[6] Such views, which provided an easily grasped populist explanation of Aum, were congruent with those of Aum's critics who, prior to the subway attack, had argued that Asahara and his lieutenants had exerted some form of "mind control" over their followers.[7] The subway attack appeared to confirm, in public perception, the accuracy of such accusations, and those who had spoken against Aum were consequently transformed into "experts" not just on Aum but on "cults" in general. These critics became articulate proponents of an "anticult" movement that was quickly able to establish itself as an authority and pressure group.

The workings of the "anticult" movement in Japan—especially its rhetoric—will not be unfamiliar to outside observers. The term "cult" (Japanese: *karuto*) has entered the Japanese language with very similar meanings and connotations to the English media use of the term. Thus, *karuto* in Japanese connotes a dangerous movement run by a manipulative and fraudulent figure who poses as a religious teacher (but whose real interests are power, money, and sex) and who "brainwashes" his devotees into following his every beck and call.

While the term *karuto* was used in Japan prior to the Aum affair, it has subsequently become dominant in public discourse. In this process, the quasi-distinction made in many Western media discussions of new movements between "religions" (genuine, upstanding movements) and "cults" (evil, fraudulent and dishonest) has become commonplace. Many Japanese religious organizations have contributed to this perception by affirming their respectability and commitment to normative values— while simultaneously condemning Aum, by giving their support to anti-cult campaigns, and by sending out warnings about "dangerous" and "false" (rival) religious movements.[8]

These perceptions about the dangers of cults have given rise to various alarmist books and articles that seek to identify the "next Aum" (that is, the next group that might become dangerous and cause social disruption). One of the groups so targeted has been Soka Gakkai. The movement was persecuted for its opposition to the wartime government's militarism but it is now the largest religious organization in Japan. Soka Gakkai, more than almost any other movement prior to Aum, had provoked public opprobrium because of its aggressive recruitment policies and its strongly developed political base. These developments had caused concern that Soka Gakkai might threaten the post-war constitutional separation of religion and state. Thus, it was not surprising that the group was one of the movements labelled by some as potentially being "another Aum."[9]

Space does not permit further discussion of all the movements or types of movement that have been labeled as "cults." It is, however, my suspicion that beneath the surface there may be a further disturbing pattern of intolerance emerging in Japan. Based on various surveys that I have done of "anticult" literature in Japanese bookshops, supplemented recently by interviews with people involved in the anticult movement in Japan, it is evident that a primary identifier or marker indicating what sort of movement may be called a "cult" relates to the degree to which the movement in question embraces normative Japanese values, especially concerning the family. Movements that encourage dissociation from the (biological) family and entry into an alternative community structure tend to be termed "cults." This is the case, for example, with the Yamagishikai, an agrarian communal movement that has attracted much opposition and criticism in recent years.

Most strikingly, however, it is also evident that the term "cult" is more readily applied in Japan to movements that come from outside the country than to those of Japanese origin. Implicit in the term "cult," in other words, are not just ideas of being deviant but also connotations of "foreign" and "not Japanese"—connotations that are implicitly leveled also at groups of Japanese origin that have non-normative orientations. Here one should note that many of Aum's characteristics were drawn from external traditions (notably Tibetan and Indian) and that it adopted a self-consciously "different" (and inherently non-normative Japanese) style.

The two movements most frequently portrayed in such terms are the Jehovah's Witnesses and the Unification Movement, both of which have been active in Japan in recent decades and both of which have acquired reputations for being socially disruptive and divisive. Both had been involved in scandals and conflicts before the Aum affair, examples including the Unification Movement's alleged role in extorting large sums of money from unsuspecting clients through aggressive spiritual purification sales schemes, and the Jehovah's Witnesses' unusual teachings concerning surgery and blood transfusions. Both, too, are seen as "foreign" movements that infringe on Japanese social sensibilities by demanding their followers' full adherence. The groups are accused of withdrawing from the normative round of rituals that are part of the Japanese religious and social calendar and aligning instead with identity groupings that are in conflict with normative Japanese social values.

The apparent identification in popular discourse of these two movements (and of "cults" in general) as highly deviant and dangerous was illustrated for me during a visit to one of Japan's largest bookshops, Kinokuniya in Shinjuku, Tokyo, in the late 1990s. There I found that books about Aum were shelved not under "Religion" but in the section on criminal organizations alongside works on the *yakuza* (Japanese gangsters) and the Mafia, and next to books on crime, serial killers, and mass murderers. Perhaps, given that Aum had killed at least twenty-five people, I should not have been too surprised at this—or indeed, given their respective death tolls, the presence there of books in Japanese on Peoples Temple and the Order of the Solar Temple. What took me aback, however, was that books denouncing the Jehovah's Witnesses and the Unification Movement were placed alongside these. It was as if the bookshop's shelving policies had been determined by the agenda of the anticult movement. It certainly reflected a disturbing pattern of thinking in Japan, in which deviance from norms in the religious context is equated with the sinister and the murderous. I would also suggest—if my observations are correct—that the prevalence, in modern Japan, of Japanocentric modes of identity discourse that are clearly anti-Western and anti-foreign[10] has, if anything, become intensified after the Aum affair, with certain movements identified as "dangerous" largely because of their foreign provenance. These subliminal associations of danger, deviance, and foreign appear, in other words, to be becoming overt in populist discourse: anticult rhetoric is at some points thus interwoven with implicitly nationalist undertones.

The Muted Voices of Academia

The emergence of the anticult movement as a force claiming authority in the sphere of new religions clearly suggests parallels with many Western countries. In Japan, too, there are various indications that some involved in the movement have used deprogramming as a means of "rescuing" NRM members[11]—although this practice has caused all manner of disputes within the anticult movement itself, and it is clear that many tensions and conflicts exist between different activists engaged in combatting what they call "cults."[12] Despite the inherent inner tensions and weaknesses within the wider anticult movement, it remains a potent and vocal public force, aided by the fact—somewhat different to the situation in the U.S., the U.K. and elsewhere—that there has been little discernible and informed response to the movement from the scholarly world.

In Japan, the voices of scholars who could provide informed perspectives have become muted almost to the point of non-existence. In part this is because of the vociferous success of "anticult" activists who were quick to claim and seize the post-Aum moral high ground. They were aided in this by failures in the academic community, notably the misinterpretations of a small number of scholars in Japan and elsewhere who appeared to give support to Aum when it was first accused of criminal behavior. Thus, a small group of American scholars visited Japan shortly after the subway attack (and at Aum's invitation) because they were concerned about possible human rights violations against Aum. While their motives were sincere, their actions reflected a tacit assumption prevalent among many scholars that NRMs accused of atrocities are normally innocent. Their visit went down very badly in a country where it was widely agreed that Aum was guilty and that it posed a serious threat to public security.

On this score, it was fascinating to note how different interest groups involved in the sphere of "cult wars" in the United States acted out similar and contrasting agendas in Japan over Aum. Hassan and his fellow anticultists leapt to unsubstantiated conclusions about brainwashing, and NRM scholars assumed that Aum must have been a victim. The visit by NRM scholars, coming on top of misjudgments by two Japanese academics, backfired because of Aum's swiftly proven guilt. It also seemed to confirm the arguments made by prominent anticult activists in Japan that academics are little more than apologists for dangerous and deviant groups.[13]

Only a very few scholars so erred, and most Western and Japanese NRM scholars made no attempt to defend Aum or to do anything other than discuss, interpret, and analyze its criminal actions. Still, the prevailing image has been of academic compliance with cults, with scholars who discuss movements such as Aum in any terms other than those of cultic deviance and evil seen as little more than apologists. It is small wonder, then, that at present the opportunity for Japanese scholars to present an alternative to the views of the anticult movement has been severely curtailed. Scholars in many Western countries are certainly not unfamiliar with such scenarios and are well aware that presenting other than condemnatory views on NRMs can bring similar accusations. However, it is clear that the voices of academics are to some extent now heard by civil authorities and law enforcement agencies in countries such as the U.K. and the U.S. In Japan, on the other hand, there appear to be no counterbalancing arguments in the debates over dangerous cults. This, in turn, has intensified the hostile environment for NRMs in the post-Aum era.

Concluding Comments

The above brief overview indicates that Japan has entered into a new era in which certain types of movements (which, it should be emphasized, have never had a good press) have come to be viewed as increasingly dangerous and suspect. Although the primary catalyst for producing this climate has been the Aum affair—which has redrawn the picture of the post-war religious world and reshaped the relationship between society and religion—other cases, such as the Hōnohana Sanpōgyō affair, have appeared to reinforce public perceptions about NRMs and deviancy. They have helped give rise to an active anticult movement which has faced relatively little opposition from the academic world. At present, the predominant trends—with a rampant press, an aggressive anticult movement, a population ready to accede to draconian laws against suspect groups, law enforcement agencies prepared to investigate religious movements, and few alternative voices capable of being heard—presage an inauspicious immediate future for emergent religious groups.

Yet I should append some caveats to this gloomy picture. It is important to note that the Japanese experiment with freedom of religion is still in its infancy and dates only from 1946. Such freedom—which includes both the freedom of citizens to follow the religious paths they wish and the freedom of religious organizations to function without state interference—comes at a price and is dependent on an implicit contract of trust. It demands that state and society should respect the freedom of religious worship, allow religious organizations to follow their own beliefs and practices, and refrain from interference in such groups. It also demands that religious movements show tolerance and respect for the safety, freedoms, and views of others and for the laws of society.

The first major challenge to this fledgling democratic understanding of religious freedoms came not from the state, the mass media, or from anticult campaigners, but from a religious movement that was incapable of accepting criticism, enduring opposition or, indeed, tolerating internal dissent. After Aum, the authorities could have taken more drastic steps or enacted even harsher laws against religious movements and still gained public approval. Yet, even in a period of moral panic and hysteria, this has not been done. The only repressive new law is directed solely at Aum. Even so Aum has retained its right to exist, and the courts have upheld the basic democratic rights of its members. The courts have rejected attempts by local authorities, for instance, to deny Aum members the right of residence or access for their children to schools. Moreover, recent court cases have upheld the rights of people who have sued members of the anticult movement over incidents of deprogramming.[14] These developments indicate that, despite the current public mood, the Japanese authorities remain committed to the tenets of religious freedom, albeit in a more qualified manner than prior to Aum. While the previous consensus is now dead and while Japanese NRMs can no longer enjoy the privilege of being virtually above the law, there are at least some indications that whatever new consensus might eventually emerge will not cause their existing rights to be wholly swept aside, and that the courts and legal system appear to affirm and guarantee legal rights that many opponents of "cults" in Japan would like to see taken away.

Notes

1. All proper names in this paper are given according to Japanese style, with the family name first and the given name second.
2. One should note that many movements, including Buddhist sects and new religions, embraced the rampant nationalism of the era: see, for example, Robert Sharf, "The Zen of Japanese Nationalism," *History of Religions* 33:1 (1993): 1–43.
3. For a fuller discussion of this and other aspects of the Aum affair see Ian Reader, *Religious Violence in Contemporary Japan: The Case of Aum Shinrikyō* (Richmond, U.K., and Honolulu, HI: Curzon Press and University of Hawaii Press, 2000).
4. Officials of the agency were widely quoted in articles in the Japanese and foreign media—especially during 1997 and 1998—that have raised fears about a resurgent Aum. However, the agency sources have invariably cited grossly exaggerated membership figures for Aum, raising suspicions that its "information" has been deliberately modified for political reasons.
5. On this case see Yonemoto Kazuhiro, *Kyōso taiho* (Tokyo: Hōjimasha, 2000), esp. 9–54.
6. For a discussion of the emergence of the anticult movement in Japan see Watanabe Manabu, "Reactions to the Aum Affair: the Rise of the 'Anti-cult' Movement," *Bulletin of the Nanzan Institute for Religion and Culture* 21 (1997): 32–48.
7. See, for example, Egawa Shōko, *Kyōseishu no yabō* (Tokyo: Kyōikushiryū Shuppankai, 1991).
8. Kōfuku no Kagaku, for example, which had already attacked various rivals as "false religions" (*jakyō*) prior to 1995, stepped up its attacks further after the Aum affair, while its leader, Ōkawa Ryūhō, gave a number of sermons in 1995 about the "dangers" of such "false religions." See Ōkawa Ryūhō, *Jinsei seikō no hissaku* (Tokyo: Kōfuku no Kagaku Shuppan, 1995), especially 163ff.
9. Noda Mineo, *Ikeda Daisaku zenmyaku no kenkyū* (Tokyo: Miyai Shobō, 1997).
10. There is plentiful material on this widespread discourse (known in Japan as *Nihonjinron* or "discussions about Japaneseness") on Japanese modes of identity. For a general overview in religious contexts see Winston Davis, *Japanese Religion and Society: Paradigms of Social Change* (Albany: State University of New York Press, 1992).
11. See Yonemoto, *Kyōso taiho*, 250ff.
12. I base these remarks especially on interviews conducted in Japan with people involved in anticult activities, in November 2002.
13. See Ian Reader, "Scholarship, Aum Shinrikyō and Integrity," *Nova Religio* 3:2 (Spring 2000): 368–82.
14. Information from Yonemoto Kazuhiro, interview with author, Tokyo, 21 November 2002.

CHAPTER 13

New Religions in Australia
Public Menace or Societal Salvation?*

JAMES T. RICHARDSON

New Religions in Australia: An Overview

New religions in Australia have had their share of controversy, although not as much as in some countries in Europe and former Communist areas.[1] Indeed, as Gary Bouma has noted, the situation with most new religious movements (NRMs) has been remarkably peaceful in Australia, which has come to be more tolerant with its new, more pluralistic approach to religious and ethnic differences.[2] However, there are some who would dispute this assessment, and who claim either that NRMs cause many problems in Australian society,[3] or that NRMs themselves suffer considerably at the hands of authorities and the media.[4] And some scholars, most notably Rowan Ireland, argue that the increasing religious and cultural diversity of Australian society might be considered a positive feature because many of the new religions, by virtue of their teachings and practices, actually contribute to a new kind of societal integration of Australian society.[5] This brief essay will attempt to assess the current situation in Australia concerning NRMs.[6]

Historical, Social, and Legal Context

One could easily argue, as does Bouma, that Australia is a land peopled by new religions on a regular basis, since it has always been a society with a heavy inflow of immigrants who carry their cultural values and practices with them. This influx of different peoples began almost immediately, because of the presence of Irish Catholics among the convicts sent to Australia in the late eighteenth century. Catholics coming to Australia either as convicts or free citizens encountered significant numbers of Methodists, Presbyterians, and Congregationalists who had joined with the dominant Anglicans to form a mostly Protestant new nation.

While many smaller religious groups were allowed to exist and even prosper in early Australia, some groups were devalued and effectively left out of the amalgam that became Australia, especially groups like the Seventh-day Adventists and Jehovah's Witnesses, which were viewed with suspicion, as were Jews.[7] That suspicion continues into the present and has spread to other, more recent religious groups, especially those making more life-changing demands on participants. However, that suspicion of certain foreign groups did not dominate public policy, and indeed the demand for workers to assist with Australia's booming economy overwhelmed such concerns, especially after World War II. Workers, no matter their religious and cultural affiliations, were desperately needed to build the Australian economy, and thus the Anglican-Protestant hegemony began to crumble under economic pressures.

Thus, a "White Australia" immigration policy, with a strong preference for British and Irish immigrants, eventually gave way to a formal policy in the 1970s that declared Australia a multicultural nation which officially welcomed all comers, as long as they were willing to fit into Australian society and become productive citizens in the growing economy. Thus we see Australia's religious demographics clearly showing a shift from the Anglican-dominated Protestant hegemony of earlier times. As Bouma notes, in 1947, the nation of 7.6 million people was 88 percent Christian, with one half of one per cent in the "other" category (Buddhists, Hindus, Jews, Muslims, Other), and the rest (11.4 percent) not claiming a religion or not answering the question.[8] By 2001, the population had grown to 18.8 million, but the rapid immigration that contributed greatly to the growth resulted in only 69 percent claiming to be Christian, a dramatic growth to 4.8 percent in the "Other" category, and a whopping 25.3 percent claiming no religion (15.5 percent) or not stating a clear preference (9.8 percent).[9]

What may seem remarkable to some is that this sort of diversity was achieved without the benefit of a federal, constitutionally-based Bill of Rights guaranteeing freedom of religion.[10] Early in Australia's history, the effort to establish a Bill of Rights that included religious freedom with the initial Constitution was beaten back by those who wanted the dominant religious traditions to exercise more control. Indeed, the religious freedom/Bill of Rights issue has been defeated twice since then by the voters, with religion being a focal point of those subsequent campaigns. The initial campaign and those since have used the United States as a problematic example of what can happen with such formal guarantees of religious freedom. Those efforts have apparently struck a resonant chord with the Australian voters, who voted 69 percent to 31 percent against adding a Bill of Rights in 1988.

The Australian Constitution does include a Clause 116 that seems modeled after the language in the United States Constitution concerning religion, but the clause is more symbolic in its meaning since it does not apply to the individual states. The clause reads:

> The Commonwealth shall not make any law for establishing any religion, or for imposing any religious observance, or for prohibiting the free exercise of any religion, and no religious test shall be required as a qualification for any office or public trust under the Commonwealth.

There is an effort currently being made to develop the legal meaning of this clause by doing something analogous to what happened with the Fourteenth Amendment to the United States Constitution. This amendment contains the famous "equal protection clause" that has been used to force federal constitutional guarantees of individual rights and freedoms upon the separate states. However, this movement, led by those—including some prominent judges—who think Australia should formally adopt and abide by international norms for human rights, has not gained momentum yet, leaving religious freedom protections mainly with the states.

Although Clause 116 does not apply to the states, it does prevent the federal government from adopting legislation establishing a religion, and it prevents the creation of federal laws that violate religious freedom. Perhaps most important, the clause makes it unlawful to discriminate in hiring for federal public service jobs, a protection that allowed many minority faith members, including particularly Catholics, to obtain respectable jobs and thus begin to climb the status ladder in Australia.

Of the six Australian states, only one, Tasmania, has a guarantee of religious freedom in its state constitution, and that protection can be overridden by legislative action. Two states (Victoria and Queensland) have statutes that afford some protections for minority faiths. New South Wales (Sydney) has explicitly rejected adding religious freedom to its anti-discrimination statutes, mainly because of opposition from traditional religious organizations, as well as gay and lesbian lobby groups.[11] This rejection occurred in the face of thorough documentation about problems being faced by a number of religious minorities in New South Wales (NSW). Included in this large study were details about the famous Lindy Chamberlain case, in which Mrs. Chamberlain, a Seventh-day Adventist, spent three years in prison after being found guilty of killing her baby at Ayers Rock (Uluru) in 1980. She was eventually freed after some extraordinary efforts by those who thought that she had been wrongly convicted, and that a dingo had actually taken the baby.[12] The study also detailed the 1978 Hilton bombing case, in which three members of the Ananda Marga group were convicted after a massive, but apparently wrong-headed and misleading campaign by the police and media to convict them of setting off a bomb that killed two people during an international conference in Sydney. Again, these defendants were eventually freed after further investigation, suggesting the existence of some checks and balances within the Australian system of justice. But they were not released before they had spent five years in prison, and one of the three was prosecuted again, unsuccessfully.

Further removed in time are some famous episodes in Australian history concerning discrimination against minority faiths. Australia became, in 1941, the second country in the world to ban the Jehovah's Witnesses (the other was Nazi Germany). After being banned under Australia's sedition statutes (and having their property confiscated), however, the Witnesses continued to operate and even doubled their membership within two years. Shortly thereafter, in June 1943, the High Court of Australia overturned the specific act under which the Witnesses were banned, making the ban inoperative.[13]

More recently, some of the controversial NRMs that have gained notoriety in other societies have also been the target of efforts at social control by Australian officials. The Family, formerly known as the Children of God (COG), experienced considerable attention from authorities at the federal level and within some states, and some 17 COG homes across Australia were raided in 1976 by immigration officials (no violations were found, however). This official scrutiny culminated in massive synchronized raids in May 1992 against Family communal homes in Victoria and NSW that resulted in 153 children being taken into custody.[14] The two states eventually failed in their efforts to have the children declared wards of the state and subsequently had to release the children and deal with various claims against the state made by The Family members affected. Again, the outcome of these cases, which engendered considerable media attention, suggests that there are some checks and balances within the Australian justice system.

The Unification Church (UC) has also garnered much attention in Australia over the past few decades, as documented by the NSW Anti-Discrimination study. Questions were raised at the federal level, as well as by the NSW government, about the operation of the UC within Australia. Specific concerns were raised about their requests to build training centers within Australia, and only after a two-year battle was the church even allowed to build a worship center. Its initial request for a residency-based ministry was denied and lost on appeal. The controversy sparked (or was sparked by) much extremely negative news coverage of the UC, focusing on claims made from overseas about activities of the UC in other societies, particularly England. UC members have also been forcibly deprogrammed, as documented in the NSW Anti-Discrimination study.

Scientology has also come in for its share of negative attention in Australia over the years. Several states have, at one time or another, indirectly banned Scientology by declaring it "psychological" and hence illegal because practitioners were not registered psychologists. This made it illegal for the organization to register as a religion, advertise, teach their doctrines, or receive payments for services rendered to individual practitioners. At one time the federal "Companies Code" prohibited the use of the terms "Scientology" and "Dianetics" in any advertising materials. Scientology also lost a major High Court case in 1983 in which it was appealing a decision that allowed the Australian Security Intelligence Organization (ASIO) to engage in ongoing surveillance of Scientology members. This surveillance involved the reporting of personal information on individual members when they applied for jobs with federal agencies. The ASIO case seemingly demonstrates little concern for the religious freedom of members of Scientology (or for religious freedom in general). However, that same year the High Court handed down a resounding victory for Scientology by overturning a Victoria Appeal Court decision that had declared with much verbiage that Scientology was not a religion for purposes of tax exemption. This High Court decision is considered the major case on the definition of religion in Australia, and its careful delineation of what constitutes a religion makes the decision one of international import.[15] More recently, a case in Victoria involved the government's attempt to define Scientology's "Purification Rundown" as a "health practice" and therefore subject to regulation. The State Supreme Court did not accept this argument. It is also worth noting that Scientology was, in 2002, invited to join an interfaith dialogue in Sydney.

Lynne Hume has written insightfully about the treatment of Wiccans and other Pagans in Australia, noting that the southern hemisphere context makes the practice of Wicca especially challenging and interesting since important ritual dates occur at opposite seasons of the year. She also applies the criteria developed in the 1983 Scientology tax case to Wicca, concluding that it meets those criteria and should be considered a religion for legal and tax purposes. She notes the changing legal climate in Australia concerning the practices of Wiccan groups, with a number of changes in various states and at the federal level making it less likely that Pagans will be prosecuted for engaging in their faith.[16] It is noteworthy also that a 1998 federal report, entitled *Article 18: Freedom of Religion and Belief*, issued a number of findings more positive toward Wiccans and Pagans, among them that, "There is no evidence to suggest that individuals or the community require specific protection from witchcraft or fortune-telling practices." The report goes on to state that any problems of fraud that might arise from such activities can best be dealt with under general criminal and civil laws, and it further recommends that states having laws against sorcery, witchcraft, fortune-telling, and enchantment (some dating from the 1800s) should repeal those statutes since "Wiccans and Pagans have the right to manifest their beliefs either individually or in concert with others in the practice of witchcraft and fortune-telling."[17]

This same federal report, *Article 18*, presents a more mixed picture when considering NRMs in general. After beginning the discussion with an examination of the terms "cult" and "new religious movement," the report opts to use both somewhat interchangeably, dismissing the extreme negative connotations of the term "cult."[18] The report then attempts to "split the baby in half," by showing some recognition of the fact that many participants in such groups join voluntarily and claim to have positive gains from so doing, while at the same time giving considerable credence to anticult views of participation, and listing several pages of alleged negative repercussions of involvement in such groups. In the end, however, the report shifts in a markedly critical direction concerning "cults" and new religions, by using the term "brainwashing" as if it had scientific meaning, and using a brainwashing-based rationale to justify some recommendations about such groups.[19] The findings include several which assume that coercion is a regular part of decisions to participate in new religions ("Coercion includes the use of covert or brainwashing techniques to recruit new members") and that guidelines or principles for what are acceptable religious practices need to be developed. The report also recommends that the Attorney General's department should convene "an interfaith dialogue" to "examine the question of methods of coercion in religious belief and practice"; to "consider whether legal limitations should be imposed on religious groups regarding coercive tactics"; and to "formulate an agreed list of minimum standards for the practice of religious groups."[20]

Given recent world events, it would be an oversight not to comment on the place of Islam in Australia, especially given that Islam is the largest non-Christian group in the country. Government actions to preempt or counter terrorism have focused particularly on religious minority groups, especially Muslims from Asia, the Middle East, and Africa. Soon after the 9/11 tragedy, a mosque in Brisbane was fire-bombed. In the wake of the Bali terrorist bombing of October 12, 2002, a number of suspected terrorist groups were raided by the Australian authorities, with most targets involving Muslims. These raids have attracted attention, both within and without Australia, and have perhaps contributed to anti-Islamic sentiments in the populace.

Discussion and Conclusions

Whether anything comes of the just-cited recommendations of the federal report entitled *Article 18* is not at all certain, especially in light of Australia's growing animus toward Islam.[21] There is evidence that the report has been shelved by the Attorney General's office, as indicated by Bouma. Apparently the Attorney General received considerable negative response to the idea of federal legislation guaranteeing more religious freedom, and then claimed that the problems uncovered were not of a magnitude as to require federal intervention.[22] Still, the report does suggest more animus exists toward new faiths in Australia than one might expect, given the long history of relative openness toward new religious groups. And the report also is relatively devoid of appreciation for the important theoretical point made by Rowan Ireland that the increasing religious diversity in Australia might actually contribute to a new type of societal integration not based on similar beliefs and values, but on a new negotiated social identity that could serve Australia and Australians well.

Australian history appears to ebb and flow with regard to religious freedom for newer and minority religious groups, with some sad chapters in that history, but also some definite bright spots, as operation of the checks and balances inherent in the Australian justice system have demonstrated on occasion. It remains to be seen whether the relatively optimistic views about Australia expressed by Bouma and by Ireland will be borne out, or whether the difficulties so well chronicled by Juliet Sheen will increase and become the way that Australians relate to and define NRMs.

Notes

*   Appreciation is expressed to Carolyn Evans, Reid Mortesen, Juliet Sheen, Gary Bouma, and Mike Hill for suggestions on this chapter.

1.   See special issue of *Social Justice Research* (12, 1999) edited by this author under the theme, "Social Justice and Minority Religions," which describes the situation in a number of European and former Communist Countries in a series of eleven articles. Also see James Richardson and Massimo Introvigne, " 'Brainwashing' Claims in Governmental Reports of Cults and New Religions in Europe," *Journal for the Scientific Study of Religion* 40 (2001): 143–68.

2.   See Gary Bouma, "Social Justice Issues in the Management of Religious Diversity," *Social Justice Research* 12 (1999): 283–96.

3.   See Rachael Kohn, "Cults and the New Age in Australia," in *Many Religions, All Australian,* ed. Gary Bouma (Adelaide: Open Book Publishers, 1997), 149–62.

4.   See Juliet Sheen, "Living within the Tensions of Plurality: Human Rights Law and Policy," in ed. Gary Bouma, *Many Religions, All Australian,* 163–82. Also see the very thorough report, written by Sheen, New South Wales Anti-Discrimination Board, *Discrimination and Religious Conviction* (Sydney: NSW Anti-Discrimination Board, 1984). On media coverage of

such issues in Australia, see James Richardson, "Journalistic Bias Against New Religious Movements in Australia," *Journal of Contemporary Religion* 11 (1996): 289–302.

5. See Rowan Ireland's thoughtful paper, "Religious Diversity in the New Australian Democracy," *Australian Religious Studies Review* 12 (1999): 94–110.

6. I am relying on my own research, some of which is cited herein, as well as some recent scholarly overviews of the area of new religious movements, including Lynne Hume, "New Religious Movements: Current Research in Australia," *Australian Religious Studies Review* 13 (1999): 27–39, and Rowan Ireland, ibid.

7. Carolyn Evans pointed out that Sir Issac Issacs, a Jew, was both a High Court Judge and Australia's first native-born Prime Minister before World War II, interesting in light of problems encountered by many Jews in Australian history.

8. See Bouma, "Social Justice Issues," 287. Australia has long allowed a question on religious identification on its federal census, which makes the kind of comparison offered by Bouma quite meaningful.

9. See Gary Bouma, "Globalization and Recent Changes in the Demography of Australian Religious Groups: 1947–2001," *People and Place* 10 (2002): 17–23.

10. See James T. Richardson, "Minority Religions ('Cults') and the Law: Comparisons of the United States, Europe, and Australia," *University of Queensland Law Journal* 18 (1995): 183–207.

11. See New South Wales Anti-Discrimination Board, 1984.

12. The movie *Cry in the Dark*, starring Meryl Streep and Sam Neill, chronicled this tragic episode.

13. The Witnesses in Germany were not so fortunate, as thousands were imprisoned and died at the hands of the Nazis.

14. See James Richardson, "Social Control of New Religions: From 'Brainwashing' Claims to Child Sex Abuse Accusations," in *Children in New Religions*, eds. Susan Palmer and Charlotte Hardman (New Brunswick, NJ: Rutgers University Press, 1999), 172–86, for details on these raids.

15. See New South Wales Anti-Discrimination Board, 1984, and Richardson, "Minority Religions ('Cults') and the Law," for more details on Scientology's treatment by governmental bodies in Australia.

16. See Lynne Hume, "Exporting Nature Religions: Problems of Praxis Down Under," *Nova Religio* 2 (1999): 287–89, and Lynne Hume, "Witchcraft and the Law in Australia," *Journal of Church and State* 37 (1995): 135–50.

17. Quotes taken from p. 66 of Human Rights and Equal Opportunity Commission, *Article 18: Freedom of Religion and Belief* (Sydney: Commonwealth of Australia, 1998). This report was supposedly a harbinger of dramatic changes in laws against various kinds of discrimination in Australia, but, as will be recounted later herein, the effort has apparently gone for naught because of pressures similar to those that have kept Australia from adopting a Bill of Rights over the years.

18. On problems using the term "cult" see Lynne Hume, "A Reappraisal of the Term 'Cult' and Consideration of 'Danger Markers' in Charismatic Religious Groups," *Colloquium* 28 (1996): 35–52; Jane Dillon and James T. Richardson, "The 'Cult' Concept: A Politics of Representation Analysis," *SYZYGY: Journal of Alternative Religion and Culture* 3 (1994): 185–98; and James Richardson, "Definitions of Cult: From Sociological-Technical to Popular Negative," *Review of Religious Research* 34 (1993): 348–56.

19. This is similar to many other governmental reports in Western Europe, which are analyzed in Richardson and Introvigne, "Brainwashing Claims in Governmental Reports." For a critique of "brainwashing"-based claims about participation in new religions see James T. Richardson, "The Ethics of 'Brainwashing' Claims," *Australian Religious Studies Review* 7 (1995): 48–56.

20. Quotes from Human Rights and Equal Opportunity Commission, *Article 18*, 81–82.

21. A more recent official report that is somewhat critical of the *Article 18* report has been called to my attention by Michael Hill. This report, produced for the Parliament of the Commonwealth of Australia by the Joint Standing Committee on Foreign Affairs, Defense, and Trade, is entitled, *Conviction with Compassion: A Report on Freedom of Religion and Belief* (November, 2000), and adopts a more critical stance toward "cults" (a term it insists on using). However, the report ends up recommending support for the idea of the Commonwealth Attorney General "convening an inter-faith dialogue to formulate a set of standards for the practices of cults" (184).

22. See Bouma, "Social Justice Issues in the Management of Diversity in Australia," 292.

PART 4

North and South America

CHAPTER 14

The Mainstreaming of
Alternative Spirituality in Brazil

ROBERT T. CARPENTER

Alternative Spirituality Within the Context
of Brazil's Religious Marketplace

Latin America has never figured prominently in the scholarly literature on new religious movements (NRMs) or related phenomena worldwide. The ubiquitous Roman Catholic presence in the region during the five centuries following the sixteenth-century conquest of the New World by Spanish and Portuguese colonial powers was a formidable obstacle for newer religions to overcome. Even so, Latin American religious culture has been more diversified than it might appear at first sight.

Nowhere has this been more the case than in Brazil, long the home of the most exuberant and variegated national religious culture in all of Latin America. The last quarter of the twentieth century saw Brazil's religious arena become even more pluralistic than it had been theretofore, as a full-fledged religious marketplace emerged for the first time in that country. The perennial religious hegemony of the Brazilian Catholic church was challenged as never before on various fronts. While some of the strongest challenges came from evangelical Protestant groups, others were mounted by entities identified either with Kardecist Spiritism or with Umbanda. (The latter is a uniquely Brazilian synthesis comprising elements of Afro-Brazilian and indigenous religious traditions, Kardecism, and even Theosophy.) By the latter part of the twentieth century, Brazil not only claimed the world's largest Roman Catholic population but also sizeable contingents of Protestants, Spiritists, and adherents of religions of African origin, in addition to some of the largest Japanese NRMs outside of Japan.

The perhaps surprising notion of Japanese new religions thriving in tropical Latin America represents just one element of a multifaceted development that was beginning to exert a profound influence upon Brazil's still emergent religious marketplace as the twentieth century drew to a close: namely, the rise of a rather diffuse and heterogeneous "alternative spirituality" cultural movement in that country. For instance, while carrying out field research in Brazil on Kardecist Spiritism, anthropologist David J. Hess attended the First International Congress on Alternative Therapies in the city of São Paulo in 1985, where he glimpsed what was already a vibrant, thriving "world of alternative Brazilian religion, science, and medicine—a Brazilian New Age which makes that of California seem bland in comparison."[1] Brazilian anthropologist and psychologist Jane Russo, in a study that she conducted concerning the rise in popularity of bodywork therapies among middle- and upper-class Brazilians about that same time, cited the emergence in Brazil during the 1980s of an "alternative complex" that was at once ecological, holistic, spiritual, and millenarian in tenor. According to Russo, this complex was directly traceable to the earlier 1960s counterculture in Brazil, as well as to a subsequent psychoanalytic boom that had taken place in the country's larger urban centers during the 1970s.[2]

The present study highlights ways in which mainstream institutions, both within and outside the cultural industries, contributed decisively during the decades of the 1980s and 1990s towards a broadening of the appeal of alternative spirituality in Brazil. Principally through the avenues of books, newsmagazines, and television programming, the general public was at least made aware of selected teachings and practices associated with alternative spirituality. As a result of this process of resource mobilization, or leveraging of social influence making use of third party assets and resources, the alternative spirituality movement was able to exert an influence upon the country's culture as a whole that greatly exceeded what would have been expected given the relatively small size of the movement's core constituency.[3] The following episode relates a prime example of this dynamic in action.

A Primetime Showcase for Alternative Spirituality

Brazilian *telenovelas* air six nights a week in prime time on major television networks, typically lasting six to eight months from opening episode to final episode. The most successful programs in this genre can attract live audiences in the millions at their peak, which indicates their considerable potential for exerting far-reaching cultural influence upon Brazilian urban society.[4]

Such was indeed the case with the *telenovela Mandala,* which was broadcast on TV Globo, Brazil's most popular television network, from October of 1987 to May of 1988.[5] Just one month prior to the *telenovela*'s debut, the Globo Network had aired a Portuguese-dubbed version of the miniseries *Minhas vidas* (*Out on a Limb*), starring Oscar-winning actress Shirley MacLaine in an adaptation of her autobiographical New Age bestseller. Clearly this had been a strategic programming move aimed at boosting the viewing audience's curiosity regarding alternative spirituality in anticipation of *Mandala*'s debut. *Mandala*'s basic plot line was an adaptation of the classical Greek Oedipus myth to a late twentieth-century Brazilian cultural setting. Nevertheless, the serial drama abounded throughout with visual and aural references to an entire zodiac's worth of manifestations of alternative spirituality. The opening and concluding episodes, for example, were filmed on site at the Valley of the Dawn, a thriving esoteric community located on the outskirts of Brasilia, the national capital.[6] They featured the protagonist, Oedipus, displaying paranormal powers amid the Valley's profusion of eclectic visual imagery featuring altars, pyramids, and oversized images of spirit guides. Virtually every episode of the *telenovela* included some reference to alternative spirituality, including crystals, UFOs, astrological charts, remote viewing, mind control techniques, Buddhist meditation practices, astral projection, and telepathy, to name just a few. The computer-generated graphics that served as the backdrop for *Mandala*'s nightly opening and closing credits depicted a cluster of the cowrie shells typically used for purposes of divination in Afro-Brazilian traditions cascading through the center of an abstract, hollow mandala as it rotated on its axis. The overall effect implied a blending of one symbol that had been introduced into Brazilian religious culture from Africa four centuries earlier and another symbol that had only recently been appropriated from South Asian religious traditions.

What was the connection between *Mandala* and the broader phenomenon of alternative spirituality that was just beginning to build momentum in Brazil at that time? The following excerpt from a public relations release issued by the Globo Network just a few days before *Mandala*'s debut sheds some light on this question, especially in the comments by the program's principal screenwriter, Alfredo Dias Gomes, concerning the country's overall religious climate at that juncture:

> At a time when people are seeking out esotericism more every day, *Mandala* takes full advantage of all the symbols. It has Tarot, astrological charts, cowrie shells, and pyramids, along with many other items that no doubt will spark the public's interest.

Dias [Gomes] concurs:

> Our people are inherently mystical. They believe in everything yet at the same
> time believe in nothing. . . . We as a people don't accept one single religion as
> our orthodoxy. We are utterly ecumenical. There are Catholics who participate
> in Macumba [a popular Afro-Brazilian tradition], Marxists who follow gurus,
> materialists who pay heed to their astrological charts, and so forth. In *Mandala*
> I have included everything that might be linked to the *telenovela*'s central
> theme: destiny. I think people are going to identify with it.[7]

This press release shows the impact that the growing presence of alternative spirituality in Brazil was having upon the screenwriter. At the same
time, Gomes's deft rendering of diverse spiritual themes over the course of
the *telenovela* made its own impact in terms of exposing the general public
to concepts and practices of alternative spirituality—an impact that certainly was amplified by the formidable publicity apparatus that stood
behind the most prestigious *telenovelas* and included the network itself,
the daily press, weekly photojournal magazines, and more specialized fan
magazines. This episode serves as one of the more prominent examples of
mainstream cultural institutions playing a key role in the spread of alternative spirituality in urban Brazil in the 1980s.

Alternative Spirituality in Relation to the Brazilian Religious Mainstream

One basic question to be addressed deals with the parameters of alternative spirituality within the religious setting of late twentieth-century
Brazil. Which traditions, beliefs, and practices could legitimately be classified as pertaining to alternative spirituality and which could not? The term
"alternative spirituality" typically denotes an eclectic constellation of religious and spiritual phenomena encompassing both beliefs and practices
appropriated at the individual level as well as full-fledged religious movements with hundreds or even thousands of adherents—as long as the phenomena under consideration are situated outside their respective culture's
religious mainstream.[8] The highly diversified character of Brazil's religious
arena made this latter determination particularly problematic. Many traditions and phenomena that warranted being included in the mainstream
in Brazil definitely would have been considered non-mainstream elsewhere in the world, even elsewhere in Latin America.

With this in mind, the term "alternative spirituality" within the Brazilian
cultural milieu of the 1980s denoted an eclectic congeries of religious and
spiritual teachings and practices derived predominantly from non-Christian,
non-Latin American, and non-African sources. These sources included such
venerable religious traditions of South Asian and East Asian origin as
Buddhism, Hinduism, and Taoism, in addition to Japanese NRMs, the Theo-

sophical family, and other metaphysical, occult, and spiritualist traditions.[9] Moreover, alternative spirituality in Brazil included a broad array of beliefs and practices related to physical and emotional aspects of healing, to divinatory techniques, and even to certain ecological issues.[10] To a limited extent, specific elements appropriated from traditions with deep roots in Latin America, such as indigenous shamanism or certain Afro-Brazilian traditions, also warranted being classified as "alternative."

Critical to the success enjoyed by the proponents of alternative spirituality in attracting the attention of the Brazilian public were their collaborative links to other spheres of Brazilian society and culture that did not necessarily have any direct stake in the dissemination of such ideas and practices. For the most part these links were with professionals in the cultural industries of publishing and the mass media. However, in certain cases there was even governmental involvement. These links are the subject of the next section below.

Allies in the Spread of Alternative Spirituality in Brazil

The Cultural Industries

A key factor in generating momentum for the spread of alternative spirituality in Brazil during the last two decades of the twentieth century was a trend that eventually became known throughout the publishing industry and beyond as the "esoteric boom." This was a significant and rather sudden increase as of the mid-1980s in the number and variety of books sold that dealt with various facets of the highly eclectic subject matter associated with alternative spirituality.[11] Brazil's publishing industry, which had suffered through prolonged doldrums in terms of overall sales, responded eagerly to the evidence of strong consumer demand for books that could credibly be marketed under the esoteric rubric. Acquisitions editor Hortênsia Cavalcanti (pseudonym) later gave me her insider's perspective regarding this dramatic development in the book trade as she described the circumstances that led to her own hiring in the mid-1980s by a major publisher in Rio de Janeiro for the express purpose of launching a new collection dedicated to different aspects of alternative spirituality.

> Brazil was just beginning to experience a boom in esoteric books. We were facing serious problems in the book trade at the time. Sales were way down. Then the publishers started to realize that there was a way out that would enable them to stay afloat. Of course, this didn't apply either to Cultrix or to Pensamento, the two São Paulo publishing houses that had always specialized in this area. Besides those two, though, everyone else had been concentrating either on fiction or on academic textbooks but not specifically on esotericism. So I decided to give it a try.[12]

During the boom's initial phase, the esoteric niche of Brazil's book trade largely remained the province of such non-Brazilian authors as Marion Zimmer Bradley, Fritjof Capra, and Shirley MacLaine, with their works being read in Portuguese translations. Those relatively few publishers who had traditionally specialized in the occult/metaphysical category in Brazil were soon joined by several new firms that specialized in areas of subject matter related to the theme of alternative spirituality. At the same time, several prominent general interest publishing houses ventured into the esoteric market niche for the first time, launching new special collections or series in their catalogues under such rubrics as "Enigmas of the Ages," "New Age," and "The Arch of Time," hiring specialists like Hortênsia Cavalcanti who were well versed in alternative spirituality to manage them.

At first publishers in the esoteric niche were loath to sign book contracts with unproven Brazilian authors. The key turning point occurred when Paulo Coelho, who had previously enjoyed celebrity status as a rock music lyricist during the 1970s, became the first Brazilian to join the elite company of bestselling occult fiction authors. Coelho's first two books, *Diário de um mago* (*Diary of a Magus*) and *O alquimista* (*The Alchemist*), became bestsellers in Brazil in 1989.[13] The latter work, an engaging tale of an Andalusian shepherd boy's journey throughout the Mediterranean region on a quixotic mystical quest, became a bestseller in several countries over the course of the ensuing decade. Once Coelho's marketability as an esoteric author had been demonstrated beyond question, several well-known general interest publishing houses became willing to assume the risk of signing relatively unknown Brazilian esoteric authors to contracts.[14]

It is important to note, however, that Coelho's rise to prominence did not occur unaided but resulted from a specific collaborative effort involving professionals in different mainstream cultural industries. Regarding television, for example, an intriguing episode linking Paulo Coelho to the Dias Gomes *telenovela Mandala* took place on November 8, 1987, just a couple of weeks into the program's eventual seven-month run on the Globo Network. The episode in question was a segment on *Fantástico,* Globo's top-rated Sunday evening variety program, one that clearly had been produced with the intent of stimulating interest in the new *telenovela.* Following some preliminary background information on the mandala as a mystical symbol found in various religions around the world, Paulo Coelho—an "authentic twentieth-century *bruxo* (wizard)," according to the narrator's voiceover—appeared on camera to comment on various appropriations of the mandala motif throughout the history of Christianity.[15]

What makes this otherwise unremarkable program segment pertinent to the issue of the role of cultural industries in the spread of alternative spirituality in Brazil is the combination of its language and its timing. At the very moment that Paulo Coelho was being presented to millions of

Fantástico viewers as an "authentic twentieth-century wizard," his most successful work, *The Alchemist,* had yet to be published; meanwhile, *Diary of a Magus,* the only Coelho book that had been released, was languishing on bookstore shelves. Apparently some promotional specialists from the publishing and television industries, in concert with the budding author's publicity agents, had been engaging in some public relations alchemy of their own in order to transmute a standard bearer of the rebellious sixties counterculture into a reassuring icon in his own right: an irenic sage who embodied the occult wisdom of the ages.

This metamorphosed image of Paulo Coelho was showcased to the public by various means in order to maximize the would-be magus's marketability. A case in point involved an article in *Manchete,* a popular weekly Brazilian counterpart to *Life* or *Look* in the United States—not a periodical that specialized in alternative spirituality at all. In June of 1988, a piece entitled, "*O despertar dos (nossos) magos*" (The awakening of [our] magi), appeared in *Manchete.* It dealt with the growing interest on the part of Brazilians in an eclectic range of modalities of magic, including astrology, Afro-Brazilian cowrie shells, Tarot cards, geomancy, Native (North) American shamanism, and Druidic rituals. The centerpiece of the article was a photograph covering two full pages that portrayed Paulo Coelho in a magician's robe, grasping a beaker amidst the swirling mists of an antiquated laboratory—the modern-day alchemist engrossed in his experiments. The photo's caption cited the titles of Coelho's first two books, both of which were still a year away from attaining bestseller status, while mentioning that the author was among a handful of Brazilians at that juncture who could truthfully claim to have completed the Camino de Santiago de Compostela pilgrimage route in Spain on foot.[16]

The foregoing examples from the publishing industry and the mass media, both electronic and print, demonstrate how alternative spirituality in Brazil benefited during the late twentieth century from the favorable national exposure it received from professionals who were trained in the most effective techniques for communicating messages to the general public. Assuredly, the collaboration between the proponents of different modalities of alternative spirituality and the culture industry specialists was driven at least in part by an underlying profit motive. For this reason, much more intriguing was the boost that alternative spirituality received from an unexpected quarter: the government of the Federal District (the Brazilian counterpart to the District of Columbia) in Brasilia.

An Instance of Governmental Backing for Alternative Spirituality

One place in Brazil where alternative spirituality as a movement met with an enthusiastic response early on was the capital city of Brasilia and its environs. By the early 1980s, a groundswell of idiosyncratic millenarianism was already building in Brasilia. Certain recurring catch phrases in the local media labeled Brasilia as "the Capital of the Age of Aquarius," "the Capital of the New Age," and "the Capital of the Third Millennium." Myths and legends circulated to the effect that Brasilia had a special destiny that had been revealed long before the city had been planned and built in the country's remote interior during the 1950s. David J. Hess took note of this singular ethos when he went to Brasilia in June of 1985 for a conference involving several groups representing diverse facets of "alternative thought"; he called the city the "up-and-coming center of Brazilian esotericism."[17] That same year, a market research firm based in Brasilia provided the following sketch of the city's prevailing religious attitudes:

> Brasilia is considered to be a mystical city. . . . This makes for a city that attracts people who are searching for mystical or religious answers. . . . This public tends to have a negative reaction toward anything that bears the stamp of a traditional style of Christianity, while tending to be quite receptive toward the language of "new" religion in new garb, such as that pertaining either to oriental or to spiritualist traditions.[18]

The alternative spirituality network's influence was visibly inscribed upon Brasilia's self-consciously modernistic landscape. Several groups identified with alternative spirituality erected eye-catching temples or pyramids that stood out far more conspicuously amid the comparatively low-rise architecture of Brasilia than they would have in any other major Brazilian city. Among the groups possessing such distinctive structures were Jodo Shinshu Pure Land Buddhism, the Ancient and Mystical Order Rosae Crucis (AMORC), and two Japanese new religious movements: Seicho No-Ie (the House of Growth) and Sekai Kyuseikyo (the Church of World Messianity). Most striking of all, however, was the Temple of Good Will, a cone-shaped, seven-sided pyramid that towered twenty-one meters above its surrounding neighborhood. Completed in 1989, the Temple of Good Will housed the Brasilia chapter of the Legião da Boa Vontade (Legion of Good Will), or LBV, a spiritualist group that had originated in Rio de Janeiro in 1950 and by the 1980s had become known throughout Brazil for its high-profile charitable activities. The Temple of Good Will was open to the public around the clock, thereby affording unrestricted access to the spiral labyrinth in its basement for meditation walks.[19]

Brasilia's readily apparent affinity for alternative spirituality found an unexpected champion in the person of José Aparecido, who served as governor of the Federal District during the mid-1980s—precisely when alternative spirituality was beginning to gain momentum in Brazil as a whole. On July 10, 1986, Governor Aparecido proposed the establishment of an "esoteric city" on Federal District government property. The governor's original proposal called for numerous alternative groups to be allocated space in a single complex in order to promote greater synergy among them. This was no isolated demonstration of support for the cause of alternative spirituality on Governor Aparecido's part. On another occasion he awarded honorific medallions to seventy representatives of Brasilia's alternative community, giving rise to the following bemused account by a journalist who had adopted that community as his particular beat:

> Never before had those walls heard a more unusual speech than the one delivered by the governor that evening: an expression of support for magic and for the alternative movement. Never before had the Burití Palace's formal protocol faced such a challenge of hosting so many strange people at the same time! There were astrologers, indigenous shamans, homeopathic healers, leaders of mystical organizations, UFO devotees, painters, mediums, paranormals, pendulum diviners, chromotherapists, . . . acupuncturists, naturopathic healers. It was truly a festival and a triumphant celebration of sorcerers and alternatives.[20]

Governor Aparecido's proposal eventually resulted in the founding of a new institution, the City of Peace/International Holistic University of Brasilia. It began functioning officially in April of 1988 as a branch of the Université Holistique Internationale in Paris, with French transpersonal psychologist Pierre Weil as its first president. Though the International Holistic University of Brasilia did not house alternative groups permanently on its campus, it became a focal point nonetheless for alternative spirituality in the Federal District through its diversified offerings of courses, seminars, workshops, and retreats. In addition, the institution set up branch offices and retreat centers around Brazil and also took the lead in promoting periodic high-profile, international conferences on holistic themes in different Brazilian cities.[21] In other words, Governor Aparecido's support for alternative spirituality at the local level in the Federal District ultimately benefited the movement at the national level.

Before leaving this particular case, it is worth noting that support for alternative spirituality in Brazil's Federal District during the latter half of the 1980s was hardly unanimous. Influential dissenting voices expressed alarm over the outright backing that the Federal District government was extending to the alternative spirituality community under Governor Aparecido. Roman Catholic Archbishop Dom José Freire Falcão sounded a warning: "We are concerned about any form of expansion of the sects."[22] A less parochial complaint was registered by a local journalist following the inauguration of the International Holistic University of Brasilia; ironically enough, given the reporter's take on the situation, his protest served as eloquent testimony to the pervasive influence that alternative spirituality had attained in the nation's capital:

> In Brasilia the alternative has become the conventional. I am deeply concerned, as a student of both sociology and psychology and as a dyed-in-the-wool Westerner. In Brasilia the holistic has now become the establishment.[23]

Such instances of condemnation of alternative spirituality and its growing influence in Brazilian society in the late 1980s on the part of a handful of opinion leaders simply confirmed how successful the collaboration between proponents of alternative spirituality professionals in such cultural industries as publishing and the mass media had been in gaining widespread public exposure at the national level. Even the atypical case of the endorsement and support received from Governor José Aparecido and his administration paid dividends far beyond the borders of the Federal District. Clearly the alternative spirituality movement was well served by its allies in other cultural spheres during the period in which it was establishing its identity on the Brazilian scene. But what were its prospects for the future?

With an Eye toward the Future: Alternative Spirituality and the Dawning of the Third Millennium in Brazil

When viewed from the perspective of the outset of the Third Millennium, a calendrical designation fraught with significance for proponents of alternative spirituality, there is every reason to expect that this particular movement will exert a profound influence on the rest of Brazil's religious marketplace and beyond, although from a much more embedded base in the broader culture than was the case during its initial phase in the 1980s. The 1990s saw the dynamic expansion and consolidation in Brazil of extensive, loosely organized alternative spirituality networks akin to the New Age networks of Western Europe and the United States.[24] Articulated at the municipal, metropolitan, and regional levels in Brazil, they typically comprised the following elements: holistic lecture and seminar centers, small groups dedicated to the study and practice of specific traditions (whether separately or in combination), bookstores, shops selling diverse accessories, alternative therapy treatment centers and clinics, and often even consulting firms.[25] This higher public profile that alternative spirituality assumed as it gained greater acceptance within Brazilian urban culture was advantageous in many ways, but it also occasioned greater opposition from certain sectors of society.

Factors Favoring the Spread of Alternative Spirituality

An unquestionable comparative advantage that alternative spirituality enjoyed within the religious marketplace as it continued to insinuate its way into the cultural mainstream during the 1990s was that its appeal tended to be concentrated disproportionately among the more affluent classes in Brazilian urban society. Referring specifically to the Brazilian context, Chilean sociologist Cristián Parker observed that

> the various centers, associations, courses, events, and initiatives—for example, yoga, acupuncture, naturism, meditation, the astral map, and Taoism—inspired by these "new age" currents seem to flourish preponderantly in certain middle-class groups and among segments of the population, especially youth, having more formal schooling.[26]

Such elective affinity between alternative spirituality and the more affluent population sectors was mirrored in the advertising and event calendars which appeared in the specialized monthly pulp periodicals that circulated within the alternative spirituality complex in greater Rio de Janeiro, for example, during the mid-1990s. Not only did these periodicals carry advertisements for bookstores, study centers, holistic institutes, and shops, but they also published schedules of pending events, including lectures, courses, and seminars across a broad range of topics in such general areas as natural therapies, divinatory techniques, magical practices, parapsychology, and the control of spiritual energies. The vast majority of the addresses corresponding to the advertisements and notices in all of the periodicals were located in shopping centers or in other commercial districts of Rio that were geared predominantly towards upscale consumers.

The nature of the advertising in these pulp periodicals points to another factor that favored the spread of alternative spirituality in Brazil: its pragmatic emphasis on principles of holistic health and recourse to diverse modalities of complementary and alternative medicine. This resonated strongly with the widespread popularity that homeopathic medicine had enjoyed in Brazil since the arrival of Kardecist Spiritism from France in the mid-nineteenth century.[27] The following were among the therapeutic approaches that were frequently advertised in the alternative spirituality pulp periodicals that circulated in Rio de Janeiro in the mid-1990s: Bach Flower Remedies, acupuncture, yoga, crystals and gemstones, color therapy, various massage techniques, aromatherapy, shiatsu, Reiki, dance and bodywork, iridology, and diverse meditation and visualization techniques.

The fact that the holistic/therapeutic dimension of alternative spirituality clearly benefited from the long-standing recourse by Brazilians of all classes to homeopathy—an alternative therapy identified with Spiritism—suggests another factor favoring the spread of alternative spirituality in Brazil. Anthropologist José Jorge de Carvalho has observed that those non-Christian religious traditions that had already been assimilated into Brazil's religious mainstream long before the appearance of alternative spirituality on the scene—most notably Afro-Brazilian traditions, Kardecist Spiritism, and

Umbanda—shared certain prominent themes with such key elements of alternative spirituality as esoteric groups and Japanese new religions; salient among these themes were the notion of spiritual evolution and the phenomenon of spirit possession.[28] Even though different currents of thought and practice within alternative spirituality addressed these themes in their own distinctive fashion, at least they were dealing with concepts that were already somewhat familiar to the general public.

Factors Potentially Inhibiting the Spread of Alternative Spirituality

As amenable as conditions were overall for the spread of alternative spirituality in Brazil during the 1990s, there were also significant countervailing factors. Some of these had to do with mainstream religious institutions; others did not.

The growing influence of the holistic paradigm in Brazilian culture during this period has already been mentioned as having contributed significantly to alternative spirituality's broad public appeal through the avenues of alternative medicine and divination. At the same time, however, the very instrumental nature of this appeal raised the specter of possible violation of the national Penal Code. Dating back to 1890, at a time when the country had been in transition from an empire to a republic, successive versions of the Penal Code had contained provisions specifically aimed at suppressing *curandeirismo*. In Brazilian usage, *curandeirismo* is an ambiguous term that can denote either faith healing or else charlatanism or quackery, depending on the context.[29] Article 157 of the Penal Code of October 11, 1890, had explicitly outlawed the practice of "spiritism, magic, and sorcery, using talismans or cartomancy to induce feelings of love or hatred, [or] providing instruction in the cure of curable or incurable diseases for the purpose of either mystifying or exploiting the gullibility of the general public." Article 158 of the same legislation had condemned the *curandeiro*, or faith healer.[30]

Even though the Penal Code had originally been promulgated near the end of the nineteenth century, it cast a shadow long enough to be a source of concern for some proponents of alternative spirituality a century later. In an interview with this author, Francisco Borges, an editor of one of the pulp periodicals that circulated within the alternative spirituality milieu in Rio de Janeiro during the mid-1990s and a practitioner of several divinatory techniques, was quite emphatic in describing the threat that he saw the Penal Code potentially posing to him and his peers:

> I see it as a huge problem. One of these days it could take away all of these gains that we've fought so hard for. Look, today the medical profession says, "Homeopathy can only be practiced by doctors," but it has denied the validity of homeopathy. Then it says, "The practice of acupuncture must be licensed,"

but it has denied the validity of acupuncture. You see? The next thing you know, the medical profession is going to declare, "Yes, it is important to study astrology, but it must be limited to psychologists." As long as we lack a sense of group or class solidarity and some organization and discipline, we're really vulnerable. . . . There is an article in the Penal Code that deals with what it calls "injury to the public's good faith," and do you know what? Astrology, cartomancy, chiromancy—they are all right there in the Penal Code.[31]

While the Penal Code posed a potential threat to practitioners of alternative spirituality, a more immediate challenge arose from within the religious marketplace itself, prompted by the movement's very success. The spirit of religious tolerance that has historically characterized Brazilian culture generally discouraged the formation of a strong anticult network of the type that developed in North Atlantic societies during the last third of the twentieth century. The Roman Catholic Church was somewhat ambivalent in its stance toward alternative spirituality. Certain luminaries among its clergy, such as liberation theologian Leonardo Boff and community activist Frei Betto, published works in alternative collections that espoused themes consistent with alternative spirituality.[32] On the other hand, Vozes, one of the principal Catholic publishing houses, issued a work entitled, *The Other Side of Modern Spiritualism: Understanding the New Age,* that warned its readers against the spiritual dangers posed by the New Age movement in Brazil.[33] Moreover, as part of a seven-volume series on "sects" by Baptist pastor Tácito da Gama Leite Filho, the official publishing house of the Brazilian Baptist Convention published three studies intended to equip its evangelical readership to contend with Asian religious traditions and occult and spiritualist groups associated with alternative spirituality.[34]

On balance, the forces arrayed against alternative spirituality paled in comparison to those within the Brazilian religious marketplace and Brazilian culture in general that imparted momentum to this particular cultural movement. Consequently, there is no reason to anticipate that alternative spirituality will not continue to flourish in the Third Millennium.

Conclusion

This study has provided a glimpse into the phenomenon of new religious movements in Brazil, the home of the most kaleidoscopic religious arena in all of Latin America, by examining selected aspects of alternative spirituality as a cultural movement, with a predominant focus on the movement's nascent phase during the 1980s. Historically, Brazilian religious culture has demonstrated an unusual capacity for assimilating elements from diverse geographical origins, most notably African traditions, French Spiritism, and North American Protestant denominations. Even so, what stands out in the case of alternative spirituality's fairly rapid trajectory from outsider status at the dawn of the 1980s to cautious acceptance on the part of Brazilian mainstream culture by the end of the decade is the critical role that certain key mainstream cultural institutions played in lending additional momentum to that process, thereby accelerating it.

The case of the mainstreaming process undergone by the alternative spirituality movement in Brazil during the 1980s is instructive for observers interested either in new religious movements as a worldwide phenomenon or in modern Latin American religions. Clearly the religious arena in Latin America is not limited to the intense competition being waged between the Roman Catholic Church and various Protestant denominations and missions. This case demonstrates that many new religious movements have been thriving in the interstices of more traditional religious institutions in the region. Furthermore, this study indicates that a full understanding of religious competition in contemporary Latin America requires a perspective that is sufficiently broad to take into account other segments of the culture that might not have a direct religious connection but can still play a decisive role in influencing the outcome.

Notes

1. David J. Hess, *Spirits and Scientists: Ideology, Spiritism, and Brazilian Culture* (University Park, PA: Pennsylvania State University Press, 1991), 2.
2. Jane A. Russo, *O corpo contra a palavra: as terapias corporais no campo psicological dos anos 80* (Rio de Janeiro: Editora UFRJ, 1993), 111–12.
3. Rhys H. Williams and N. J. Demarath III, "Cultural Power: How Underdog Religious and Nonreligious Movements Triumph against Structural Odds," in *Sacred Companies: Organizational Aspects of Religions and Religious Aspects of Organizations*, eds. N.J. Demarath III, Peter Dobkin Hall, Terry Schmitt, and Rhys H. Williams (New York and Oxford: Oxford University Press, 1998), 364–77.
4. Joseph Straubhaar, "Telenovelas," in *Encyclopedia of Latin American History and Culture*, editor in chief Barbara A. Tenenbaum, Vol. 5 (New York: Charles Scribner's Sons, Macmillan Library Reference USA, Simon & Schuster Macmillan; New York: Simon & Schuster and Prentice Hall International, 1996).
5. Dias Gomes, *Mandala* (Rio de Janeiro: Rede Globo de Televisão, 1987–88), *Telenovela*.
6. José Jorge de Carvalho, "An Enchanted Public Space: Religious Plurality and Modernity in Brazil," in *Through the Kaleidoscope: The Experience of Modernity in Latin America*, ed. Vivian Schelling (London and New York: Verso, 2000), 280–82.
7. "*Mandala*—Boletim de Programação da Rede Globo," 10 October 1987, 4.
8. Timothy Miller, "Introduction," in *America's Alternative Religions*, ed. Timothy Miller (Albany: State University of New York Press, 1995), 1–10; Jon P. Bloch, *New Spirituality, Self, and Belonging: How New Agers and Neo-Pagans Talk about Themselves* (Westport, CT, and London: Praeger Publishers, 1998), 1–2, 7–10.
9. Luiz Eduardo Soares, "Religioso por natureza: cultura alternativa e misticismo ecológico no Brasil," in *Sinais dos tempos: tradições religiosas no Brasil*, ed. Leilah Landim, Cadernos do ISER 22 (Rio de Janeiro: ISER—Instituto de Estudos da Religião, 1989), 121–44; Leilah Landim, ed., *Sinais dos tempos: diversidade religiosa no Brasil*. Cadernos do ISER 23 (Rio de Janeiro: Instituto de Estudos da Religião, 1990); Leila Amaral, "Nova Era: um movimento de caminhos cruzados," in *Nova Era: um desafio para os cristãos*, eds. Leila Amaral, Gottfried

Kuenzlen, and Godfried Danneels (Coleção: Atualidade em Diálogo; São Paulo: Paulinas, 1994), 11–50; Alberto Moreira and Renée Zicman, eds., *Misticismo e novas religiões*, 2ª ed. (Petrópolis: Editora Vozes; Bragança Paulista: Instituto Franciscano de Antropologia da Universidade São Franciscano, 1994); Peter B. Clarke, "Japanese New Religious Movements in Brazil: From Ethnic to 'Universal' Religions," in *New Religious Movements: Challenge and Response*, eds. Bryan Wilson and Jamie Cresswell (London and New York: Routledge, 1999), 197–210.

10. Denis M.S. Brandão and Roberto Crema, *O novo paradigma holístico: ciência, filosofia, arte e mística*, 2ª ed. (São Paulo: Summus Editorial, 1991); Jane Araújo Russo, *O corpo contra a palavra*, 112–13.

11. Interviewees who concurred regarding the factuality of an "esoteric boom" that had arisen in the Brazilian publishing industry during the mid-1900s included Hortênsia Cavalcanti (pseudonym for an editor of an esoteric series at a Brazilian publishing house), interview by author, Rio de Janeiro, 11 August 1995; Jorge Gomes (pseudonym for an editor of an esoteric series at a Brazilian publishing house), interview by author, Rio de Janeiro, 5 September 1995; Lázaro Leão (pseudonym for an esoteric bookstore owner), interview by author, Rio de Janeiro, 9 September 1995; and Socorro Pires (pseudonym for an editor of an esoteric series at a Brazilian publishing house), interview by author, Rio de Janeiro, 20 May 1996.

12. Hortênsia Cavalcanti (pseudonym), interview by author, Rio de Janeiro, 11 August 1995.

13. Paulo Coelho, *O diário de um mago*, 107ª ed. (Rio de Janeiro: Rocco, 1995); *O alquimista* (Rio de Janeiro: Rocco, 1988).

14. Socorro Pires (pseudonym), interview by author, Rio de Janeiro, 20 May 1996.

15. *Fantástico*, Rede Globo, 8 November 1987.

16. Marina Nery, "O despertar dos (nossos) magos," *Manchete*, Ano 37, Numero 1886 (11 junho 1988): 60–7.

17. David J. Hess, *Spirits and Scientists*, 118–19.

18. Assessor, "Centro de Cultura Cristã: planejamento de comunicação," Brasília, 1985, 4.

19. José Jorge de Carvalho, "An Enchanted Public Space," in *Through the Kaleidoscope*, ed. Schelling, 283–86.

20. Dioclécio Luz, *Roteiro mágico de Brasília*, vol. II (Brasília: Cultura Gráfica e Editora, 1989), 248.

21. Ibid., 244–54; Robert T. Carpenter, "Religious Competition and the Spread of Alternative Spirituality in Brazil," (Ph.D. dissertation, University of California, Santa Barbara, 2001), 228.

22. Luz, *Roteiro mágico de Brasília*, vol. II, 248.

23. Paulo Carneiro, "Holística ou a oficialização do mistério," *JOSÉ* 11:612 (16–22 April 1988): 16.

24. Danny L. Jorgensen, *The Esoteric Scene, Cultic Milieu, and Occult Tarot* (New York and London: Garland Publishing, 1992); Michael York, *The Emerging Network: A Sociology of the New Age and Neo-Pagan Movements* (Lanham, MD: Rowman & Littlefield Publishers, 1995).

25. Amaral, "Nova Era: um movimento de caminhos cruzados," in *Nova Era*, eds. Amaral, et al; Paul Heelas and Leila Amaral, "Notes on the 'Nova Era': Rio de Janeiro and Environs," *Religion* 24 (1994): 173–180; José Guilherme Cantor Magnani, "Esotéricos na cidade: os novos espaços de encontro, vivência, e culto," *São Paulo em Perspectiva* 9:2 (April/June 1995): 66–72; Carpenter, "Religious Competition and the Spread of Alternative Spirituality in Brazil"; Tavares Fátima Regina Gomes, "Feiras esotéricas e redes alternativas: algumas notas comparativas dos circuitos cariocas e parisienses," *Rever* 1 (January 2001).

26. Cristián Parker, *Popular Religion and Modernization in Latin America: A Different Logic*, Trans. Robert R. Barr (Maryknoll, NY: Orbis Books, 1996), 158.

27. David J. Hess, "The Many Rooms of Spiritism in Brazil," *Luso-Brazilian Review* 24:2 (Winter 1987): 15–34.

28. José Jorge de Carvalho, "An Enchanted Public Space," in *Through the Kaleidoscope*, 278.

29. Hess, *Spirits and Scientists*, 129.

30. Código Penal de 1890, Decreto de 11 de outubro de 1890 (Rio de Janeiro: Imprensa Nacional, [1890]). The entire text of Articles 157 and 158 can be found in Yvonne Maggie, *Medo do feitiço: relações entre magia e poder no Brasil* (Rio de Janeiro: Arquivo Nacional, 1992), 22–3.

31. Francisco Borges, [pseudonym], interview with author, Rio de Janeiro, 12 September 1995.

32. Leonardo Boff and Frei Betto, *Mística e espiritualidade*, 2ªed., Coleção Arco do Tempo (Rio de Janeiro: Rocco, 1994); Leonardo Boff, *Nova era: a civilização planetária*, 2ªed., Série Religião e Cidanania (São Paulo: Editora Ática, 1994); Frei Betto, *A obra do artista: uma visão holística do universo* (São Paulo: Editora Ática, 1995).

33. Ricardo Sasaki, *O outro lado do espiritualismo moderno: para compreender a Nova Era* (Petrópolis: Editora Vozes, 1995).

34. Tácito da Gama Leite Filho, *Seitas orientais*, Seitas do Nosso Tempo, Vol. 2 (Rio de Janeiro: Junta da Educação Religiosa e Publicações da Convenção Batista Brasileira [JUERP], 1987); *Atitudes ideológicas e filosóficas*, Seitas do Nosso Tempo, Vol. 6 (Rio de Janeiro: JUERP, 1992); *Fenomenologia das seitas*, Seitas do Nosso Tempo, Vol. 7 (Rio de Janeiro: JUERP, 1992).

CHAPTER 15

The Fate of NRMs and their Detractors in Twenty-First Century America

J. GORDON MELTON

At the beginning of the twenty-first century, the United States has emerged as the most religiously pluralistic society that ever existed. Over two thousand different primary religious groups (denominations) exist in the U.S. across the spectrum of the world's religions. During the nineteenth century, the diversification of religion was primarily within the Christian community; the sixteen Christian churches that existed at the nation's founding generated more than 300 new denominations a hundred years later. Toward the end of the nineteenth century, all of the major world's religions had also established their initial centers, although they were relatively minuscule. From 1880 to the present, there is a steady decade-by-decade increase in the number of new religions present in American society, including both new Christian denominations and the wide spectrum of Buddhist, Hindu, Muslim, and even Jewish groups. The growth of new religions has continued unabated during times of social unrest and relative calm, war and peace, good economic times and bad.[1]

American pluralism has experienced a notable extension due to the modern revival of the Western Esoteric tradition. Occultism, all but counted out as a factor in Western culture at the beginning of the nineteenth century, experienced a remarkable comeback in the nineteenth century with the founding of Spiritualism and Theosophy, the growth of astrology, and the rising belief in reincarnation. The growth was capped in the 1980s by the New Age movement, which drew many to esoteric beliefs while simultaneously creating a fresh image for what had heretofore been dismissed as mere occultism.

This very pluralistic culture was founded upon the legal tradition of religious freedom embedded in the First Amendment of the U. S. Constitution (the phraseology of which would later be incorporated into the constitutions of the various states) wedded to other powerful constitutional guarantees such as freedom of speech and assembly.[2] These guarantees were further established by the Fourteenth Amendment, which asserted, "No state shall make or enforce any law which shall abridge the privileges or immunities of citizens of the United States; nor shall any state deprive any person of life, liberty, or property, without due process of law; nor deny to any person within its jurisdiction the equal protection of the laws."

America also possesses a strong emphasis upon individualism with an accompanying attitude of "live and let live" that has promoted an ever-growing tolerance of life style differences. Yet, however tolerant, the American public has always had its limits, and the testing of the boundaries of accepted behavior has been a constant source of tension in the culture. The twentieth century saw major turmoil over the acceptance of the working woman, the move of African Americans into the middle class, and the presence of a visible lesbian/gay/bisexual/transgender community.

The dynamic changes of American society did not leave the mainstream religious community unscathed. American Christianity was deeply split in the first decades of the twentieth century by the fundamentalist-modernist controversy. That controversy was imposed across all denominations, with theological differences often coinciding with deeply held convictions about acceptance or rejection of the changes in American society and the importance of social ethics versus personal morality. In the last half of the twentieth century this split manifested as a choice between an emphasis on ecumenism or evangelism. Americans exported this division worldwide through the realignment of groups either with the World Council of Churches or the World Evangelical Fellowship.

Several factors have correlated with the growth of American pluralism over time. One factor has been immigration. As in other countries, the majority of the new religions in the United States have been imported by immigrants from around the world. Although some of these religions remain confined to an ethnic community, the majority have reached out for acceptance in middle America, especially as the ethnic community Americanized. While overall growth has not been affected, the passing of different immigration laws has very much changed the development of particular religions. Second, population growth has created an ever-increasing pool of potential recruits for new groups. This population growth has been accompanied by the increasing urbanization of the American public. The anonymity of city life provides private space wherein new and very different groups can survive without constant public scrutiny.

New Religions in the Late Twentieth Century

The dynamic of American religion, manifest in the continual production of new religious groups, has also created the problem of distinguishing new religious movements (NRMs) from other kinds. The term "new religious movements," of course, was imported from Japan where it was used to distinguish the spectrum of new religions that emerged following the imposition of an American-style religious freedom on the country in 1945. Over the next twenty years, a variety of formerly suppressed groups and a host of newly founded groups emerged to claim significant portions of the population. The term was imported to the United States to describe the new Asian groups that came into the country following a 1965 change in the immigration laws and the new Christian groups that arose to evangelize the baby boom generation just coming of age at the end of the 1960s.

New religions exist in contested space, some because of their unique beliefs and others because of different behavior patterns (such as high-pressure evangelism, communalism, a variant sexual ethic, or separatist social organization). A few new religions have stood out for their involvement in illegal and/or violent activity. Also, as the name implies, new religions are relatively new on the religious landscape. Just as people fear the unknown in general, so the very unfamiliarity of new religions often breeds anxiety when they initially appear. For the purposes of this essay, "new religious movements" shall refer to those religious groups that have made their initial appearance in American society since World War II and those that primarily target young adults as recruits.

The ferment surrounding the baby boomers (communalism, drug use, life on the streets) attracted the attention of social scientists, while the visible pool of religiously unattached youth attracted a variety of evangelists and missionaries. Japan had weathered its transition to an extreme pluralism in a relatively peaceful manner, but the peculiar situation of the early 1970s in America gave birth to the modern cult awareness movement. Among the problems facing the baby boomers was unemployment; the American economy proved unable to accommodate the sudden increase of new people entering the job market. This gave young street people an added incentive to join high-demand religious groups whose life included, along with commitment to the group, a job, friends, and a place to live.

Such high-demand groups provided a new context for the resolving of adolescent dilemmas concerning career, sexuality, and religious commitments. The use of religious groups as springboards to personal autonomy seemed destined to place them in conflict with parents who saw them as competitors for the hearts of their offspring.

Out of the hundreds of NRMs that emerged at this time, a few high-demand groups (the Unification Church, the International Society for Krishna Consciousness, Divine Life Mission, The Way International, for example), which sought to grow by building a cadre of full-time employees to spearhead an intense evangelistic effort, attracted the ire of parents. They rejected the notion of their sons and daughters dropping promising careers in business or the professions to live and work with a new, questionable, low-status religion.

The 1970s can be seen as the first phase of a new cult awareness movement, the term "cult" being adopted from Evangelical Christians as the appropriate label for the despised new religions. Through the 1970s, numerous parents' groups sprang up across the United States, and members sought an effective means to get their children out of NRMs and reoriented toward a more acceptable career and lifestyle. From the 1970s to the present, the history of the conflict of new religions and American culture has been written in the efforts (largely unsuccessful) of anticultists to entice the government to support their crusade and in their varied activities to advance their agenda in light of the government's refusal to become involved. Initially, the parents' groups focused upon legal redress in the courts through conservatorship laws, which enabled relatives to remove an adult convert from a group (but which quickly proved a dead end), and upon deprogramming, an extra-legal tactic that involved the kidnapping of a group member and his/her subjection to intense psychological pressure to renounce the group. Parents soon learned that they needed the assistance of a wide variety of professionals to assist them in the development of a secular understanding of their dilemma. Courts and law enforcement agencies were quite unresponsive to parental upset over adult children joining fringe religions.

Everything changed in November 1978, with the deaths at Jonestown. Though the Peoples Temple was a congregation in a mainline denomination, it was quickly transformed into the epitome of a dangerous cult. The parents' groups, however, discovered that they were unable to react effectively to the Jonestown deaths. They lacked a national organization. Over the next few years, they created two organizations—the Citizens Freedom Foundation, an activist group that promoted deprogramming and a variety of initiatives to attract popular support, and the American Family Foundation (AFF), which would specialize in research and education on the cult issue. Within a few years, CFF evolved into the Cult Awareness Network (CAN).

With the CFF in place and public revulsion over Jonestown cresting, the number of deprogrammings rose dramatically, along with the development of rehabilitation centers at which people who had been successfully deprogrammed could receive therapy aimed at consolidating their decision to leave the group and reenter mainstream society. Anticultists undertook a variety of initiatives at the state level, and sympathetic legislators attempted to find a means of bringing the government into the controversy as allies of the parents. These initiatives were uniformly defeated by a coalition of civil libertarians and leaders from older religious groups who saw the new legislation as a threat to their own existence.

Because they have not been involved directly in deprogrammings, the many court cases, and the legislative initiatives that have been generated by the several cult awareness organizations, the role of the hundreds of Evangelical Christian countercult groups in shaping public opinion about new religions has been largely ignored. However, it would be hard to conceive of the successes of cult awareness efforts in the 1980s without the massive campaign against the new religions propagated by organizations such as the Christian Research Institute, Spiritual Counterfeits Project, and Eastern Christian Outreach. These groups have, irregardless of the ups and downs of the secular cult controversy, continued to produce a massive wave of literature condemning what they see as deviant religions while simultaneously creating a significant Internet presence.[3]

The Brainwashing Controversy

As the legislative thrust moved to its conclusion, several professionals who had adopted the cult awareness perspective came forward with psychological rationales to justify action against a select number of religious groups. These professionals were not motivated by theological concerns, but rather by what they perceived as the unjustified manipulation of recruits by NRMs and the resulting psychological harm this caused. While a spectrum of positions emerged, the most popular proved to be the "coercive persuasion" theories articulated by psychologist Margaret Singer, popularly known as "brainwashing." Singer and her colleagues began to suggest that the particular recruitment procedures and the spiritual practices of the groups (the use of meditation, chanting, mantras, and so forth) overrode the free will of the members and caused them to stay in cults against their better judgment.[4] It was argued by many that prolonged membership in the groups could do irreparable mental and even physical harm.[5]

If cults altered individual personalities and actually harmed their members, then deprogramming was justified. Brainwashing theories provided the intellectual support for the practice. Such support was necessary as attention shifted from the legislative halls to the courts, where people who had been successfully deprogrammed launched civil suits against the groups they had formerly joined. Juries, responding to brainwashing arguments, handed down multi-million-dollar judgments. Those opposed to NRMs were unable to gain a knockout ruling, however, as judgments tended to be reversed or sharply reduced on appeal. But it seemed only a matter of time.

Some of Singer's professional allies attempted to establish a task force within the American Psychological Association (APA) to prepare a lengthy presentation of the "coercive persuasion" argument, which would be reviewed by the APA in its usual manner. The acceptance of such a report by the APA would not establish her theory, but would grant it status as a more than acceptable hypothesis. This plan, however, backfired. When the report was submitted and reviewed in 1987, it was unanimously rejected. As summarized in a brief memo to the task force members, the reviewers denounced the task force's approach as methodologically flawed and lacking in scientific rigor. That ruling would radically limit the use of brainwashing theory and lead to the demise of both deprogramming and the Cult Awareness Network.[6]

The prominent role given to the brainwashing hypothesis in the 1980s placed a number of scholars who studied new religions in the middle. While not particularly supportive of the groups that they studied, they had seen no evidence among the groups that something like brainwashing was occurring, or, from a theoretical point of view, that such a phenomenon even existed. They came to believe that brainwashing was an unscientific hypothesis and, as the number of court cases multiplied, became ever more vocal. Following the APA action, both the American Sociological Association and the Society for the Scientific Study of Religion issued supportive statements.

As the court cases proceeded, the search began for an appropriate case to present the psychological and sociological consensus concerning the popular brainwashing hypothesis. That case came in 1989 in *US v. Fishman*, a criminal case in a federal court, in which the defendant Fishman attempted to plead that his crimes were committed due to the debilitating influence of his membership in a cult. Two extensive reports refuting the brainwashing hypothesis, based in part upon the APA evaluation, led the court to deny testimony on the subject. In an opinion published in 1990, the court gave legal support to the position that brainwashing theory as applied to new religions had no scientific standing. That ruling would be sustained by similar rulings in several other cases. It essentially brought to an end the typical civil cases of the 1980s in which groups were sued primarily by a deprogrammed former member bringing charges of brainwashing.

CAN had already seen the problems associated with deprogramming, and though quietly continuing to support it, publicly began to nurture the rise of what was termed "exit counseling." Exit counselors adopted many of the arguments used by deprogrammers (both psychological and logical) to break the allegiance of members of NRMs, but rejected the use of physical force. Following the Fishman ruling, most activists saw the handwriting on the wall and withdrew from further deprogramming activity. Over time, exit counseling matured into a new profession, thought reform counseling (using a term made popular by psychiatrist Robert J. Lifton).

At this point, one of the more prominent new religions, the Church of Scientology, experienced a breakthrough in its ongoing legal battles. The Internal Revenue Service finally ended its lengthy review of the church's tax status and many corporate entities and, unable to find any substantial reason for continuing to question its religious or charitable nature, granted it full tax-exempt status. The ruling freed a significant amount of funds and personnel within the church, which now targeted the Cult Awareness Network as the major cause of its problems. Through a host of corporate affiliates, individual Scientologists filed lawsuits. Although none of these lawsuits ever came to trial, all allowed depositions to be taken. During 1993–94, several dozen officials and employees of CAN were interviewed, and a detailed understanding of the organization developed.

The information from the Scientology depositions (and the primary lawyer working with the church, Rick Moxon) was made available to one Jason Scott, a member of a Pentecostal church in Seattle, Washington, who had been deprogrammed by Rick Ross. Ross had been brought into the case by referral from CAN's Washington State representative. Scott sued Ross for damages and received a large negative judgment. During the trial, Ross was unable to enter substantial testimony on brainwashing to justify his actions. More important, using the information from the Scientology depositions, Moxon was able to make the case that CAN was involved. CAN was given a million dollar judgment that forced it into bankruptcy the next year. The ruling was sustained on appeal, and, adding insult to injury, a coalition of groups that had been publicly designated as "cults" by CAN pooled resources and purchased CAN's name, logo, and 800-telephone line. The coalition now operates a new CAN through a Scientology-controlled corporation in Los Angeles.

New Religions since Fishman/Scott

The rulings in the Fishman and Scott cases ended the practice of deprogramming in the United States. Though the problems faced by new religions are by no means settled, minority and otherwise unpopular religions no longer feel that simply by following their normal program of recruitment and worship, they will be called into court and accused of brainwashing their members. They still have to face a somewhat hostile press, however, and the several violent incidents associated with the Branch Davidians, Solar Temple, Heaven's Gate, and the Movement for the Restoration of the Ten Commandments have added "violent tendencies" to the top list of charges thrown at them.

The Scott decision did not completely end the legal problems for new religions, however, and they have been forced into court on a variety of issues, especially divorce cases in which one partner in the marriage is a former member of the group. In addition, ex-members have continued to bring grievances against their former associates into court. Two examples include a sexual abuse charge in a recent case against the Ananda Church of Self Realization, and ongoing litigation filed against the International Society for Krishna Consciousness by some young adults who grew up in the movement. Attempts have been made to bring brainwashing into many of these cases, though this charge is frequently withdrawn when the Fishman documents are presented to the court. At the same time, other new religions, such as the Wiccans and Neopagans, pushing for public acknowledgement of their religion, have filed a variety of cases charging religious discrimination, most notably against school boards that have banned the wearing of pentagrams by students.

While decimated by the Fishman and Scott decisions, cult awareness activists filled the vacuum left by the fall of CAN and organized the Leo J. Ryan Foundation (named for the congressman killed at Jonestown). Together with sympathetic members of the AFF, these activists have attempted to develop new programs to continue their crusade. One aspect of their efforts is the further secularization of the concept of cult. During the 1980s, CAN theorists argued that cults were pseudo-religions distinguished from real religions by their use of brainwashing. They had also argued that a few other kinds of groups could manifest cult-like characteristics. In the 1990s, these theorists began to argue that cults were not primarily religious, but rather a peculiar type of social group. While some cults happened to be religious, cults also took the form of political and psychotherapy groups and could manifest anywhere. They now claimed that their program was not aimed at destructive religious groups, but at any group that manifested a set of cult characteristics. This was a further attempt to get around the problems of the First Amendment that continually blocked any attempt to gain government backing for their cause.

In 1999, using this slightly revised perspective, the Ryan Foundation capitalized on several controversial incidents involving religious groups at the University of Maryland to ask the State of Maryland to mandate the establishment of cult counseling and information resources throughout Maryland's university system. The implication was that cult specialists would be hired to train counselors and write anticult material. This new effort was brought to light when a commission was appointed by the Governor of Maryland, and when William Stuart, an anthropologist at the University of Maryland, alerted his scholarly colleagues concerning the importance of what was occurring. During the summer of 1999, the commission listened as various speakers rehashed the cult/brainwashing controversy of the 1980s. The commission report, though somewhat ambiguous, was mildly favorable to demands that the university administration act. However, the legislature never considered the report, and to date no further action has grown out of it.[7]

Having received favorable mention in the commission's final report, members of the Ryan Foundation generally lauded the effort of their education director Ron Loomis and others who had led the Maryland effort. It was their general assessment that the commission hearings had been a valuable learning experience; the commission initiative also clearly indicated a direction they could follow in the future. State legislatures are now being monitored for any possible repeats of the Maryland hearings.

The new millennium, however, finds the cult awareness movement in the United States in some disarray. Among its long-term problems is its inability to generate a base of empirical research supporting the existence of either (1) thought control in NRMs as something above and beyond the normal working of social influence noticeable in any group, or of (2) any measurable harm done to members of such groups. Moreover, in contrast to the 1980s and the theoretical unity found in Margaret Singer's presentation of thought control, today no single theory of how thought control might work has gained more than modest support.[8] A few have attempted to reclaim brainwashing as a reality,[9] while others search for a perspective built around undue social influence. This theoretical disunity (as well as the defensive battle CAN was fighting for its own existence) made it impossible for the movement to capitalize on the several incidents of violence (Heaven's Gate, Aum Shinrikyō, and the Solar Temple) that so energized the cult awareness movement worldwide.

The cult awareness movement received an unexpected boost in 2002 with the election of Philip Zimbardo as president of the American Psychological Association. Though not primarily known for his opinions on cults and brainwashing, during his term he called for a review of the evaluation of the DIMPAC Report and a new effort to research what have been labeled "destructive cults of hatred." It is yet to be seen if he will receive any support from his colleagues.[10]

Among the barriers to any revival of brainwashing theories is the continued massive amount of ongoing research on new religions now being pursued by more than a hundred scholars in the United States and at least that many more elsewhere. Annually, contributions to the field appear in books and articles void of any reference to the brainwashing issue, which has been found to lack any utility in generating insights about the diverse world of new religious groups.[11]

At the same time, the increase in numbers and membership in NRMs that began in the 1880s has proceeded through the 1980s and 1990s as if the cult awareness movement had never existed. In the 1980s, some groups were quite fearful of CAN, but that fear disappeared during the 1990s. Currently, the cult awareness movement is seen as little more than a meddlesome nuisance.[12] Multinational groups are convinced that any "cult" problem they may now have exists in Europe.

The Effects of 9/11

The bombing of the Pentagon and World Trade Center in 2001 produced two noticeable alterations in the world of NRM studies that seem likely to have lasting influence. First and foremost, it removed NRMs from center stage as the most controversial set of religions. Given the last decade of terrorist violence that is now a part of the mass consciousness in the U.S., the violence associated with new religions appears secondary and is being so treated. Not least among the immediate changes has been the shift in focus of law enforcement agencies, especially the FBI, to potential terrorist organizations. While that shift has stalled the ongoing dialogue between NRM scholars and law enforcement personnel, the gains made in the years since Waco remain in place, as was clearly indicated by the call for assistance that occurred during the sniper shooting incidents that gripped the Washington, D.C., area in the fall of 2002.

9/11 also called attention to the neglect of Islamic groups by NRM scholars, a further indication of the balkanization of religious studies and the boundaries that exist between NRM studies and other specializations, so vividly illustrated in the 1990s with Japanese religions studies. A year after 9/11, efforts to overcome the barriers between NRM studies and Islamic studies became evident both in the October 2002 issue of *Nova Religio* and in the various presentations in the New Religious Movements Group and Millennialism Studies Group sessions at the American Academy of Religion.

NRM scholars and anticultists are now discussing terrorist violence together with the violence associated with new religions. In the wake of 9/11, some superficial attempts were made to equate Al Qa'ida with groups such as the Branch Davidians and Heavens Gate, and exit counselors offered to deprogram Al Qa'ida and Taliban suspects being held in Cuba. Meanwhile, more serious discussions were developing quietly on the relationship between, for example, Aum Shinrikyō and modern Islamic movements. Both movements have demonstrated the destruction that can be inflicted by a very small group, as well as the price they must pay when the larger society reacts.

Notes

1. Information on the continued growth of America's new religions can be found in the various editions of J. Gordon Melton, *Encyclopedia of American Religions* (Detroit: Gale Group, 7th edition, 2002).

2. Over 2,000 laws have been passed by the state and federal governments that spell out in some detail the nature of church-state separation in the United States, most speaking to areas in which the government may not meddle, and a few to areas in which cooperation is allowed (such as chaplains for the armed forces or church-run government programs). Most recently, a massive faith-based initiative program proposed by the Bush administration promises greatly to extend government-religion cooperation.

3. Douglas E. Cowan, *Bearing False Witness?: An Introduction to the Christian Countercult* (Westport, CT: Praeger, 2003), 239.

4. The brainwashing controversy has generated a considerable literature, including Dick Anthony, "Religious Movements and 'Brainwashing' Litigation: Evaluating Key Testimony" in *In Gods We Trust: New Patterns of Religious Pluralism in America*, eds. Thomas Robbins and Dick Anthony, 2nd ed. (New Brunswick, NJ: Transaction Press, 1989), 295–344; James T. Richardson and David G. Bromley, eds., *The Brainwashing/Deprogramming Controversy* (Lewiston, NY: Edwin Mellen Press, 1983); James T. Richardson, "A Social Psychological Critique of 'Brainwashing' Claims about Recruitment to New Religions," in *The Handbook of Cults and Sects in America*, eds. David G. Bromley and Jeffrey K. Hadden, vol. 3 (Part B) (Greenwich, CT: JAI Press, 1993), 75–97; and James T. Richardson, "Sociology and the New Religions: 'Brainwashing,' the Courts, and Religious Freedom," in *Witnessing for Sociology: Sociologists in Court*, eds. Pamela J. Jenkins and Steve Kroll-Smith (Westport, CT, and London: Praeger, 1996), 115–34. A recent overview of the controversy can be found in J. Gordon Melton, "Brainwashing and the Cults: The Rise and Fall of a Theory," posted at http://www.cesnur.org/testi/melton.htm.

5. On this point, see Flo Conway and Jim Siegelman, *Snapping: America's Epidemic of Sudden Personality Change* (New York: Lippincott, 1979).

6. The texts of the relevant material relative to the APA and brainwashing may be found at http://www.cesnur.org/testi/APA_Documents.htm.

7. A large selection of materials relevant to the Maryland hearings can now be found on the Internet at the New Religions site established by the late Jeffrey Hadden at the University of Virginia: http://cti.itc.virginia.edu/~jkh8x/soc257/cultsect/mdtaskforce.htm.

8. Current thinking on brainwashing/mind control within the cult awareness movement can, for example, be found in Michael Langone, ed., *Recovery from Cults* (New York: W. W. Norton & Company, 1993); Margaret Thaler Singer with Janja Lalich, *Cults in Our Midst* (San Francisco: Jossey-Bass Publishers, 1995); and the more popular presentation of Steven Hassan, *Releasing the Bonds* (Somerville, MA: Freedom of Mind Press, 2000).

9. Most notable in attempting to revive brainwashing as a consideration by social scientists have been Benjamin Zablocki and Stephen Kent, though to date they appear to have found little sympathy. See their essays in Benjamin Zablocki and Thomas Robbins, eds., *Misunderstanding Cults* (Toronto: University of Toronto Press, 2001).

10. Melissa Dittman, "Cults of Hatred," *Monitor on Psychology* (November 2002): 30–33.

11. For a current assessment of opinion on new religions by scholars, see David G. Bromley and Jeffrey K. Hadden, eds., *The Handbook on Cults and Sects in America*, 2 vols. (Greenwich, CT: JAI Press, 1993); John A. Saliba, *Understanding New Religious Movements* (Grand

Rapids, MI: William B. Eerdmanns, 1996); Philip Jenkins, *Mystics and Messiahs: Cults and New Religions in American History* (New York: Oxford University Press, 2000); and David G. Bromley and J. Gordon Melton, *Cults, Religion and Violence* (Cambridge, U.K.: Cambridge University Press, 2002).

12. Like mainline groups, all new religions are aware that they may face problems from the illegal and immoral actions of individual leaders and members (from child abuse to financial fraud) and that if they are brought into court for criminal or civil proceedings they may have to respond to allegations of brainwashing or thought control.

CHAPTER **16**
New Religions and the Anticult Movement in Canada

IRVING HEXHAM AND KARLA POEWE

Introduction

Canadians pride themselves on valuing tolerance, multiculturalism, and religious pluralism. Consequently, new religions are treated relatively well in Canada where, apart from the odd news report about a "dangerous cult," they receive relatively good treatment and are seen as a legitimate expression of belief. This article provides an overview of recent historical factors affecting the treatment of new religions in Canada, paying particular attention to a short period of intense anticult activity in the early 1980s. It concludes by suggesting that current tolerant attitudes towards new religions may be as ill informed as were earlier hostile attitudes.

Twenty-five years ago, Canadians in general and the Canadian media in particular were highly hostile towards new religions and new religious movements (NRMs). Evidence of this hostility can be seen today by anyone who borrows the now forgotten book, *Moonwebs*,[1] from a library. Written by Josh Freed, a talented producer working with the Canadian Broadcasting Corporation (CBC), *Moonwebs* painted an unflattering portrait of the Unification Church of Sun Myung Moon.[2] Nor was Freed alone. Newspapers articles, and radio and television reports all deemed new religions such as the Unification Church and the Hare Krishna movement "dangerous cults" in need of close scrutiny if not outright government regulation.

Contrast the hostility towards new religions in the late 1970s and early 1980s with the mild reception given to claims about human cloning by the Raelian sect in late 2002 and early 2003.[3] Although the headline in Canada's *National Post* described the group as a "cult," in the article itself it was called a "sect," and the criticism of its actions was very mild indeed. In fact, another Canadian journalist described the whole episode as "a nice break from weapons of mass destruction."[4] Clearly, Canadian attitudes towards new religions have changed dramatically over the last twenty-five years. To understand this change and the current non-debate about new religions we need to take a closer look at the whole history of cults in Canada.

The Historic Background

It is arguable that Jan Karel van Baalen, a Christian Reformed minister serving in Edmonton, Alberta, did more than any other writer to shape contemporary attitudes toward new religions in Canada by identifying them as "cults."[5] His book, *The Chaos of the Cults*, became a bestseller in North America, a standard text in both academic and public libraries, and remained in print until the 1980s. Van Baalen never defines what he means by the word "cult." Instead he says new religions are "essentially pagan."[6]

If van Baalen helped create the negative popular image of cults, another Canadian, S. D. Clark, provided academics with what became one of the standard studies of sects in 1948.[7] Like van Baalen, Clark never defines his terms, and his *Church and Sect in Canada* is essentially a history of Canadian churches prior to 1900. It was Clark's student, W. E. Mann, who produced the first real sociological study of new religions in Canada. Although inadequate by contemporary standards, his definitions were a major contribution at the time to the discussion of religious groups. Mann defines a church as "a religious structure which has become well accommodated to the secular world, and is, for the most part, aligned with the middle and upper classes." Sects were viewed as "institutions of social and religious protest, as bulwarks of certain disadvantaged social groups in their struggle against the social power, moral conventions, and ethos of the middle classes, and against institutionalised formalized religion."[8] He defined cult as "a religious group that looks for its basic and peculiar authority outside the Christian tradition," to which he added, "whereas sects emphasize recovery of primitive, first-century Christian doctrine, cults tend to blend alien religious or psychological notions with Christian doctrine with a view to obtaining a more 'adequate' or 'modern' faith."[9] He then listed common characteristics found in cults including a "post-scientific outlook" and a lack of "emotional manifestations" and "ascetic tendencies."[10]

Using this framework, Mann produced an essentially historical account of religious movements in the Canadian province of Alberta, with particular emphasis on the 1930s and the rise of evangelical Christian groups that he labelled "fundamentalist." On first reading, Mann's account seems essentially descriptive and non-judgmental. Indeed, throughout the book he argues that both cults and sects serve important social functions including the integration of both immigrant and rural groups into urban societies.[11] Yet underlying his apparently positive assessment is a deeper level of criticism; he implies that people who join sects or cults are "inclined to neurosis and neurasthenia" caused by deep-seated social and psychological needs.[12] He also argues that many members profit personally from their role in these groups. Thus, although he saw the groups he studied as socially beneficial in the context of a developing society, his dependence on deprivation theory leaves the reader with the distinct impression that sects and cults ought not to appear in normal societies such as those found in eastern Canada.[13] Therefore, although Mann does not attack new religions, he lays the groundwork for future attacks based on claims about psychological manipulation and the exploitation of members.

Finally, in the late 1960s and early 1970s, Walter Martin's *The Kingdom of the Cults* became a bestseller in Canada, where it could be found in most public libraries.[14] Consequently, when newspaper reporters were asked to write a story about some "strange new religion," very often the only work they could find that was remotely on topic was Martin's book. As David Virtue, the religion editor for *The Province* in Vancouver, said, "I was asked to write a story on the Hare Krishna movement which was active in Vancouver. When I went to the library there were no books on the topic. The closest I could get to the Krishnas were the groups discussed by Martin in his book. So I called them a 'cult' following his example. After all there were no other experts to be found."[15]

Cults and the Canadian Press until 1980

When new religions came to the attention of the Canadian public in the early 1970s, most Canadians seemed rather amused by the appearance of their members on city streets, and local newspapers gave them relatively fair coverage. This observation can be verified by studying the archives of Canadian newspapers. For example in Saskatchewan, the Saskatoon *Star-Phoenix* ran a number of stories about new religions in the mid-1970s which saw "cults" in terms of curious, but not dangerous, new religions.[16] The paper even reprinted an article from the *Toronto Star* by Tom Harpur that rejected the practice of "deprogramming."[17] Later it warned, "Cult 'rescuers' may expand to Canada," and took a negative view of deprogrammers as well as a positive view of the Hare Krishnas.[18] Similar findings appear in most other Canadian newspapers of the period.

Things began to change in 1978 with the successful deprogramming of Benji Carroll. This event involved Montreal reporter Josh Freed, who later wrote *Moonwebs* and made the film, *Ticket to Heaven*, based on the book.[19] Before the book was published, Freed wrote several sensational articles for *The Montreal Star*[20] that "exposed" the "Moonies." Shortly after these disclosures, the *Star-Phoenix* also ran a story about two young women in Boston who apparently killed themselves and their pets in the belief that they were entering the realm of Greek mythology. This appears to be the first cult suicide story of recent times.[21]

The negative publicity that gradually attached itself to "cults" led University of Saskatchewan's United Church of Canada Chaplain Colin Clay to write a "confidential report" for the Saskatchewan government and to give interviews to the press warning about "dangerous cults."[22] In September 1979, the Saskatchewan government rejected Clay's report and refused to establish the "deprogramming centre" he recommended.[23] Clay strongly disputed the government's decision, causing the Minister of Education to explain that it was Clay who originally initiated contact with the government by claiming "several hundred young people in Western Canada" were "involved in cults." After examining his report, the government rejected his findings for lack of solid evidence.[24]

Following this rejection of his work, Clay organized the first national conference on cults in Canada at the University of Saskatchewan. He invited a number of prominent Americans involved in deprogramming, including Gifford Cappellini and Barbara Underwood. Herbert Richardson and Darrol Bryant from the Universities of Toronto and Waterloo also attended this meeting, but when they attempted to ask questions during the question period they were silenced and ordered to leave. Later they gave their own press conference stating that Clay was actually "selling deprogramming."[25] In the wake of these events during the late 1970s, the Canadian media slowly began to publish negative stories about new religions.

Canadian Academics and "the Cults" from 1955 to 1980

Professor James Penton played an important role in changing the attitudes of academics to minority religions in Canada through the publication of *Jehovah's Witnesses in Canada: Champions of Freedom of Speech and Worship.*[26] Penton documented the persecution of Jehovah's Witnesses in Canada generally, and in Quebec in particular, from the founding of the movement until the 1960s. This shocking indictment established Penton both as a scholar and champion of religious liberty. In the mid-1970s, Penton emerged as an active defender of the rights of new religions.

In 1977, Herbert Richardson responded to the growth of deprogramming in the United States and its introduction to Canada by organizing two conferences in cooperation with the American Civil Liberties Union. The first was held in New York on February 5, the second at the University of Toronto on March 18. Following these meetings Richardson produced a sourcebook exposing deprogramming.[27] These conferences led to the founding of the small academic pressure group, Canadians for the Protection of Religious Liberty, in 1977. The well-known Mennonite scholar R. J. Sawatsky served as the group's first president.

Richardson also founded the Edwin Mellen Press in 1978, which he launched by organizing a major session at the Annual Meeting of the American Academy of Religion in New Orleans and by publishing *A Time for Consideration: A Scholarly Appraisal of the Unification Church*.[28] During the conference, news about Jonestown broke and Richardson began a high profile career as a leading academic spokesman defending new religions. Shortly afterwards, Darrol Bryant issued *Deprogramming and Media Coverage of New Religions*, a short booklet that was scheduled to become the first volume in a Documentation Series on *Religious Liberty in Canada*. None of the other projected volumes appeared.[29]

The Canadian Anticult Craze 1979–1982

From 1977 onwards, various parents' groups, often encouraged by university chaplains, formed across Canada to promote deprogramming and encourage legislators to pass restrictive laws against religious conversion. Anticult organizations with names like the Toronto-based COMA or Council on Mind Abuse were founded in Montreal, Toronto, Winnipeg, Vancouver, and various other cities. Most of these groups were founded by an individual or a small group of concerned people. Only in Montreal, Toronto, and Saskatoon do they appear to have attracted more widely based support, and today only the Montreal group, which is supported by the local Jewish community, continues to exist. Unfortunately, no one has studied the rise and decline of these movements in Canada, although Pauline Côté recently published a good overview of political and legal issues concerning new religions in Canada that deals with some of these topics.[30]

In October 1978, the government of Canada's largest province, Ontario, announced the establishment of a commission to investigate new religions led by the well-known civil libertarian, Daniel G. Hill. The commission was hailed as a victory by the growing anticult movement and greeted with alarm by most academics, established churches, and members of various new religions.

The Hill Commission led both sides to organize letter-writing campaigns. Interestingly, the official spokespersons of groups as diverse as the Mennonites, the Lutheran Church in America, the Jehovah's Witnesses, various Baptist conventions, and the United Church of Canada wrote open letters to Hill warning against the danger of restricting religious liberty.[31] Only members of the Society of Friends appear to have supported the anticult movement.[32]

When the Hill Report appeared in June 1980, anticult activists were disappointed because it concluded that while occasionally some individuals may suffer harm as a result of the activities of religious groups, there was no evidence that members of the general public were in danger from new religions.[33] Consequently Hill and his fellow investigators recommended that the government reject calls for anticult legislation and other measures aimed at restricting the activities of religious groups.

Before the publication of the Hill Report, anticult stories multiplied in the Canadian media following claims by a Vancouver family that their son had been "brainwashed" by the Moonies. This story, which appeared in slightly different versions in numerous newspapers across Canada, was followed by other sensational stories about the Moonies and other groups.[34] This spate of anticult atrocity stories continued until mid-1982, when these tales suddenly disappeared from the press. The progress and decline of such stories, which were often syndicated across Canada, can be seen from their frequency in newspapers such as Regina's *Leader Post*. Significantly, most of these stories concern or at least mention "Moonies."[35]

Given the fact that *Moonwebs* appeared early in 1980 followed by Freed's highly successful film, *Ticket to Heaven*, in 1981, it is tempting to speculate that this intense anticult activity was the result of a skillful publicity drive by Josh Freed.[36] As a journalist he was in a position to promote stories that helped both his book and the subsequent film. If this is so it also explains why interest in "cults" dropped off so dramatically following the film's release. Unfortunately, we will probably never know whether Freed created or capitalized on the Canadian cult craze of the early 1980s. All we can do here is note the relationship between the appearance of these stories and the release of his book and film.

Cults in Canada since 1983

Daniel Hill's devastating debunking of the emerging anticult movement's claims and his equally caustic criticisms of deprogramming deflated the emerging Canadian anticult movement. Four years later, a well publicized study by Saul Levine, an established psychiatrist working at Toronto's Children's Hospital, showed the lack of scientific support for notions of brainwashing and the often harmful effects of deprogramming on those who underwent the process.[37]

Equally important for media perceptions of the role of NRMs in Canadian life was the work of Reginald Bibby who, from the mid-1980s, began publishing regularly updated statistics concerning religious groups in Canada.[38] Canadian academics such as Irving Hexham, Karla Poewe, Lorne Dawson, and Susan Palmer contributed to a more tolerant ethos by publishing books that took a sane view of cults and recognized the need to protect religious liberty.[39] The work of these NRM scholars was given wide coverage by the media. Similarly, a significant number of Canadian sociologists including Fredrick Bird, Merlin Brinkerhof, Marleen Mackie, Raymond Currie, Joan Townsend, Nancy Nason-Clark, and Douglas Cowan have been active in organizations like the Society for the Scientific Study of Religion and have published numerous academic papers providing solid information about the activities of new religions in Canada. The reputations and publications of these scholars have been crucial to the public perception of NRMs in Canada. Whenever the national radio or television network, the CBC, or other stations want academic comment on "the cults," they are more often than not likely to get a moderate and well-informed response from these academics.

The one exception to the generally neutral tone of most Canadian academics and their rejection of anticult rhetoric is Stephen Kent.[40] Kent has been outspoken in his criticism of many new religions, particularly Scientology, and works closely with various anticult groups. Although Kent's views are widely known, few Canadian academics agree with his findings and most disagree quite strongly because of his tendency to use the testimony of ex-members.

Following the 1979–1982 anticult scare, occasional stories have appeared in the Canadian mass media about "cults." But, with a few exceptions, they have been relatively restrained, in spite of the publicity surrounding the Solar Temple in Quebec and both the Branch Davidians and Heaven's Gate in the United States. Significantly, no major story appeared highlighting the deaths of Canadians in any of these incidents or claiming that these tragedies proved the need for anticult legislation.[41] Thus, Canadian academics, whose views are taken seriously by the media, played an important role in encouraging responsible reporting about NRMs in Canada. It is safe to say that Canada lives up to its image as a tolerant and highly livable society with a strong tradition of political liberalism; the anticult movement remains relatively weak.

Conclusion

Susan Palmer has described new religions as "baby religions" that, like human babies, "can be heartbreakingly adorable or intensely annoying."[42]

What most Canadian observers seem to have forgotten is that a baby who gets hold of a box of matches can easily burn the house down. Not only are babies cute and annoying but they may also be very dangerous to themselves and others. New religions are no different. They may be cute but they are also potentially very dangerous socially and need to be treated with care.[43] In the case of old religions we have had hundreds of years to learn how their followers are likely to react in critical situations. With new religions we are entering the unknown.

Today Claude Vorilhon, who is better known as Rael, the founder and "prophet" of the atheist and non-profit Raelian movement, advocates peace and the welfare of humanity.[44] How do we know that he has not already received a telepathic message informing him that ordinary humans are dross and that Raelian clones deserve to inherit the Earth? Since he already advocates a world government based on what he calls "geniocracy," or rule by a Raelian elite, this may not be too farfetched a thought.[45]

Therefore, it is conceivable, although unlikely, that already scientists affiliated with Cloneaid, a Raelian-inspired human cloning service, are developing a mutated virus to induce male infertility. Since such an act would not kill existing humans, which is against Raelian ethics, it may be perfectly acceptable within the group's otherwise high moral code. How do we really know? The truth is we do not know what they are really planning. All we know is that the group, like a baby with a box of matches, is playing with some potentially dangerous scientific tools. This is why the complacency and acceptance that has replaced earlier hostility and rejection towards new religions is equally wrong and potentially dangerous. What we need today is a new skepticism that respects the freedom of belief and association but looks closely at the implications of NRM actions and teachings for society as a whole.

Notes

1. Josh Freed, *Moonwebs: Journey into the Mind of a Cult* (Toronto: Dorset Publishing, 1980).
2. Freed's major television production on the Unification Church was a CBC documentary, *Ticket to Heaven*, which appeared as a home video in 1982.
3. Araminta Wordsworth, "Scientists sceptical, angry over cult 'clone.' Alleged birth of Eve renews call for ban on human cloning," *The National Post*, 28 December 2002.
4. Margaret Wente, "Hel! The Raelians stole my brain," *The Globe and Mail*, 9 January 2003.
5. Jan Karel van Baalen, *The Chaos of Cults* (Grand Rapids, MI: Eerdmans, 1938).
6. Ibid., 18–20.
7. S. D. Clark, *Church and Sect in Canada* (Toronto: Toronto University Press, 1948).
8. W. E. Mann, *Sect, Cult and Church in Alberta* (Toronto: University of Toronto Press, 1955), 5.
9. Ibid., 6.
10. Ibid., 7–8.
11. Ibid., 154–58.
12. Ibid., 86–7, 101, 111.
13. Ibid., 29–35, 66, 153–55.
14. Walter Martin, *The Kingdom of the Cults* (Minneapolis: Bethany Fellowship, 1965).

15. Private conversation with David Virtue, June 1977.
16. *Star-Phoenix* (Saskatoon), 10 November 1977, 17 December 1977.
17. Ibid., 5 April 1975.
18. Ibid., 29 January 1977.
19. Josh Freed, *Moonwebs*; *Leader-Post* (Regina), 13 July 1981.
20. *Star-Phoenix* (Saskatoon) 6, 7 March 1978.
21. Ibid., 10 May 1979.
22. Ibid., 1 May 1979.
23. Ibid., 7 September 1979.
24. Ibid., 13 September 1979.
25. Ibid., 24 September 1979.
26. James Penton, *Jehovah's Witnesses in Canada. Champions of Freedom of Speech and Worship* (Toronto: University of Toronto Press, 1976).
27. Herbert Richardson, *Deprogramming: Documenting the Issues* (Toronto: private publication, 1977).
28. M. Darrol Bryant and Herbert W. Richardson, eds., *A Time for Consideration: A Scholarly Appraisal of the Unification Church* (Toronto: Edwin Mellen Press, 1978).
29. M. Darrol Bryant, ed., *Deprogramming and Media Coverage of New Religions* (Toronto: Canadians for the Protection of Religious Liberty, 1979).
30. Pauline Côté, "From Status Politics to Technocratic Pluralism: Toleration of Religious Minorities in Canada," *Social Justice Research* 12:4 (December 1999): 253–82.
31. *Toronto Star*, 31 October 1978. File letters dated 21 February, 25 April, 1 May, 14 May, 30 May, 1979.
32. The Friends Committee fact sheet, "Bondage not Religion," 1 October 1981, mentions their support for anticult legislation in 1980 and attacks both Herbert Richardson and Canadians for the Protection of Religious Liberty.
33. Daniel Hill, *Study of Mind Development Groups, Sects and Cults in Ontario* (Toronto: Government Printer, 1980).
34. E.g., *Kelowna Daily Courier*, 10 March, *Cape Breton Post*, 11 March, *Thunder Bay Chronicle*, 11 March, and *Sherebrook Record*, 19 March, 1980.
35. Cf. *Leader Post*, 24, 28 September 1979; 14 January, 19 February, 10, 22 March, 7 April, 2 June, 13 July, 22, 29 August, 15 October, 1980; 2, 11 April, 29 June, 7, 13, 20 July, 1982; 26 August, 14 September, 17, 22, 26 October, 20, 23 November, 1981; 9 March and 13 July, 1982.
36. See notes 15 and 16.
37. Saul Levine, *Radical Departures: Desperate Detours to Growing Up* (San Diego: Harcourt, Brace and Jovanovich, 1984).
38. Cf. Reginald Bibby, *Fragmented Gods: The Poverty and Potential of Religion in Canada* (Toronto: Irwin, 1987); idem, *Unknown Gods: The Ongoing Story of Religion in Canada* (Toronto: Stoddart, 1993); and idem, *The Bibby Report: Social Trends Canadian Style* (Toronto: Stoddart, 1995). A new book updating these figures is due in the near future.
39. Cf. Irving Hexham and Karla Poewe, *Understanding Cults and New Religions* (Grand Rapids, MI: Eerdmans, 1986) and *New Religions as Global Cultures* (Boulder, CO: Westview Press, 1997); Lorne L. Dawson, ed., *Cults in Context* (Toronto: Canadian Scholars Press, 1996) and *Comprehending Cults* (Toronto: Oxford University Press, 1998); Susan J. Palmer and Charlotte E. Hardman, eds., *Children in New Religions* (New Brunswick, NJ: Rutgers University Press, 1999).
40. Hexham and Poewe are highly critical of certain aspects of new religions although they strongly argue that "understanding precedes criticism," and they defend the right of new religions to propagate their views and receive full protection under the law. Thus they reject Kent's arguments while recognizing that not all new religions are necessarily socially harmless.
41. *The Alberta Report*, now known as *The National Report*, is a Canadian *Time*-type magazine and a good source for observing the attitude of reporters to new religions over time. Almost without exception the stories written in this otherwise highly conservative magazine are sympathetic towards members of new religions and highly critical of attempts to restrict religious freedom. Other Canadian newspapers and magazines display a similar restraint when dealing with new religions. Cf., *The Alberta Report*, 27 March, 18 and 25 September, 1981; 8 February, 15 March, 3 May, 1982; 6 February 1984; 28 January 1985; 21 August 1989.

42. Susan Palmer, "Caught Up in the Cult Wars: Confessions of a Canadian Researcher," in *Misunderstanding Cults: Searching for Objectivity in a Controversial Field*, eds. Benjamin Zablocki and Thomas Robbins (Toronto: University of Toronto Press, 2002), 101.
43. Cf. Karla Poewe, "Scientific Neo-Paganism and the Extreme Right Then and Today: From Ludendorff's *Gotterkenntnis* to Sigrid Hunke's *Europas Eigene Religion*," *Journal of Contemporary Religion* 14:3 (October 1999): 387–400.
44. This is found on the official website of the movement at www.rael.org.
45. See "SCIENTISTS FROM ANOTHER PLANET CREATED ALL LIFE ON EARTH USING D.N.A.," published by the International Raelian Movement, www.mt.net/~watcher/raelmsg.html.

PART 5

Theoretical Considerations

CHAPTER 17

New Religious Movements and Globalization

JAMES A. BECKFORD

Introduction

Debates about globalization are different from many other social scientific debates because their origins owe much to studies of religion. At a time when sociological accounts of religion exercise little influence over discussions of change and continuity in social life, it is rare indeed for a major strand of sociological theorizing to emerge in large part from ideas about religion. Roland Robertson's pioneering attempts to delineate "globality" and "the global circumstance" were, from the very beginning, inseparable from questions about the past and future of religion.[1] Then Peter Beyer critically assessed the relevance of ideas about globalization to a range of religious phenomena.[2] More recently, Karla Poewe,[3] and Hexham and Poewe[4] investigated the potential for charismatic Christianity and other faith movements to develop into global forms of religion. In short, questions about religion have been integral, if not always central, to the development of a significant amount of social scientific thinking about globalization. Nevertheless, many writers on globalization still overlook or neglect religion in their preoccupation with the political, cultural, or economic dimensions of the phenomenon.[5] This chapter will try to remedy these weaknesses by highlighting the association between new religious movements (NRMs) and globalization.

I aim to achieve two things in this chapter. First, I consider the ways in which NRMs can be understood in the context of debates about globality. Second, I outline some of the implications of the global circumstance for the development of NRMs. The space available does not permit me to elaborate or illustrate my arguments at length, but I have discussed them in more detail elsewhere.[6]

NRMs and the Context of Globality

"Globalization" is a contested concept, but the following list of its defining characteristics captures most of the features that social scientists tend to emphasize:

1. the growing frequency, volume, and interconnectedness of movements of ideas, materials, goods, information, pollution, money, and people across national boundaries and between regions of the world;
2. the growing capacity of information technologies to shorten or even abolish the distance in time and space between events and places in the world;
3. the diffusion of increasingly standardized practices and protocols for processing global flows of information, goods, money, and people;
4. the emergence of organizations, institutions and social movements for promoting, monitoring, or counteracting global forces, with or without the support of individual nation-states;
5. the emergence in particular countries or regions of distinctive or "local" ways of refracting the influence of global forces.[7]

This "generic" conception of globalization often underpins claims that the process is unique to late modernity and that it depends heavily on new information technologies. While these claims are true, they represent only a partial view of a more complex reality, especially where religion is concerned. For example, early Protestant forms of religious thought, feeling, and action helped to lay the ideological and institutional foundations for worldwide systems of social, political, economic, and cultural relations. Early modern campaigns to extend the influence of Protestantism, Catholicism, and Islam around the world also created networks that facilitated the growth of such globalizing phenomena as intercontinental trading in slaves, international trade in goods and services, colonialism, and imperialism. The roots of globalization go back to the early modern period in Europe and the Middle East.

Since the mid-nineteenth century, some religious movements have also boosted the process of "making the world a smaller place" by establishing systematic and standardized programs for attracting, inducting, and mobilizing recruits in many different countries. The Watchtower movement of Jehovah's Witnesses, the Church of Jesus Christ of Latter-day Saints, the Christian Science Church, and the Seventh-day Adventist Church all exemplify this thrust toward the worldwide diffusion of fairly uniform beliefs, practices, and forms of organization. At the same time, these religious movements have energetically campaigned for notions of religious freedom and the protection of religion from "interference" by the state, thereby indirectly contributing to the diffusion of doctrines of universal human rights—often in the face of violent opposition and persecution. The case of Jehovah's Witnesses in the Nazi era in Germany in the 1930s, in the United States in the 1940s, in Quebec in the 1950s, and in communist countries during the Cold War is exemplary.

Furthermore, the NRMs that emerged in the mid-twentieth century have made strenuous efforts to crystallize forms of global consciousness. For example, the Unificationist movement, the Church of Scientology, Transcendental Meditation, and Soka Gakkai International (SGI) all stress the interconnectedness of human actions and social institutions at a global level.[8] They deliberately aspire to overcome national boundaries of ideology, religion, ethnicity, and citizenship in their drive toward a peaceful and harmonious world that is unified by what they consider to be universal values.

Nevertheless, as Robertson has made clear, these would-be universal values are often conveyed by means of particularist ideologies.[9] Religious movements have their own, highly distinctive ways of defending and promoting values that, they claim, have universal applicability. As a result, the freedom that Jehovah's Witnesses demand for the right to practice their religion in private and public is not necessarily the same as the freedom demanded by freethinkers, Quakers, or Muslims. Nor is the social justice sought by movements such as the Nation of Islam entirely compatible with the ideals of the Baha'is.[10] In other words, each movement's ideology places a highly particular meaning on concepts that may appear to be universal in meaning.

This is one of the reasons why some NRMs, especially those operating in the former Soviet Union, are perceived as a threat to societal integrity. It is ironic, but the fact that NRMs articulate discourses of individual freedom, social justice, and freedom of religion makes them suspect in the eyes of competitors and opponents. It is unusual for NRMs to be seen as disinterested purveyors of universalistic ideals. Thus, agencies of the Russian Orthodox Church and supporters of the pre-Revolutionary status enjoyed virtually uniquely by the church have fought hard to prevent NRMs from enjoying the benefits of newly won freedoms. Marat Shterin and James Richardson have shown how recent legislation in Russia discriminates against "non-traditional" religious groups in an effort to prevent the country from losing its distinctive identity in an increasingly globalized world.[11]

The public reaction to NRMs in such a highly centralized state as France is all the more hostile for the very reason that opponents accuse the movements of disingenuously abusing the sacred doctrines of rationality and rights on which the French republic was founded.[12] Both Russia and France are also countries in which hostility to NRMs owes much to fear of American imperialism in the guise of globalization. In this sense, NRMs are partly the incidental victims of cross-national struggles for power and sovereignty in the post-communist, globalizing world. "Collateral damage" is another way of describing the repercussions on NRMs.

The response of many NRMs to aggressive opposition is to try to justify their claim to freedom by arguing that human history has been unfolding in a providential fashion and that the moment has come to sweep away outdated religious beliefs and practices in order to usher in a new universal dispensation. This is central to the Unificationist movement's strategy for completing the messianic task begun, but not completed, by Jesus Christ. It is also close to the Baha'i view that history has reached a crucial turning point and that an era of worldwide peace is at hand.[13] This is a highly positive version of a theme central to many accounts of globalization, namely, the necessity for globe-wide ideas and institutions to replace ideas and institutions rooted in separate nations and states.

The prospect of a new global order is also central to many variants of the Human Potential and New Age movements and Scientology. All these very different kinds of NRM nevertheless share a conviction that human beings have, perhaps for the first time, come into possession of the knowledge required to free them from traditional structures of thought and action. Hence, the confidence of the Maharishi Mahesh Yogi, founder of Transcendental Meditation, and of Werner Erhard, the founder of *est* (now largely re-configured as the Landmark Trust), that the state of the entire world would improve if a sufficient number of people became sufficiently energetic and disciplined about their spiritual practice. Such movements hold out the prospect of globalization based on a combination of liberal individualism and discipline—the very ingredients of modernity, according to Peter Wagner.[14]

Not all NRMs subscribe to the same—entirely undifferentiated—model of globalization, however. For example, the Rashtriya Swayamsevak Sangh (RSS), a religio-ethnic-political movement that emerged in India in 1925, is engaged in forging a "world Hindu" identity. It aims to specify and strengthen the place of Hindus in the emerging global order partly through the agency of the Vishwa Hindu Parishad (VHP) or World Hindu Council, and the Bharatiya Janata Party (BJP). It has much more to do with exclusive collective discipline than with inclusive, liberal individualism. In fact, the RSS and the VHP give the impression that Hinduism is expanding to take up the new opportunities provided for it by globalization. But their strategy is not to argue that individuals should be free to choose between different faith options in a pluralistic democracy or to opt for some generic, brand-free global faith. On the contrary, their aim is primarily to strengthen collective identity and consciousness among Hindus—albeit at a global level. According to Daniel Gold,

> Postcolonial Hindu fundamentalism can thus appear as a new colonialism of the victors. In representing an emergence of Indic group consciousness in new forms shaped by the colonial experience, it can easily lead to a tyranny of the majority. For it keeps the Western idea of religious community as an ideally homogeneous group, but abandons the ideas of equality among communities and protections for minorities introduced with the secular British administration: a flourishing, united Hindu Nation should need no legal protection for any special group.[15]

In short, Hindu nationalism uses a highly distinctive rhetoric in which the notion of "world" Hinduism assumes great importance, but it actually aspires towards a global order that is anything but homogeneous or standardized. It is a vision of globality in which Hinduism survives as an independent, major component pursuing its own ends and transcending national boundaries.

A closely related facet of this highly particularist model of globalization is the extent to which the RSS and the VHP are able to elicit support from Indians and the descendants of Indians living in diasporic communities outside India.[16] There is at least a possibility that, in the name of a certain kind of globalization, Hindu nationalism may actually foment particularist and separatist ideas among Hindus living as minorities all over the world. It is ironic that globalized processes of communication and finance may make it correspondingly easier for them to support the Hindu nationalist cause inside India.

I need to sound a note of caution at this point, however. It is necessary to make a clear distinction between the *global aspirations* of some NRMs and their *transnational modes of operation*. I mean that, in practice, the direction and control of the movements tend to remain centered on one particular country—or among the nationals of one particular country—even when their operations extend virtually worldwide. As a result, there can be no mistaking the Japanese character of SGI, the Korean character of the Unificationist movement, the American character of Scientology, or the

Swedish character of the Word of Life movement.[17] The Baha'is and ISKCON are ambiguous cases in so far as control of them is dispersed across several countries. This is for ideological reasons in the case of the Baha'is and for reasons to do with internal conflicts in the case of ISKCON.[18] The Universal Church of the Kingdom of God is also ambiguous because its Brazilian character has been significantly refracted by social and cultural forces in southern Africa.[19]

In other words, the study of NRMs and older religious movements leads me to be cautious about some of the wilder claims that are made about the standardizing and individualizing effects of globalization. I have tried to show that, while some of these movements purvey ambitious ideas about globality, there is also a strong tendency for them to represent the universal in particularist terms. Another way of putting this is to say that some NRMs are seizing the opportunity to exploit the image and the reality of globalizing circumstances in order to enhance their appeal and their power. But they try to do this in ways that are firmly grounded in non-global cultures and forms of organization. This means that NRMs construct and use notions of globality for their own purposes—but they do not necessarily subscribe to the idea of globalization as I sketched it at the beginning of this chapter.

Implications of Globalization for NRMs

Although NRMs may operate with unusual ideas about the global circumstance, the movements are still subject to the forces that are closer to the center of social scientific understanding of globalization. Leaving aside the movements' highly variegated interpretations of globality, I now want to investigate some aspects of the impact that globalization—as I defined it near the beginning of this chapter—has had on them. I group the impacts in two general categories. The first category contains the positive opportunities that globalization offers to NRMs for enhancing their work. The second contains the obstacles that are all the more challenging to NRMs precisely because they have to operate in globalizing conditions. In short, my aim is to assess the balance of advantages and disadvantages that globalization presents to NRMs.

Advantages

One of the reasons why many NRMs are currently able to entertain such high hopes and positive expectations about their place in a globalizing world order is that crucial social and technological developments have given them new opportunities and encouragement. It is worth adding, however, that religious movements have often pioneered applications of new technology, beginning as early as the sixteenth century C.E. with early

Protestants' experimentation with printing technologi(
First World War, for example, the predecessors of Jeh(
veloped a traveling show that depicted the "Photo-Dr
colored images and sound. They subsequently adapte(
tions technologies such as portable phonographs for
evangelism, public address systems mounted on car
mitter on Staten Island, New York. Other modern religious
such as the Seventh-day Adventists and the Mormons, invested heavily in
the use of medical technologies in support of their missionary work in
Africa and South America.

Meanwhile, Soka Gakkai International and other new religions of
Japan have effectively exploited mass communications technologies.
Forensic investigations of Aum Shinrikyō's activities have shown that
this movement was actively engaged in neurological research as well as in
the refinement of systems for the delivery of chemical weapons.[20] In fact,
the association between the Raelians and the highly controversial issue of
human cloning is only the latest in a long line of medical, scientific, and
technological experiments conducted by NRMs. Indeed, experimenting
with consciousness, unconsciousness, and all forms of spiritual experience is central to the mission of NRMs ranging from "UFO cults" to healing movements in many parts of the world. The *locus classicus* is the
Church of Scientology's use of a simple skin galvanometer, called an E-
meter, in its auditing processes. In 1963, the U. S. Food and Drug Administration seized a number of E-meters during a raid on Scientology
premises on suspicion that the machines were in contravention of laws
regulating the practice of medicine.

The Internet has had the effect of accelerating and extending the circu-
lation of the ideas which fuel the experiments that NRMs conduct not only
in spiritual matters but also in social relations. It has certainly created fresh
opportunities for publicity and proselytism. The number of web pages
controlled by NRMs, for example, expanded rapidly and massively in the
1990s to the point where it was no longer an exaggeration to consider that
some NRMs enjoyed global outreach.[21] Similar claims can be made with
confidence about charismatic and Pentecostal currents in Christianity.[22]
What is less clear is how successful NRMs have been in turning the Internet
to their advantage as a means of publicizing their beliefs or activities and of
recruiting new members. Dawson and Hennebry quote an article that appeared in the *New York Times* only days after the Heaven's Gate movement
suicides in Southern California claiming that "The Heaven's Gate suicides
can only amplify fears that, in some quarters, may be already bordering on
hysteria. The Internet, it seems, might be used to lure children not only to
shopping malls where some 'sicko' waits, but into joining UFO cults."[23]
Moreover, a headline in the Japanese daily newspaper, *The Mainichi*, in

ary 2003 claimed, "AUM uses sultry Net sirens to lure male members." he allegation was that some female members of Aum Shinrikyō were trying to lure men into the movement by offering a matchmaking service on its website. Anticultists have not been slow to ratchet up this type of anxiety. Nevertheless, Bainbridge acknowledged that having web pages conferred prestige on even the most insignificant NRM by giving the impression that it had worldwide significance.[24] Even substantial movements could benefit from the ease with which the Internet enabled them to contact their existing members. And, according to Jeffrey Zaleski, the nature of disembodied communication on the Web is such that "the lonely," "the shy," and "the outcasts" are more likely to associate themselves with a NRM than would otherwise be the case.[25]

Another advantage of the Internet is that it has made it easier and more economical for NRMs to remain in communication with politicians, lawyers, and academics who share concerns about the treatment of religious minorities. There is a constant stream of communications by e-mail, user lists, syndicated distribution lists, and web pages. "Cult watchers" and suspected sympathizers can be kept abreast of the latest developments in, for example, legal cases or the preparations for major events. The Family has gone further than most NRMs by establishing its highly valuable WorldWide Religious News service that supplies digests of news stories from all over the world free of charge on a daily basis by e-mail. They have recently added omnibus editions of the stories grouped by region of the world. But perhaps the web pages left by the members of the Heaven's Gate movement who "transited" to another reality in March 1997 are the most arresting example of innovative exploitation of the Internet.

Disadvantages

Exploiting new information technologies brings risks, costs, and disadvantages to NRMs. First, there are good grounds for doubting whether the Web actually serves as an effective tool for recruiting new members. Dawson and Hennebry, and Mayer offer empirical evidence that casts doubt on alarmist claims about the capacity of NRMs to boost their recruitment potential by exploiting the Web.[26] Bainbridge adds a number of theoretical reasons for suspecting that disembodied proselytism is likely to fail—given what we already know about the importance of social relations and social networks in the recruitment process.[27] Moreover, the proliferation of religious websites may simply encourage searchers to keep on searching instead of being content with any particular NRM.

Second, NRMs that rely heavily on the Web as a means of informing the public about their beliefs and practices run the risk that opponents, apostates, and ruthless competitors will steal or parody their material. This makes it correspondingly more difficult for NRMs to prevent or to stanch any unwanted "leakage" of their ideas to the outside world or to dissident "insiders." The idea of "anticult terrorism via the Internet" is not an exaggeration.[28] The Church of Scientology, for example, has been at the center of bitter legal disputes about ownership of the copyright of material that its opponents and detractors have posted on the Web. Similarly, the Japanese movement Sukyo Mahikari has attracted a large number of dissident and/or oppositional websites.[29] And all NRMs stand to lose credibility if public interest grows in websites that are really parodies of their particular brand of religion, such as the Church of the Mighty Gerbil and Thee Church Ov MOO.[30]

Third, there can be no doubt that the Internet has enabled anticult activists to strengthen their opposition to NRMs. Indeed, Web search engines are just as likely to direct browsers toward sites that are critical of NRMs as they are toward the movements' own sites. Anticult sites have the further advantage that they can aggregate negative commentary on large numbers of NRMs in a wide variety of countries, thereby enhancing the impression that all "cults" are the same.[31] Journalists and program makers may also be drawn to these sites because they offer quick and convenient access to opinion that is easily digestible, especially if it is infused with the vitriol of apostates' experiences. In France, the stakes are even higher because agencies of the state have also seized the opportunity to publish extensive anticult materials on official websites. It seems to me, then, that the balance of advantage on the Web possibly tilts toward the anticultists at present.

Leaving the Internet aside, globalization is also likely to affect NRMs by encouraging agencies of the state, legal authorities, and international agencies to harmonize their responses to the issues raised by NRMs. For example, repeated efforts have been made to establish Europe-wide criteria and procedures for identifying and controlling religious movements. As the intensity of transnational activity of many kinds increases, the pressure mounts to achieve agreement at a supra-national level on ways of responding to problems in a uniform fashion. The simultaneous deaths of members of the Solar Temple movement in several different countries in 1997 gave rise to tensions between their respective police and security forces.

Conclusions

My argument is in several parts. The first is that, while many NRMs cultivate truly global ideas and aspirations, their modes of operation remain "merely transnational." Second, the ideas and images of globality that NRMs convey are indelibly marked by their origins in particular cultures. Third, the advent of the Internet is a mixed blessing for NRMs because the instrumental advantages that accrue to them are probably outweighed by the countervailing opportunities that it creates for their opponents, detractors, and dissidents to attack them. It would be unwise, therefore, to assume that global forces have completely transformed the conditions in which NRMs operate. But globalization has undoubtedly intensified and accelerated some of the conflicts in which NRMs have long been embroiled.

Notes

1. Roland Robertson, "Globalization, Politics and Religion," in *The Changing Face of Religion*, eds. James A. Beckford and Thomas Luckmann (London: Sage, 1989), 10–23; *Globalization: Social Theory and Global Culture* (London: Sage, 1992); Roland Robertson and J. Chirico, "Humanity, Globalization and Worldwide Religious Resurgence: A Theoretical Exploration," *Sociological Analysis* 46:3 (1985): 219–42.
2. Peter Beyer, "The Global Environment as a Religious Issue: A Sociological Analysis," *Religion* 2 (1992): 1–19; *Religion and Globalization* (London: Sage, 1994).
3. Karla Poewe, ed., *Charismatic Christianity as a Global Culture* (Columbia: University of South Carolina Press, 1994).
4. Irving Hexham and Karla Poewe, *New Religions as Global Cultures: The Sacralization of the Human* (Boulder, CO: Westview Press, 1997).
5. James A. Beckford, *Social Theory and Religion* (Cambridge, U.K.: Cambridge University Press, 2003).
6. Ibid.; "Religious Movements and Globalization," in *Global Social Movements*, eds. R. Cohen and S. Rai (London: Athlone Press, 2000), 165–83; and "Religious Interaction in a Global Context," in *New Religions and Globalization: Theoretical and Methodological Perspectives*, ed. Armin Geertz (Aarhus, Denmark: Aarhus University Press, 2003).
7. James A. Beckford, "Religious Movements and Globalization," in *Global Social Movements*, 170.
8. David G. Bromley and Anson D. Shupe, *The Moonies in America* (Beverly Hills, CA: Sage, 1979); George D. Chryssides, *Exploring New Religions* (London: Cassell, 1999); Roy Wallis, *The Road to Total Freedom: A Sociological Analysis of Scientology* (London: Heinemann, 1976); William Sims Bainbridge, *The Sociology of Religious Movements* (New York: Routledge, 1997); Karel Dobbelaere, *Soka Gakkai: From Lay Movement to Religion* (Salt Lake City: Signature Books, 2001).
9. Roland Robertson, *Globalization: Social Theory and Global Culture*.
10. M. Gardell, *Countdown to Armageddon: Louis Farrakhan and the Nation of Islam* (London: Hurst, 1996); Margit Warburg, "Religious Groups and Globalisation: a Comparative Perspective," in *Challenging Religion*, eds. James A. Beckford and James T. Richardson (London: Routledge, 2003), 47–55.
11. Marat S. Shterin and James T. Richardson, "Local laws restricting religion in Russia: Precursors of Russia's new national law," *Journal of Church and State* 40:2 (1998): 319–41.
12. James A. Beckford, " 'Dystopia' and the Reaction to New Religious Movements in France," in *Regulating Religion: Case Studies from Around the Globe*, ed. James T. Richardson (New York: Kluwer Academic, forthcoming); Danièle Hervieu-Léger, *La Religion en Miettes ou la Question des Sectes* (Paris: Calmann-Lévy, 2001).
13. Peter Smith, *The Babi and Baha'i Religions: From Messianic Shi'ism to a World Religion* (Cambridge, U.K.: Cambridge University Press, 1987).
14. Peter Wagner, *A Sociology of Modernity: Liberty and Discipline* (London: Routledge, 1994).
15. Daniel Gold, "Organized Hinduisms: From Vedic Truth to Hindu Nation," in *Fundamentalisms Observed*, eds. Martin Marty and Scott Appleby, vol. 1 (Chicago: University of Chicago Press, 1991), 580.
16. Chetan Bhatt, *Liberation and Purity: Race, New Religious Movements and the Ethics of Postmodernity* (London: UCL Press, 1997).
17. Simon Coleman, *The Globalisation of Charismatic Christianity: Spreading the Gospel of Prosperity* (Cambridge, U.K.: Cambridge University Press, 2000).
18. Burke E. Rochford, Jr., "Analysing ISKCON for Twenty-five Years: A Personal Reflection," *ISKCON Communications Journal* 8:1 (2000): 33–36.

19. D. Lehmann, "Charisme et possession en Afrique et au Brésil," in *La Globalisation du Religieux*, eds. Jean-Pierre Bastian, Françoise Champion, and Kathy Rousselet (Paris: L'Harmattan, 2001), 139–52; A. Mary, "Globalisation des pentecôtismes et hybridité du christianisme africain," in *La Globalisation du Religieux*, 153–68.

20. Ian Reader, *Religious Violence in Contemporary Japan* (Honolulu: University of Hawaii Press, 2000).

21. Irving Hexham and Karla Poewe, *New Religions as Global Cultures*.

22. Karla Poewe, ed., *Charismatic Christianity as a Global Culture*; David Martin, *Pentecostalism: The World Their Parish* (Oxford: Blackwell, 2002).

23. Lorne L. Dawson and J. Hennebry, "New Religions and the Internet: Recruiting in a New Public Space," *Journal of Contemporary Religion* 14:1 (1999): 17–39.

24. Bainbridge, *The Sociology of Religious Movements*, 155.

25. Jeffrey P. Zaleski, *The Soul of Cyberspace: How New Technology is Changing Our Spiritual Lives* (New York: HarperCollins, 1997).

26. Dawson and Hennebry, "New Religions and the Internet"; Jean-François Mayer, "Religious Movements and the Internet: The New Frontier of Cult Controversies," in *Religion on the Internet: Research Prospects and Promises*, eds. Jeffrey Hadden and Douglas Cowan (New York: JAI Press, 2000), 249–76.

27. Bainbridge, *The Sociology of Religious Movements*.

28. Massimo Introvigne, "So Many Evil Things: Anti-cult Terrorism via the Internet," in *Religion on the Internet*, eds. Hadden and Cowan, 277–306.

29. Mayer, "Religious Movements and the Internet," in *Religion on the Internet*, eds. Hadden and Cowan.

30. Dawson and Hennebry, "New Religions and the Internet."

31. Eileen Barker, *New Religious Movements: A Practical Introduction* (London: HMSO, 1989).

CHAPTER **18**

Apocalypse 9/11

JOHN R. HALL

The attacks of September 11, 2001, were abhorrent to modern civilized life.[1] Yet moral condemnation does not provide adequate grounds for understanding the struggle between Al Qa'ida and the U.S.-led coalition. Those who planned and carried out the attacks succeeded, probably more than they anticipated, in altering political agendas, economic realities, and social life around the globe. With the military actions against the agents and sponsors of terrorist, rebel, and state violence in Afghanistan, Pakistan, the Philippines, Iraq, and elsewhere; the seemingly interminable conflict in Israel and Palestine; and the obliquely linked rumblings of war in Syria, Iran, and North Korea, global history is taking a sharp turn into a new era. Yet for all that has been written, we do not yet well understand the import of these manifold developments. In part, we are in the midst of history unfolding, and thus lack that retrospective capacity to chart events in relation to one or another coherent narrative keyed to outcome. Yet precisely when history remains open, it is important to try to understand an *encompassing* historical transformation. One way to explore current global history is to consider the ways it might involve "apocalyptic war."

The American-led confrontation with international Islamicist insurgency has quickly become a hinge upon which contemporary history turns. Certainly both governments and Islamicist organizations plan (and steel people to anticipate) more moments of reckoning, involving not only Al Qa'ida and its allied networks in various countries, but also the broader "axis of evil" identified by U.S. President George W. Bush. An attack by a

265

stateless entity on the scale of 9/11 is without precedent, and the ensuing events have not constituted anything like a conventional war. Is the world caught up in apocalyptic war? On the face of it the question seems grandiose. In religion, apocalypse typically symbolizes some divinely ordained and inexorable process. Sociologically, however, we need to understand that even apocalyptic history is open-ended. Apocalyptic war is "socially constructed" or "deconstructed," depending upon the actions taken by various parties to a situation. In the most extreme cases, the established social order itself comes to define its struggle in apocalyptic terms, or acts in ways that lead others to believe that it has joined such a struggle.

Time, the Established Social Order, and Apocalypse

Theorists of narrative have recently emphasized that the course of unfolding history is affected by imaginary constructions ("stories") developed by its participants.[2] The distinction between "ideology" and "utopia" offers a useful way to identify such narrative imaginaries, because it affirms that narratives structure both the actions of (ideological) supporters of an established social order as well as those of (utopian) opponents who seek to bring a new social order into being. Thus, ideologists and utopianists are locked in struggle over the meaning of history. From the perspective of a prevailing ideology, utopian visions are fantastic, unrealizable, and morally abhorrent, but for the utopianists, these assertions are themselves ideological, and they would lose their force if a transcendent social order were achieved. In other words, an ideology is a utopia about an existing social order.[3]

Utopian thought is strongly ordered by orientations toward time. Some utopias posit gradual progress; others become centered on the here-and-now or a return to a golden past. Still others orient collective action by way of *apocalyptic* time, which posits the end of one era of history (or indeed, the end of history altogether) and the onset of God's dispensation, in whatever form it will take.[4] Many utopian groups that live out apocalyptic imaginaries seek converts to greet the rise of the new millennial kingdom. Others, like the Shakers, retreat from society at large to wait passively for the new era. However, apocalyptic imaginaries also have framed trajectories of extreme violence. In recent years, these have included the 1978 murders and mass suicide of Peoples Temple in Jonestown, Guyana, Heaven's Gate's collective suicide in a plan to reach the "next evolutionary stage above human," and Aum Shinrikyō's 1995 sarin poison gas attack in the Tokyo subway system.[5]

Although these episodes of apocalyptic violence pale in comparison to the attacks of September 11, 2001, Georg Simmel reminds us that the same social form can manifest on quite different scales and within different structures of social organization. Thus, continuities between sectarian apocalyptic violence and political terrorism had received increasing attention, even before 9/11.[6] In turn, the image of apocalypse gained a new currency with the attacks of 9/11.

Yet how might we delineate such a religiously charged phenomenon as "the Apocalypse" sociologically? One approach is to "translate" the term for sociological purposes. In Greek, *apokalyptein* means "disclose." This could suggest not just "revelation" in the prophetic sense, but more profoundly, the sudden manifestation of ultimately powerful forces that envelop collective social life. Sociologically, then, the apocalypse differs from the religious time of God's final judgment, some final Armageddon that happens *to* human beings. Rather than "the end of the world," the Apocalypse is "the end of the world as we know it," that is, a disjuncture brought on by social forces and human actions, in which dramatic events reshape the relations of many individuals at once to history.

Ordinary time and apocalyptic time are two different kinds of *social* time that arise and intermingle in human history. The German social critic Walter Benjamin captured this possibility when he wrote of an historical present shot through with "chips of messianic time."[7] And that is the enduring image of September 11, 2001—a brilliantly beautiful morning on the East Coast of the United States that was punctured by a tableau of terror.

Yet Benjamin's image of messianic time bears unpacking, for the temporal structure of the Apocalypse is complex. How does the Messiah come? When, for whom, and to accomplish what? Of course sociologists cannot answer such questions directly: we are researchers, not prophets. What we can do is to look to historical moments when apocalyptic imaginaries animate social action, when people in various quarters act out one or another apocalyptic narrative. Such narratives, when they arise, often manifest on multiple fronts. Thus, a generalized climate of apocalyptic expectation sometimes emerges when people confront social or economic dislocation, or during calendrical shifts such as the passage to the third millennium. More intensively, the most radical apocalyptic narratives call on people to transcend their everyday lives, to undergo a rebirth of self and act in relation to special historical circumstances through collective social action conducted in sectarian organizations of true believers. In turn, the actions of such groups can amplify the general apocalyptic *zeitgeist*.[8] In these dialectical processes, apocalyptic temporal imaginaries can give rise to historical temporalities that are themselves apocalyptic.[9]

Sociologically, there are three broad narrative constructions of apocalyptic time: 1. anticipation of impending doom; 2. escape to a refuge safe from the unfolding apocalypse; and 3. the unfolding apocalypse of war.

The first two of these are important in relation to a generalized apocalyptic *zeitgeist*. However, it is apocalyptic war that would punctuate historical time.[10] But what is apocalyptic war? War is hell, but all wars are not the same. The narrative of the generic "apocalyptic warring sect" (as I term it) posits a struggle by the forces of good against those of evil as the necessary pathway to a post-apocalyptic tableau of salvation. The end of history can come only through a conflict in real historical time, and the warring sect makes inaugurating such a conflict its sacred enterprise.

Apocalyptic war is thus not conventional war: it tends to play out as an extreme form of terrorism. However, not all terrorism is apocalyptic, and apocalyptic war is not adequately understood if it is reduced to terrorism—a term easily saturated with political meanings and agendas. Charles Tilly has usefully defined terrorism as "asymmetrical deployment of threats and violence against enemies outside the forms of political struggle operating within some current regime." Apocalyptic war is sacred terror. In it, strategic actions become strongly infused with symbolically transcendent "religious" meanings. To identify apocalyptic war as sacred, however, requires a sociological caveat: action within strongly countercultural milieus opposing an existing social order cannot be neatly divided between the religious and the non-religious. A given countercultural movement, if it proves viable, brings to the fore questions of ultimate meaning, and thus bears a religiously prophetic and sacred quality, even if it is broadly secular in orientation.[11]

To consider whether current history is constructed through apocalyptic narratives, we need to address two connected issues. First, we must ask whether Al Qa'ida's ideology, actions, and *modus operandi* approximate the apocalyptic warring sect as an ideal type. Second, we need to consider how the temporal constructions of Al Qa'ida intersect with the collective actions of the U.S. and its allies in the established global order.

Al Qa'ida's Jihad as Apocalyptic War

As Max Weber observed nearly a century ago, religion represents a special case of status honor that, for participants, is "nourished most easily on the belief that a special 'mission' is entrusted to them. . . . Their value is thus moved into something beyond themselves, into a 'task' placed before them by God."[12] Religion under Western monotheism, in Weber's account, develops a possibility of "holy war, i.e., a war in the name of a god, for the special purpose of avenging a sacrilege." In Weber's genealogy of the construct, the ancient Hebrew idea of a promise that God's chosen people would be elevated "above other nations" provided a legitimating framework. In turn, the Christian Augustine (354–430 C.E.) affirmed a doctrine of forced conversion. But Islam was the first religion to establish a connection between "religious promises and war against religious infidelity," aiming at "the subjugation of the unbelievers to political authority and economic domination of the faithful." Yet, under traditional Islam, Weber held, "if the infidels were members of 'religions with a sacred book,' their extermination was not enjoined," for they could make useful economic contributions to Islamic society, through tribute or taxation.[13]

The ideology of Al Qa'ida in essence promotes a holy war avenging a sacrilege. Over the years, Osama bin Laden and his associates developed explicit doctrines that animate their movement, most notably, the September 1996 "Declaration of Jihad against the United States." Their ideology identifies a series of sacred transgressions, identifies a particular strategy of rectification, and envisions a utopian era once their strategy has been fulfilled. The transgressions include: the stationing of U.S. troops in Saudi Arabia near the holiest Muslim cities; the U.S.-led 1991 war against Iraq after it invaded Kuwait; the Israeli control of the city of Jerusalem; and most generally, the end of the Ottoman empire some 80 years ago. As sociologist Jeff Goodwin has observed, these transgressions and the wider hegemony that they represent are matters of geopolitics, but they are refracted through a lens of religious meaning.[14] For bin Laden and the radicalized Islamicist movement, they require a specifically religious response of jihad, or holy war.

Jihad is a complex Islamic doctrine, subject to varying definitions in both Muslim theological debate and scholarly analysis.[15] Historically, the ethical and legal routinization of Islam over the centuries tended to codify the limits to wars against "religions with a sacred book" that Weber noted in early Islam, and placed limiting interpretations on jihad. During the twentieth century, however, Islamicist movements began to reconstruct the theology of jihad in response to contemporary historical conditions, especially the British declaration of a protectorate in Egypt during World War I and the end of the caliphate and establishment of secular rule in Turkey in the 1920s.

A radicalized anti-modern construction of jihad emerged within the Egyptian Muslim Brotherhood founded in 1928 by Hasan al-Banna. Al-Banna initiated the push to establish a true Islamic state organized on the basis of *sharia*, or Islamic law. How to establish such a state was a question open to alternative strategic answers. A key Brotherhood thinker of the 1950s, Sayyid Qutb, argued that not only non-Islamic states, but even secular Muslim ones were to be regarded as infidel states to be overthrown by violence. Another Egyptian, Abt al-Salam Faraj, subsequently extended Qutb's doctrine. Faraj insisted that jihad is not subject to codified Islamic legal restraints—for example, prohibiting the killing of non-combatants— and that it does not require a *fatwa*, or religious ruling affirming approval by Muslim authorities. Moreover, for Faraj, according to sociologist Charles Seligman, jihad is no longer simply a series of battles between soldiers; it can draw on "deception and deceit, surprise attacks, trickery and large scale violence."[16]

Available evidence suggests that Egyptian Islamicists Qutb and Faraj were central figures in the broad movement that constructed a radicalized theology of jihad, and that a key conduit of these ideas to Al Qa'ida was Ayman al-Zawahiri, a doctor who participated in the Egyptian movement and later became a close associate of Osama bin Laden.[17] Congruent with the formulation of Faraj, jihad in bin Laden's movement became a doctrine of war, in which both killing the enemy and being willing to die oneself are religious duties that receive divine blessing. As a jihad commander in the mountains of Pakistan reportedly said, "We prefer to die in honor than live in humiliation."[18]

In essence, bin Laden's movement seeks a postapocalyptic restoration of the Islamic caliphate, untainted by secular rule or external hegemony. The path to that restoration requires a holy war. Whereas previously, Islamic fundamentalists had directed their hostilities toward the "nearest enemy," namely, insufficiently Islamic states that govern territories where Muslims live, bin Laden reversed the hierarchy of enemies by asserting that "if the United States is beheaded, the Arab Kingdoms will wither away."[19] In this formulation, jihad is no longer "contained" within nationalist struggles. It becomes oriented to an epochal redirection of world history. This sacred struggle, however, is simultaneously a strategic one, directed against "the Crusaders"—the Christian West, with the United States as the foremost representative of its hegemony in Muslim states. The transcendent character of the struggle is evidenced by a young Pakistani's comment, "Jihad will continue until doomsday, or until America is defeated, either way."[20]

Al Qa'ida's *ideology* is clearly apocalyptic. Yet questions remain as to whether the group's *organization* and *actions* are specifically apocalyptic, and in turn, whether any specifically apocalyptic characteristics would matter in its struggle against the United States and the West. The temporal structure of apocalyptic ideology promises transcendence to eternity through victory. But the temporal structure of action by the "apocalyptic warring sect" takes a different form, "of an imminent and decisive Manichean battle between the forces of good and evil." As I wrote in 1978,

> the sectarian mission involves a struggle with opposing forces in historical time. A band of true believers, who become certified as charismatic warriors through a process of rebirth, act alone or in concert with a wider underground network of sympathizers and similar bands. These warriors engage in the moment-to-moment coordination of guerilla-style action in pursuit of strategic, symbolic, and terrorist missions. The members of the sect come out of the

quiescent masses to act in historical significance far out of proportion to their actual numbers. . . . [T]he successful execution of actions related to missions and contingency plans depends on interpersonal trust, the development of high proficiency at various technical and strategic skills, and acts of commitment and bravery which place mission ahead of personal survival.[21]

In October 2001, Harvard professor Michael Ignatieff described the perpetrators of the 9/11 attacks in similar terms:

> What we are up against is *apocalyptic nihilism.* The nihilism of their means—the indifference to human costs—takes their actions not only out of the realm of politics, but even out of the realm of war itself. The apocalyptic nature of their goals makes it absurd to believe they are making political demands at all. They are seeking the violent transformation of an irremediably sinful and unjust world. Terror does not express a politics, but a metaphysics, a desire to give ultimate meaning to time and history through ever-escalating acts of violence which culminate in a final battle between good and evil.[22]

Professor Ignatieff's comment overreaches in one sense: even if apocalyptic war is a metaphysical construct, myths can mobilize people to acts of violence that have strategic ends.

In the case at hand, apocalyptic war is unconventional war not just because it involves a struggle that pits police and intelligence operatives against underground cells. Rather, the strategies of conflict mounted by Al Qa'ida target the established global order itself, manifestly in the destruction of the World Trade Center, but also against the postmodern simulacratic construction of the world as a tourist destination, generalized source of entertainment, and available domain for the spread of Western culture—from Christian missions to McDonald's. The struggle of Al Qa'ida not only exceeds conventional political violence (to recall Tilly's definition of terrorism), it positions terror as a technique in civilizational struggle. In the early twentieth century, Georges Sorel argued that violence—as a challenge to the ideological construction of the established order—nurtures the myth that change is possible.[23] While the *goal* may be unreachable, *having* the goal can be consequential. Put differently, apocalyptic "religious" violence may be simultaneously strategic and sacredly symbolic.[24]

Yet the religious yoke of apocalyptic war typically wears lightly. As Max Weber observed concerning warriors for the faith—from Muslims and Crusaders to Sikhs and Japanese Buddhists—"even the formal orthodoxy of all these warrior religionists was often of dubious genuineness."[25] Participants in a holy war will be a diverse lot, varying in their religious sophistication and commitment. The sources of jihad as a doctrine among alienated religious thinkers and members of Arab professional classes show that the movement did not originate among the poor, the ignorant, or the dispossessed. Still, like medieval Christian crusaders, Al Qa'ida's frontline operatives participate in a struggle infused with religious meaning without being saints themselves. In these terms, Al Qa'ida is not untypical among warring sects.[26]

Yet what leverage does analyzing Al Qa'ida as an apocalyptic sect yield? After all, military strategy substantially depends on the assets and vulnerabilities of parties to a conflict. For terrorism in general, maneuvers are dictated by the realities of a conflict in which one party is comprised of an underground network of operatives. In the case at hand, they do not depend on whether Al Qa'ida approximates the warring sect as an ideal type. Rather, strategic time is the constitutive temporal organization of all kinds of conflict. Thus, there are fluid theoretical lines of transition between the warring sect as a type and warring cadres more generally. Yet the theoretical distinctions about warring sects do throw into relief two features relevant to understanding Al Qa'ida—internal organization and external context.

Organizational Structure

In the early months after 9/11, the U.S. government was at pains to demonstrate that responsibility for the attacks did not rest with the nineteen hijackers alone, or even with their immediate handlers. In effect, designating the responsible organization as Al Qa'ida warranted a war against it, and implicated any individual or group associated with it, or providing financial support—including nation-states giving safe harbor to its members—as a party to the larger struggle. Yet these legal and political rationales do not provide an adequate basis for understanding Al Qa'ida as an organization.

There can be no doubt about the degree to which terrorist actions as complex as those of 9/11 are tightly organized and coordinated, but both the strategy of operating underground and the demands of terrorist operations require a *decentralized* and *disaggregated* organization open to reconstitution, rather than a tightly integrated top-down organization. These general features of the apocalyptic sect characterize both the funding as well as the structure of Al Qa'ida. Although its financing remains incompletely understood, Al Qa'ida evidently engages in the "spoils communism" common to warring sects, but elevated to a global level. The sources of funds are said to range from Osama bin Laden's personal wealth and business operations to support from Saudi princes and other wealthy Muslims, Muslim mosques and charities, and, perhaps, profits from heroin trafficking. Resources flow to the network through diverse channels, often disguised as to their nature and address.[27]

As for organization, Al Qa'ida was forged out of alliances between a number of previously existing organizations, it is loosely connected with a wider network of groups and cells, and its form has continued to undergo transformation as conditions change. The list of signatories to the 1998 "International Islamic Front for Jihad on the Jews and Crusaders" numbers jihad groups in 21 countries, from Bosnia and Croatia to the Philippines.[28] The alliance is extensive in its reach, and it operates on an unprecedented global scale. Al Qa'ida enjoyed a physical sanctuary in Afghanistan as long as the Taliban ruled, but the training programs there created something of a jihadist diaspora, spreading operatives literally into every continent and region of the world.

Depiction of the network as centralized in command structure would not well capture either the independent cell structure common to warring sects or the complexities of how the 9/11 attacks were undertaken.[29] Nor does it adequately take into account the degree to which success of actions depends on commitment to mission rather than authority as a basis of co-ordination. In the aftermath of 9/11, the counterterrorist efforts of the U.S. and its allies have taken their toll on Al Qa'ida and they have forced jihadist cells (further) underground. Still, there has been a continuing stream of terrorist actions both strongly and weakly associated with Al Qa'ida, including bombings, military attacks and skirmishes, and assassinations of both governmental and other Westerners. Beyond these concrete acts, pre-emptive arrests in the U.S. suggest the existence of "sleeper cells" already established there. These developments demonstrate that jihad has not been shut down. Rather, quasi-independent cells and autonomous groups have continued to coordinate with one another, apparently sometimes on the basis of witnessing public acts and statements, rather than direct communi-cation.[30] Like warring sects more widely, Al Qa'ida has operatives and allies capable of playing off the actions of one another.

Countercultural Milieu

What may be called the wider countercultural milieu of militant Islam fur-ther differentiates Al Qa'ida from conventional military organizations, as well as terrorist organizations that lack a strong apocalyptic ideology. Con-ventional military organizations typically receive the patriotic support of their own homeland, but the boundaries between the military and other social actors are clearly demarcated. Terrorist organizations lacking legiti-macy among a wider populace may coerce cooperation by individuals and groups in the territory where they operate, but once again, the boundaries between the terrorists and others are distinct.

By contrast, participants in an apocalyptic warring sect are the most highly committed people in a countercultural social milieu that offers both direct infrastructural support and the indirect "moral" support of a much wider population who find themselves sympathetic to the sect's ideology. Sometimes, a state can pin down and eliminate an isolated terrorist organization, but the warring sect with broad countercultural support is much more difficult to repress. In these terms, Al Qa'ida is clearly not a maverick terrorist organization, isolated from any wider public. What is most unsettling for the so-called war on terrorism is that the group is intricately connected with a complex network of other militant Islamic organizations, Islamic schools, and Muslim patrons. Beyond these relatively tangible networks, Al Qa'ida enjoys extensive support within a much broader Islamicist "apocalyptic" counterculture.[31]

Apocalyptic War and the Established Social Order

For an apocalyptic thesis to add anything to a more conventional analysis of resources and strategies in conflict, the distinctive features of apocalyptic war must make a difference for the nature of a conflict and its trajectory. Although the two distinctive features of warring sects that I have identified—decentralized organization and connection to a wider counterculture—could simply be empirically noted, the apocalyptic analysis locates these features within an encompassing "sociologic." Decentralization and countercultural support are not independent features: they tend to reinforce one another.

Apocalyptic war does not unfold as a one-sided series of terrorist actions. Rather, it is an *interactive* process. Thus, Hall, Schuyler, and Trinh observed, "States face a delicate situation: they are duty bound to control the acts of strategic apocalyptic war, but to the degree that they do so, they become apocalyptic actors themselves. The problem that states confront is how to act strategically without feeding images of the state as an actor in an apocalyptic drama."[32] The possibilities can be charted between two poles. In the *asymmetric* case, the central interaction occurs between an apocalyptic sect and the security forces of an established social order. Here, the sect points to actions by agents of the dominant social order to justify its own acts, and when the established order responds with force, the sect seizes upon this response to legitimate its claim among a wider countercultural audience to indeed be the vessel of God in a holy struggle against evil. By contrast, in *symmetric* apocalyptic war, both parties are able to assert roughly equivalent claims of legitimacy, typically operating out of different territorial strongholds. The very boundaries of state-like monopolies on power are thus at stake in symmetric apocalyptic war.

The military and diplomatic mobilization initiated by the United States against Al Qa'ida has been enormous. Yet it may not bring success against an apocalyptically oriented opponent. Both organizational decentralization and countercultural support make the military goal of defeating Al Qa'ida extremely difficult, so difficult as to have led strategic planners to question whether this goal is an adequate basis for responding to Al Qa'ida. Given decentralization, conventional military action against terrorists cannot achieve victory on the battlefield, and so the U.S. and its allies have developed a distinctive antiterrorist strategy. This strategy operates on multiple fronts that are relatively distant from Al Qa'ida itself—tightening security, controlling immigration, and aggressively gathering and filtering intelligence. At the core of the strategy is a combination of police-like work to apprehend network participants and interrogate them under military conditions, and in turn use this intelligence to hunt down additional network participants, capturing them if possible, but targeting them for remote assassination (for example, by unmanned missile-firing Predator aircraft) if direct capture is deemed unfeasible. Beyond the immediate strategy lies a longer-term goal—of discrediting terrorism as a *modus operandi*. Yet what this goal entails remains unclear.[33]

In the campaign against Islamicist jihad, the U.S. and its allies face the dilemma of how to deal with warring sectarians without mobilizing *other* Muslims to take up their cause, and without destabilizing other governments—such as Pakistan, Iraq, the Philippines, and Morocco through military initiatives that, in the eyes of some Muslims, confirm the validity of Osama bin Laden's brief against Western hegemony. The key question about any strategy adopted by the allies concerns whether its successes at decimating networks of cells associated with Al Qa'ida produce the unintended consequence of fueling and hardening support for the apocalyptic struggle among the sects' sympathizers. During the initial effort against Al Qa'ida, the U.S. steered clear of using Pakistan as a platform for invasion and defeat of the Taliban. But subsequent actions, and the doctrine of preemptive strike that undergirds them, put the U.S. at risk of radicalizing Muslims who might otherwise reject jihad.[34]

The allies have dented the capacity of Al Qa'ida to operate effectively. But to date, they have not contained jihad. It is worth noting that the warring sect does not pursue an unfolding series of actions, but instead seeks to mount effective actions at strategic moments. A period of relative quiescence thus may not mean much. So long as ideological commitment is sustained, a sect can continue to conduct devastating operations even under extremely compromised conditions. 9/11 itself was undertaken by a small number of operatives, 19 men directly, and the cost of the attacks, variously estimated at less than $500,000, is minuscule compared to the resources estimated to be at the disposal of militant Islamicist organizations.[35]

The German analyst Carl von Clausewitz once famously described war as "the pursuit of politics by other means." Implicit in this definition is the idea that war can be won. Once the probabilities of victory become remote and the costs of continued war insupportable, rational strategists will seek political solutions to end war. Politics is a game of strategy, bluff, and compromise. With war as extreme politics, peace is possible.

Is apocalyptic war different? The alternatives depicted by Michael Ignatieff are stark: total victory or death. Yet, as Mark Juergensmeyer describes what he calls "cosmic war," victory would be hard to define, since the goals of religious terrorists are often murky, grandiose, or both. Given the totalistic revolutionary visions that animate the apocalyptic warring sect, defeat would be unthinkable, yet conversely, their chances of any final "victory" in any concrete historical sense seem slim to nonexistent.[36] With the jihad announced by Al Qa'ida, victory would amount to nothing less than a reordering of the global geopolitical order, by the elimination of Western—and especially U.S.—hegemony directly or by proxy in lands that the jihadists deem Islamic. Yet precisely the remoteness of this goal—and indeed, the Western refusal to countenance it as an issue—enhances the sanctity of the goal for those drawn to the Islamicist cause.

In turn, there is reason to wonder whether the agenda of the established order does not *itself* bear features of a holy war. Indeed, a smattering of public figures suggest that Americans *ought* to see the conflict in these terms.[37] In the early days after September 11, George W. Bush formulated his announced war against terrorism as a "crusade." The Afghan military operation was initially named "Infinite Justice." The U.S. administration quickly backed away from these narrative formulations. However, in early 2002, President Bush sought to define a more encompassing and coherent enemy than the liminal and difficult to defeat Qa'ida network. To do so, he designated an "axis of evil" that included Iraq, Iran, and North Korea—nation-states historically hostile to or disconnected from one another that nevertheless fit a U.S. policy category of posing a threat to the hegemony of the prevailing global order. Bush thus invoked an encompassing historical struggle between good and evil, the forces of light and the forces of darkness.[38] Of course, the U.S. also has formulated its agenda in other terms, and the degree to which this particular ideological frame drives U.S. action is an open—and at present historically open-ended—question. Yet the structure of the ideology is unmistakable: it is itself apocalyptic.

Invoking a "holy war" at all is a tack fraught with difficulties, for it frames conflict in terms that mirror those of Al Qa'ida. In effect, insofar as the U.S. and its allies let the conflict become defined by Al Qa'ida as an apocalyptic one, they aid Al Qa'ida in its efforts among its Muslim audience to legitimize its struggle as a holy war. When rhetoric—and even more, events on the ground—reconstruct the conflict in these terms, in the Islamic world, it increasingly becomes viewed as a *symmetric* one between *two* apocalyptic parties—each claiming good, righteousness, and God on its side—rather than a conflict between a global order in which Muslims share a stake versus a fringe Islamicist movement whose acts of terror will be rejected as illegitimate by most Muslims. In other words, the conflict of civilizations that Samuel Huntington proclaimed is not simply an empirical description: its validity hinges on whether the forces of Islamic jihad are able to sustain the legitimacy of their struggle among Muslims at large.[39]

Muslim societies face basic alternatives, either finding pathways toward a version of modernism that somehow accommodates Islam to secular institutions, or reasserting Islam as the crucible that will envelop the social order, including its modernized features. Certainly the West is not in a position to force that choice. But sentiments in the Muslim world will be affected by Western policies—from strategies of fighting terrorism, to dealing with the Palestinian-Israeli debacle, to war with Iraq, to political alliances with client regimes, to repression of Islamic parties in politics. The problem, as starkly posed by Michael Ignatieff, is whether the United States will begin to look in the Muslim world the way Louis XVI looked in France in 1789.[40]

The construction of the struggle as a *symmetric* apocalyptic war would place opponents of terrorism in a position remarkably similar to that of the jihadists themselves. Each side becomes party to a crusade, whether explicitly declared, as with Al Qa'ida, or more ambiguously invoked, as with the Bush administration.[41] The implications of this construction become evident if we recall Juergensmeyer's account of the prospects for those who undertake a cosmic war: defeat is unthinkable, yet conversely, victory in any concrete historical sense is extremely unlikely. A holy war, by whatever name, would replace the Cold War against the "Evil Empire" (as Ronald Reagan called the Soviet Union) to become the reigning transcendent meaning of history. For the West, this trajectory unveils an Orwellian prospect: jihad and the war against it fuel one another in ways that substantially alter the social fabric of modernity, eroding civil liberties, consolidating an international security state and a culture of surveillance, providing fertile ground for a re-emergent "secular fundamentalism" of patriotic nationalism, and yielding a new focus for what Richard Hofstadter famously called "the paranoid style in American politics"—directed at the Muslim Other.[42]

Globally, the project of fighting a posited "axis of evil" promotes a militarized climate rather than fostering conditions for pursuit of any positive agenda directed toward political stability, social and economic development, and dealing with the pressing global problems of poverty, disease, and ecological degradation. To the extent that the struggle against terrorism becomes a *cause célèbre* that the U.S. promotes as the dominant axis of international relations, it distracts states and NGOs from any agenda that would work to resolve serious world problems on other than a military basis.

Beyond the Apocalypse

Terrorism is nothing new. But in the postmodern circumstance, what was once "propaganda of the deed" undertaken by lone individuals and "primitive rebels" has fused simultaneously with long-available religious ideologies of apocalyptic war and emergent technological and scientific possibilities of mayhem. In the latter twentieth century, a series of religious sects—from Peoples Temple to Aum Shinrikyō to Falun Gong—demonstrated anew that sects are capable of engaging states in struggles of historical significance. Now, the attacks of September 11 and the response of the U.S. and its (nervous) allies potentially elevate apocalyptic war to a global scale.

However, the challenge for the forces that embrace the Enlightenment vision (if not its spotty record of actualization to date[43]) is not how to "win" an apocalyptic war. Such wars are not readily winnable. Rather, the challenge is to move the historical moment *beyond* the time of apocalyptic war, beyond the cycle of violence in which apocalyptic warriors point toward attacks by the U.S. as vindication of the righteousness of their own cause.

One commander in the Hezbul Mujahadeen, Kiramat Ullah, was quoted soon after 9/11 as saying, "We would be very happy if America attacked Afghanistan, because now all Muslims are divided. If America attacked, it would unite the Muslim world."[44] Like most utopian visions, the goal of a united Islam has a grandiose flair. Although the apocalyptic wish for a counterattack was fulfilled, it did not unite the Muslim world. But the geopolitical agenda pursued by the U.S. and its allies seems to have further radicalized segments of the Muslim population already predisposed toward the apocalyptic view—across the Islamic world from North Africa to Indonesia, and in other societies around the globe.[45] As of this writing (October 2003), this apocalyptic view continues to be reinforced by events. The U.S. strategy, in one private intelligence assessment, is heavily weighted toward a relentless gathering of intelligence and overwhelming use of force. The calculation must be that the U.S. cannot worry about whether its actions tend to legitimate the Islamicist view that the U.S. is a "crusader" state. In this calculation, overwhelming military force is supposed to "render perception immaterial."[46]

Whatever the prospects of eliminating terrorist organizations militarily, an apocalyptic analysis suggests that the U.S. faces a much more formidable task. A holy war cannot be won just through intelligence, military and police action, and efforts to eliminate the financial resources of the enemy networks. In addition, and more centrally, countering jihad means undermining its utopian appeal to wider Muslim audiences. To date, there are reasonable grounds to wonder whether even more Muslims have been radicalized. Reversing this development would require far more fundamental policy shifts toward the Middle East and Islam than have been seen to date.

The most contentious debates in the wake of 9/11 centered on whether quasi-imperialist actions by the West, and specifically, the United States, somehow "caused" the attacks.[47] But this formulation is too crude in the extreme: it asks the wrong question. Rather, the issue is whether long-term policies of the West helped foster (or failed to undermine) a political and social climate in the Islamic world where jihad could gain such wide appeal. In its global extension, the West has had two principles—capitalism and democracy—that have sometimes seemed incompatible. In many situations, democracy has been compromised in favor of access to markets tied to regimes that lack political legitimacy among their populations. The consequences are unfortunate. As Charles Tilly has argued, when foreign powers prop up an authoritarian regime through military and economic aid, this support obviates the necessity of that regime to bargain with its constituency.[48] Obviously, jihadists do not embrace a Western vision of democracy. The point is this: Western lack of commitment to the construction of political and economic institutions that can claim broad legitimacy in states with large Muslim populations creates conditions favorable to apocalyptic readings of history. Yet the West stands to lose a great deal if such readings become widespread. The Cold War was sustained for four decades even in the absence of deep religious meanings. By comparison, apocalyptic war is far more intractable. Crusades operate in the *moyen durée*, not *le temps court*, of history. An apocalyptic war cannot be won. Strategies to win such a war are more likely to fuel it. The goal, instead, must be to act outside of, and thus move beyond, the end of apocalyptic history. How to do so is the world-historical challenge at the beginning of the twenty-first century.

Notes

1. The research for this essay was supported in part by a University of California–Davis Faculty Research Grant. Earlier versions of the paper were presented at the Institute for Governmental Affairs, UC Davis, 10 October 2001; the Conference on Religions and Violence, Canadian Ministry of Foreign Affairs, in cooperation with the University of California Institute for Global Conflict and Cooperation, Ottawa, Canada, 5 April 2002; and the Center for Comparative Social Analysis Workshop, University of California–Los Angeles, 30 January 2003. I am grateful to these audiences and to Penney Alldredge, Janet C. Broome, and Kelvin L. White for their comments and suggestions, and I especially thank Penney Alldredge for invaluable research assistance.

2. Margaret Somers, "Deconstructing and reconstructing class formation theory: narrativity, relational analysis, and social theory," in *Reworking Class*, ed. John R. Hall (Ithaca, NY: Cornell University Press, 1997), 73–105; John R. Hall, with Philip D. Schuyler and Sylvaine Trinh, *Apocalypse Observed: Religious Violence in North America, Europe, and Japan* (London: Routledge, 2000), chap. 2.

3. Karl Mannheim, *Ideology and Utopia* (New York: Harcourt, Brace, and World, 1937).

4. Ibid.; John R. Hall, *The Ways Out: Utopian Communal Groups in an Age of Babylon* (London: Routledge & Kegan Paul, 1978).

5. Hall, Schuyler, and Trinh, *Apocalypse Observed.*

6. Georg Simmel, *The Sociology of Georg Simmel* (New York: Free Press, 1950), 22. On continuities between sectarian and political terrorism, see Hall, Schuyler, and Trinh, *Apocalypse Observed*, 200.

7. Walter Benjamin, "Theses on the philosophy of history," 153–64 in *Illuminations* (New York: Harcourt, Brace, and World 1968 [1940]), 263.

8. Hall, Schuyler, and Trinh, *Apocalypse Observed*, chap. 1.

9. On socially constructed temporalities of history, see John R. Hall, "The time of history and the history of times," *History and Theory* 19 (1980): 113–131.

10. Anticipation has long been a stock-in-trade of conversionist salvation sects predicting "the end of the world," and escape has historically been associated with the formation of one or another "post-apocalyptic" utopian communal movement that seeks to transcend historical time, as it were, by establishing a timeless tableau of heaven that is metaphorically located *after* the apocalypse; Hall, *The Ways Out*, 206 and Chap. 3. Groups bearing a post-apocalyptic ideology are enhanced in their capacity to sustain the commitment of participants; see John R. Hall, "Social organization and pathways of commitment: types of communal groups, rational choice theory, and the Kanter thesis," *American Sociological Review* 53 (1988): 679–92.

11. Charles Tilly, "Terror, Terrorism, Terrorists," *Sociological Theory* (forthcoming, 2003). A more conventional definition, pointing to violence by nonstate actors targeting noncombatants in order to instill fear, approximates the U.S. statutory one used in compiling statistics; see Paul R. Pillar, *Terrorism and U.S. Foreign Policy* (Washington, D.C.: Brookings Institute Press, 2001), 13. On Osama bin Laden as something else than a "mere terrorist," see T.L. Friedman, "No mere terrorist," *New York Times* [hereafter *NYT*], 24 March 2002. On the unconventional character of apocalyptic religiosity, see Hall, *The Ways Out*, 7.

12. Max Weber, "The Social Psychology of the World Religions," in *From Max Weber: Essays in Sociology*, eds. H. H. Gerth and C. Wright Mills (New York: Oxford University Press, 1946 [1919]), 276–77.

13. Max Weber, *Economy and Society*, Guenther Roth and Claus Wittich, eds. (Berkeley: University of California Press, 1978), 473–74. The degree to which Islamic doctrines of the Koran and *Hadith* (interpretive traditions) actually protected communities of Jews and Christians (*ahl al-dhimma*) in practice has been historically variable, as have been interpretations of the theology itself.

14. Jeff Goodwin, "The empire strikes back: the geopolitical roots of 9/11," lecture, UC Davis Center for History, Society, and Culture, Davis, California, 12 November 2002.

15. J. Lelyveld, "All suicide bombers are not alike," *NYT*, 28 October 2001, explores the debate concerning jihad.

16. Charles Seligman, "Religious visions and sacred terror: the case of Islam," paper presented at the annual meetings of the Society for the Scientific Study of Religion, Salt Lake City, Utah, November 2002, 14.

17. On Zawahiri and his connection to both Qutb and bin Laden, see N. MacFarquhar, "Islamic jihad, forged in Egypt, is seen as bin Laden's backbone," *NYT*, 4 October 2001; Lawrence Wright, "The man behind bin Laden," *The New Yorker*, 16 September 2002, 56–85.

18. Quoted in J.F. Burns, "Americans battling closer to Qaeda bunkers," *NYT*, 6 March 2002.

19. Anonymous, *Through Our Enemies' Eyes: Osama bin Laden, Radical Islam, and the Future of America* (Washington, D.C.: Brassey's, 2002), 48–49; "Anonymous," who wrote a "primer for civil servants" about Al Qa'ida (xiii), is well connected to U.S. government circles.

20. Anonymous, *Through Our Enemies' Eyes*, Chapter 4, offers a detailed discussion of Al Qa'ida ideology; see also J. Miller, "A nation challenged," *NYT*, 9 October 2001. Consistent with this ideology, in 2003, bin Laden called for jihad in opposition to the U.S.-led war

against Iraq, despite the fact that Saddam Hussein is a secular ruler of a Muslim country; Neil MacFarquhar, "Tape attributed to bin Laden urges Muslims to stand with Iraq," *NYT*, 12 February 2003, A16. Pakistani quoted in J.F. Burns, "Bin Laden stirs struggle on meaning of jihad," *NYT*, 27 January 2002.

21. Hall, *The Ways Out*, 206–7.
22. Michael Ignatieff, "On the brink of war: it's war—but it doesn't have to be dirty," *The Guardian* [London], 1 October 2001.
23. Georges Sorel, *Reflections on Violence* (New York: Collier, 1961 [1921]).
24. John R. Hall, "Religion and Violence: Social Processes in Comparative Perspective," in *Handbook for the Sociology of Religion*, ed. Michele Dillon (Cambridge, U.K.: Cambridge University Press, 2003), 359–81.
25. Weber, *Economy and Society*, 475.
26. What is notable about participants in such groups is the *metanoia*, or what Black Panther Huey Newton dubbed "revolutionary suicide"—the metaphoric social death of the individual, who sheds a previous identity enmeshed in everyday life to be reborn to a struggle in which physical death is accepted as virtually inevitable, and certainly preferable to the dishonor of defeat; see Hall, *Gone From the Promised Land* (New Brunswick, NJ: Transaction, 1987), 135–36. On the culture of martyrdom among Muslims, see J. Lelyveld, "All suicide bombers are not alike."
27. Anonymous, *Through Our Enemies' Eyes*, Chap. 3; William F. Wechsler and Lee S. Wolosky, co-directors, Independent Task Force, "Terrorist financing" (New York: Council on Foreign Relations, 2002).
28. Wright, "The man behind bin Laden," 81.
29. Among the many analyses of the planning and execution of the 9/11 attacks, see especially Judith Miller and Don Van Natta, Jr., "In years of plots and clues, scope of Qaeda eluded U.S.," *NYT*, 9 June 2002; Douglas Frantz with Desmond Butler, "Sept. 11 attack planned in '99, Germans learn," *NYT*, 30 August 2002; Richard Bernstein, with Douglas Frantz, Don Van Natta, Jr., and David Johnston, "On path to the U.S. skies, plot leader met bin Laden," *NYT*, 10 September 2002; and James Risen and David Johnston, "F.B.I. account outlines activities of highjackers before 9/11 attacks," *NYT*, 27 September 2002. On post-9/11 shifts toward even greater decentralization, see John Diamond and Kevin Johnson, "Al-Qaeda considered as dangerous as before 9/11," *USA Today*, 1 November 2002, and Peter L. Bergen, "Al Qaeda's new tactics," *NYT*, 15 November 2002. Despite the strategic advantages of independent-cell organizations, even they are vulnerable: Wright, "The man behind bin Laden," 78, notes that the Egyptian Islamic Jihad's "blind-cell" structure was compromised in 1993, when Egyptian authorities arrested the group's membership director, who possessed a computer with a membership database.
30. *NYT*, 15 June 2002, 1. On sleeper cells as a fifth column, see R.G. Powers, "The evil that lurks in the enemy within," *NYT*, 16 June 2002.
31. Countercultures, of course, can manifest varying degrees of tension with mainstream society and the state. Charles Kurzman, "Bin Laden and other thoroughly modern Muslims," *Contexts* (Fall/Winter 2002), cites a Gallup Poll suggesting that 15 per cent of Muslims regarded the 9/11 attacks as morally justified. In terms of democratic politics, this would be a small percentage. Nevertheless, numerically, it would include millions of people. The taking of such a position, unthinkable in the West, is a gauge of countercultural alienation among a substantial segment of the Muslim population.
32. Hall, Schuyler, and Trinh, *Apocalypse Observed*, 200.
33. David Johnston and David E. Sanger, "Yemen killing based on rules set out by Bush," *NYT*, 6 November 2002; Seymour Hersh, "Manhunt: the Bush administration's new strategy in the war on terrorism," *The New Yorker*, 23 and 30 December 2002, 66–74. On the long-term strategy, see Eric Schmitt, "Pentagon draws up a 20-to-30 year antiterror plan," *NYT*, 17 January 2003; Schmitt speculates that meeting the long-term goal would require "addressing the economic or political conditions that foster terrorist activities," but he does not quote any source on this point.
34. The doctrine of preemptive action has multiple sources, but its most recent assertion, prior to the Bush administration policy (*NYT*, 17 June, 20 July 2002), came from the Israeli government, initially in its dealings with millennialist Christians; see Hall, Schuyler, and Trinh, *Apocalypse Observed*, 201.

35. Anonymous, *Through Our Enemies' Eyes*, 31.

36. Mark Juergensmeyer, *Terror in the Mind of God: The Global Rise of Religious Violence* (Berkeley: University of California Press, 2000), 162.

37. Thus, conservative commentator Daniel Pipes, in *Militant Islam Reaches America* (New York: Norton, 2002), warns Americans of the need to awaken to a struggle that extends beyond Al Qa'ida to Islamicists more generally. American Christian public figures such as Jerry Falwell and Franklin Graham have depicted Islam as militant at its core, and even "evil"; see Michael Wilson, "Evangelist says Muslims haven't adequately apologized for Sept. 11 attacks," *NYT*, 15 August 2002.

38. A detailed discussion of the symmetric dualisms of bin Laden and Bush is provided by Bruce Lincoln, *Holy Terrors: Thinking about Religion after September 11* (Chicago: University of Chicago Press, 2003), Chap. 2.

39. Samuel Huntington, *The Clash of Civilizations and the Remaking of World Order* (New York: Simon and Schuster, 1996).

40. Writing before 9/11, the scholar of the Islamic and Arab worlds, Bernard Lewis, already described the basic alternatives in *What Went Wrong? Western Impact and Middle Eastern Response* (New York: Oxford University Press, 2001). The dilemma that moderate Muslims face when the civilizational divide is exacerbated is described by Khaled Abou El Fadl, "Moderate Muslims under siege," *NYT*, 1 July 2001. On the issues posed for the West, see especially Rohan Gunaratna, *Inside Al Qaeda: Global Network of Terror* (New York: Columbia University Press, 2002), and Michael Ignatieff, "Is the human rights era ending?" *NYT*, 5 February 2002.

41. Lincoln, *Holy Terrors*, 32.

42. Richard Hofstadter, *The Paranoid Style in American Politics* (New York: Knopf, 1965).

43. On the Enlightenment and contemporary social formations and politics, see Peter Wagner, *A Sociology of Modernity: Liberty and Discipline* (London: Routledge, 1994), and Thomas de Zengotita, "Common ground: finding our way back to the Enlightenment," *Harper's*, January 2003, 35–44.

44. *NYT*, 7 October 2001.

45. The play of that struggle is open to debate. Some observers, such as Judith Miller ("Naming the evildoers," *NYT Book Review*, 29 September 2002) and Charles Kurzman (in "Bin Laden and other thoroughly modern Muslims," *Contexts* [Fall/Winter 2002]) argue that militant Islam has crested in its appeal. But the "Arab Human Development Report 2002" warns of intellectual stagnation in Arab society; see Barbara Crossette, "Study warns of stagnation in Arab societies," *NYT*, 2 July 2002. And recent analyses suggest that under democratic elections, Islamicist parties have been gaining power not only in Pakistan and Turkey, but also in Bahrain and Morocco; see Neil MacFarquhar, "War and politics: Islamists gain votes as U.S. acts," *NYT*, 6 November 2002. Similarly, survey research conducted in 2002 in certain countries with majority Muslim populations—Egypt, Jordan, Indonesia, Lebanon, Turkey, and Senegal—reveals opposition to the U.S.-led war against terrorism among majorities of the populations; see Adam Clymer, "World survey says negative views of U.S. are rising," *NYT*, 5 December 2002.

46. STRATFOR, "Emerging Bush doctrine reshaping U.S. strategy," http://www.stratfor.com/standard/analysis_view.php?ID=203273 (accessed 25 February 2002).

47. Notably, Edward Rothstein challenged postmodern relativism in the early months after 9/11 in his essay, "Attacks on U.S. challenge the perspectives of postmodern true believers," *NYT*, 22 September 2001, A17. Later, he depicted unnamed "international commentators and American intellectuals" as arguing that "terrorism is caused by social and economic injustice"; Rothstein, "Cherished ideas refracted in history's lens," *NYT*, 7 September 2002. For a retort, see Stanley Fish, "Postmodern warfare: the ignorance of our warrior intellectuals," *Harper's*, July 2002, 33–40.

48. Charles Tilly, *Coercion, Capital, and European States, A.D. 990–1990* (Cambridge, MA: Blackwell, 1990).

CHAPTER 19

Establishments and Sects in the Islamic World*

MARK SEDGWICK

According to Islamic tradition, the Prophet Muhammad predicted that, just as the Jews and Christians had, the Muslims would split into a number of *firqas* (sects).[1] This prediction is reported in various versions, usually giving the number of sects into which Islam would divide as seventy-three, and usually consigning all save one to the fires of hell.[2] Since this prediction, various Muslim writers have compiled accounts of sects, sometimes called heresiographies by Western scholars.[3] The earliest known such work dates from the ninth century A.D.; Islamic heresiogra-

*This article is a revised version of my "Sects in the Islamic World," which appeared in *Nova Religio* 3 (2000), 195–240, and was based on a paper, "New Religious Movements in the Muslim World," given at the Twelfth International Congress of CESNUR (the Center for Studies on New Religions), held in Turin (Italy), 10–12 September 1998. I have made two main types of change to the original "Sects in the Islamic World." Firstly, my revisions take account of comments on my original article made by Jeff Kenney, William Shepard, and Amira Sonbol in *Nova Religio* 6 (2002): 137–64; my response to those comments, "Sects and Politics," was published in the same volume of *Nova Religio*, 165–73. Secondly, I have shortened the article. I have added discussion of Al Qa'ida, but removed discussion of several other sects, as well as discussion of the relationship between sects and the public authorities, and discussion of the persecution of what this article terms "post-Muhammadan denominations."

I would like to thank: Eileen Barker for introducing me to the most useful concept of "denominationalization," which led to the evolution of the original paper into an article; the peer reviewers of "Sects in the Islamic World" (especially Jeff Kenney); and William Shepard, whose "'Denomination' as a Label for Some Islamic Phenomena?" (*Nova Religio* 6: 155–64) is the source of the key concept of "establishment" used in this article.

phies in more or less the classic format continue to appear today, and examples can also be found on the Internet.[4] Following the prediction of the Prophet, many Muslim heresiographers have devoted considerable ingenuity to ensuring that the sects they deal with number seventy-two (the seventy-third normally being the author's own), evidently on two mistaken assumptions: that the number seventy-three should be taken literally,[5] and that no further sects would arise after the heresiographer's own time.

In fact, new religious movements—or sects and cults—continue to arise in the Islamic world, as everywhere else. An immediate problem for their student, however, is one of definition. Although the Arabic word *firqa* is commonly translated into English as "sect," the word generally used today to translate "sect" into Arabic is not *firqa* but *ta'ifa*. Neither word really means "sect," as we will see. This is hardly surprising: exact correspondences between words in English and Arabic are far less frequent than between English and, say, French, and there are significant differences between the nature and organization of Islam and of Christianity. Despite this, this article argues that religious bodies in the Islamic world can be analyzed using the standard sociological terms and concepts already established in Western contexts, albeit with some modifications. A "standard" classification of the main types of religious bodies in the Islamic world is established below on this basis. It is hoped that this classification will in future make possible better understanding of the development over time of bodies in the Islamic world, and more productive comparisons with bodies and processes of development observed and studied elsewhere.

This article takes as its starting point a tripartite classification of religious bodies into "church," "sect," and "cult"[6] that was first established in a Western context. Few terms can be more overtly Christian than "church." This has in the past discouraged their application to Islam: although the terms "church" and "sect" were used in writing about Islam in the late nineteenth and early twentieth centuries, they generally created confusion, and have since almost wholly disappeared from serious literature on Islam.[7] In his recent *Social Dimensions of Sectarianism*, Bryan Wilson warned against applying the conclusions of observations made in one culture to another culture, emphasizing that "it is important not to project onto bodies outside the Christian ambit characteristics that are part of the cultural baggage of Christian religiosity,"[8] and Islamologists are generally careful to eschew culturally alien terms. Unless attempts are made to place Islamic phenomena within some sort of common scientific terminology, however, Islamic studies are doomed to continuing isolation.

Concepts

As long ago as 1911, Ernst Troeltsch (1865–1923) hypothesized that the sect-type/church-type division was probably a general one in monotheistic religions, and speculated that "it may well be supposed that similar phenomena occur within Islam."[9] As we will see, Troeltsch was right, at least in terms of his own definition: "If objections are raised to the terms 'Church' and 'Sect' . . . ," wrote Troeltsch, "we would then have to make the distinction between institutional churches and voluntary churches."[10] His idea of a "voluntary church" has a major problem, which was pointed out by H. Richard Niebuhr in 1929 ("by its very nature, the sectarian type of organization is valid only for one generation. The children born to the voluntary members of the first generation begin to make the sect a church"),[11] by Joachim Wach in 1947 ("it cannot be denied that people join a church and are born into a sect")[12] and again by Bryan Wilson in 1990 ("in all growing movements, there are always some new . . . members").[13] The fact that no religious body can remain entirely voluntary forever does not, however, invalidate Troeltsch's distinction between voluntarism and institutionalism. As we will see, religious bodies in the Islamic world do follow this basic distinction, as in the West.

A second basic distinction derives from a more recent observation, made in the 1980s in response to the increasing marginalization of institutional churches in the modern West. This led Rodney Stark and William Sims Bainbridge to define the sect in terms of "the degree to which a religious group is in a state of tension with its surrounding sociocultural environment,"[14] an approach with which Bryan Wilson concurs.[15]

Institutional Bodies

There is no established institutional church in Islam. Neither, however, is there an established institutional church in the United States, and the use of "denomination" to replace "church" in response to this unusual feature of American religious life is of considerable assistance in applying Troeltsch's dichotomy to the Islamic world.

"Denomination" and "church," however, are not quite the same thing. As William Shepard has pointed out, there are important differences between medieval churches that claimed universal authority and constituted the local religious "establishment," and contemporary American denominations that "generally accept their competitors as equally legitimate."[16] The main difference, though, is not so much between different types of religious bodies as between different environments. Just as there may be political pluralism or a single-party state, so there may be religious pluralism or an established religion. Just as the same political party may participate in a pluralistic system or constitute the political establishment in different environments (the obvious comparison is between the French and Soviet Communist Parties in 1975), the same religious body may be one denomination among others (such as the Roman Catholic Church in the United States today) or may constitute the religious establishment (the Roman Catholic Church in seventeenth-century Spain). An established church, then, is the religious equivalent of the ruling party in a one-party state.

Whether a party operates in a pluralistic system or monopolizes power makes a great difference to that party, but in either case it remains what political scientists would call a political party. Similarly, a denomination remains a denomination whether it constitutes the religious establishment or operates within it (though the two different environments have important implications here too). The fundamental difference is in the environment, not the party or denomination. Where there is a monopolistic religious or political system, the environment is under the control of the established church or ruling party, and all parties and denominations other than those that constitute the establishment will find themselves excluded, in a state of high tension with both their environment and the political or religious establishment—or even with both, given the tendency for religious and political authority to coalesce in monopolistic systems.

There is some sort of establishment even within a pluralistic system. Such an establishment has only minimal organization, whether the establishment be liberal democracy or monotheism (a non-pluralistic establishment, in contrast, has the organizational characteristics of the denomination or the party that constitutes it). Even in a pluralistic system, however, the possibility of tension between a denomination or party and the establishment or environment remains. In contemporary Germany, the political establishment is liberal democracy, and the religious establishment is Judeo-Christian monotheism. Non-democratic parties and polytheistic denominations are generally tolerated, but both are excluded from their respective establishments. In extreme cases, they may be rejected and persecuted, as—for example—are the Unification Church ("Moonies") and various neo-Nazi parties.[17]

In general, a religious denomination may: (1) constitute the establishment; (2) be part of a pluralistic establishment (in which case it is an "accepted denomination"); (3) be excluded by the establishment (in which case it is either an "alien denomination" or a "rejected denomination," depending on the degree of tension between it and its environment). Where a single denomination constitutes the establishment, it may exercise significant control over the general sociocultural environment. In pluralistic systems, the reverse tends to be true, with the sociocultural environment playing a central role in defining the nature of the establishment. When a denomination is rejected, it is rejected primarily by the sociocultural environment. Persecution, however, is done by an establishment.

Voluntary Bodies

In addition to voluntarism, Troeltsch identified two further characteristics of the sect: that it be organized and that it be oriented towards a "fellowship principle," that is, that the members of a sect "aim at a direct personal fellowship" unavailable in the institutional church.[18] The fellowship-principle is distinct from voluntarism. A voluntary body need not necessarily be oriented inwardly, towards direct personal fellowship. As we will see below, it may also be outward-oriented, concentrating more on its mission to those outside than on its own fellowship. Similarly, "organization" is not the same as "institutional." When Troeltsch used the word "institutional," he did not mean so much "organized as an institution" as "not voluntary; part of the established framework." A voluntary religious body may be highly organized, loosely organized, or barely organized; these possibilities are all independent of its other characteristics. For Troeltsch, degree of organization was the basis of the distinction between sect and cult. He distinguished the sect from "epidemic infections which are based upon the transference of strong passions from one person to another" and from mysticism, "a purely individualistic emphasis upon direct communion with God, which . . . in itself feels no need of fellowship." However, whilst "in itself mysticism has no fellowship-principle at all; its only idea of fellowship is intercourse between like-minded souls," "as soon as [mystics] wish to organize themselves into a community they follow the example of the sect-type."[19] To paraphrase, a cult becomes a sect when it ceases to be barely organized.

The prime characteristics of a sect, then, are: (1) its voluntary nature; (2) its orientation towards the "fellowship-principle"; (3) its coherent organization; and (4) tension between it and its sociocultural environment or between it and the local religious establishment.

Expanding slightly on the first and last of these four characteristics, Bryan Wilson identifies five "specific sociological indicia of the sect." According to Wilson, a sect: (1) is "exclusivistic" in relation to the prevailing norm; (2) "maintains a degree of tension with the world"; (3) is a voluntary body; (4) has a possibility of "discipline . . . even expulsion"; and (5) is for its members a "primary source of social identity."[20]

Two of the three "indicia" which Wilson has added are in effect articulations of voluntarism. Voluntarism implies exclusivity, and (for obvious

I.	Voluntarism
II.	Exclusivism
III.	Fellowship-principle
IV.	"Primary source of social identity"
V.	Organization
VI.	Discipline
VII.	Tension

Fig. 19.1. Specific characteristics of the sect.

reasons) expulsion from a voluntary body is easier than expulsion from an institutional body. Wilson's third new characteristic, a sect's primary role as a source of social identity, is both a result of voluntarism and tension, and a means of sustaining tension. It might in some ways be equated to commitment.

It is not clear why Wilson does not include among his "indicia" either Troeltsch's fellowship-principle or his requirement for a minimal degree of organization. Since my analysis of sects in the Islamic world indicates that both are relevant, we will add these two characteristics back to Wilson's five "indicia," making seven "specific characteristics of the sect" for use below (see Figure 19.1). The two characteristics found both in Troeltsch and in Wilson (voluntarism and tension) are by common consent the most important. They will, therefore, be the basis of the two continua which will be our principal test of sectarianism.

One possible characteristic which will not be used is that implied in the term which is coming to replace "sect" and "cult" in much scholarly usage, including the title of this volume: new religious movement or "NRM." "New" is in a sense shorthand for "voluntary and in tension," since membership of a new body can only be voluntary, and since novelty is associated with, and is sometimes a source of, tension. In the West, sects are generally new and in a state of tension with their environment, while denominations are generally older and uncontroversial. As we will see, this is not always the case in the Islamic world, where some religious bodies are in a state of tension with their environment despite being old and institutional, and where new and voluntary bodies may be uncontroversial. What matters is not novelty in itself, but voluntarism and tension. Novelty, then, will not be treated as a "specific characteristic" of the sect (though it will be used to distinguish between two forms of one particular type of sect).

Evolution

In the view of Wilson, "the evolution of religious movements—often represented as 'from sect to church'—is a social process that has suffered . . . theoretical over-generalization." Wilson is here referring primarily to "denominationalization,"[21] a concept usually ascribed to H. Richard Niebuhr's 1929 *The Social Sources of Denominationalism*. Wilson stresses that "there is . . . no normal or typical pattern of sectarian or denominational development" and comments that "Niebuhr overlooked the uniqueness of American history."[22] Wilson's warning against assuming an invariable pattern is timely, but his criticism of Niebuhr is less well founded, since Niebuhr in fact saw the highly specific environment of the American western frontier as the defining characteristic of American religious history. His central thesis is not that sects are destined to be transformed into denominations, but that "doctrines and practice change with the mutation of social structure, not vice versa." As the frontier disappeared, "the frontier sect becomes a rural church"—a rural church which continued to differ in important ways from the long-established urban churches of the East Coast, thus giving rise to the *problem* of denominationalism which caused Niebuhr to write his book in the first place.[23] I would not myself go so far as Niebuhr: more than mutation of social structure is needed to explain changes in doctrine and practice. An understanding of the implications of structures, however, is crucial to understanding changes in doctrine.

Although partly based on a misreading of Niebuhr's work,[24] the concept of "denominationalization" is well-known and useful, especially when applied to the reduction of tensions between a sect and its environment, as, for example, by Ronald Lawson in his excellent study of Seventh-day Adventist responses to the Waco siege.[25] Similar reductions of tension can frequently be observed in the history of sects in the Islamic world, as will be seen below. Movement in other directions, including from one type of sect to another, will also be observed.

Religious bodies in the Islamic world, as elsewhere, may be divided into denominations (accepted, alien or rejected), sects, and cults. The relationship between these categories and our two most important variables is shown in Figure 19.2. The locations of denominations, sects, and cults in this figure follow from the definitions already examined, except that cults are here classified as low tension. This does not follow logically from our

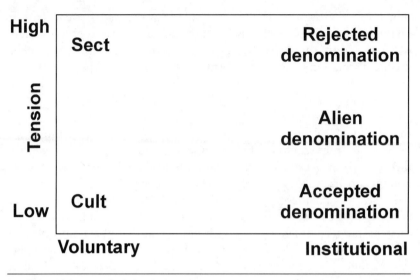

Fig. 19.2. Main types of religious body.

definitions, but in practice it usually seems to be the case, certainly in the Islamic world. The reasons for this fall beyond the scope of the current article, but may be that some degree of visible distinctness (and thus organization) is required before there can be tension between a body and its environment. If a body is barely organized, as, for example, with individual elements of the contemporary Western "cultic milieu,"[26] tension tends not to arise.

Denominations in the Islamic World

The closest Arabic term to "denomination" is *madhhab*, a word normally but inadequately translated as "school of law." In 1900, there were five main *madhhab*s, four Sunni and one Shi'i;[27] today there are either five or six, a question which presents certain complications that will be avoided by concentrating on the situation in 1900.[28] A *madhhab* is concerned with the *sharia*, a concept for which "law" is the usual—but again an inadequate—translation. The *sharia* does cover matters that would in the West be classed as law (civil, criminal and family), but in its widest sense it describes all the prescriptions for how a Muslim should live and worship, including matters that would in the West be classed as ritual, ethics, and even table manners. A *madhhab* is a "school" in the sense that Jungian analysis is—it comprehends assumptions, methodology, and a body of accumulated conclusions. In practice, the *madhhabs* differ largely on details. The Shafi'i *madhhab*, for example, holds that it is permitted to keep working dogs but not pet dogs, on the basis of its reading of a particular set of *hadiths* (reports of the words and actions of the Prophet). The Maliki *madhhab*, in contrast, allows the keeping of dogs as pets by preferring to apply the broad principle that no living thing is unclean.

Any ordinary Muslim follows the conclusions of a particular *madhhab*, normally the *madhhab* that predominates in the area where the Muslim is domiciled. Thus an Egyptian from Lower Egypt (the Delta) will normally follow the Shafi'i *madhhab*, while an Egyptian from Upper Egypt will normally follow the Maliki *madhhab*. In Cairo, where there are many immigrants from Upper Egypt, followers of both *madhhabs* are to be found, and people normally follow whichever *madhhab* they learned from their parents as a child.

It was once popular, especially in British colonial reports, to translate *madhhab* as "sect," and the word is sometimes used thus in modern Turkish and Malay.[29] Even in Arabic, the word is sometimes used in this way, as in "*madhhabs* of the heretics" (a phrase which appears in the title of a recent Arabic heresiography).[30] This, however, is a secondary rather than primary use: a *madhhab* cannot be described as a sect, since it has almost none of the characteristics of a sect (as shown in Figure 19.1). As it is almost universally agreed amongst Sunni Muslims that all the four Sunni *madhhabs* are equally "right," no Sunni *madhhab* is in tension with anything—rather, they together constitute the pluralistic Sunni religious establishment. Since there is only one Shi'i *madhhab*, that one *madhhab* constitutes on its own the monopolistic Shi'i establishment. There is nothing "exclusivistic" or voluntary about a *madhhab*; though it is possible to change one's *madhhab*, this happens very rarely. It is impossible to be expelled from a *madhhab*; and the only significant class of persons for whom it is in any sense a "primary source of social identity" are the scholars who specialize in it.[31]

A *madhhab* is a denomination, then, but differs from a denomination as the concept is normally understood (and as denominations exist in the West). Firstly, it is not a hierarchically organized body. The full-time personnel of one of the Sunni *madhhabs*—the scholars who specialize in it—are not in any formal relation with each other. Each *madhhab* has a number of senior and respected scholars—Muftis—who may, in response to questions, issue *fatwas* giving their view on particular questions of interpretation or practice, but a Mufti has no authority (other than that conferred by his learning) over any other scholar, or over a follower of his *madhhab*. The *fatwas* he gives are not even binding.[32] The situation is a little different for the single Shi'i *madhhab*, however, since the Shi'i equivalent of a Mufti, the *marja-e taqlid* (pattern of emulation) does have binding authority over his followers. This gives Shi'i Islam a more hierarchical organization than Sunni Islam, with interesting implications, as we will see below. Arguably, Shi'i Islam has a pluralistic establishment composed of denominations made up of the followers of each *marja-e taqlid* (of whom there are currently about twenty).

This lack of hierarchical organization in Sunni Islam does not mean that there is no organization at all. Individual educational institutions have directors, for example, and those directors have authority similar to that of a university president in the West. Scholars dominate religious education and preaching, and dominated the criminal and civil law in the pre-modern period, by virtue of their education and training, and as a consequence of their class consciousness: scholars regarded themselves as constituting a class and sometimes acted as a class, rather as any other group—merchants, for example—might.

The second crucial difference between a *madhhab* and a typical Western denomination is that "lay" (that is, non-scholarly) members of a *madhhab*, though in a sense subject to its jurisdiction for some legal purposes,[33] are not organizationally dependent on it for their religious practice. Muftis, scholars and the *marja-e taqlid* have no sacral functions. In principle, any adult, sane Muslim can perform any ritual act within Islam.

The *madhhab*, then, can be described as a denomination. Like a Western denomination, it is an independent repository of religious authority, a freestanding system for producing interpretations of the religious system of which it is part. The functions performed by Western and Islamic denominations within their respective establishments are also broadly similar.

The *madhhabs* we have been considering so far are all what I have termed "accepted denominations." There are also various types of alien and rejected denominations in Islam. The single Shi'i *madhhab*, for example, may constitute the religious establishment in Iran, but in Sunni Egypt it is an alien denomination, just as Greek Orthodoxy was an alien denomination in seventeenth-century Spain. Similarly, the Maliki *madhhab* may be an accepted denomination in Egypt, but in Iran it is alien. In a country such as Iraq, which in its 2003 borders is mostly Shi'i but has a Sunni minority that once monopolized political power, there are two competing religious establishments, rather as there were two competing religious establishments in Ireland under British rule (the once politically powerful Sunni minority in Iraq corresponding to the once politically powerful Protestant minority in British Ireland).

In addition to these denominations that are alien in one place though accepted in another, there are several rejected denominations—Coptic Orthodox Christians in Egypt, Jews in Morocco, Sikhs in Pakistan, Baha'is in Iran, and various others. These rejected denominations fall into three categories on the basis of their status within Islamic law, categories which may usefully be adopted as sociological categories.[34] Christians and Jews are *ahl al-kitab*, "people of the book,"[35] granted certain privileges by Islamic law. In terms of legal status, the *ahl al-kitab* come second after Muslims, while "pre-Muhammadan" "idolaters" such as Hindus come third.[36] At the very bottom are "post-Muhammadans."[37] Islam recognizes a sequence of prophets that includes Moses and Jesus and culminates in Muhammad. It is a central tenet of Islam that Muhammad was the last prophet, who brought the perfect religion, and that there will be no more prophets after him until the end of time. Periodically, however, sects have emerged in the Islamic world recognizing post-Muhammadan prophets,[38] some of which have later become denominations. Most of the so-called "Muslim sects" with which the non-specialist is familiar are in fact "post-Muhammadan" denominations of this kind. Examples include the Ahl-i Haqq, found in Kurdistan, for whom the Divine Essence manifested itself after the time of the Prophet Muhammad in the form of Sultan Suhak (fifteenth century),[39] the [Qadiyani] Ahmadiyya, and the Baha'is.[40] Post-Muhammadan denominations are generally in a far greater state of tension with their environment than are the *ahl al-kitab* or "idolaters."

Cults in the Islamic World

One of Colin Campbell's hypotheses concerning cults is that they and the "cultic milieu"[41] "flourish . . . in relation to (a) the amount of 'alien' culture contact and (b) the disintegration of dominant indigenous culture."[42] Although the dominant culture of the Islamic world is far from disintegration, there has been considerable "alien" culture contact for certain groups within Islamic countries, usually the higher socioeconomic classes. There are Egyptians who, without ever having lived outside Egypt, are more comfortable reading in a European language than in their own, and it is of people such as these that the Islamic cultic milieu mostly consists. Campbell's cultic milieu "includes deviant belief-systems and their associated practices,"[43] and an Egyptian who reads widely in a European language will inevitably encounter a variety of "deviant belief-systems," among them Christianity. Christianity is unlikely to be very attractive,[44] and so it is usually of non-Christian Western deviant belief-systems that the contemporary cultic milieu in the Islamic world consists. In a sense, Campbell's definition of the cultic milieu as "the cultural underground of society"[45] could almost be reversed: in a socioeconomic sense, the cultic milieu of many Islamic countries is found in the cultural high ground.

There is less of a truly indigenous cultic milieu for the lower socioeconomic classes in the Islamic world than in the West, however. Campbell's Western cultic milieu "substantively . . . includes the worlds of the occult and the magical, of spiritualism and psychic phenomena, of mysticism and New Thought, of alien intelligences and lost civilizations, of faith healing and nature cure."[46] Of these, only New Thought, alien intelligences and lost civilizations could be classed as "deviant" in an Islamic context; all the other elements are part of the cultural mainstream, not of any special milieu.[47] If the requirement that a cult be somehow "deviant" is removed, however, the Islamic world is full of cults. The two most frequent types of non-deviant cult are loosely organized groups of devotees of a particular saint[48] and enthusiasts of particular healers or casters-out of spirits.

Sects in the Islamic World

This article proposes a classification of sects in the Islamic world into three categories: the *firqa* (literally, part or division), the *tariqa* (path), and the *ta'ifa* (section). This classification (shown in Figure 19.3) is a pragmatic one, reflecting the need to define clusters of sectarian bodies that actually occur. The extent to which these three types of sect display the seven specific characteristics shown in Figure 19.1 varies, but all show a sufficient number of characteristics to be described as a "sect." The two most im-

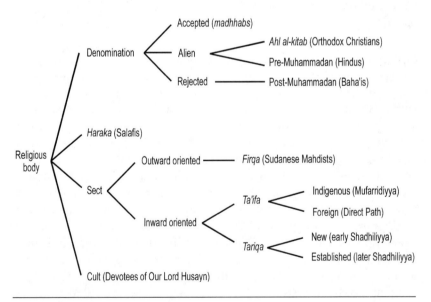

Fig. 19.3. Classification of religious bodies.

portant types are the *firqa* and the *tariqa*;[49] the closest to the archetypal contemporary Western sect or NRM is the *ta'ifa*. The *firqa* must be distinguished from a nonsectarian entity—the *haraka*, or movement—that in some ways resembles it. The *haraka*, though not a sect, is discussed below for the sake of completeness.

The first division is between sects that display one of our most important specific characteristics, the fellowship-principle, and sects that lack this characteristic. The *firqa* (like the nonsectarian *haraka*) claims a monopoly over the proper interpretation of Islam and is therefore oriented outwards towards those for whom it has a message (the entire community of Muslims). Although lacking one important specific characteristic of the sect (the fellowship-principle), the *firqa* displays all the other six, and may be described as an outward-oriented sect.

The *tariqa* and *ta'ifa*, in contrast, display all the seven specific characteristics of the sect. Both are inward-oriented, in the sense that they are oriented towards the fellowship-principle and in the sense that they are more concerned with members of the sect than those outside, that is, are not outward-oriented. The major difference between them is that the *tariqa* arises in a Sufi context. It is for this reason that different terms are used; almost the only point on which consensus currently exists in the definition of religious bodies in the Islamic world is that a body of Sufi origin is a *tariqa*. A further and more important distinction—which is not part of the consensus—must be made between new and "established" *tariqas*, since these two types of *tariqa* display important differences. Novelty is not used in any other definition, since *firqas* and *ta'ifas* are too unstable to become "established" without changing into something else (normally a nonsectarian body or a *tariqa*). In the same way, a unique distinction is made between *ta'ifas* of indigenous and foreign origin, since those of foreign origin have certain special attributes. This distinction is not made for other types of sect, since no cases are known of *firqas* or *tariqas* of foreign origin.[50]

Our three types of sect vary in the degree of tension between them and their environment and in their degree of voluntarism, as is shown in Figure 19.4. The differences in tension within the two pairs (*firqa* and *ta'ifa / tariqa*) arise for different reasons. As has been said, the *tariqa* is a specifically Sufi phenomenon, and tends to stay relatively close to the generally accepted teachings and practice of its environment; the *ta'ifa*, on the other hand, often departs from them radically and is therefore in a much higher state of tension with its environment. In contrast, there is little difference in the (usually significant) degree to which the outwardly-oriented *firqa* and the nonsectarian *haraka* tend to depart from "accepted teachings and practices." The difference in tension between them arises largely because the

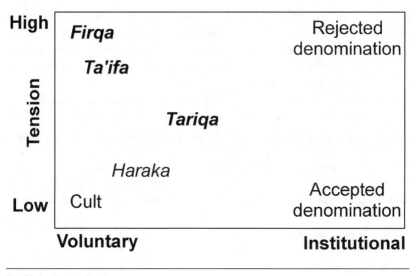

Fig. 19.4. Types of sect.

---

haraka is barely organized and so is in a much lower state of tension with its environment than the *firqa*.

The system of classification proposed above differs both from various systems used by individual Western scholars and by individual scholars writing in Arabic. Arabic, although not the first language of most Muslims, has until recently had no rival as the language of scholarship and religion throughout the Islamic world.[51] As the language of the Qu'ran, it will probably always remain the only language of Islamic theology. However, there is a lack of unanimity among these scholars, and usage of the various Arabic terms for "sect" is not consistent.[52] In modern Arabic usage, the English word "sect" is normally translated as *ta'ifa* in, for example, newspaper reports of the activities of the Japanese Aum Shinrikyō NRM or the Order of the Solar Temple.[53] *Ta'ifa* is not, however, a precise term. It is also used to refer to a variety of other religious bodies, such as the Franciscans or Roman Catholics, and even to ethnic groups such as the Kurds, or artistic ones such as the Impressionist Movement. When referring to a sect, *ta'ifa* is usually qualified by the adjective *diniyya* (religious). In many contexts, its meaning is close to "minority."[54] The word most used by scholars writing in Arabic, today as in the classical period, is *firqa*.[55] This might be translated into English as "division,"[56] but again there is little or no consensus regarding meaning.

Outwards Orientation: Firqas *and* Harakas

The term *firqa*, as has been seen, was that used in the Prophet Muhammad's well-known prediction that the Muslims would split into sects. *Firqa* literally means little more than "part," and as we have seen is today often applied fairly indiscriminately to all varieties of religious bodies, including post-Muhammadan denominations. This article, however, will use *firqa* to denote an organized sectarian body which claims a monopoly over the proper interpretation of Islam, which is consequently outward-oriented, and usually in a state of high tension with its environment. Tension is usually so high, in fact, that the *firqa* is inherently unstable; as we will see, a *firqa* normally either quickly becomes something else, or vanishes.

Firqas differ from the standard definition of sect in that, since their avowed mission is to the whole of Islam (or even all humanity) and their orientation is outwards, they are not typically much interested in any "fellowship." They are, however, exclusivistic voluntary bodies, with possibilities of discipline, and are for their members a "primary source of social identity." On this basis, they are clearly sects within much the usual sense of the word.

A *haraka* (literally, "movement") is distinguished from a *firqa* by its lack of organization. It is generally in a state of far lower tension with its environment than a *firqa*, even though its message may be equally radical. This may well be because only an organized body can threaten and resist a state. The implications of the differences between the nineteenth-century Salafi *haraka* and the *madhhabs* as then established, for example, were dramatic and have since had far-reaching consequences,[57] but the degree of tension between the Salafis and their environment was low, probably because they were at the time only barely recognizable as a group of any sort. The members of a *haraka* have no great interest in any fellowship save of the purely intellectual kind, are not usually in a state of great tension with their environment, and are not exclusivistic. Since a *haraka* is barely a group, possibilities of discipline are very limited. A *haraka* displays the standard characteristics of a sect (as shown in Figure 19.1) only in so far as it is a voluntary body and may be a "primary source of social identity" for its members. The same is true of many non-religious bodies. Not all outward-oriented bodies in Islam are sects.

The names of many early *firqas* might themselves be translated as "sect." The earliest was the Kharijites, literally "leavers" or "dissenters," tightly-organized communities of purists in the seventh century who rejected the emerging religious and political consensus shortly after the death of the Prophet, and on numerous occasions fought against the political and religious establishments which embodied that consensus.[58] The Kharijite *firqa* is the prototypical sect in Islam. Not only is it the earliest Islamic sect, but in the late twentieth century, the term "Khariji" was sometimes applied to various contemporary groups, with little or no reference to theology, to mean "sectarian extremist."

From a Sunni perspective, the Shi'a were the second important *firqa*, arising out of the same period of ferment as the Kharijites.[59] Shi'a is the noun derived from *shi'i*, which literally means "partisan" or "sectarian," and came to be applied to those defined by their devotion to the murdered Caliph Ali and to his son Husayn, who was martyred at the battle of Karbala in 680 after unsuccessfully attempting to seize the Caliphate back from the Umayyads. The early Shi'a differ from the Kharijis, however, both in being less tightly organized and in being more political in their orientation. The Sunni establishment had an obvious interest in portraying them as a *firqa*, but in fact they were initially more of a *haraka* and became a denomination at about the same time that the Sunni *madhhabs* emerged.

The Shi'a are the origin of a number of subsequent *firqas* that later became denominations. Not all Shi'a recognized the standard line of twelve Imams in succession to the Prophet Muhammad, starting with Ali and ending with the disappearance of the Imam Muhammad al-Mahdi in 874. The Ismaili *firqa* of the Shi'a, for example, recognized only seven Imams. The Ismailis established a Fatimid Caliphate of their own in what is now Tunisia, moving east to rule Cairo from 969 to 1171. Further *firqas* split off from the Fatimids. The Nizaris (1101) established a statelet based on Alamut (Syria), becoming famous in the West as the "Assassins,"[60] and the Druze (1021), Bohras, and the followers of the Aga Khan also all derive from the Fatimid Ismailis.

All these Shi'a *firqas* have survived to the present time and have become denominations of one sort or another. The status of accepted denomination being a more comfortable one than that of alien or rejected denomination, some of these one-time *firqas* have at points presented themselves, or have been presented by their friends, as *madhhabs*. In practice, their scientific classification would probably vary from time to time and place to place, as the degree of tension between them and their environment has varied.

There is an important political and military aspect to all these early *firqas*, largely as a result of the close identification of religious and political establishments in the first centuries of Islam. This close identification is not quite the same as the alleged absence of separation of church and state in Islam, a deficiency which was much discussed during the nineteenth century and remains a staple of many discussions today. In fact, separate religious and political establishments are identifiable almost immediately after the death of the Prophet. It is not the case that there was no separation between them, but rather that there was only rarely conflict between them. In this the history of Islam differs significantly from the history of Christianity. The early Christian religious establishment was almost immediately in conflict with the Imperial Roman political establishment, and conflict between religious and political establishments has frequently recurred in Western history, from medieval struggles between royal and ecclesiastical authority to battles over secularism in France that were resolved only at the start of the twentieth century. L. Carl Brown has argued most convincingly that the relative absence of such conflicts from Islamic history is because "the organizational arrangements of Muslim religious specialists, or ulama, makes an *institutional* confrontation between Muslim church and Muslim state virtually impossible."[61] Brown also points out that the exception to this is Shi'i Islam, where a more hierarchical organization has made possible more conflict between religious and political establishments (a conflict which the religious establishment won during the Iranian revolution).

The close identification between Sunni religious and political establishments, then, is in part a consequence of the religious establishment's inability to challenge the political establishment. It is not, however, an exclusively Sunni phenomenon. As was said above, there is a tendency for religious and political authority to coalesce in monopolistic systems—when competition between the two establishments does not prevent it. There are numerous examples of this in Western history. In Spain under Franco, for example, the religious and political establishments stood closely together; the conflict between French religious and political establishments during the later nineteenth century was partly the consequence of an earlier close alliance between the religious establishment and a different political establishment.

For our purposes, the most important implication of close relations between religious and political establishments is that conflict with one tends to lead to conflict with the other. The Kharijite *firqa* challenged the religious establishment of its time and, as a consequence, came into conflict with the political establishment as well. The Shi'a, though more of a *haraka* than a *firqa*, were initially in conflict with the early Islamic political establishment, and so came to be in conflict with the religious establishment as well. In both cases, conflicts with the political establishment resulted in military confrontation.

Many more recent *firqas* have also been involved in armed conflict. These *firqas* can be divided into two categories, those deriving from a divinely inspired leader (such as the Babis, the Sudanese Mahdists, or the [Qadiyani] Ahmadis),[62] and those which placed little or no emphasis on divine communication, such as the Wahhabis and the Muslim Brotherhood. Each of these proposed a new variety of Islam, and all became involved in armed conflict.[63]

The story of the Sudanese Mahdists starts with a self-proclaimed Mahdi, Muhammad Ahmad (c. 1840–85). According to Sunni eschatology, the Mahdi will proclaim himself shortly before the end of time, and then lead an insurrection which will briefly establish a reign of righteousness on earth. Any self-proclaimed Mahdi, then, poses a challenge to both political and religious establishments. The political establishment in the Sudan at the time of Muhammad Ahmad was an Ottoman-Egyptian regime, which almost immediately dispatched a small force to arrest Muhammad Ahmad. The authorities had, however, misjudged the situation, and their small force was easily defeated by the supporters of the Mahdi.[64] Conflict between the Mahdists and the political establishment escalated until, in 1885, the Mahdists captured the Sudanese capital (Khartoum) and beheaded the governor, Gordon Pasha (a British soldier in Ottoman-Egyptian service). Muhammad Ahmad died shortly afterwards.

Egypt was at the time in a state of internal turmoil as a result of the deposition of the Khedive Ismail in 1879 and the military occupation of Egypt by the British in 1882. Under these circumstances, no force was sent to reestablish Ottoman-Egyptian authority, and the Mahdists continued in control of the Sudan until 1896, when Anglo-French competition led to the dispatch of an Anglo-Egyptian army under nominal Egyptian command. This army defeated the Mahdist forces decisively—the British had machine guns and the Mahdists did not, and the battle of Omdurman (1898) is a classic case of "asymmetrical warfare."[65] The British exhumed Muhammad Ahmad's corpse and severed his head from his body.

The Mahdist state was later adopted as a symbol by Sudanese nationalists, but in fact the supporters of the Sudanese Mahdi were attracted to Mahdism for a variety of reasons, none of which were national. Some reasons for supporting the Mahdiyya were undoubtedly religious—the conviction that the *sharia* should be enforced, or the belief that Muhammad Ahmad really was the Mahdi. Other reasons were economic: the Ja'aliyyin tribe and the Danaqla were prominent amongst the earliest supporters of the Mahdi and had suffered severely from the Ottoman-Egyptian government's disruption of the slave trade, in which they had been very active. There were political reasons, too, for attraction to Mahdism. The Baqqara were the third major group among the Mahdi's earliest supporters, and as nomads had resented and resisted the Ottoman-Egyptian government's attempts to restrict their traditional autonomy and force them to pay taxes.[66]

It is clear from this example that the origins of a *firqa* are one thing, and the reasons for the presence or absence of wide support for a *firqa* are another thing. Separating the analysis of the *firqa* itself from analysis of the support for the *firqa* is one way of resolving the old argument about political and economic causes of sectarian revolt. "At times of crisis in the Islamic world," wrote Holt and Daly in their *History of the Sudan*, "the appearance of a *mahdi*, claiming divine sanction to overthrow the old order and set up a new theocracy, is a not uncommon development."[67] This view of eschatological movements as a response to social and economic crisis goes back at least to Weber, and is often used to explain the origins of Western sectarian movements. It might, however, be more correct to say that at times of crisis a person claiming to be a Mahdi is much more likely to be taken seriously than at other times, that when people are generally content with "the old order" they have little interest in "a new theocracy" or any other new system. In much the same way, radical revolutionaries whose message has no religious content whatsoever can be found in most places, but it is only under special circumstances that they attract significant support. The origins of the Bolshevik party belong to intellectual history; growth of support for it in 1917 must be explained in terms of the hunger for bread and peace generated in Russia by the First World War, just as the growth of support for the Sudanese Mahdi must be explained in different terms from those used to explain the motivations of the Mahdi and of his closest followers.

Other contemporary bodies which might be classified as *firqas* include Islamist groups such as Jihad in Egypt, Hamas in Palestine, and Al Qa'ida. These are often referred to as "political Islam," and Hamas is also commonly described as a political party. This description is not wrong: a *firqa* is often a political or military entity as well as a religious body. The one does not exclude the other.

Al Qa'ida displays almost all the characteristics of the *firqa*. It is outward-oriented. Membership is voluntary and a primary source of its members' identity. It is exclusivistic and organized, and the possibility of discipline clearly exists. The only question is over the degree of tension between Al Qa'ida and its environment. Whilst the Taliban were in power in Afghanistan and defined the religious establishment there, Al Qa'ida was arguably a denomination more than a *firqa*. In post-Taliban Afghanistan and in the context of the wider Islamic world, though, Al Qa'ida is clearly not a denomination, but it is still not clear to what extent it is in a *firqa*-like state of tension with its environment. Some degree of hostility towards America and the West in general was already found in Al Qa'ida's environment in mid-2001, and this hostility has since became much more widespread and pronounced as a result of America's perceived "war on Islam."[68] Few Muslims endorsed the attacks of 9/11, but many Muslims—perhaps the majority of Arabs—refused to accept Al Qa'ida's ultimate responsibility for those attacks.[69] This refusal partly reflected an Arab desire to avoid responsibility,[70] but it also reflected a reluctance to condemn Al Qa'ida, a reluctance which suggests that Al Qa'ida and its wider environment were not in a state of great tension. At the time of this writing, Al Qa'ida is certainly in a state of high tension with the various Arab political establishments, but—as we have seen—the environment matters more than the establishment.

In order to place Al Qa'ida properly in its wider context, some further analysis is required. In the same way as there is a basic division between denomination and sect (with cult as a less important third category), there is a basic division in political science between political party and interest group. Political parties, in the classic definition, "have as their primary goal the conquest of power or a share in its exercise," while interest groups "endeavor . . . to exert influence on those who wield power."[71] To the extent that Al Qa'ida aims at the conquest of power, it is a political party. Otherwise it would follow that it must be an interest group, aiming to exert influence on the American government.

This is a somewhat surprising conclusion, but interest groups are commonly classified on the basis of their "methods of action," including methods which we normally associate with "open" lobbies, but also "corruption" and even intimidation. The classic example of intimidation is "the writing of threatening letters to deputies,"[72] but terrorism is—in essence—no more than a particularly violent form of intimidation.

Interest groups may also be classified, on the basis of the scope of their activities, as local or global. The growth in the number and importance of interest groups which operate on a global scale (groups such as Greenpeace or Amnesty International) was one characteristic of late twentieth-century globalization. Al Qa'ida, if considered an interest group, would be one of the few global interest groups of non-Western origin.[73]

Inwards Orientation: Ta'ifas and Tariqas

Most sects in the Islamic world have not aimed at the regeneration of the entire community of Muslims or claimed to be the unique repository of "true" Islam. Most are oriented inwards, towards the "fellowship-principle." These less spectacular but far more frequent sects fall into two main categories, the ta'ifa and the tariqa. As will be seen, a further distinction is necessary, that between new and established tariqas.

The closest equivalent of the tariqa in the West is the monastic order, a body which is not normally regarded as sectarian for the very good reason that, although voluntary and very much oriented around the fellowship-principle, it is organizationally integrated into a denomination.[74] Since the denominations of Islam are barely organized, however, a tariqa is of necessity organizationally autonomous, and so cannot be treated as part of a denomination. Although Sufism is commonly and correctly described as mysticism, a tariqa is clearly an organized community, and so is a sect in Troeltsch's definition.

A distinction must be made between the new and the established tariqa because the attributes associated with the two differ significantly. A tariqa typically starts with a small group following a single charismatic figure (such as Abu Hasan al-Shadhili, 1196–1258) who is regarded by his followers as a *wali*, that is, someone especially close to God. At this stage, the new *tariqa* probably has no name, and membership is entirely voluntary. The *tariqa* (or the *wali* who is its *shaykh* or leader)[75] is not only the primary source of social identity for these members but also the most important thing in their lives. The *tariqa* is exclusivistic by virtue of the degree of commitment expected from members and may also be exclusivistic as a result of formalized requirements for admission.

An additional attribute of the new *tariqa* is that, even though its focus is its *shaykh* rather than its teaching or practice, either teaching or practice will often differ in some way from that generally accepted in the relevant environment at the time. Some degree of tension with its environment may often result from this difference, and also from the exclusivism and commitment of the new *tariqa*'s members, the followers of the new *shaykh*. The new *tariqa*, then, displays all seven of the specific characteristics of the sect.

As time passes, a variety of denominationalization often occurs. If the *tariqa* survives, membership becomes less voluntary: people join it more because of its position in a locality, or because of a family connection, than because of the *shaykh*. After a few generations, the *shaykh* will be a less charismatic successor of the *tariqa*'s founder, and the degree of commitment required of his followers will have declined. By this point, the *tariqa* has normally acquired a name (such as the "tariqa Shadhiliyya"); many of the unusual features of the new *tariqa* which originally caused tension will have faded.[76] The established *tariqa* will be a secondary source of social identity, and sometimes as weak a source as the soccer team one supports. As a body aiming at fellowship but not in tension with its environment, the established *tariqa* will often continue for centuries as an integral part of that environment and is barely a sect any more. It continues to display something of each of the specific characteristics of the sect, but only in attenuated form. In many ways, it is closer to the denomination than the sect. It is not a denomination, however, because it is a body to which one may belong in addition to a *madhhab*, not as an alternative to a *madhhab*.

Ultimately, a *tariqa* will cease to be a sect at all in one of two ways. Established *tariqas* tend to split very frequently on the death of their *shaykhs*, and after a few centuries there are a large number of groups still describing themselves as "tariqa Shadhiliyya" but having no significant links with each other and often having very different attributes. At this stage, the name "tariqa Shadhiliyya" indicates lineage, not a sectarian body, nor indeed a

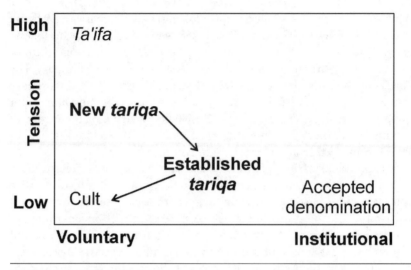

Fig. 19.5. Development of *tariqas*.

recognizable body of any kind. It has given rise to new, distinct sects, each one of which must be described more precisely, as for example "the Shadhiliyya of Shaykh Mahmud in the town of Qina."

Splits in a *tariqa* have been seen by some scholars as a form of failure, which indeed they would be for certain other forms of organization, such as political parties or *firqas*. The objectives of a *tariqa*, however, are very different. A mass organization under tight central control may advance the outward-oriented objectives of a *firqa*, but not those of a *tariqa*. The splitting of an established *tariqa* into new *tariqas*, then, may be compared to the bursting forth of seed from a ripe pod, and equated not with failure but with success. For a *tariqa*, failure is when the process of quasi-denominationalization continues until the *tariqa* has lost all the characteristics of a sect including organization, in which case what remains resembles either a cult, or has become nothing more than a form of sociability.[77]

The *tariqa* is an established and respectable part of the Islamic religious landscape. No Muslim would welcome the existence of *firqas*, but the *tariqa* is as desirable as the *madhhab*.[78] As a result, many *ta'ifas* often represent themselves as *tariqas*. They can, however, be distinguished from *tariqas* either in terms of their non-Sufi origins,[79] or in terms of the distance between their teachings and practice and those generally accepted amongst Sufis.[80] Thus the Mufarridiyya of Makmun Yahya, an Indonesian from Sumatra, called itself a *tariqa*, despite expressing views generally rejected by Sufis (and indeed all Muslims).[81] Makmun Yahya allegedly claimed to be the Imam Mahdi for the Muslims, Jesus for the Christians and father of all man for those without religions. [He further] claimed that . . . every prayer and act of repentance to Allah must be through the Angel Kuranaz and [himself] before they could be accepted by Allah. [He] never performed the Friday and Congregational prayers because he claimed to perform these [in Mecca].[82]

I have no information about the origins of the Mufarridiyya, but the heterodoxy of the teachings[83] here reported is sufficient to distinguish it from a *tariqa*. The Mufarridiyya, then, should almost certainly be classified as a *ta'ifa*. A claim such as this to be the Mahdi implies a mission to the whole of Islam and is at first sight characteristic of a *firqa*, not a *ta'ifa*. In fact, however, what matters is whether the sect is really outward-oriented or whether the claimant's significance is restricted to a small and well-defined group of followers, as it seems to have been with Makmun Yahya. In this case, the sect should be described as a *ta'ifa*, since it is in reality inward-oriented. Of course, in their earliest years many *firqas* would be defined as *ta'ifas* on this basis, since the significance of the leader of any new sect is initially restricted to the leader himself and his first followers. No sect, then, can emerge as a fully grown *firqa*, and it is for this reason that the successful *ta'ifa* may be said to develop into a *firqa*. Most *ta'ifas*, however, simply fade away. Few if any become denominations directly, perhaps because the heterodoxy of their teachings and practice creates too large a gap between them and their environment.

One variety of *ta'ifa* that deserves special mention is the *ta'ifa* of foreign origin. The Middle East lies next to Europe, and there has always been cultural transfer from the West, including transfer of sects and NRMs. Although no Western NRMs have grown to any great size in the Middle East, there have been and are instances of small groups following NRMs that have been studied in other contexts. Western NRMs of "Eastern" origin (such as the Theosophists) have of course existed in the Islamic world, but there have also been various foreign imports connected with the special nature of the cultic milieu in the Islamic world discussed above. The first Masonic lodges were established in the Ottoman world in the early eighteenth century, although it was only in the nineteenth century that they began to attract significant numbers of Muslims;[84] and both Swedenborg and Papus's Martinism reached the cosmopolitan port city of Salonika at the start of the twentieth century.[85] Shortly afterwards, a Spiritist Association was established in Cairo,[86] and there are various reports of Egyptian Muslims today following figures such as "Shaykh Silver Birch," a Westerner who was evidently at some point adopted into a Native American tribe.[87] The Spanish-based NRM New Acropolis has been expanding slowly in Egypt since the mid 1990s.[88]

Many such *ta'ifas* of foreign origin remain in a state of low tension with their environments, despite what might be described in Islamic terms as almost total heterodoxy. An interesting example of this is the Direct Path. This is led by Professor Fulan,[89] a Muslim Egyptian academic who has for many years been following the teachings of a neo-Hindu guru, Krishna Menon. He teaches a "direct path"[90] to enlightenment, based on Advaita Vedanta but independent of any religious practice. Although Professor Fulan insists that he teaches "no dogma" and "no beliefs," his followers constitute a *ta'ifa*. They assemble once a week in two groups to hear of the Direct Path. One group is warned in English against the "straitjacket" of religion and religious practice in discourses with frequent references to Western esoteric writers and Hindu and Buddhist teachings; the other, larger group is given a modified version of the same message in Arabic in the context of reading and interpretation of the Qu'ran.[91] Qu'ran reading and interpretation is a standard activity throughout the Islamic world, and groups engaged in it may be found in mosques everywhere. The English-language group is small, consisting of a mixture of Westerners resident in Cairo and Egyptians who have spent years abroad and are thoroughly Westernized, and usually meets in the apartment of an American follower of Professor Fulan. The Arabic-language group is larger, drawn mostly from the Egyptian military and civil elite, and meets in the professor's own house.

For over twenty years, Professor Fulan has been teaching these two different messages to two different groups. His English-language message

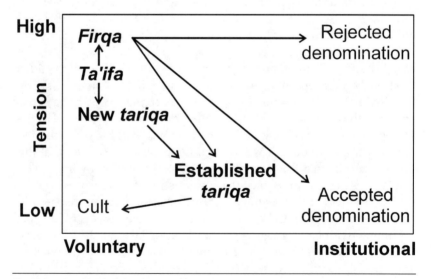

Fig. 19.6. Development of sects.

corresponds most directly to the teachings of his guru; of his Arabic-language version, he says: "I have to express myself in that language," that is, the language of Islam.[92] An informant who went to a meeting of the Arabic-language group when it was addressed by Krishna Menon's successor as guru (while on a visit to Egypt) reports that the guru's message, which was not re-expressed in Qu'ranic or Islamic terms, caused mounting dismay and resistance among his audience.

The Direct Path, then, although a *ta'ifa* of foreign origin,[93] presents itself mostly as an Islamic body—not just in order to avoid persecution, but also to gain access to its audience.

Conclusion

We have now seen how religious bodies in the Islamic world, like religious bodies in the West, can accurately and productively be classified as denominations, sects, or cults. We have also seen how religious bodies (like political ones) can usefully be analyzed in terms of their relationship with their religious (and political) establishment.

We have also seen that the three types of sect we identified (or five, if one includes the subdivisions of *tariqa* and *ta'ifa*) are properly classified as sects in much the standard (Western) scientific sense. Not all of these sects display the seven specific characteristics shown in Figure 19.1 in equal measure or in the same way, but all are clearly different from denominations and cults.

Finally, we have been able to use the system of classification established in this article to illuminate change. We have seen how the types of sect which are most sectarian—the new *tariqa* and the *ta'ifa*—are those which may most frequently transform themselves into other types of sect (if they survive). The *firqa*, in contrast, only rarely remains in any way sectarian, because of its inherent instability.

Notes

1. Singular *firqa*, plural properly *firaq*. English plurals are however used in this article, along with simplified transliteration.
2. Most of these versions are given in Abd al-Qahir ibn Tahir al-Baghdadi, *Al-farq bain al-firaq*, trans. and ed. Kate Chambers Seelye (New York: Columbia University Press, 1920), 21–22. *Hadith* reports often differ somewhat from each other; their historical reliability is a vexed question with which this article does not need to concern itself. What matters for our present purposes is that almost all Muslims accept *hadith* such as this as reliable.
3. For example, Steven I. Judd, "Ghaylan al-Dimashqi: The Isolation of a Heretic in Islamic Historiography," *International Journal of Middle East Studies* 31 (1999), 172. "Heresy" is, however, a concept which has no exact equivalent in Islam. In this article, "Muslim," "Islamic," and "Muhammadan" are used as in Arabic, with "Islamic" denoting the religion, "Muslim" denoting an adherent of the religion, and "Muhammadan" denoting the Prophet Muhammad.

4. The ninth-century work is the *Kitab firaq al-shi'a* of Al-Hasan ibn Musa al-Nawbakhti (d. 899). At least five heresiographies were published in Cairo in the late 1980s and 1990s, four by Egyptian academics and one in a more popular series. An example of an Internet heresiography is Ijaz A. Rauf, "73 Divisions in Islam and One True Jama'at," available at http://www.real-islam.org/73.htm [October 2002]. This is an especially interesting example, being prepared by a member of the [Qadiyani] Ahmadiyya, a body which most other Muslims would consider a sect.

5. Ibn Khaldun (d. 1406) warned that "numbers [such as these] are not to be taken literally; the intended sense is rather that of magnitude" (*Al-muqaddima*, quoted in Lawrence I. Conrad, "Seven and the *tasbi*': On the Implications of Numerical Symbolism for the Study of Medieval Islamic History," *Journal of the Economic and Social History of the Orient* 31 [1988]: 42–73). Conrad demonstrates that, in almost all cases, it is wrong to take literally numbers involving sevens.

6. The usefulness in an Islamic context of the more recent concept of "new religious movement" is considered later.

7. A recent exception to this is Fuad I. Khuri, *Imams and Emirs: State, Religion and Sect in Islam* (London: Saki Books, 1990).

8. Bryan R. Wilson, *The Social Dimensions of Sectarianism: Sects and New Religious Movements in Contemporary Society* (Oxford: Clarendon Press, 1990), 3.

9. Ernst Troeltsch, *The Social Teaching of the Christian Churches* (1911; London: George Allen & Unwin, 1931), 340, n. 165b.

10. Troeltsch, *Social Teaching*, 340, also n. 165b.

11. Helmut Richard Niebuhr, *The Social Sources of Denominationalism* (1929; Cleveland: Meridian, 1957), 19.

12. Joachim Wach, *Sociology of Religion* (London: Kegan Paul, Trench, Truber & Co, 1947), 199.

13. Wilson, *Social Dimensions of Sectarianism*, 108.

14. Rodney Stark and William Sims Bainbridge, *The Future of Religion* (Berkeley: University of California Press, 1985).

15. Wilson, *Social Dimensions of Sectarianism*, 52.

16. William Shepard, " 'Denomination' as a Label for Some Islamic Phenomena?," *Nova Religio* 6:1 (2002): 156, 158–59.

17. I do not mean to criticize the treatment of neo-Nazi parties in Germany. There are many justifications for their persecution. Legal disabilities and official hostility do, however, constitute persecution.

18. Troeltsch, *Social Teaching*, 331.

19. Ibid., 348.

20. Wilson, *Social Dimensions of Sectarianism*, 1–2.

21. Denominationalization might be defined as the transformation of a sect into a denomination.

22. Wilson, *Social Dimensions of Sectarianism*, 105, 107.

23. Niebuhr, *Social Sources*, 21, 145, 181–84. In the preface to his book, Niebuhr, a Yale theology professor for 31 years, explains that "The effort to distinguish churches primarily by reference to their doctrine and to approach the problem of church unity from a purely theological point of view appeared . . . to be a procedure so artificial and fruitless that [the author] found himself compelled to turn from theology to history, sociology, and ethics for a more satisfactory account of denominational differences" (p. vii).

24. His famous observation on page 19, quoted above in that context, is more than anything else a comment on a fairly obvious problem with Troeltsch's definition of a sect as "voluntary." One might suspect that page 19 is now more widely read than later sections of the book.

25. "Seventh-day Adventist Responses to Branch Davidian Notoriety: Patterns of Diversity within a Sect Reducing Tension with Society," *Journal for the Scientific Study of Religion* 34 (1995): 323–42. This is perhaps a better example than the more frequently used one of the Mormons, since the Mormons originally had what has been described as "a well-founded fear of persecution."

26. See Colin Campbell, "The Cult, the Cultic Milieu and Secularization," *A Sociological Yearbook of Religion in Britain* 5, ed. Michael Hill (London: SCM Press, 1972): 119–36.

27. There were more in antiquity, but only the five which survived are relevant for our present purposes.

28. In certain countries such as Egypt, the significance of the *madhhab* has declined over the last century to the point where many (perhaps most) Egyptian Muslims are not aware which *madhhab* they are following, though in practice almost all continue to follow one on many points. For example, the position of the hands at various points in the ritual prayer varies from *madhhab* to *madhhab*; anyone who prays will adopt one of the four alternative rulings, usually that of his family. One might, however, argue that what has really happened is that a single "Sunni *madhhab*" has been formed out of some or all of the four standard Sunni *madhhab*s, or even that a new "neo-Salafi *madhhab*" is fast establishing a monopoly position.

29. Standard dictionaries give *mazhab* as a Malay word for "sect," and *mezhep* as a Turkish word for "cult." These translations are, however, of limited interest; *ibadet* and *tapinma* are also given as Turkish words for cult. The etymology of the former is "worship" (from Arabic), and of the latter "idolatry" (*tapi*, an idol).

30. Barakat Muhammad Murad, *Madhahib al-zanadiqa wa aqaid al-batiniyya fi al-fikr al-Islami* (Cairo: al-Sir, 1992).

31. In some parts of the Islamic world, differences in *madhhab* correspond with other differences. For example, landowners in Upper Egypt in the nineteenth century tended to follow the Hanafi *madhhab* while the peasantry was almost entirely Maliki. In such circumstances, however, *madhhab* serves more as a marker than a source of identity.

32. It is, however, frowned upon for a Muslim to obtain a variety of *fatwas* from different Muftis until he gets the answer he wants. The status of a *fatwa* differs somewhat between Sunni and Shi'a Islam.

33. For example, different rules govern inheritance in different *madhhabs*.

34. Theological distinctions may produce social realities. To varying extents, most contemporary Islamic states in theory treat people as citizens with equal rights, irrespective of their religion. In practice, however, the classifications derived from Islamic law often matter more.

35. So called since they have also received divine revelations, recorded in the Torah and the New Testament. It is the Qu'ran's confirmation of this revelation that matters, much more than monotheism as such.

36. In practical and popular terms, Jews have in recent years become somewhat confused with Israelis, and their status has suffered accordingly. The relationship between Zionism and Judaism in popular perceptions, however, falls beyond the scope of this article.

37. "Muhammadan" is used in this article (as it is in Arabic) exclusively as an adjective denoting the Prophet Muhammad, and not to denote Islam. The expression "Mohametanism" was once used to denote Islam, but has been generally and properly rejected as both offensive to Muslims and inaccurate: the role of the Prophet in Islam is very different from the role of Christ in Christianity.

38. "Post-Muhammadan" is not the same as "post-Islamic." Post-Muhammadan prophets regard themselves as successors to Muhammad and Jesus, in the same way that Islam sees Muhammad as the successor to Jesus and Moses. Not all post-Islamic prophets are post-Muhammadan. A person who claimed to be the Jewish Messiah, for example, would not be post-Muhammadan, and would be regarded by Islam as principally the concern of the religion which gave rise to him.

39. The previous manifestation was actually that of Ali rather than Muhammad, which adds a further twist. See Ziba Mir-Hosseini, "Inner Truth and Outer History: The Two Worlds of the Ahl-i Haqq of Kurdistan," *International Journal of Middle East Studies* 26 (1994): 267–85. For Muslims, of course, Muhammad was human, not a manifestation of the Divine Essence.

40. Both of these are discussed in detail in my original "Sects in the Islamic World."

41. Campbell argued that individuals often belonged not so much to a single cult as to a milieu, a web of different but interconnected cults.

42. Campbell, "Cult," 130.

43. Ibid., 122. "Deviant," Campbell means, in the terms of the "dominant . . . culture."

44. Christianity is well known in most Islamic countries, as an identity if not as a theology, being much mentioned in the Qu'ran, and perhaps more importantly as a consequence of the colonial experience. In some countries, such as Egypt and Syria, there are also signifi-

cant Christian minorities. For a Muslim, then, Christianity is from an early age a very present "other."

45. Campbell, "Cult," 122.

46. Ibid.

47. The exception to this is perhaps the *zar*, which is generally regarded as deviant and also contains significant syncretic elements. One might speak of a popular *zar*-cultic milieu. There is an extensive literature on the *zar*.

48. In Cairo, for example, the Devotees of Our Lord Husayn organize a "table of the Most Merciful" (free meals for the poor during the Ramadan fast) and raise money for the restoration of mosques.

49. The *firqa* is associated with reform, and the *tariqa* with renewal. See Wael B. Hallaq, "Was the Gate of Ijtihad Closed?" *International Journal of Middle East Studies* 16 (1984): 3–41, for an interesting discussion of these two concepts.

50. One exception is the Maryamiyya, a *tariqa* of French and Swiss origin, most active in the West but also with a presence in Iran. See my *Against the Modern World: Traditionalism and the Secret Intellectual History of the Twentieth Century* (New York: Oxford University Press, forthcoming 2004).

51. The rival is of course now English, a language which many contemporary non-Arab Muslim scholars and intellectuals are more likely to speak than Arabic.

52. For a discussion of the system of classification used by Khuri in *Imams and Emirs*, see my "Sects in the Islamic World," 205–06, and for the various systems used by scholars writing in Arabic, see 207–08.

53. The word *ta'ifa* was used thus by *Ittihad* [United Arab Emirates] on 5 and 26 January 1996, *Al-sharq al-awsat* [London] on 25 February 1996; *Al-Balad* [Saudi Arabia] on 9 January 1996, and by *Al-Ahram* [Cairo] on 18 January 1996. The Solar Temple is referred to in Arabic as "the religious *ta'ifa* of sun worshipers" (incidentally, "sun worshiper" is the Arabic for "sunflower").

54. As, for example, in a Kuwaiti newspaper report on the *bidun* (a category of stateless persons long resident in Kuwait), or an Egyptian newspaper report on the reception given by the Prime Minister to the visiting leader of the Bohras (*Al-Ahram*, 28 January 1999).

55. Some other terms are little used today. See D. Gimaret, "Milal wa'l-Nihal," *Encyclopedia of Islam*, new ed., vol. 7 (Leiden: Brill, 1960–2002), 54–55.

56. In journalistic Arabic, however, *firqa*'s chief meaning is now military ("division," as in "armored division") and it is consequently rarely applied to religious bodies.

57. Albert Hourani's *Arabic Thought in the Liberal Age, 1798–1939* (Cambridge, U.K.: Cambridge University Press, 1983) is now somewhat outdated, but remains a classic account. Among the implications was the creation of what may be seen as a new denomination.

58. The Kharijites are treated in all standard works on the emergence of Islam.

59. One of the earliest known works of Islamic heresiography was entitled, "The Book of the *firqas* of the Shi'a," the *Kitab firaq al-shi'a* of Al-Hasan ibn Musa al-Nawbakhti (d. 899).

60. Most of the delightful stories relating to the Assassins which were once so popular sadly have little basis in reality.

61. L. Carl Brown, *Religion and State: The Muslim Approach to Politics* (New York: Columbia University Press, 2000), 31.

62. The Babis and the [Qadiyani] Ahmadis are discussed at length in my "Sects in the Islamic World," but are not dealt with here for reasons of space.

63. For a fuller consideration, see my "Sects in the Islamic World." In this article, I limit myself to exploring one single example.

64. Peter Malcolm Holt, *The Mahdist State in the Sudan, 1881–1898: A Study of its Origins, Development and Overthrow* (Oxford: Oxford University Press, 1958), 47–48.

65. The Mahdists lost some 11,000 dead and 16,000 wounded; the Anglo-Egyptian army lost only 49 men (and 382 wounded). P.M. Holt and M.W. Daly, *The History of the Sudan from the Coming of Islam to the Present Day* (London: Weidenfeld and Nicolson, 1979), 112.

66. Holt and Daly, *History of the Sudan*, 88–89.

67. Ibid., 88.

68. The reasons for the interpretation of American and Israeli activities during 2002 and after as a war on Islam fall beyond the scope of this article. It is clear, however, to any observer of the Arab world that this interpretation is very widespread.

69. Whilst it is generally accepted that there were Arabs at the controls of the planes, there is a widespread conviction that someone else must have been behind the plot—as always, Israeli intelligence is a favorite candidate for anything that causes loss to the Arabs.
70. One significant immediate reaction of many Arabs on 9/11was fear—fear of what America might do in response.
71. Maurice Duverger, *Party Politics and Pressure Groups: A Comparative Introduction* (1968, translated New York: Thomas Y. Crowell, 1972), 1.
72. Duverger, *Party Politics*, 121–22.
73. That there are few interest groups of even local scope in the Islamic world results most importantly from the hostility of various authoritarian regimes to the existence of such independent groups.
74. This raises the interesting question of whether the shift in focus from church to society made necessary by secularism might indeed turn Christian monastic orders into sects. Characteristics such as celibacy and poverty may not produce any tension between an order and the Catholic Church, but they are increasingly foreign to contemporary Western secular society.
75. *Wali* is a rank or spiritual station; *shaykh* is a function. Great *shaykh*s are almost always *walis*, but there is no requirement for a *shaykh* to be a *wali*, and many *walis* never function as *shaykhs*.
76. These features may in some cases have been no more than the unusual degree of commitment to the founding *shaykh*.
77. The rejected post-Muhammadan denomination the Ahl-i Haqq (mentioned above) evidently derives from a Sufi *tariqa*, but this is an unusual course. A classic example of the trajectory of a *tariqa* away from sectarian tension is the Tariqa Muhammadiyya, a new *tariqa* that became established and "respectable." The Tariqa Muhammadiyya is discussed in my original "Sects in the Islamic World"; this discussion is omitted here for reasons of space.
78. This is sometimes emphasized by referring to the *tariqa* as a *mashrab* (a spiritual spring), rhyming with *madhhab*. Many Sufi practices were, however, attacked by the Wahhabis and the Salafis, and as a result of these attacks (and also of socioeconomic changes associated with mass urbanization and other aspects of modernity) the word *tariqa* has in some circles ceased to have positive value.
79. A Sufi *shaykh* has normally been authorized to act as such by his own *shaykh*. The chain of such authorizations is recorded, and in some ways corresponds to the concept of apostolic succession in Catholic Christianity.
80. As has been said, the distance between their teachings and practice and those generally accepted by Muslims (including Sufis) is often great, and thus a source of tension. What matters for distinguishing between the *ta'ifa* and the *tariqa* is, however, the distance between the (Sufi) *tariqa* and the (non-Sufi) *ta'ifa*.
81. On this basis, many *ta'ifas*, although found and originating in the Islamic world, are not themselves especially "Islamic." This article, of course, deals not with "Islamic sects" but with "sects in the Islamic world."
82. Pusat Islam, "Tarekat Mufarridiyah," available http://www.islam.gov.my/ppi/makmun.html [October 2002].
83. That is, in general terms, and so also in Sufi terms.
84. Thierry Zarcone, *Mystiques, philosophes et francs-maçons en Islam: Riza Tevfiq, penseur ottoman (1868–1948), du soufisme à la confrérie* (Paris: Institut français d'études anatoliennes d'Istanbul, 1993), 177, 203–4 (Turkey), 268 (Iran), 222–23, 235 (Egypt).
85. Paul Dumont, "La franc-maçonnerie d'obédience française à Salonique au début du XXe siècle," *Turcica* 16 (1984): 83–86.
86. The *Jam'iyya al-Ahram al-ruhiyya* of Ahmad Fahmi Abu'l-Khayr. See Fred De Jong, "The Works of Tantawi Jawhari (1862–1940): Some Bibliographical and Biographical Notes," *Bibliotheca Orientalis* 34:3/4 (1977): 154–56 and 159–60.
87. My information on this group is vague and second-hand.
88. Private information.
89. This is not his real name.
90. Consisting of a "upward path," the realization that the absolute is not that which is experienced, and a "downward path," seeing the object and subject as being the same, equally nonexistent.

91. Comments on the English-language group are based on personal observation in February 1998 and discussions with one follower of the professor over a longer period. Comments on the Arabic-language group, which I was not allowed to visit, are based on discussions with this follower and with another informant who had visited the Arabic-language group some years before.

92. Address to the English-language group, 14 February 1998.

93. It might, however, alternatively be classified as a cult, since it is not a primary source of identity for any of its members and since members of the English-language group are mostly members of the local cultic milieu, and even the international cultic milieu. One member of the group spoke of visits to a variety of NRMs in England and France, from which she had just returned.

CHAPTER 20

Research on New Religious
Movements in the Post-9/11 World

BENJAMIN ZABLOCKI AND J. ANNA LOONEY

In this chapter, we review some selected social science research on new religious movements (NRMs) in North America. We think that there may be a paradigm shift occurring in the study of NRMs associated roughly with the turn of the century but accelerated by the earthshaking terrorist events of September 11, 2001. We do not claim to be sure of the exact nature of this paradigm shift but hope to suggest here a few of its likely dimensions.

Although we will cite the work of certain researchers in connection with twentieth-century perspectives and others in connection with those perspectives we see emerging in the twenty-first century, we have no intention of thus classifying any particular scholar as either "old fashioned" or "avant garde." It seems more reasonable to assume that almost all NRM researchers, to some degree, are going through a simultaneous transition in the way they perceive and analyze NRMs. Nor is it our intention to imply that this emerging perspective is a response to deficiencies in the twentieth-century view of NRMs. Rather, it appears to us to be a way of building on the significant accomplishments of NRM research in the second half of the last century.

We confine our discussion mostly to NRMs in North America because that is the region we know the best. But we do not thereby mean to argue that North America is ahead of other areas of the world in this intellectual transition. It may well lag behind. Indeed, if we had to pick a single exemplar of this emerging way of looking at NRMs, our choice would be Jean-François Mayer, a European scholar, whose recent work has been with

NRMs in Africa. Many of us American scholars have been slow to catch on to his more global and more social-movement-oriented approach.

The contours of the emerging paradigm are not yet clear, but we wish to suggest four specific dimensions as candidates for attention in this regard. First, it seems as if NRms are becoming nrMs in the eyes of the academy. In the twentieth century, the emphasis in the study of NRMs was on their newness and on their *sui generis* religious nature. The social movement aspect of these entities was sometimes noted but rarely emphasized. The quantum leap in global consciousness precipitated by 9/11 has propelled us into seeing that our field of research can benefit from being looked at as a part of the larger field of social movements. At the same time, we have come to recognize that there is nothing particularly new or exclusively religious about many of the ideologies driving these movements. Distinctions among ideologies that are purely religious, those that are purely political, and those that are purely cultural are difficult and often impossible to draw. A relocation of NRM research within the social movement field might be salutary for both fields. Curiously, social movement scholars have tended to concentrate on political movements, leaving NRM scholars to attend to religious movements. A growing realization of the artificiality of this very Protestant sharp distinction between the political and the religious is likely to lead to progress in understanding both sorts of social movements. In this regard, parallel arguments by Doug McAdam and others identified with the social movements field should be noted.[1]

Second, it seems that theories focusing on *structure* are giving way to theories focusing on *process*. Taxonomic treatments of NRMs as well as the functionalist and culturalist[2] explanatory theories that predominated in the twentieth century are beginning to give ground to theories that attempt to account for the social and cultural *mechanisms* used by NRMs for attaining cohesion and control, and for mobilizing resources. To put it another way, "why" questions are making room for equally important "how" questions. In this way, attention is shifting from the structural characteristics of NRMs to the social processes whereby they continuously create and maintain themselves.

Third, an important but distracting concern with litigation and government policy regarding NRMs that severely polarized the research community in the twentieth century has begun to recede. Scholars have thus been given an opportunity to take off their inevitably polarizing expert-witness hats and return to their more accustomed roles as detached observers. Input from twentieth-century NRM scholars was crucial in helping policy makers and courts get an initial handle on how to deal with new religious movements. But now these agencies have had time to develop their own models and their own standard operating procedures, leaving academics free to spend more time simply looking, listening, and learning.

Fourth, North American researchers have begun, especially since 9/11, to join their colleagues in the rest of the world in perceiving social phenomena globally and transnationally. The very publication of this volume is a landmark event in this evolution of awareness. However, this does not mean that we are yet at the point where we are able to undertake the extensive collaboration necessary to conduct rigorous comparative studies of NRMs across national boundaries. Hopefully that day will not be long in coming. Organizations like CESNUR have already attempted, with some degree of success, to provide the infrastructure needed for such undertakings.

Let us look at the way this shift has begun to manifest itself in the study of NRMs. We will limit ourselves to examining how attention seems to be shifting in four areas that have long been of major concern to researchers: 1. tolerance of NRMs by the surrounding society; 2. the problem of ideological disconnection between the NRM and society; 3. the management of charisma within NRMs; and 4. the social and psychological characteristics of joiners, stayers, and leavers.

Toleration of NRMs by Society

Sociologists of religion face a challenge in attempting to observe and explain the role of religious toleration in collective life. Emile Durkheim's theory that religion is the collective expression of moral community offers a useful starting point for beginning an inquiry into the social tension that arises in a culture with diverse religious systems, like the United States.[3]

The American Constitution and the Bill of Rights comprise the kind of collective expression of moral community that Durkheim specifies in *The Elementary Forms of Religious Life.* These founding principles represent the most universal expression of an American formula for dealing with religion—that is, accommodating the choices citizens make in exercising their Constitutional freedom to affiliate, believe, and practice whatever type of religion they wish. This basic freedom has been held sacred by succeeding generations; it is carved in our monuments and upheld in our courts of law. In a sense, the American commitment to the principles articulated in its founding documents represents a religion in itself, in much the same way that a country might be dominated by one state-sanctioned religion.

At the same time, there is a deeply held belief that the exercise of one's own freedom should not impinge upon the health, safety, or guaranteed freedoms of others. To this end, Americans collectively abide by laws and regulations that ensure the rights of others. The boundary between the exercise of personal freedoms and the responsibility of the collectivity to protect its vulnerable members from harm is not always clear; the lack of clarity and consensus is the opportune place for tension to emerge.

Public opinion is not the only obstacle to acceptance faced by NRMs. Thomas Robbins describes the murky waters NRMs tread in their efforts to establish themselves in a locked-down, competitive religious marketplace.[4] Entrepreneurial efforts so admired in secular businesses can be the scourge of religious movements. Robbins astutely points out that asset-rich institutional churches assume an air of self-righteous indignation when pointing to the aggressive recruitment and expansion strategies of NRMs, but what other means do small innovative religious groups have of gaining a toehold in society? Robbins is not alone in observing that NRMs are highly dependent on monies raised from non-members through direct solicitation; moreover, they often press their advantage of avoiding state regulation because they are religious institutions.[5]

Seeing NRMs as arising out of larger, more complex social movements may be helpful in resolving disputes over toleration. Exemplifying a shift to a social movement perspective, the argument is made that popular alarm over the proliferation of "cults" is unwarranted. Stark and Finke were prophetic voices in contending that the growth of NRMs in North America is part of a pattern of gradual, long-term, linear shifts in religious participation in the United States.[6] These scholars attack the assumption that religious affiliation comes from an irrational human impulse; individuals join churches that seem relevant to them in a particular social context. Stark and Finke fault church historians and sociologists alike with failing to analyze rigorously church membership rates for the last half of the twentieth century. Rather than an explosion of cults in the 1960s and 1970s, they find a continuous presence of NRMs whose true number was more accurately counted in the hundreds rather than in the thousands.[7]

Stark and Iannaccone have stressed the need to understand, not only the reasons, but the actual interactive mechanisms that determine the cultural receptivity of society to cults and sects. They argue that "the economic/rational choice approach to religion is possibly the most powerful and comprehensive social scientific approach that scholars have at their disposal."[8] They criticize the trend toward idiosyncratic explanations that have short-changed existing theory and offer instead a series of propositions that explain the relationships between regulation and competitive tension in the religious economy. Of particular importance is their analysis of the cultural niche filled by sects and cults; although both sects and cults exist in tension with mainstream religious institutions, "sects function to revive conventional religious traditions, while cults attempt to dislodge and replace conventional religious traditions."[9] Cults impose "costly demands" on their affiliates through sacrifice and stigma; the benefits—fellowship with like-minded believers now, and eternal salvation later—make cult membership "a good bargain" according to the rational choice paradigm.[10]

NRMs are often created as part of an ongoing experimental process rather than rigidly conforming to *a priori* theological scripts. The case of the Unification Church arguably fits Robert Wuthnow's observation that NRMs can be viewed as social experiments designed to correct problems with existing institutions.[11] The Unification Church has actively sought to accommodate cultural expectations in the United States; the Reverend Moon has remade his public image in keeping with normative concerns. He has weathered the storms of negative publicity surrounding ex-member accounts as well as his personal troubles with the IRS to emerge as the leader of a new religion that has endured.

How much toleration of religious diversity is optimal? This, of course, is not a question that social scientists are competent to answer. But a polarized academic community divided between those advocating a high level of toleration[12] and those demanding a high level of surveillance[13] has impeded the achievement of consensus even at the descriptive level. Researchers who emphasized too much either the strengths or weaknesses of any particular NRM ran the risk of putting themselves out of favor with either proponents or opponents of unconditional toleration.

Between these two extreme positions has emerged a field of inquiry that attempts to explain or describe the cultural ambivalences in the tension that surrounds NRMs in American society.[14] For example, one of the attractive features of many NRMs to individual seekers is the alternatives they offer to unsatisfying social institutions—particularly the nuclear family and the traditional church. Many scholars have found that NRM affiliates find answers to their personal troubles.[15] NRMs often promoted religious practices that produced satisfying and/or relaxing spiritual states without the use of drugs or therapies. Such "solutions" can be seen as either helpful to society in solving social problems or harmful in that they undermine the effectiveness of more traditional ways of solving these problems. Turf battles emerge when social welfare experts, counselors, and other paid professionals sense that charismatic groups are stepping into their territory.

Finally, North American sociologists have struggled to understand how other societies deal with the difficult issues arising from the need to balance tolerance with regulation. Recent debates in the pages of *Nova Religio* about the German treatment of Scientology show an example of this. Our post-9/11 consciousness may help us come to understand that "one size fits all" approaches to the toleration-regulation questions don't sufficiently respect cultural differences across nations. At the same time, sympathetic review of how nations other than our own are dealing with this issue may turn out to be useful in coping with the American situation.

The Problem of Ideological Disconnection

Ideological diversity is healthy for open democratic societies. However, ideological disconnection occurs when this diversity becomes so extreme that co-existing subcultures no longer are able to even agree on the basic symbols of discourse. Mark Juergensmeyer has chillingly documented the ease with which difference can become disconnection in the ideological sphere.[16] Unfortunately, new religious movements are particularly at risk for both benign and virulent ideological disconnections from the larger society.

A fundamental disconnection between committed members of apocalyptic NRMs and the rest of the human collectivity arises from vastly different belief systems. Members of these NRMs embrace a values system that is other-worldly or "world rejecting,"[17] while traditionally religious and secular individuals tend to affirm and preserve the material world. This is not to say that adherents of mainstream culture do not rely on religious beliefs to guide and comfort them, but rather that their spiritual convictions are not perceived as threats to the present social order. Moreover, mainstream believers tend to keep their religious beliefs private, or at least subordinate to their public, civic deportment.

Our typical twentieth-century approach to understanding ideological disconnection focused on identification of specific ideological traits in NRMs. For example, Robbins and Anthony argued that internal factors within the particular NRM provide clues for anticipating the degree of ideological disconnection that could lead to violence. They identify four elements that may contribute to a group's propensity toward violence:

> [T]he endogenous potential for violence is likely to be enhanced when communal groups are energized by a fervent millenarian vision, and when the membership has totalistic psychological characteristics, and when the group is under the direct personal control of a charismatic leader with an exalted messianic self-conception and a determination to resist any encroachments on his authority or constraints on his freedom of action.[18]

Indicative of a more social-movement and process-oriented perspective, John Hall has argued that the devil always lies in the details.[19] He maintained, for example, that while the Peoples Temple and the Branch Davidians can both be seen as ideal-type apocalyptic sects, they each had significantly different ways of ideologically disconnecting from the larger society. Jim Jones invoked Huey Newton's dark vision of society as an inescapable net of oppression for minorities and the poor, while David Koresh preached within a well-established Adventist tradition replete with apocalyptic theology. Both leaders responded to external pressures in terms of their ideological beliefs. In November 1978, Jim Jones, beset with physical, mental, and emotional ailments, concluded that his cause was lost and that the "revolutionary suicide" of his followers in Jonestown was the best option in the face of mounting opposition.[20] Fears of the repeat of a "Jonestown model" at the Waco standoff contributed to well-documented tragic blunders by the authorities.[21]

Michael Barkun has shown how disconnecting mechanisms come to feed on themselves and thus become more extreme over time. For example, in his work on the Christian Identity movement, Barkun found that the group's theology justifies the use of force against God's enemies (whom they identify as "Jews, non-whites and government above the local level").[22] In an effort to separate themselves from social contamination, Christian Identity groups draw impenetrable boundaries between believers and "others":

> The very act of withdrawal increases the likelihood of pressure from the state. For the more radical the withdrawal, the greater the probability that those who withdraw will ignore, circumvent, or violate the complex network of laws and regulations the state has put in place.[23]

Jeffrey Kaplan, who has also done extensive research on White Supremacist groups, exemplifies in his research the importance of taking a social movement approach with a transnational perspective in order to understand these groups. He demonstrates, in his *Encyclopedia of White Power*,[24] that the interlocking directorates and the interweaving of charismatic influences among these groups is dense and complex; and that only a perspective that allows these groups to be understood in relation to the larger social movement they represent can have any hope of explaining them. His work and Barkun's also illustrate the vagueness of the line separating the political from the religious.

Juergensmeyer has demonstrated that radical groups that sanction terrorism occupy marginal positions within their religious denominations.[25] These radicals are frightening because they are convinced that they are following God's mandates and thus fulfilling the destinies divinely ordained for them. Juergensmeyer found that religious radicals around the globe are similar in three ways:

1) They refuse to compromise their beliefs with social conventions (a trait that sets them apart from mainstream religious organizations);

2) They reject the boundaries between private beliefs (religion, in this instance) and public forms (civil society and its institutions); and

3) They believe that the faith they are practicing is purer and truer to their religious heritage than conventional practice; moreover,

their religious practices contribute to the cosmic struggle of good against evil.[26]

While some NRMs turn their violence outward, other groups enact violent behaviors against their own members. The conflagration of the Branch Davidian compound is an example of both inward-turning and outward-reacting violence. Anthony and Robbins find that "totalistic cults" sometimes tend to be volatile, although this volatility does not necessarily result in destruction of human life.[27] When put in a position where no alternatives seem available, a cult leader may invoke a violent ending (Jim Jones' dire interpretation of the events following Congressman Ryan's murder, for instance).

Ideological disconnection does not only occur over the issue of violence. In fact, it is most likely to occur in NRMs over issues of marriage and sexuality. Unusual sexual and marriage practices within NRMs can be highly alarming to society. Wright and D'Antonio assert that regulation of sexual intimacy within a cult group "helps engender social cohesiveness and maximize social control."[28] Whether the charismatic leader restricts sexual intimacy or encourages nontraditional sexual behaviors, the effect is the same in terms of creating a tightly knit group.

Wright and D'Antonio claim that restriction of sexual practices is more common in the NRMs they studied than is freedom of sexual behavior. Charismatic leaders seem to recognize that directives on sexual practices are powerful ways "to heighten individual commitment and social control, thus enhancing the movement's chances to succeed."[29] Members of the Unification Church, for instance, are taught to refrain from sex before marriage and even abstain from intimate relations for a specified time after marriage. Reverend Moon exercises divine wisdom in arranging marriages between members, demonstrating that God's hand is firmly at work in building the perfect family; to this end, he secures the cooperation of his members by exercising spiritual authority in the most intimate areas of personal relationships.

When sexual practices within NRMs deviate from traditional dyadic relationships, mainstream society tends to respond with varying degrees of concern, especially if the reputed practices seem bizarre and unnatural in conventional terms. Bhagwan Sri Rajneesh was among the most controversial cult leaders in encouraging sexual freedom, claiming that sexual energy was the "fundamental source of all human energy," and repression of this energy was the "source of most individual problems."[30] In her study of Rajneeshpuram, Goldman found that the commune's practices of collective meditation and therapy sessions resulted in "profound friendships and absorbing love affairs" among Bhagwan's devotees. Even so, through interviews with members, Goldman heard the women asserting love for their spiritual master that was on a higher plane than physical intimacy: "Their love for Bhagwan was the central, shared bond that cemented their friendships and romances with one another."[31]

Members of certain NRMs confess deep love for their leaders, assertions that cause outsiders to question the sexual practices within the group.[32] For instance, Tabor and Gallagher describe David Koresh's curious blend of celibacy and polygamy.[33] Sexual practices within the Branch Davidian compound progressed from traditional dyads to newly interpreted conjugal relationships where all the members, male and female, were "wedded" to the Lamb of God. One of the wives who survived the Waco assault said that Koresh regarded sex as a spiritual matter; he was obeying God in having sexual relations with his wives. The Children of God is a well-known NRM often cited for their sexual recruitment practices.[34] What appears to be license from the outsider's point of view may in fact be ideologically purposeful.

The Management of Charisma

Beginning with the works of Max Weber, sociologists have been acutely aware of the centrality of charisma for the understanding of social and cultural change.[35] However, Weber's concerns have led to a tradition of research focusing on the personal characteristics of the charismatic leader on the world stage and the routinized forms taken by charismatic collectivities after the deaths of these leaders. From its beginnings, NRM scholarship has been concerned rather with the management of charisma in its raw, unbridled, and non-routinized manifestations. Twentieth-century scholars quickly pointed out the necessity of turning away from an exclusive concern with the biographies of charismatic leaders to a parallel concern with the structural characteristics of networks of charismatic followers both among themselves and in relationship to the leader.[36] But only recently has attention been drawn to the *process* of the charismatic relationship.[37] In the works of these more recent writers, charismatic relationships are looked at not only as structural facts with distinguishing social-network signatures, but as open-ended ongoing processes of identity formation for both followers and for leaders. Moreover, scholars are beginning to look at the passage of time and how it affects the relationship between the charismatic leader and his long-term followers.

Charismatic, high-demand movements have much in common whether they are religious or political. Charismatic religious movements are more similar to charismatic political movements than they are to other religious movements that are not structured around charismatic authority. Recent research has described the power of charismatic leaders of all types to create very similar looking totalistic groups.[38] For instance, Amy Siskind describes how the therapist/leaders at the Sullivan Institute crossed ethical boundaries in directing the client/members regarding choice of careers, decisions about relationships and child-bearing, and personal financial planning.[39]

On the complex global stage, charismatic actors cannot so easily be classified into religious or political categories. Ironically, this was pointed out over 25 years ago in a book by Irving L. Horowitz that has not had nearly the influence that it deserved.[40] This book, entitled *Science, Sin, and Scholarship: The Politics of Reverend Moon and the Unification Church*, was perceived, in the highly polarized climate of its day, as being anticult. It therefore was given the cold shoulder by many scholars concerned with creating a climate of toleration for NRMs. Horowitz's book, however, can more usefully be read as a well-documented account of how a visible religious collectivity might be just one cog in a transnational movement with a geopolitical agenda.

More recently, Irving Hexham and Karla Poewe have again mounted a powerful argument for the importance of studying NRMs as transnational phenomena.[41] And Lifton, of course, has given us a persuasive case study demonstrating that the leaders and the members of a new religious movement themselves may not be sure where to draw boundaries between religion and politics.[42]

The importance of looking at charismatic influence in NRMs as a process rather than as a structural form of authority is illustrated in recent works by Dawson, Davis, Lifton, and Zablocki.[43] Dawson carefully operationalizes Wallis' concept of deviance amplification.[44] Using this concept, he demonstrates the fragility of the continuous process of testing that charismatic leaders must go through, and the many ways in which it can implode or explode. Davis presents a close analysis of the way this led to mass suicides in the Heaven's Gate community. Lifton provides another sort of process model, this time from a psychoanalytic perspective. And Zablocki looks at the process by which the subjective experience of being trapped in the net of charismatic relationships can lead at times to an atmosphere of hopelessness and despair.[45]

Charismatic leadership is essential for many if not all forms of cultural innovation. However, it is clearly a double-edged sword. Much twentieth-century research on NRMs was hampered by a polarized need to see the charismatic cup as either full of nectar or full of poison. Freed from these constraints, contemporary scholarship in this field is increasingly able to develop theories that cope both with the creative power and the destructive potential of charisma.

Joiners, Stayers, and Leavers

Finally we come to a set of issues that may well be the most thoroughly studied and the least thoroughly understood of any within the rubric of

NRM studies. What sorts of people join new religious movements? Do they come from one common pool of "seekers," or are those who join Scientology and those who join the Moonies as different as apples and oranges? How long do those who join tend to stay? Do they join voluntarily, or are they manipulated into joining? What kinds of factors distinguish those who stay from those who leave? Do leavers have an easy or a tough time readjusting to mainstream society? Hundreds of books and articles have been written about these and related subjects. But few robust and replicable empirical conclusions have emerged from all this research.

Here, perhaps more easily than in the other areas we have looked at, we can see clearly the value of a paradigmatic adjustment. Very likely, we have been asking our questions in the wrong way. Because many NRMs band together in communal living arrangements or at least separate themselves from society by blatantly distinctive modes of dress or demeanor, we tend to assume that they are well-bounded social entities like families or business firms with well-defined criteria of membership and non-membership. Had we from the beginning emphasized the M in NRM, we would have learned from the social movements literature the importance of concepts such as "publics" and "civic arenas" which are:

> fractured, contentious, and multi-sectorial [and in which] coalitions are complex, fractious, and fragile constructions. . . . [which] involve cross-cutting and often contending organizational sectors, which must overcome their routine . . . segmentation in order to forge joint actions.[46]

Joiners of NRMs are an unremarkable lot in terms of personal background characteristics and measurable psychological traits. On this point, at least, there seems to be widespread agreement. The search for a religious seeker profile has gone on for years with no apparent success. The reason for this was pointed out early on in an article by Lofland and Stark.[47] Seekership, according to these authors, is largely a contextual and relational property whose determinants are not to be found at the individual level. Yet the search continues to go on in an effort to identify those at most "risk" for conversion.

We know surprisingly little about the characteristics associated with likelihood of long-term staying in membership roles in NRMs. Bainbridge made an important discovery that the probability of staying is very small early in the careers of new members but becomes much larger if they survive their first two or three years of membership.[48] But many more questions remain to be answered. Do rates of staying vary with age, with gender, with educational background? Are rates similar across NRMs, or does each NRM have its own retention profile? Do long-term stayers experience subjective restraints that eventually make them feel stuck?[49] Further, our current tendency to emphasize the social movement aspect of many

NRMs suggests that we pay more attention to a neglected category—people whose daily involvement with a NRM comes to an end (because of demands of career, marriage, or family) but who stay involved on a more superficial basis as fellow-travelers and perhaps financial contributors.

Our understanding of leavers has probably been the category most obscured by the polarized cult wars of the twentieth century. Many monographic accounts of specific NRMs notoriously make no attempt to investigate leavers. An example is the otherwise fine recent investigation of the Children of God by Bainbridge.[50] When leavers are studied, they are usually only looked at once, shortly after exiting the NRM.[51] A few researchers have attained fascinating results by studying ex-members after a lapse of membership of a decade or more.[52] More such research with a long-term perspective on post-NRM careers would be very useful. Investigators are further hampered by the negative attitudes taken by NRM leaders toward any attempts to interview ex-members. Bromley[53] and Johnson[54] among many other have labeled all those who left their NRMs under less than friendly terms "apostates," and this label has been used to cast doubt on the veracity of data collected from them. It has thus been a widespread practice until recently to ignore data gathered from leavers. There have been, however, some notable exceptions; in his work on the Holy Order of MANS/Christ the Savior Brotherhood,[55] Lucas "triangulates" ex-member accounts with the accounts provided by present members, outside observers, and documentary sources. He argues that ex-member accounts are as valuable (and as liable to distortion) as those by present members. Zablocki, too, has analyzed leaver responses and found them to be no more unreliable than data gathered from stayers.[56]

As we learn to view the religious life as a process, at once highly private and inner-looking and at the same time involving heroic investments of self into the public sector, we may come to understand why questions of joining, staying, and leaving must be asked with greater subtlety and more shades of gray.

Conclusions

In this chapter, we have briefly discussed what we see as an intellectual evolution in the way NRMs in North America are viewed by those who study them. Such an evolution is highly promising for the future of NRM research. It involves an emphasis on the social movement aspects of NRMs (and a de-emphasis on their putative "newness" and their exclusively religious nature). The emerging social movement emphasis may allow this overly insular field to benefit from exchanges with colleagues in the sociological subspecialty called "social movements," which has hitherto defined social movements primarily as political mobilizations.

The new paradigm also involves asking "how" questions as well as "why" questions, and a heightened awareness of religious movement participation as an open-ended process of identity formation, extending inwardly toward the formation of personal identity and outwardly to the formation of social identity. This intellectual evolution is helpful in putting the cart back behind the horse where it belonged from the beginning. Although we ultimately all want structural explanations of NRMs, we have neglected to first pay sufficient attention to the mechanisms they use to survive and prosper. Without understanding how they do what they do, we will never have more than a superficial understanding of why they take the forms they take and behave in the startling ways they have sometimes behaved.

Most important, this evolution promises the end of a severe and undignified polarization that has damaged the reputation of the entire field and prevented legitimate accomplishments from being taken as seriously as they deserve in the wider academic community. The misunderstandings that fostered this polarization may never be fully overcome but they may, nevertheless, wither away as the political and juridical pressures causing them diminish in importance. We are confident that, if they do, the various sides in these intellectual debates will find that they have had much more in common in their goals all along than they would ever have believed.

The final dimension of this evolution we have discussed is the most exciting to us—the evolution of a truly global perspective and perhaps even a global and transnational methodology. New religious movements are not exclusively an American phenomenon, but those in America do have distinctive American characteristics that are worth understanding. So, of course, do those in Japan, in Nigeria, in Russia, in Israel, and in South America. Systematic comparative work transcending national boundaries and national cultural perspectives is sorely needed. This, in our opinion, is the most important and challenging task for us in the years ahead.

Notes

1. Doug McAdam, "Culture and Social Movements," in *New Social Movememnts: From Ideology to Identity*, eds. Enrique Larana et al. (Philadelphia: Temple University Press, 1994).
2. See Raymond Boudon and François Bourricaud, "Culturalism and Culture," in *A Critical Dictionary of Sociology*, eds. R. Boudon and F. Bourricaud (Chicago: University of Chicago Press, 1986).
3. Emile Durkheim, *The Elementary Forms of Religious Life*, trans. Karen E. Fields (New York: The Free Press, 1995), 44.
4. Thomas Robbins, "New Religious Movements on the Frontier of Church and State," in *Cults, Culture and the Law: Perspectives on New Religious Movements*, eds. Thomas Robbins, William C. Shepherd, and James McBride (Chico, CA: Scholars Press, 1985).
5. Ibid., 98; E. Burke Rochford Jr., "Accounting for Child Abuse in the Hare Krishna: Ethnographic Dilemmas and Reflections," in *Toward Reflexive Ethnography: Participating, Observing, Narrating*, eds. David G. Bromley and Lewis F. Carter (Amsterdam: JAI Press, 2001), 157–79.

6. Rodney Stark and Roger Finke, "A Rational Approach to the History of American Cults and Sects," in *Religion and the Social Order*, vol. 3A, eds. David Bromley and Jeffrey K. Hadden (Greenwich, CT: JAI, 1993).

7. Ibid., 116.

8. Rodney Stark and Lawrence R. Iannaccone, "Rational Choice Propositions about Religious Movements," in *Religion and the Social Order*, eds. Bromley and Hadden, 241.

9. Ibid., 251.

10. Ibid., 249.

11. Robert Wuthnow, "The Cultural Context of Contemporary Religious Movements," in *Cults, Culture, and the Law*, eds. Robbins, Shepherd, and McBride.

12. David Bromley and Thomas Robbins, "The Role of Government in Regulating New and Nonconventional Religions," in *The Role of Government in Monitoring and Regulating Religion in Public Life*, eds. James Wood and Derek Davis (Waco, TX: Davison Institute of Church-State Studies, 1993).

13. See Margaret T. Singer with Janja Lalich, *Cults in Our Midst* (San Francisco: Jossey-Bass, 1995).

14. See, for example, Marc Galanter, *Cults: Faith, Healing, and Coercion* (New York: Oxford University Press, 1999); Benjamin Zablocki and Thomas Robbins, "Finding a Middle Ground in a Polarized Scholarly Arena," in *Misunderstanding Cults: Searching for Objectivity in a Controversial Field*, eds. Benjamin Zablocki and Thomas Robbins (Toronto: University of Toronto Press, 2001); William Sims Bainbridge, *The Endtime Family: Children of God* (Albany: SUNY Press, 2002).

15. See John Lofland, *Doomsday Cult: A Study of Conversion, Proselytization, and Maintenance of Faith* (Englewood Cliffs, NJ: Prentice-Hall, 1966); David G. Bromley, Bruce C. Busching, and Anson D. Shupe, "The Unification Church and the American Family: Strain, Conflict, and Control," in *New Religious Movements: A Perspective for Understanding Society*, ed. Eileen Barker (New York: Edwin Mellen, 1982); William Sims Bainbridge, *The Sociology of Religious Movements* (New York: Routledge, 1997); and Marion S. Goldman, *Passionate Journeys: Why Successful Women Joined a Cult* (Ann Arbor: University of Michigan Press, 1999).

16. Mark Juergensmeyer, *Terror in the Mind of God: The Global Rise of Religious Violence* (Berkeley: University of California Press, 2000).

17. Thomas Robbins and Dick Anthony, "Sects and Violence: Factors Enhancing the Volatility of Marginal Religious Movements," in *Armageddon in Waco*, ed. Stuart A. Wright (Chicago: University of Chicago Press, 1995).

18. Ibid., 252.

19. John Hall, "Public Narratives and the Apocalyptic Sect: From Jonestown to Mt. Carmel," in *Armageddon in Waco*, ed. Wright.

20. John Hall, *Gone from the Promised Land: Jonestown in American Cultural History* (New Brunswick, NJ: Transaction Books, 1987).

21. James D. Tabor and Eugene V. Gallagher, *Why Waco? Cults and the Battle for Religious Freedom in America* (Berkeley: University of California Press, 1995).

22. Michael Barkun, "Millenarians and Violence: The Case of the Christian Identity Movement," in *Millennium, Messiahs, and Mayhem: Contemporary Apocalyptic Movements*, eds. Thomas Robbins and Susan J. Palmer (New York: Routledge, 1997), 249.

23. Ibid., 253.

24. Jeffrey Kaplan, "The Roots of Religious Violence in America," in *Misunderstanding Cults*, eds. Zablocki and Robbins; *Encyclopedia of White Power* (Walnut Creek, CA: Altamira Press, 2000).

25. Juergensmeyer, *Terror in the Mind of God*, 216.

26. Ibid., 221.

27. Dick Anthony and Tom Robbins, "Religious Totalism, Exemplary Dualism, and the Waco Tragedy," in *Millennium, Messiahs, and Mayhem*, eds. Robbins and Palmer.

28. Stuart Wright and William V. D'Antonio, "Families and New Religions," in *Religion and the Social Order*, eds. Bromley and Hadden, 228.

29. Ibid., 228–29.

30. Lewis Carter, *Charisma and Control in Rajneeshpuram: The Role of Shared Values in the Creation of a Community* (Cambridge, U.K.: Cambridge University Press, 1990), 3.

31. Goldman, *Passionate Journeys*, 221.
32. Hall, *Gone from the Promised Land*.
33. Tabor and Gallagher, *Why Waco?*
34. Bainbridge, *The Endtime Family*.
35. Max Weber, *The Theory of Economic and Social Organization* (New York: The Free Press, 1964).
36. See, for instance, Leon Festinger et al., *When Prophecy Fails* (Minneapolis: University of Minnesota Press, 1956); John Lofland, *Doomsday Cult*; Benjamin Zablocki, *The Joyful Community* (Chicago: University of Chicago Press, 1971), and *Alienation and Charisma* (New York: The Free Press, 1980); and Raymond Bradley, *Charisma and Social Structure* (New York: Paragon Press, 1987).
37. See, for instance, Carter, *Charisma and Control in Rajneeshpuram*; Robert J. Lifton, *Destroying the World to Save It: Aum Shinrikyo, Apocalyptic Violence, and the New Global Terrorism* (New York: Henry Holt, 1999); Winston Davis, "Heaven's Gate: A Study of Religious Obedience," *Nova Religio* 3 (2000): 241–67; Lorne Dawson, "Crises of Charismatic Legitimacy and Violent Behavior," in *Dramatic Confrontations*, eds. David Bromley and J. Gordon Melton (Cambridge, U.K.: Cambridge University Press, 2002); and Janja Lalich, *Bounded Choice: True Believers and Charismatic Cults* (Berkeley: University of California Press, forthcoming 2004).
38. Juergensmeyer, *Terror in the Mind of God*.
39. Amy Siskind, "Telling Tales, Naming Names: My Experience as Apostate and Ethnographer of the Sullivan Institute/Fourth Wall Community," in *Toward Reflexive Ethnography*, eds. Bromley and Carter, 194.
40. Irving L. Horowitz, *Science, Sin, and Scholarship: The Politics of Reverend Moon and the Unification Church* (Cambridge, MA: MIT Press, 1978).
41. Irving Hexham and Karla Poewe, *New Religions as Global Cultures* (Boulder, CO: Westview Press, 1978).
42. Lifton, *Destroying the World to Save It*.
43. Dawson, "Crises of Charismatic Legitimacy and Violent Behavior"; Davis, "Heaven's Gate"; Lifton, *Destroying the World to Save It*; and Benjamin Zablocki, "Exit Cost Analysis: A New Approach to the Scientific Study of Brainwashing," *Nova Religio* 1 (1998): 216–49.
44. Roy Wallis, "The Social Construction of Charisma," *Social Compass* 29 (1982): 25–39.
45. Zablocki, "Exit Cost Analysis."
46. Ann Mische and Philippa Pattison, "Composing a Civic Arena: Publics, Projects, and Social Settings," *Poetics* 27 (2000):163–64.
47. John Lofland and Rodney Stark, "Becoming a World Saver: A Theory of Conversion to a Deviant Perspective," *American Sociological Review* 54 (1968): 862–74.
48. Bainbridge, *The Sociology of Religious Movements*.
49. Benjamin Zablocki, "Toward a Mystified and Disinterested Scientific Theory of Brainwashing," in *Misunderstanding Cults*, eds. Zablocki and Robbins.
50. Bainbridge, *The Endtime Family*.
51. See Stuart Wright, *Leaving Cults: The Dynamics of Defection* (Washington, D.C.: SSSR Monograph Series, 1987), no. 7; James R. Lewis and David G. Bromley, "The Cult Withdrawal Syndrome: A Case of Misattribution of Cause?" *Journal for the Scientific Study of Religion* 26 (1987): 508–22.
52. Marion Goldman and Lynne Isaacson, "Enduring Affiliations and Gender Doctrine for Shiloh Sisters and Rajneesh Sannyasins," *Journal for the Scientific Study of Religion* 38 (1999): 411–22; and Julius Rubin, *The Other Side of Joy: Religious Melancholy Among the Bruderhof* (New York: Oxford University Press, 2000).
53. David G. Bromley, "The Social Construction of Contested Exit Roles: Defectors, Whistleblowers, and Apostates," in *The Politics of Religious Apostasy*, ed. David G. Bromley (Westport, CN: Praeger, 1998).
54. Daniel Johnson, "Apostates Who Never Were: The Social Construction of Absque Facto Apostate Narratives," in *The Politics of Religious Apostasy*, ed. Bromley.
55. See Phillip Charles Lucas, *The Odyssey of a New Religion: The Holy Order of MANS from New Age to Orthodoxy* (Bloomington, IN: Indiana University Press, 1995); "Shifting Millennial Visions in New Religious Movements: The Case of the Holy Order of MANS," in *The Year 2000: Essays on the End*, ed. Charles B. Strozier (New York: New York University Press,

1997); "From Holy Order of MANS to Christ the Savior Brotherhood: The Radical Transformation of an Esoteric Christian Order," in *America's Alternative Religions*, ed. Timothy Miller (Albany: State University of New York Press, 1995); "The Eleventh Commandment Fellowship: A New Religious Movement Confronts the Ecological Crisis," *Journal of Contemporary Religion* 10:3 (1995): 229–41; and "Social Factors in the Failure of New Religious Movements: A Case Study Using Stark's Success Model," *SYZYGY: Journal of Alternative Religion and Culture* 1:1 (Winter 1992): 39–53.

56. Benjamin Zablocki, "Reliability and Validity of Apostate Accounts in the Study of Religious Communities," presented at the annual meetings of the Association for the Sociology of Religion, New York, New York, 1996.

CHAPTER 21

Cults, Porn, and Hate

Convergent Discourses on First Amendment Restriction

THOMAS ROBBINS AND DICK ANTHONY

Introduction

This paper attempts to extend and contextualize themes originally introduced in an earlier article.[1] That paper identified marked similarities among arguments for excluding from the protection of the First Amendment egregious behaviors in three communicative realms: the persuasive and ritual practices of "cults," sadistic pornography, and racist "hate speech."

In all three communicative sub-areas, problematic speech behaviors have been identified which are viewed by the First Amendment restrictionists as going beyond "only words" and amounting to insidious instruments of domination producing coerced or compulsive behavior on the part of "victims." The effects of pornography, racist "hate speech," and cultist indoctrination have been viewed as "visceral" in the sense that they are not mediated by an individual's cognitive processes but rather bypass such processes and undermine the critical intellect, thereby eroding the foundations of personal autonomy. Irrational and subcognitive, the effects of pornographic sexual stimulation, provocative hate speech, and alleged quasi-hypnotic cultic techniques to alter consciousness are not viewed primarily as expressions of ideas but rather as somewhat drug-like forces which produce psychic disequilibrium and erode self-control. The alleged irrational and subcognitive quality of these communicative behaviors and their consequent coercive effect on the recipients of communications are said to disqualify these acts from the full protection that the First Amendment accords "free speech" and religious "free exercise."

In the earlier paper we expressed our unease with these restrictionist discourses that propose to narrow the scope of the First Amendment and exclude more types of communicative behavior from constitutional protection. Observers have noted that an implicit *rationality* criterion potentially disadvantageous to minorities (whose speech is more likely to be viewed as subrational) seems to be entailed.[2] The received distinction between speech acts and non-speech acts appears to be relativized and replaced by indeterminate standards of rationality, coerciveness, compulsiveness, and so on. In this paper we somewhat diminish the previous paper's emphasis on continual "rebuttal." We restate more clearly and succinctly the basic thesis regarding the interrelationship of three restrictive First Amendment discourses, and we additionally attempt to contextualize the convergent exclusionary First Amendment discourses in terms of the increasing ambiguity of moral boundaries in American society and the increasingly problematic location of personal responsibility. We also relate these First Amendment arguments to divergent conceptions of liberty.

Cults and Pornography

The First Amendment protects "the free exercise of religion." Clearly implicit (and occasionally made explicit) in arguments supporting the exclusion of "cult indoctrination" from constitutional protection is the notion that the insidious and coercive nature of persuasive communications in "cults" renders the quality of spiritual expression therein essentially *unfree*. As such, psychologically coercive religion does not qualify for the protection vouchsafed only to the *free* exercise of religion. "The language of the First Amendment," affirms Richard Delgado, "does not support absolute protection for all religious beliefs ... logically the amendment protects [only] freely held religious belief."[3]

Catherine MacKinnon has made a somewhat similar point regarding pornography and the protection of free speech:

> The most basic assumption underlying the First Amendment adjudication is that, socially, speech is free. . . . Free speech exists. The problem for government is to avoid constraining that which, if unconstrained by government, *is* free. This tends to presuppose that whole segments of the population are not systematically silent prior to government action.[4]

In effect, the argument is being made that pornography, which degrades and intimidates women while hyper-stimulating men and thus instigating compulsive male aggressive behavior, does not constitute truly *free* speech and, moreover, actually imperils the cultural climate necessary for guaranteeing free speech for women.

Beyond the convergence of theoretical rejections of the applicability of the protective shield of the First Amendment—pornography is not "free speech" and brainwashing cultism is not "free exercise of religion"—there are marked similarities in the particular explanations as to why cultic and pornographic communications are not truly "free." To some degree, in both areas allegations are made that problematic communications are *subcognitive* and subrational and impact primarily emotions and instincts in a manner which actually subverts personal autonomy and maintains little connection with "the free marketplace of ideas."

Delgado and other writers see "cult indoctrinees" becoming disoriented and even *incapacitated* through a combination of poor diet, sleep deprivation, manipulated social bonding, appeals to fear and guilt, behavioral conditioning and, above all, dissociative and trance states induced through "hypnotic" processes associated with meditation, repetitive chanting, glossolalia, and other experiential rituals. These processes are said to enhance suggestibility and impair judgmental and cognitive functions. Regression to infantile cognitive states and loss of capacity for complex or critical thought are sometimes said to be involved.[5]

Some of the arguments mustered to support the notion that pornography is not authentic "free speech" warranting the protection of the First Amendment also emphasize the dynamics of emotional arousal and visceral excitation and the consequent subcognitive and subrational quality of pornographic communications. As Ronald Dworkin points out, MacKinnon, in her book, *Only Words*, appears to embrace a somewhat mechanistic psychology of coercive arousal:

> She says that much pornography is not just speech—it is not "only words"— because it produces erections in men and provides them with masturbatory fantasies. (She warns her readers never to "underestimate the power of an erection.") Her view of the psychology of emotional arousal is mechanical—she thinks men who read pornography "are sexually habituated to a kick, a process that is largely unconscious and works as primitive conditioning, with pictures and words as sexual stimuli." In any case she thinks that pornography's physiological power deprives it of First Amendment protection: "An orgasm is not an argument," she says, "and cannot be argued with. Compared with a thought it raises far less difficult free speech issues, if it raises any at all."[6]

As another critic comments, MacKinnon believes "that because pornography is 'noncognitive' expression, it can be regulated on a lesser showing of justification than would be required for regulating speech at the First Amendment's 'core.'"[7]

Themes of visceral communication and coercive hyper-arousal are also featured in an interesting, posthumously published article by a former civil liberties lawyer that directly cites pornography and cult indoctrination as unworthy recipients of First Amendment protection:

> What occurs as the mind absorbs photographs of women being tied up with spiked leather masks and torso straight jackets, with knives stuck up their bodies and representations of ecstasy on their faces? What have the anxious acts of a person, young or old, who has not had enough protein or sleep, who has been deprived of contact with family, privacy, ideas or influences other than the cult's, deprived of the opportunity for reality-testing and under enormous peer pressure, what has all this to do with the exercise of religion (if we give the term the reasonable meaning it had when the First Amendment was adopted or even the common-sense meaning it has today)? . . . We make a knee-jerk application of classical First Amendment principles to an event which is different in basic quality from those which stimulated the basic concept and the subsequent case law.[8]

MacKinnon, Stender, Delgado, and others are clearly stating that there is some inherent quality of pornographic or cultic communications, or the way in which their effects are produced (for example, subcognitive emotional arousal), which distinguish such communicative and expressive practices from those "free" practices which are legitimately protected under the First Amendment. Like cultist mind control, pornographic stimulation is said to enhance *suggestibility* and thus to more or less *compel* certain behaviors.

Pornography and Hate Speech

The arguments mustered in support of the argument that pornography does not represent truly *free* speech include the proposition that pornographic communications are really inimical to free speech because they in effect "silence" women. Pornography allegedly does this by depicting women as degraded and sexually masochistic such that women are inhibited from speaking out on behalf of their dignity and autonomy or else they cannot, where demeaning objectification of women is pervasive, obtain a hearing.[9] A similar argument is also made with respect to the posited ineligibility of racist and sexist "hate speech" for the protection of the First Amendment. This argument extrapolates the more conventional premise that some raucous speech is insupportable in some contexts because it silences or "drowns out" other speech. Aggressive heckling or shouting a speaker down at a public meeting constitute relatively non-problematic examples. More civil libertarian resistance may be anticipated to the application of the "drowning out" argument to speech that negatively stereotypes other speakers and therefore "silences" them. "Speech," notes Michaelman, "can degrade the fair value of other peoples' speech by summoning up perceptions of them (quite apart from their messages) as human types unworthy to be heard or credited—that is by exploiting cultures of oppression to induce prejudgment."[10] Charles Fried, a critic of "the new first amendment jurisprudence" represented by MacKinnon, Michaelman, et al., paraphrases this view: "Some speech must be shut down in the name of free speech."[11]

In this view, hate speech and pornography diminish their victims' sense of self-worth and thus disempower them and undercut their participation in public discourse. Such wounding and disempowering speech may thus be legitimately throttled to empower other potential speakers to enhance the diversity of speech. Arguments of this nature generally place some emphasis on the *emotive* quality of highly objectionable hate speech. Indeed, it is sometimes argued that it is the visceral nature of extreme hate speech (epithets, for example) which reduces the victim to silence or inarticulate helplessness:

> Assaultative racial speech functions as a preemptive strike. The racial invective is experienced as a blow, not a proffered idea, and once the blow is struck, it is unlikely that dialogue will follow. Racial insults are undeserving of first amendment protection because the perpetrator's intention is not to discover truth or initiate dialogue but to injure the victim.[12]

Reference is obviously being made here to the "Fighting Words" doctrine.[13] "When racial insults are hurled at minorities, the response may be silence or a flight rather than a fight." Women and minorities often report they find themselves speechless. "The pre-emptive effect of further speech is just as complete as with fighting words."[14] The visceral emotional response of victims of "assaultive speech" thus precludes counter-speech. Attack "produces an instinctive, defensive reaction," thus, "When one is personally attacked with words that denote one's subhuman status and untouchability, there is little (if anything) that can be said to redress either the emotional or reputational injury."[15]

We note here that this is a rather *deterministic* argument. Assaultive hate speech is said to have a predictable, indeed one might say *coercive* impact such that victims are in effect rendered "speechless." Fighting words are said to produce a compulsive arousal effect on the humiliated recipient such that if violence ensues, the responsibility is assigned to the assaultive speaker. Fighting words can thus be censored or negatively sanctioned to maintain peace and order.

The arguments about the compulsive consequences of "assaultive speech" have clear parallels with the arguments affirming the coercive effects of cultic rituals and persuasive speech, as well as with the formulations about violent pornography "silencing" women and mechanically (that is, coercively) arousing men. In all three discourses, *subcognitive emotional arousal is said to undercut personal autonomy* such that the (largely) verbal behaviors which produce arousal cannot be treated as truly *free* speech or religious exercise. Psycho-emotional compulsion is viewed as negating First Amendment protection.

A second significant aspect of these exclusionary discourses entails the *social science* dimension. This is particularly conspicuous with respect to anticult arguments that rely on clinical analyses and on invocations of research on "brainwashing," "coercive persuasion," "thought reform," and so on.[16] The social science angle is somewhat less conspicuous in the two free speech discourses; nevertheless, the arguments regarding the subcognitive coercive-compulsive effects of pornography and hate speech are at least quasi-scientific. They posit a deterministic psychodynamic of such a compulsive or coercive quality that personal autonomy, rationality, and free will become inoperative. *Social science thus becomes the arbiter of civil liberties and constitutional protections* that are properly applicable only to contexts of *free* speech and religious practice and not to psycho-domination and compulsive arousal. Social science adjudicates autonomy, which is deemed essential to freedom.

Two additional issues must be noted at this point. The exclusionary First Amendment discourse regarding "cults" is purportedly *libertarian.* Both sides claim to be vindicating true "freedom of religion" which, in the view of those who want to exclude cultic indoctrinational practices from the scope of the First Amendment, requires prior "freedom of mind" or the capacity (allegedly nullified by cultic indoctrination) to exercise autonomy and "free exercise." In contrast, the exclusionary discourses involving pornography and racist assaultive speech possess both "libertarian" and "egalitarian" variants. The former version argues the inapplicability of the First Amendment's protection of free speech to putatively "unfree" communications. The egalitarian argument, however, potentially concedes the applicability of the Constitution's protection of free speech, but maintains that libertarian considerations must be balanced by considerations of equal protection of the laws and equal opportunity. In her recent book on pornography, MacKinnon[17] evokes a conflict between the constitutional values of *liberty* and *equality,* "the law of equality and the law of the freedom of speech are on a collision course in this country."[18] It is now necessary, according to MacKinnon, for the law to compensate for its recent one-sided emphasis on liberty.

The necessity of balancing liberty and equality is also maintained by defenders of hate speech censorship, who urge that understanding the damage produced by assaultive speech "requires a reconsideration of the balance that must be struck between our concern for racial equality and freedom of expression."[19] For Ronald Dworkin, however, this "balancing" logic represents an ominous appeal "to the frightening principle that considerations of equality require that some people not be free to express their tastes or convictions or preferences anywhere."[20]

Before we conclude by contextualizing some of these issues in terms of shifting cultural standards, one additional point must be made. Dworkin suggests that some arguments mobilized on behalf of the censorship of pornography or assaultive speech implicitly appeal to a conception of freedom of speech as a *positive liberty*.[21] In a famous essay, Isaiah Berlin defined "positive liberty" as the power to control one's destiny and attain one's goals or to participate in collective decision-making and societal control. It is contrasted with "negative liberty," which denotes simply the absence of restraint or obstruction (generally by the state) on one's action.[22] Negative liberty is generally seen as a *freedom from state action* while positive liberty is often viewed as being established through state action. Positive liberty is often seen as being threatened by an impediment or *incapacity* such as ignorance, poverty, or inequality, which the state may be called upon to remove.

Robbins has argued that those who wish to legalize deprogramming through conservatorships and guardianships (granted to parents of adult cultists) are implicitly positive libertarians who believe that "the courts must make possible the exercise of religious liberty by removing the incapacitating effects of mind control."[23] Somewhat similarly, Catherine MacKinnon sees pornography as promoting a kind of mind control whereby male sexual supremacy is institutionalized through the eroticization of male dominance and female submission.[24] Pornography constructs images of male and female for an aroused male audience whose mental degradation of women, reinforced by pornography, shapes the roles, options, and outcomes available to women in society. "Pornography, on this view, denies the positive liberty of women; it denies them the right to be their own masters by recreating them, for politics and society, in the shapes of male fantasy."[25] Criticizing this argument, Dworkin maintains that American First Amendment values are fundamentally grounded in the ideal of negative liberty. "Freedom speech, conceived and protected as a fundamental negative liberty, is the core of the choice modern democracies have made, a choice we must now honor in finding our own ways to combat the shaming inequalities women still suffer."[26]

As noted above, conceptions of positive liberty are potentially friendly to the dynamic action of the state aimed at removing impediments such as poverty, illiteracy, racism, class domination (and possibly even mind control)—all of which incapacitate individuals to exercise positive freedom. Thus Owen Fiss explicitly argues that the state becomes "the friend rather than the enemy" of freedom when it acts to suppress pornography, hate-speech, and unlimited political campaign contributions (the latter allegedly "drowns out" the voices of the poor), thereby empowering women, minorities, and poor persons to speak. The state properly "silences the voices of some in order to hear the voices of others."[27] In contrast, from the standpoint of negative liberty, forceful state action to enhance positive liberty by censoring obnoxious, prejudicial speech must be viewed as anti-libertarian.

Finally, it is important to note that there is an arguable affinity between conceptions of positive liberty and *social science*. It is social science that informs positive libertarians of the impediments which are blocking the fulfillment of positive freedom (of religion, speech, and so forth) and of what needs to be done to remove them, for example, how sociocultural conditions might be transformed to enhance the capabilities or opportunities so vital to positive liberty.

Conclusion

In his recent book, *Antichrist*, Bernard McGinn notes that many persons today cannot conceive of a totally evil (or totally good) person. "In our own century, when psychological and sociological accounts of human motivation have done so much to explain why people do good acts while others seem driven to commit evil, we are loath to think that any human being could be completely good or evil."[28]

"Good" and "evil" seem no longer clearly identifiable in a deepening climate of moral ambiguity. Responsibility for individual problems, failures, and disasters is becoming harder to pin down, and issues involving conflicting claims about responsibility often become highly contentious and politicized, for example, debates over "date rape."[29]

In some ways this moral ambiguity reflects shifting norms and cultural standards as yesterday's consensually stigmatized behaviors such as abortion and homosexuality become acceptable as well as objects of fierce moral debate. Such debate also surrounds new candidates for stigmatization such as "homophobia," "sexism," "political correctness," or smoking. Moral boundaries may be becoming less distinct.

The expansion of social science has played a role here. Social science, and in particular psychology-psychiatry, has been fertile in developing deterministic *explanations* for actions and outcomes which might otherwise—and more traditionally—be seen to reflect personal failings, weaknesses, and moral turpitude. What is entailed here is in part the mitigation of criminal and moral responsibility through deterministic conceptualizations which suggest that an alleged transgressor and moral defective might be more fairly viewed as a victim.

This pattern is relevant not only to the adjudications of criminal responsibility but also to broader areas of social policy and psychiatric diagnosis. Psychiatric diagnostic patterns have emerged that skeptics claim "medicalize character" or represent the "medicalization of everyday misery" and the "medicalization of deviance." While removing the deviant stigma from homosexuality and other conditions, the official *Diagnostics and Statistical Manual of Mental Disorders* has identified various "personality disorders" and other conditions, some of which, such as "oppositional defiance disorder," arguably convert deviant behavior from a volitional transgression of norms into involuntary conditions of victimization sometimes requiring accommodation as well as neutralization of deviant stigma. One theater in which accommodation and even compensation are worked out is the Americans with Disabilities Act (ADA), which provides protections for the civil rights of individuals with disabilities in the areas of employment, public accommodation, transportation, telecommunications, and public services. What were once thought of as faults or character flaws become "psychological disorders" requiring accommodation or compensations.

In our view, the pervasive moral ambiguity and indeterminacy of responsibility is profoundly unsettling. Moral boundaries seem to have dissolved. The convergent discourses on excluding cultic indoctrination, violent pornography, and racist hate speech from the protection of the First Amendment reflect an attempt to construct new moral boundaries which, however, will accept the modern psychologizing of moral arguments. The new boundaries are grounded in the concept of *coercion*, which, however, is expanded to include psychological coercion. The latter is seen to be particularly evident in "visceral" communications that operate at an emotional level and bypass or undercut vital cognitive and judgmental processes. The idea of the presumptive personal autonomy of individual actors, which arguably has been a basic tenet of the legal system, is weakened by these discourses that view individual autonomy as a frail reed which cannot resist emotional bombardment, erotic stimulation, and nasty, hateful provocation. While quite compatible with conceptions of positive liberty, these discourses are inimical to the idea of negative freedom and, moreover, have implications for an expansion of governmental regulation in the direction of the "therapeutic state."[30]

Social science will necessarily be vital to the construction of new moral boundaries, which is to say, psychologists, psychiatrists, and other "experts" will discern when individuals subjected to the "coercively" overpowering effects of cultic indoctrination, pornographic arousal, and racist vituperation have thereby lost their autonomy and been deprived of the capacity of exercising self-control and positive freedom. It may be objected, however, that the "scientific" conceptual frameworks which are employed to decipher the nature and effects of ("cultic") religion are themselves possessed of a "religious" or ideological quality such as to disqualify them as objective arbiters of social control, particularly in matters of religion.

Although this paper deals with the interrelationship of three exclusionary First Amendment discourses, the authors' long-term interest has involved critical evaluation of conceptualizations (or transvaluation) of religious conversion as "brainwashing."[31] This transvaluation is arguably reductive and is grounded in theoretical foundations whose objectivity—and perhaps even secularity—is open to question.

Finally, we will note that in our view, these discourses and the premises from which they operate ultimately *deepen rather than resolve the present climate of moral ambiguity.* The indeterminacy of moral responsibility is not diminished but is enhanced by psychologizing, as subtle psychological nuances are always debatable. Received civil libertarian distinctions such as that between speech and action are relativized to the ultimate detriment, in our view, of the protection of civil liberties, which may require that certain distinctions remain intact.

Notes

1. Dick Anthony and Thomas Robbins, "The Contested Authenticity of 'Free Exercise,' and 'Free Speech': The Convergence of Anti-Cult, Anti-Porn and Anti-Hate Speech Discourses," in *The Issue of Authenticity in the Study of Religions; Religion and the Social Order,* vol. 6, ed. Lewis Carter (Greenwich, CT: JAI Press, 1996), 25–46.
2. Ibid.; Kenneth L. Karst, *Law's Promise, Law's Expression* (New Haven: Yale University Press, 1993).
3. Richard Delgado, "When Religious Exercise is Not Free," *Vanderbilt Law Review* 375 (1984): 1071–1115, 1091–92. In an earlier, influential treatise Delgado argued that cultic threats to personal autonomy present a compelling state interest in overriding the expected First Amendment protection for religious freedom. See Richard Delgado, "Religious Totalism: Gentle and Ungentle Persuasion Under the First Amendment," *So. Cal. Law Review* 51 (1977): 1–99. The innovative supplementary argument that the First Amendment doesn't even apply to psychologically coercive cultic religiosity is made explicit in his later 1984 article. Interestingly, Delgado has also been active in discourses limiting First Amendment protection for racist hate speech. See Richard Delgado, "Campus Antiracism Rules," *Northwestern Law Review* 85 (1991). See also Delgado, "Words that Wound: A Tort Action for Insults, Racial Epithets and Name-Calling," *Harvard Civil Rights-Civil Liberties Law Review* 17 (1982).
4. Catherine MacKinnon, "Pornography, Civil Rights and Free Speech," in *Pornography: Women, Violence and Civil Liberties,* ed. Catherine Itzin (New York: Oxford University Press, 1992), 456.
5. Delgado, "Religious Totalism." See also Flo Conway and Jim Siegelman, *Snapping: America's Epidemic of Sudden Personality Change* (Philadelphia: Lippincott, 1978).
6. Ronald Dworkin, *Freedom's Law: The Moral Reading of the American Constitution* (Cambridge, MA: Harvard University Press, 1996), 233. See Catherine MacKinnon, *Only Words* (Cambridge, MA: Harvard University Press, 1993).
7. Karst, *Law's Promise, Law's Expression,* 48.
8. Fay Stender, "Some Rigors of our Time: The First Amendment and Real Life and Death," *Cultic Studies Journal* 41 (1987): 1–17. Ms. Stender had defended Black Panthers. After being shot by a friend of a client, she began to reconsider her civil libertarianism. Events such as the 1978 mass suicide/homicide in Jonestown and neo-Nazis being allowed to

march in Illinois, led her to write an essay questioning "knee-jerk" civil libertarian support for pornography, neo-Nazis, and alleged mind-controlling "cults" such as the Unification Church. Her essay was published posthumously in an anticult journal with rejoinders by civil libertarians.

9. See Catherine MacKinnon, *Feminism Unmodified: Discourses on Life and Law* (Cambridge, MA: Harvard University Press, 1987).

10. Frank Michaelman, "Liberties, Fair Values and Constitutional Method," in *The Bill of Rights in the Modern State*, eds. Geoffrey Stone, Richard Epstein, and Cass Sunstein (Chicago: University of Chicago Press, 1992), 97–114. See also Frank Michaelman, "Conceptions of Democracy in American Constitution Argument: The Case of Pornography Regulation," *Tennessee Law Review* 56:291 (1989): 303–04.

11. Charles Fried, "The New First Amendment Jurisprudence: A Threat to Liberty," in *The Bill of Rights in the Modern State*, eds. Stone, et al., 225–54.

12. Charles Lawrence, "If He Hollers Let Him Go: Regulating Racist Speech on Campus," *Duke Law School Journal* 431 (1990): 431 ff. See also Lawrence's, "The Id, The Ego and Equal Protection," *Stanford Law Review* 37 (1987): 317 ff.

13. Delgado, "Campus Antiracism Rules"; Lawrence, "If He Hollers Let Him Go." Interestingly, Delgado has supported restriction of First Amendment participation for both cult indoctrination and racist hate speech.

14. Lawrence, "If He Hollers Let Him Go," 452.

15. Ibid., 453.

16. See Dick Anthony and Thomas Robbins, "Law, Social Science and the 'Brainwashing' Exception to the First Amendment," *Behavioral Sciences and the Law* 10:1 (1992): 5–29.

17. MacKinnon, "Pornography, Civil Rights and Free Speech."

18. Quoted in Dworkin, *Freedom's Law*, 234.

19. Lawrence, "If He Hollers Let Him Go," 457.

20. Dworkin, *Freedom's Law*, 235.

21. Ibid., 457.

22. Isaiah Berlin, *Four Essays On Liberty* (New York: Oxford University Press, 1968).

23. Thomas Robbins, "New Religions, Brainwashing and Deprogramming," *Religious Studies Review* 114 (1985): 361–70. On the other hand, William Shepherd argues that the government has an affirmative duty to enhance religious freedom by suppressing coercive deprogramming transpiring under private (non-governmental) auspices. This seems like a positive liberty argument against deprogramming. Shepherd, *To Secure the Blessings of Liberty: Constitutional Law and the New Religious Movements* (New York: Crossroad; Chico, CA: Scholars Press, 1985).

24. MacKinnon, *Only Words*.

25. Dworkin, *Freedom's Law*, 221.

26. Ibid.

27. Owen Fiss, "Free Speech and Social Structure," *Iowa Law Review* 71 (1986): 1405 ff. See also Fiss, "State Activism and State Censorship," *Yale Law Journal* 100 (1991): 2087 ff.

28. Bernard McGinn, *Antichrist: Two Thousand Years of Human Fascination with Evil* (San Francisco: HarperSanFrancisco, 1994).

29. Arguments have been advanced to the effect that a woman who appears to submit voluntarily to a sexual act may actually be psychologically coerced and thus not responsible and in effect raped or assaulted.

30. Thomas Robbins, "Cults and the Therapeutic State," *Social Policy* (May/June 1979): 42–46.

31. Anthony and Robbins, "Law, Social Science and the 'Brainwashing' Exception to the First Amendment."

Conclusion

The Future of New and Minority Religions in the Twenty-First Century: Religious Freedom under Global Siege

PHILLIP CHARLES LUCAS

New and minority religious communities in any culture or nation face an uphill battle for survival. This is because these communities often challenge or reject the normative order of society. Thus, judicial systems, legal systems, mainstream religions, political parties, and concerned citizens' groups (such as countercult and anticult movements) are compelled to address the challenge posed by new and minority religions both to their own position in the social hierarchy and to the normative order of society in general. Each participant in the normative order constitutes a constellation of social forces that can repress, critique, persecute, and battle new and minority religions. As the essays in this volume bespeak, these constellations of social forces have grown bolder and more capable in the wake of violent events associated with the Branch Davidians, Aum Shinrikyō, the Solar Temple, Heaven's Gate, and the Movement for the Restoration of the Ten Commandments, and following the events of 9/11 and the subsequent "war on terror."

The United Nations General Assembly adopted the Universal Declaration of Human Rights in 1948. Its Article 48 reads: "Everyone has the right to freedom of thought, conscience and religion; this right includes freedom to change his religion or belief, and freedom, either alone or in community with others and in public or private, to manifest his religion or belief in teaching, practice, worship and observance." These and similar rights are enshrined in the federal constitutions of many nations around the world. In practice, however, these rights have a rather tentative status in most countries and, as recent history has amply demonstrated, religious freedoms can be diluted and even terminated when a nation or society feels threatened in some way.

In this concluding essay, I argue that abrogations of and limitations on religious freedom are increasing in nations and regions around the world. Especially given the prospect that the "war on terror" is likely to be long-term, these abrogations and limitations pose a very real threat to the freedoms articulated in Article 48 of the Universal Declaration of Human Rights. The effects of this increasing repression and dilution of religious freedom will be felt not only by new religious movements (NRMs) but by minority religious communities of all stripes, for example, by Baptists and Assemblies of God members in Belgium, by Pentecostals in France and Russia, by Wahhabi-influenced Muslims in the traditionally Islamic nations of the former Soviet Union, by communities of Sunni Muslims in Great Britain and the U.S., and by Jehovah's Witnesses and Scientologists almost everywhere.

There are five principal factors that are responsible for the increasing repression of new and minority religious communities around the world: 1. the end of Cold War, with its resultant shift from battles between capitalist democracies and their secular atheist (Communist) enemies to clashes between religion-based civilizations and their agents; 2. the attack by Muslim extremists on the World Trade Center on September 11, 2001, the subsequent ratcheting up of the international "war on terror" by the government of the U.S. and its allies around the world, and the Islamic diaspora, which has created large and vocal Muslim communities in many Western nations; 3. the sensational episodes of violence involving new religions during the late twentieth century, and the subsequent growing perception (in, for example, China, Japan, and France) that minority religions can constitute a danger to social order; 4. the diminution of academic influence in societal cult/sect debates and the concurrent internationalization of the anticult and countercult movements, along with these movements' increasingly close relationship with political, judicial, and mainstream religious forces in nations around the world; and 5. a resurgent nationalism in countries that are struggling to build a coherent national identity following radical regime changes, and the simultaneous efforts of traditional, "national" churches to regain cultural hegemony by colluding with nationalist political forces. Each of these factors plays a significant role in the increasingly repressive climate for new and minority religions around the globe.

The End of the Cold War and the Emerging Clash of Religion-Based Civilizations

The period of the Cold War (1948–1989) was marked by dueling ideologies, a weapons race, strategies of "containment," and by "proxy wars" in various parts of the world. From the viewpoint of the Western industrialized democracies, Communism represented an atheistic political ideology that threatened Western-style human freedoms, capitalist economies, and traditional religious beliefs and values. Western countries prized their traditions of religious freedom and saw themselves as defending a way of life that at its root was sanctioned by a divine order, however conceived. In a sense, to have a religion—any religion—was a mark of virtue and superiority, and it gave religious believers the hope that their God would triumph in the end over the Communist "evil empire" of nonbelievers. In this climate, freedom of religion—even for minority religions and NRMs whose beliefs one did not share—was seen as a societal good. Attempts to suppress or limit the religious freedoms of these groups mostly met with effective opposition by the majority in the Western democracies.

The end of the Cold War inaugurated a period of disorientation and uncertainty in the lives of nations and in the world of geopolitics in general. By the mid-1990s, however, various constellations of political, religious, and economic forces began to present an emerging new paradigm for geopolitics. This emerging paradigm was articulated most forcefully in Samuel Huntington's influential book, *The Clash of Civilizations and the Remaking of World Order*, which argued that the wars of the twenty-first century would be fought between blocs of countries with either an Islamic-based civilization, a Chinese-based civilization, or a Christian-based civilization. While this is not the place to argue the merits or limitations of this provocative thesis, it is fair to say that our present world geopolitical order looks more and more as if its fissures and tensions will develop along the broad civilizational axes postulated by Huntington. What is most significant about this development for our present purposes is that at least some of the wars in the post-Cold War era may well be fought between nations and blocs of nations that embrace competing *religious* heritages. This is not to say that any "Christian" nation in the West does not have significant minorities of non-Christians in its midst, only that the majority in these countries—and certainly their power elites—share a Christian or "post-Christian" worldview that is very different from, for example, a traditional Islamic or Chinese worldview.

Another way of understanding this shift is to propose the following thesis: the uncertainty, secularism, interrogation of metanarratives, questioning of authority, and fluid pluralism that seemed to define the "post-modern era" between 1965 and 1995 has given way to a new era of autocratic certainty, resurrected metanarratives—whether they be American or Christian Triumphalism, or Islamicist visions of a resurgent Islamic theocracy in the Middle East and Central Asia—and exclusivism that are often based on traditional religious belief. The most vocal forces now seem to be those that view the world as an apocalyptic battleground between religious good and religious evil. These forces embrace a clear and certain vision of those who constitute the children of light and those who constitute the children of darkness. Political, military, and religious leaders seem convinced of the moral superiority of both their worldviews and their actions in the world.

As a result of this emerging paradigm, people of traditional religious faith are now often viewed as potentially dangerous enemies—in a way even more dangerous than the Communist ideologues of the Cold War era, because they believe that their acts of violence are divinely sanctioned. This has forced governments around the world to reconsider the whole issue of religious freedom in their respective societies. Suddenly, limitations on these rights seem "necessary" and "prudent" to ensure national security. Moreover, the demonization of whole blocs of people—defined often in religious terms—now occurs more and more often in the rhetoric of religious and political leaders.[1]

The Attack on the World Trade Center and the "War on Terrorism"

The previous macro-development has been greatly exacerbated by the attack on the World Trade Center on September 11, 2001 and the resulting "war on terror." It is now clear that for U.S. President George W. Bush, the attack on the World Trade Center and on the Pentagon changed everything. His avowed primary mission is now to protect and defend the U.S. from further terrorist attacks. In the U.S., this has resulted in a massive reallocation of resources away from education, health care, and other social programs toward all manner of defense-related activities. It has also resulted in the passing of the Patriot Act by Congress, which gives the government sweeping powers to apprehend and capture potential terrorists both at home and abroad. For the first time in U.S. history, the CIA and FBI have the power to conduct domestic surveillance of religious communities that are suspected of harboring terrorist elements. Moreover, those suspected of being enemy combatants in the "war on terror" can be apprehended and imprisoned without regard for civil liberties such as the right to legal counsel, the right to a speedy trial by a jury of one's peers, and the right to face one's accusers. Muslim citizens from various nations of origin have been apprehended and held for extended periods of time without being charged with a crime and without being able to communicate with family and loved ones.[2] Evidence exists of Muslims being "profiled" as potential terrorists and prevented from entering the U.S. as students, workers, or tourists. Muslim beneficence organizations are now subjected to rigorous scrutiny following evidence that some of these organizations acted as conduits to fund terrorist cells both at home and abroad. Sensational arrests of Muslims accused of involvement in domestic terror cells are regular features of the daily national news.

In early 2003, the Bush Administration prepared a bold sequel to the Patriot Act, entitled the Domestic Security Enhancement Act of 2003. This sequel would give the government broad new powers to increase domestic intelligence-gathering and surveillance, while simultaneously decreasing judicial review of these activities and public access to information. The bill is currently under advisement, but clearly demonstrates the direction the U.S. government is tending with regard to civil freedoms and the "war on terror."[3]

The U.S. is not alone in privileging matters of national defense over civil and religious freedoms. As Brian Williams' article makes clear, former Soviet Islamic republics such as Uzbekistan and Turkmenistan have increasingly used the fear of terrorism as a pretext for the brutal repression of religious minorities, and Russia itself has ravaged the breakaway Islamic republic of Chechnya because of national security concerns.[4] In Hong Kong, now united with the People's Republic of China, a controversial anti-subversion law designed to protect China "from acts of subversion, treason, sedition, and secession" marshalled such vociferous opposition from members of NRMs, pro-democracy political parties, and workers' rights groups that the measure was rescinded. These groups feared the law would be used to jail members of political and religious opposition groups.[5] China has been uncharacteristically cooperative with U.S. authorities in the international war on terrorism, both because of its large Muslim minority in its western provinces and because of its fear of Falun Gong.

The fear of Islamic extremism represents a particular conundrum for the nations of Western Europe. This is because large Muslim populations now live in countries such as France, the United Kingdom, Belgium, Germany, Spain, and Italy. The articles in this volume on Western Europe all mention the growing Islamophobia in these countries, fears that had more to do with preserving cultural purity and access to jobs and limited resources in the pre-9/11 era, but that now increasingly are related to fears of Islamic-inspired domestic terrorism. High-profile arrests of suspected Islamic terrorists in Spain, Italy, France, Germany, and the United Kingdom are becoming common news items in the European press, further stoking public anxieties. It is important to state that these fears are not without some foundation, and that acts of terrorism by Islamic extremists *do* occur and *will continue* to occur well into the foreseeable future throughout the world. The Iraq War of 2003 and the continued bloodletting in Israel are just two of the factors providing future fuel—justly or unjustly—for the grievances that lead to these terrorist acts. To date, Western European nations have refrained from passing draconian legislation that would limit the religious rights of their Muslim populations. As we will see when we consider the present legislation against "sects" in some of these countries, however, these rights may be hanging by a thread—a thread that may break with the next instance of domestic terrorism. Any move to limit the religious freedom of Muslims in Western Europe will have to take into consideration the increasing size and influence of the aggregate Muslim populations in western European countries and the potential for widespread social upheaval if governments move to limit the civil rights of a large minority population in their midst.

The upshot of the international "war on terror" is that concerns for domestic security will increasingly trump concerns for religious freedom even in societies with long histories of religious toleration such as the U.S. and Canada. In nations without such traditions, for example Russia, China, and Uzbekistan, the prospects for religious freedom are considerably bleaker. Nowhere will these limits to religious expression be more noticeable than in nations' responses to new religious movements.

Sensational Episodes of Violence in NRMs and Public Perceptions of the Growing Threat to Public Order Posed by New and Minority Religions

A further factor in the growing repression of new and minority religions around the world is the public fear that has resulted from sensational episodes of violence involving NRMs during the late twentieth century. These episodes have radically altered public opinion concerning NRMs, and minority religions in general, and have placed enormous pressure on politicians to pass legal measures designed to protect the citizenry from "violent and dangerous" NRMs in their midst. In France and Belgium, the shock and horror of the Solar Temple murder/suicides has spawned a growing political, press, and legal campaign to "combat" new religions. As Danièle Hervieu-Léger and Susan Palmer document, the French authorities and press have launched a veritable witch-hunt against "*sectes*" that includes: 1. a governmental commission created in 1998 to combat "threats to individual liberties and public safety posed by sects"; 2. publication of a notorious "*liste*" of 173 groups that merit public surveillance; 3. the issuance of official reports detailing the scope of the "sectarian threat"; 4. the attempted passage of legal measures by the French Assembly to incorporate the ambiguous notion of "psychological manipulation" into the Penal Code; 5. the establishment of judicial parameters that enable anticultists, using biased evidence and "research," to obtain legal judgments against NRMs with relative ease; 6. a ban on NRMs advertising or opening religious centers near schools, hospitals, or retirement homes; and 7. the sensationalization of NRM malfeasance in the popular press.[6] This governmental "battle against sects" has resulted in French security authorities monitoring the weekly services of Pentecostals, Catholic Charismatics, Baptists, Mormons, Jehovah's Witnesses, as well as more obscure NRMs such as the Aumists, Scientologists, and Raelians.[7] French Assembly member Catherine Picard, a co-author of the new anticult law, has gone so far as to declare, "Proselytizing is not authorized by the French government. When religious groups talk about having the right to proselytize, the local government may authorize such activities but in reality such practices are illegal."[8]

In Belgium, Willy Fautré has documented the establishment of an official surveillance of sects and of a state interministerial agency to combat their influence.[9] These actions began in 1996 with the creation of an enquiry commission comprised of members of 11 political parties. The commission held public hearings to which various magistrates, police and intelligence officials, academics, journalists, former sect members, and anticultists were invited to testify. Groups suspected of "sectarian activities" were not invited to participate, nor were they informed of the accusations leveled against them during public and nonpublic sessions of the commission. Rather, the 71 suspected groups were asked to refute, in written form, their sectarian character, and to state their objectives and purpose. In April 1997, the commission issued its voluminous report, which it admitted contained accusations that it was unable to verify. Although the Belgian parliament adopted only the conclusions and recommendations of the report, it published the entire text, including a list of 189 suspect groups that became a kind of "black list." One year later, in June 1998, the parliament adopted the *Law Regarding the Establishment of an "Information and Advisory Center" on Harmful Sectarian Organizations and an Administrative Coordination Cell.*[10]

The work of the Information and Advisory Center is supported from behind the scenes by the Roman Catholic Church and secular humanists of various stripes, the same coalition that has colluded in the repressive French legislation passed during the late 1990s. The center's stated goals include the protection of citizens from groups that have "dangerous" doctrines, beliefs, teaching methods, and health practices. It does this by collecting and publishing information on "harmful sectarian organizations," answering public queries, giving support and guidance to institutions and juridical consultants, and funding research.[11] Fautré observes that at least one group, the Anthroposophical Society (which is involved in both alternative healing practices and alternative schooling for its children), has successfully sued a federal entity that printed a brochure with unfounded accusations against the society. However, he foresees the "antisect train" in Europe gathering speed, with those who resist the return to "philosophical and religious conformity" increasingly "exposed to public condemnation" and denied their freedom of thought and religious expression.[12]

Evidence to support Fautré's predictions appeared in a June 1999 report by the Parliamentary Assembly of the Council of Europe that is critical of sects and that advocates the creation of "information centers" and a European Observatory to monitor NRM activity. The council is composed of 40 member states, and its action may presage the passage of increasingly repressive legislation across Europe on the French and Belgian model.[13] Already, the French and Belgian commissions have influenced anticult reports in Catholic areas such as Spain and the Swiss canton of Geneva, particularly with regard to notions of "brainwashing" and "mental manipulation." James Richardson and Massimo Introvigne have detailed the ways these notions—embedded within various terms—have found their way into the official reports on "sects" issued by countries such as Italy, France, Germany, Spain, Switzerland, and Sweden. Uncritical notions of "mental manipulation" legitimate calls in these countries to protect "victims" (recruits) of NRMs with new antisect legislation and strict penalties that include heavy fines and imprisonment for NRM leaders.[14]

Ian Reader's article in this volume details the ways that issues of religious freedom in Japan have been affected in the wake of the Aum Shinrikyō gas attacks in March 1995. In this case, societal shock and horror was augmented by Aum's multi-pronged attacks on various nonmember targets of the Japanese public. The aftermath of these attacks has been profound and unsettling for Japanese NRMs. The attacks have raised serious questions about: 1. the limits of religious freedom for groups viewed as "inimical to normative social values"; 2. the tax benefits given to religious movements; and 3. the ways that NRMs acquire wealth.[15] The anticult movement has grown in size and influence in the wake of the Aum events, and the press has become a watchdog in the public effort to "expose 'deviant' religious groups."[16] Although calls for stern new measures to regulate NRMs have not resulted in sweeping changes in Japanese law, a law was passed in 1999 that required Aum to keep authorities informed of its activities and membership. The Public Security Investigation Agency was given a three-year extension of this monitoring activity by the Public Security Examination Commission (PSEC) in January 2003, despite legal objections from Aum lawyers.[17]

In a hopeful sign for advocates of religious freedom, the Tokyo District Court in 2001 held that "it is necessary to prove that there exists a specific danger that an act of indiscriminate mass murder may be committed" in order to justify governmental surveillance on a group. The court also held to a strict application of the Antisubversive Activities Law of 1952 and stated, "if there is no such danger, then restrictions on the freedom of religion cannot be permitted." Although the court ruled that surveillance was only constitutional if applied in a limited manner, it approved continued surveillance of Aum, largely of because of Shōkō Asahara's putative lingering influence over Aum's members.[18]

The PSEC's 2003 decision to extend the Aum surveillance for another three years was based on several factors, including claims that Aleph (Aum's new name) is still under Asahara's influence, that senior members of Aum still hold leadership positions, and that changes in the group's doctrines have been cosmetic. Most objective viewers would agree that, under the circumstances, continued surveillance of Aum is rational and justifiable on public security grounds. It appears that in Japan at least, the judiciary is taking great care to limit infringements on religious freedoms by legislators and public security agencies who may be overreacting to public pressures.[19]

The Peoples Republic of China, on the other hand, continues to ramp up its historical repression of new religions such as Falun Gong. While Scott Lowe's article in this volume gives the historical and cultural context for the government's tendency to crack down on NRMs that become influential in Chinese society, erstwhile hopes for an amelioration of this tendency in the twenty-first century appear headed for disappointment. The Chinese government's actions against Falun Gong include: 1. a campaign to demonize the group's leaders and teachings; 2. sensational reports of suicide attempts by, and rape and mistreatment of, Falun Gong followers; 3. arrests and imprisonments of group members; 4. attempts to link Falun Gong to other dangerous NRMs such as Aum Shinrikyō and the Order of the Solar Temple; and 5. the creation of the China Anti-Cult Association in November 2000. The association is composed of academics from across disciplines whose avowed mission is to: 1. promote the spirit of science and humanity; 2. safeguard the dignity of the law; 3. respect the freedom of belief; and 4. create a common front from people of various walks of life "to oppose any cult which aims to threaten the security of people's lives and property, disturb the public order," and thwart law enforcement efforts. Most significantly, the association has consulted with anticult NGOs and NRM scholars from around the world to further its efforts to sponsor symposia and research, publish "anti-cult books, journals and audio-visual products," and thus educate the Chinese people on the "dangers" China faces from "cult" organizations. The commission claims that "cults" represent an "international threat to social development around the world" and calls for international support of its "anti-cult campaign . . . to completely eradicate cult[s as] a social poison."[20]

Fears of both NRMs such as Falun Gong and Islamic extremism in its Western provinces presage continued suppression of new and minority religions in China. China's growing influence as a world economic power will likely embolden it to apply pressure on nations to restrict protests by followers of the Dalai Lama and Falun Gong during state visits of Chinese officials. Documented efforts in this direction have already been successful in countries as diverse as Iceland, Lithuania, and Australia.[21]

Given the continued existence of what Catherine Wessinger describes as "fragile," "assaulted," and "revolutionary" millennial movements in the world, the twenty-first century can expect more traumatic episodes of sensational violence committed against and by these movements.[22] Al Qa'ida, according to some scholars, is just one example of this potential in the contemporary world.[23] Public shock and outrage will surely increase in our era of instant communication, as image after image of the victims of these events are broadcast around the clock, and as media pundits, anticultists, and politicians call for increased surveillance and control of NRMs to protect the public. The proper response to NRM violence requires a balanced concern for both religious freedom and public safety, but this balance will be difficult to maintain, even in nations with strong traditions of religious freedom, as public fears rise. In nations where religious freedom has been historically curtailed, we can expect more and more sophisticated legal, judicial, and police actions against NRMs in the future, whether episodes of NRM violence affect them directly or not.

The Internationalization of the Anticult and Countercult movements and the Lessening Influence of Academics in NRM Debates

As many of the articles in this anthology detail, the anticult and countercult movements have become internationalized to a significant degree during the late twentieth century. Italian NRM scholar Massimo Introvigne has convincingly documented the extent to which anti- and countercult groups now reach an international audience through websites, publications, conferences, and the global travels of activists who consult with NRM information centers and local law enforcement officials, politicians, and anti- and countercult crusaders.[23] The well-established factual and theological biases of anticult and countercult research mean that public officials in nations around the world, who are attempting to formulate effective policies to protect their citizenry from NRM abuse, often base their efforts on unreliable information. For every country such as Italy, Denmark, or Germany that welcomes the research of respected academic scholars in their official deliberations, there are countries such as France and China that severely limit academic voices in legal and judicial proceedings. In Japan, which has arguably suffered from NRM violence more than any other country with the possible exception of the U.S., NRM scholars had their credibility damaged by naïve pronouncements concerning Aum Shinrikyō both before the sarin gas attack of March 1995 and in its immediate aftermath. The upshot of this damaged credibility was to "virtually silence" the more balanced voice of academic researchers in the post-Aum public debates in Japan.[24] This curtailment of academic voices in public debates can also be observed in France, where non-hostile social-scientific research into NRMs has long been marginalized in the academy, and where scholars who dare to offer balanced perspectives on NRMs are regularly pilloried for their efforts in the public press and in anticult literature.

The dangers this state of affairs poses for minority religions and NRMs are significant. In parliamentary commissions and reports, legal debates, judicial proceedings, intelligence agency assessments, news reporting, and public education, the more balanced perspectives of academic specialists in the study of NRMs are becoming less and less a factor. There are notable exceptions to this trend—the efforts of James Richardson, Eileen Barker, Massimo Introvigne, Gordon Melton, and Jean-François Mayer in official forums throughout the Western world deserve special mention—but given the forces arrayed against minority and new religions—law enforcement officials, secularist legislators, mainstream church officials, the public media, anti- and countercult movements, and public opinion—the voices of academicians provide a scant counterbalance. The continuing influence of "brainwashing" and "mental manipulation" notions—notions that have lost much of their influence in the U.S. because of the careful critiques leveled against them by competent social scientists—in the reports of state commissions investigating how to deal with the dangers of NRMs in Europe provides evidence to support this contention. As Richardson and Introvigne conclude, the thorough critique of brainwashing notions published by scholars from around the world "is usually missing" from these reports. These brainwashing notions "appear to be driving policy recommendations" even in countries that value religious freedom and pluralism and where NRMs are not seen as a threat.[26] In the future, many countries will continue to underfund research into NRMs and to steer scholars away—through various disincentives—from non-hostile yet critical NRM research. Even scholars in countries where NRM research is tolerated and accepted, such as Canada, the United Kingdom, Australia, and the U.S., may find themselves facing institutional and public pressures to curtail or even bias their research should future acts of violence or terror attributable to NRMs occur in their nations.

Resurgent Nationalism and the Simultaneous Efforts of Traditional "National" Churches to Regain Cultural Hegemony

A final factor that contributes to the increasing repression of new and minority religions around the world is a resurgent nationalism in countries that are struggling to build a coherent national identity following radical regime changes. Nationalist forces have, in some cases, made common cause with traditional, "national" churches that seek to regain cultural hegemony by eliminating "nontraditional" religions from their midst. Nowhere are nationalist and traditionalist religious forces stronger than in Russia and in the nations that make up the former Soviet Union. As Marat Shterin's article in this anthology recounts, the fall of the Soviet Union started off with a flowering of religious freedoms in the former Communist world. Missionaries from both traditional minority religions and NRMs flooded into Eastern Europe, Russia, and the former Soviet Muslim Republics of Central Asia. The 1990 Law on Freedom of Religion extended religious freedom to all residents of Russia for the first time in Russian history. Provisions of the 1993 Constitution of the Russian Federation extended these freedoms by abolishing compulsory registration of religious groups and by ensuring the ideological neutrality of the state and the equality before the law of all religions.[27]

As the new post-Soviet national entities struggled to reconstruct themselves politically, economically, and socially, one potential axis of coherent identity, nationalism, emerged as a strong contender. To peoples reeling from political upheaval, economic meltdown, the collapse of their social services safety net, and a pervasive sense of moral and spiritual decay, nationalist voices made a persuasive case for national rebuilding: "We must found our new nation on the traditions of Russian civilization and its historically established 'ethno-religious balance.' We must be very careful of foreign influences, especially those from America. Since new 'sects' can threaten our 'cultural and political integrity,' we must restrict the activities of foreign missionaries, who may be agents of American imperialism. Above all, we must protect our national purity from outside pollution."[28]

Traditional "national" religions, such as the Russian Orthodox Church, joined with these nationalist political forces in an effort to reestablish the hegemony over religion that they had long exercised in the pre-Communist past. Russia's 1997 Law on Freedom of Conscience and Religious Associations establishes the priority of "Russian historical faiths," especially Russian Orthodoxy, within the Russian religious economy. The second tier of religions—which are granted full legal rights as registered *organizations*—are those that have been present in Russia at least fifteen years. All other religions, including NRMs only recently in Russia, are granted restricted rights to operate as *groups*.[29] As Shterin details, the forces of Orthodoxy and nationalism have continued to draft laws designed to extend the privileges of "traditional religions" and to restrict all other faith communities. The situation is even more dire in the many Russian "regions," where the legitimacy of new Russian Federation laws may be very tentative. In reality, NRMs and minority faiths are often at the mercy of local officials, regional police and security agencies, and Orthodox diocesan authorities.[30]

Belarus has followed in Russia's footsteps. In October 2002 its parliament passed the most restrictive religion law in Europe. The law, which was strongly supported by the Russian Orthodox Church leadership, 1. outlaws unregistered religious activity; 2. requires the prior censorship of all religious literature; 3. bans foreign citizens from leading religious organizations; 4. restricts religious education to faiths that have ten registered communities, one of which dates to at least 1982; 5. bans all but occasional religious meetings in private homes; 6. requires all religious organizations to apply for reregistraton within two years.[31] Many religious communities have expressed their opposition to the new law. The executive chairman of Belarus's Helsinki Committee voiced the concerns of many, predicting that many communities would lose their official registration and that small religions would be hard pressed to spare both the time and resources to deal with the bureaucratic red tape involved. Many Russian Orthodox priests and laypeople oppose the bill, but the leadership of the church has reportedly suppressed all dissent.[32]

In the former Soviet republic of Georgia, nationalists and advocates of established religions have raised the specter of "brainwashing" to foment public fears about NRMs such as the Jehovah's Witnesses. Human rights watchdog groups have reported that local security officials repeatedly harass nontraditional religious minorities and that police have joined Orthodox extremists' attacks on minority religions.[33] The Jehovah's Witnesses, for example, have documented at least 80 incidents of mob attacks in the past two years and now meet only in private homes. National leaders often brand Witnesses as alien interlopers. In Armenia, the head of the police issued a secret decree ordering that all non-Armenian Apostolic Church members be removed from police work. A Jehovah's Witness who was fired from her job in the accounts department of a local police station was told, "Your being a Jehovah's Witness and working in the police is incompatible."[34] The influence of the Armenian Apostolic Church over public policy is extensive and growing. Turkmenistan, as mentioned earlier, has a draconian policy on religion freedom. All religions other than "official" Islam and Russian Orthodoxy are effectively banned. Jews, Lutherans, Roman Catholics, and Muslim minority groups are regularly detained, beaten, fined, and imprisoned for practicing their religions.[35] The U.S. Commission on International Religious Freedom, a U.S. Congress-sponsored monitoring group, has cited Turkmenistan as a serious violator of religious freedom. The Turkmen President Saparmurat Niyazov justifies his nation's laws controlling religion on the grounds of protection of national traditions and beliefs: "Everyone can follow whatever faith he wants, but a foreigner has no right to spread an alien faith in our country. This is not freedom. Rather, this is inflicting harm upon our nation's religion."[36] In these former Soviet republics, the rhetoric of nationalism is being used to continue a 70-year-old tradition of official atheism and repression of minority religions. It will certainly take time for these practices and attitudes to change.[37]

As Danièle Hervieu-Léger and Susan Palmer explain in their articles, France's repressive religion laws also have a great deal to do with French nationalism and the Roman Catholic Church's historical hegemony over religious belief and practice. In the wake of America's war with Iraq, hostility to all things "American" can be expected to grow in France. Missionary churches and foreign NRMs will increasingly be viewed as agents of American imperialism and will incite public approval for measures designed to limit their influence.

Conclusion

The future for NRMs and minority religions is not bright, given current trends around the world. A constellation of factors—the "war on terrorism," insecure national identities, state-church traditions, fears of cultural imperialism, anti-religion secularists, an increasingly sophisticated transnational countercult and anticult movement, the Muslim diaspora, and declining membership in mainstream religions—are combining to bring forward sweeping new limitations on the freedoms of minority and new religious movements in nations throughout the globe. Islands of relative freedom continue to exist, including Brazil, Italy, and Canada, but the same forces that are leading to repression in nations such as France, Russia, and the U.S. could threaten religious liberties even in those countries should circumstances change. Complicating this situation is the undeniable fact that some NRMs *do* pose a danger both to their own members and to societies at large. As J. Christopher Soper has written, "The tension between new religious movements and political institutions is an old story." In the end, the question becomes "How far can . . . [democratic societies] go in permitting religiously motivated behavior that is contrary to societal welfare or norms?"[38]

It is my view that the societal good that results from freedom of religious conscience and freedom of religious association far outweighs the societal harm a few of these movements bring upon societies on rare occasions. Most nations have sufficient legal mechanisms at their disposal to investigate and prosecute actual wrongdoing when it occurs in NRMs. Thus, the legislation currently under consideration in European nations such as Russia, Belarus, France, Belgium, and Spain appears a draconian overreaction to a few sensational episodes of NRM violence and to growing fears of cultural "pollution" that stem from globalization and the recent "sole superpower status" of the U.S.

I am aware that my views are heavily influenced by the fact that my own cultural location is North America, with its strong traditions of religious freedom, toleration, and pluralism. I am also aware that nations such as China and Russia, which have very different historical experiences with religious pluralism, may have to find a *modus vivendi* with their new and minority religious populations that will fall short of the full freedoms enshrined in the United Nations' Universal Declaration of Human Rights. Unless bold and assertive steps are taken by supporters of religious freedom to combat the growing forces of repression around the world, however, even citizens of nations such as the U.S. and Canada may soon find their basic religious rights threatened in ways that were inconceivable even a decade ago. The repression of religious freedom in any country, regardless of its history, is a cause for concern. The increasing, systematic repression of new and minority religions across cultures and nations at the beginning of the twenty-first century should be a cause of the gravest concern for all supporters of the fundamental human right of freedom of religious belief and practice.

Notes

1. An example of this demonization is found in the comments of Reverend Franklin Graham, the son of evangelist Billy Graham, who recently called Islam an "evil religion." He was chosen to preach on Good Friday, 2003, at the Defense Department, in spite of protests by Muslims at the Pentagon. Sue Pleming, "Pentagon Muslims Angered by Rev. Graham Invitation," http://reuters.com/newsSearchResultsHome.jhtml;jsessionid= XXYBNN24VBFW4CBAEOCFEY?qtype=a&position=1&query=Franklin+Graham&x= 34&y=9, accessed 15 April 2003.
2. For one example of this treatment of American Muslims, see "Muslims Protest Man's Detention without Charge," *Daytona Beach News Journal,* 20 April 2003, 5a.
3. Charles Lewis and Adam Mayle, "Justice Dept. Drafts Sweeping Expansion of Anti-Terrorism Act," http://www.publicintegrity.org/dtaweb/ report.asp?ReportID=502&L1=10&L2= 10&L3=0&L4=0&L5=0, accessed 20 April 2003.
4. See Brian Glyn Williams, "Crushing Wahhabi Fundamentalists in Central Asia and the Caucasus: Sub-plot to the Global Struggle Against Al Qa'ida or Suppression of Legitimate Religious Opposition?" in this volume.
5. Katherine Maria, "Protesters Disrupt Hong Kong Legislature," *Voice of America News,* 26 February 2003; Helen Luk, "Hong Kong's Security Chief Unveils Text of Planned Anti-Subversion Law," Associated Press, 13 February 2002.

6. See Danièle Hervieu-Léger, "France's Obsession with the 'Sectarian Threat'," and Susan J. Palmer, "The *Secte* Response to Religious Discrimination: Subversives, Martyrs, or Freedom Fighters in the French Sect Wars?" in this volume.
7. "Using the equivalent of America's FBI, the French secret police have increased their scrutiny on minority groups across France," CBN News, 19 June 2002; "A Close-up: France Targets Churches as Cults," CBN News, 19 June 2002.
8. Ibid.
9. Willy Fautré, "Belgium's Anti-Sect War," *Social Justice Research* 12:4 (December 1999): 377–92.
10. Ibid., 377–79.
11. Ibid., 388–89.
12. Ibid., 380.
13. Ibid., 377.
14. James T. Richardson and Massimo Introvigne, " 'Brainwashing' Theories in European Parliamentary and Administrative Reports on 'Cults' and 'Sects'," *Journal for the Scientific Study of Religion* 40:2 (June 2001): 143–75.
15. Ian Reader, "Consensus Shattered: Japanese Paradigm Shift and Moral Panic in the Post-Aum Era," 191.
16. Ibid.
17. "Japan Security Agency Wants No Let-Up on Aum Cult," Reuters, 2 December 2002, http://story.news.yahoo.com/news?tmpl=story&u=/nm/20021202/wl_nm/japan_aum_dc_1, accessed 4 December 2002; "Aum must prove itself 'harmless'," *The Japan Times*, 8 February 2003.
18. Ibid.
19. Kiyotaka Iwata, "Aum kept under watch and at arm's length," *Asahi News*, 22 February 2003.
20. Announcement entitled, "Introduction of the China Anti-Cult Association," 26 March 2001, received as a fax.
21. Ted Anthony, "China Pushes against Dissent Abroad," Associated Press, 8 July 2002; Helen Luk, "Hong Kong's Security Chief Unveils text of Planned Anti-Subversion Law," Associated Press, 13 February 2002; Katherine Maria, "Protesters Disrupt Hong Kong Legislature," *Voice of America News*, 26 February 2003.
22. Catherine Wessinger, *How the Millennium Comes Violently: From Jonestown to Heaven's Gate* (New York: Seven Bridges Press, 2000).
23. See, for example, Mark Sedgwick, "Establishments and Sects in the Islamic World," 302; and David Cook, "Suicide Attacks or 'Martyrdom Operations' in Contemporary *Jihad* Literature," *Nova Religio* 6:1 (2002): 7–44.
24. Massimo Introvigne, "Anti-Cult and Counter-Cult Movements in Italy," in *Anti-Cult Movements in Cross-Cultural Perspective*, eds. Anson Shupe and David Bromley (New York: Garland, 1994), 171–97; "The Secular Anti-Cult and the Religious Counter-Cult Movement: Strange Bedfellows or Future Enemies?," in *New Religions and the New Europe*, ed. Eric Towler (Aarhus, Denmark: Aarhus University Press, 1995), 32–54; "Blacklisting or Greenlisting? A European Perspective on the New Cult Wars," *Nova Religio* 1:3 (October 1998): 16–23; "So Many Evil Things: Anti-Cult Terrorism via the Internet," in *Religion on the Internet: Research Prospects and Promises*, eds. Jeffrey K. Hadden and Douglas E. Cowan (Amsterdam: JAI Press, 2000), 277–306; "Moral Panics and Anti-Cult Terrorism in Western Europe," *Terrorism and Political Violence* 12:1 (Spring 2000): 47–59.
25. Ian Reader, "Consensus Shattered: Japanese Paradigm Shift and Moral Panic in the Post-Aum Era," 192, 199.
26. Richardson and Introvigne, " 'Brainwashing' Theories in European Parliamentary and Administrative Reports on 'Cults' and 'Sects'," 162.
27. See Marat Shterin, "New Religions in the New Russia," 101–102.
28. Ibid.
29. Ibid.
30. Ibid., 103.
31. Felix Corley, "Belarus: Repressive Religion Law gets President's Signature," *Keston News Service*, 31 October 2002.
32. Ibid.

33. Robert McMahon and Don Hill, "East: Soul-Searching—Former Communist Nations Still Resistant to New Religions," Radio Free Europe/Radio Liberty, 3 May 2002.

34. The worker was reinstated on a technicality in the secret decree after a court hearing. Felix Corley, "Armenia: Police Reinstate Jehovah's Witness—for Now," Forum 18 News Service, 25 April 2003.

35. Don Hill, "East: Soul-Searching—Western Missionaries Attract Mistrust, As Well As Believers," Radio Free Europe/Radio Liberty, 3 May 2002.

36. Robert McMahon and Don Hill, "East: Soul-Searching—Nations Often Differ on How to Regulate Religions, If At All," Radio Free Europe/Radio Liberty, 3 May 2002.

37. Robert McMahon, "East: Soul-Searching—U.S.-Based Missions Struggle to Spread the Faith," Radio Free Europe/Radio Liberty, 3 May 2002.

38. J. Christopher Soper, "Tribal Instinct and Religious Persecution: Why Do Western European States Behave So Badly?" *Journal for the Scientific Study of Religion* 40:2 (June 2001): 177.

Index